Confucius, Rawls, and the Sense of Justice

Confucius, Rawls, and the Sense of Justice

ERIN M. CLINE

FORDHAM UNIVERSITY PRESS

New York 2013

Library of Congress Cataloging-in-Publication Data

Cline, Erin M.
    Confucius, Rawls, and the sense of justice / Erin M.
Cline. — 1st ed.
        p. cm.
    Includes bibliographical references (p.   ) and index.
    ISBN 978-0-8232-4508-6 (cloth : alk. paper)
    1. Justice (Philosophy) 2. Confucius. 3. Rawls, John,
1921–2002. I. Title.
    B105.J87C55 2013
    172'.2—dc23
                                            2012029099

Printed in the United States of America
15 14 13   5 4 3 2 1
First edition

For Michael

CONTENTS

List of Abbreviations   ix
Acknowledgments   xi

Introduction   1
1. Methods in Comparative Work   28
2. The Sense of Justice in Rawls   74
3. The Sense of Justice in the *Analects*   119
4. Two Senses of Justice   168
5. The Contemporary Relevance of a Sense of Justice   211
Conclusion   265

Notes   273
Bibliography   335
Index   351

CP   John Rawls. *Collected Papers*, ed. Samuel Freeman. Cambridge, Mass.: Harvard University Press, 1999.

JF   John Rawls. *Justice as Fairness: A Restatement*, ed. Erin Kelly. Cambridge, Mass.: Harvard University Press, 2001.

LP   John Rawls. *The Law of Peoples*. Cambridge, Mass.: Harvard University Press, 1999.

PL   John Rawls. *Political Liberalism*. New York: Columbia University Press, 1993, 1996.

TJ   John Rawls. *A Theory of Justice, Revised Edition*. Cambridge, Mass.: Belknap Press of Harvard University Press, 1999.

ACKNOWLEDGMENTS

I owe debts of gratitude to many who helped in various ways and at different stages of this project. I thank P. J. Ivanhoe for encouraging me to write a new book that reflected my evolving ideas about justice and Confucianism instead of simply revising my previous work on this topic, for conversations about the shape of this project, and for his extremely insightful comments and suggestions on multiple drafts of the manuscript. P.J. and his wife, Hong Jiang, are among the most generous people I know, and I am deeply grateful for their continued friendship and support. I also thank Bob Baird, who provided invaluable training in the rigors of reading Rawls, and who originally suggested that I explore the capacity for a sense of justice more intensively. As my work evolved following the completion of my Ph.D., he continued to offer encouragement and helpful feedback. He has taught me more than I could possibly express here, and I am truly thankful for the support Bob and his wife, Alice, have provided. I hope this book honors the memory of their daughter Kathy's tireless work for social justice. I also want to thank Michael Puett, who read and commented on the entire manuscript, offered encouragement, and helped me to find the right publisher. I have great admiration for him as a scholar, and even greater admiration for him as a person.

I want to express my heartfelt thanks to Ronnie Littlejohn, who was an incredibly supportive mentor and a decisive influence in my decision to study Chinese and comparative philosophy. I am also grateful to Henry Rosemont, who encouraged and supported me both as an undergraduate and as a graduate student. When I initially began to work on the subject of justice in relation to Confucianism, his probing questions helped me to strengthen and refine my views. Thanks are also due to the following individuals for their comments on various parts of the manuscript at various stages of its development: Steve Angle, Daniel Bell, Mark Berkson, Eric Hutton, Craig Ihara, Leigh Jenco, Sungmoon Kim, David Mungello, John P. Reeder Jr., Stuart Rosenbaum, Aaron Stalnaker, Justin Tiwald, and Bryan Van Norden. I also want to thank an anonymous reviewer for

Fordham University Press for helpful comments and suggestions on the entire manuscript. I presented material from this book in many different forums over the years, and I am grateful to audiences at the City University of Hong Kong, Fairfield University, Georgetown University, the Oregon Humanities Center, the University of Oregon, and the annual meetings of the American Academy of Religion, the American Philosophical Association, and the Association for Asian Studies for helpful comments and questions that influenced the final form of this work. For my discussion of the Nurse-Family Partnership in Chapter 5 I am indebted to conversations with Tom and Carole Hanks, from whom I initially learned of the program. I thank the journal *Dao* for permission to include portions of my "Confucian Ethics, Public Policy, and the Nurse-Family Partnership," a more focused precursor to part of Chapter 5. I also thank *Dao* for permission to include work that appeared in an earlier form as an article entitled "Two Senses of Justice" (Volume 6.4, 2007: 361–81), which is an early formulation of some of the ideas I develop in this book. The feedback I received from the editor, Huang Yong; two anonymous referees for *Dao*; and the commentators and members of the audience at the *Dao* Best Essay Award panel at the APA contributed greatly to the development of this work.

Thanks to Georgetown University, the Oregon Humanities Center, and the University of Oregon for grants and fellowships that supported the writing of this book. I owe special thanks to my colleagues at Georgetown University and the University of Oregon for encouragement throughout the process of seeing it to completion. I am particularly grateful to Mark Unno for his advice and for his unfailing generosity and friendship.

I want to express my appreciation to the entire editorial team at Fordham University Press. I am especially grateful to Helen Tartar, my editor, for her advice and encouragement, and to Thomas Lay for his invaluable assistance. I also thank Eric Newman for providing excellent copy editing and for his guidance and attention to detail throughout the editing process.

Finally, I want to express my profound gratitude for the support and encouragement given to me by my family, including my parents, Michael and Dorothy Cline; my brother, Kelly; and my sister-in-law, Jamie. To my children, Patrick and Bridget, whose untutored spontaneity provided plenty of opportunities for unplanned breaks from my work, I am also grateful. What I am most proud of about this book is that I completed it with two children under the age of three, something that would have been absolutely impossible without a truly extraordinary spouse. I dedicate this book to my husband, Michael Slater, for sharing the joys and challenges of parenting with me, for giving me strength when I am struggling, and for reading and greatly improving every draft of everything I write. You have exceeded every expectation and hope I ever had of what a husband could be.

Introduction

... the institutions of society favor certain starting places over
others. These are especially deep inequalities. Not only are they
pervasive, but they affect men's initial chances in life; yet they cannot
possibly be justified by an appeal to the notions of merit or desert.

—JOHN RAWLS (*TJ* §2, P. 7).

In a state that has the Way, to be poor and of low status is a cause for
shame; in a state that is without the Way, to be wealthy and honored
is equally a cause for shame.

—*ANALECTS* 8.13

As several scholars of Confucianism have noted, remarkable differences
exist between the structure and content of the work of modern liberal philosophers like John Rawls, who concern themselves primarily with discussions of justice, equality, and freedom, and the work of classical Confucian
philosophers, who focus mainly on self-cultivation and virtues that are nurtured, at least initially, largely in the context of the family. An awareness of
these differences might lead one to doubt that there is any value in trying
to compare these views. What might philosophers who devote enormous
time to discussions of self-cultivation and the family have in common with
a philosopher concerned primarily with "the fact of reasonable pluralism"
in a modern liberal democracy? This book argues that the central concerns
of the Confucian *Analects* and Rawls's work intersect in their emphasis on
the importance of developing a sense of justice, and that despite deep and
important differences between their accounts of a sense of justice, this in-
tersection is a source of significant philosophical agreement. However, this
book does not simply compare and contrast two views by examining their
similarities and differences; it also offers a larger argument concerning the

reasons why comparative work is worthwhile, the distinctive challenges comparative studies face and approaches to resolving those difficulties, and how comparative work can accomplish distinctive and significant ends—which is a necessity for and sheds light upon the central argument of the book. This work argues that a comparative study of the capacity for a sense of justice in the *Analects* and Rawls can help us not only to better understand each of their views but also to see new ways to apply their insights, especially with respect to the contemporary relevance of their accounts.

Why should philosophers working in the distinct fields of political philosophy, ethics, and Chinese philosophy be interested in a *comparative* study of Rawls and early Confucianism, as opposed to independent studies of their views on a sense of justice? In order to appreciate the answer to this question, we must first delve a bit deeper into the respective backgrounds of the sources and thinkers under study. The influence of Rawls and Kongzi is unparalleled in some important respects. Rawls is the most important political philosopher of the second half of the twentieth century, and the *Analects* is the text that is most closely associated with the founder of Confucianism, which has had a remarkably wide-ranging and pervasive cultural influence in East Asia.[1] Rawls, of course, is an American philosopher following in the contractarian tradition of liberalism that shaped the U.S. Constitution. As anyone familiar with his work knows, Rawls's fifty-year career was guided by the belief that a just society is realistically possible.[2] It is not an understatement to say that *A Theory of Justice* is one of the most influential works in moral and political philosophy written in the twentieth century. Considered as a whole, Rawls's work has probably evoked more commentary and attracted wider attention than any other twentieth-century work in moral or political philosophy. Yet despite the enduring interest in Rawls's work, there have so far been no in-depth studies of his moral psychology. This work aims to help to fill this gap in the literature by focusing on a neglected aspect of his view, namely his account of the capacity for a sense of justice.

On the other side of this comparative study is Kongzi 孔子, who lived from 551 to 479 B.C.E.[3] Born in the state of Lu, located in what is now Shandong Province in the People's Republic of China, Kongzi lived and taught during the latter part of the Zhou 周 dynasty, also known as the "Eastern Zhou" (*Dongzhou* 東周 770–256 B.C.E.). Unlike the earlier part of the Zhou dynasty (the "Western Zhou," *Xizhou* 西周 1122–771 B.C.E.), the Eastern Zhou was not a time of peace and stability. To the contrary, it was a time of extreme political turbulence characterized by violence and warfare both between and within different states.[4] After resigning from an executive position as the "minister of crime,"[5] Kongzi devoted his life to the belief that there was still hope for a stable, harmoniously functioning society. He worked to transmit the cultural forms of the Western Zhou, which he took to be the central ideas and practices of a humane society, to his students and contemporaries while striving to embody them in his own conduct. Kongzi became one of the most influential figures in the latter part of the Eastern Zhou. The period following his death, known as the Warring States Period (*Zhanguo shidai* 戰國時代 403–221 B.C.E.), is sometimes called the era of the "100 schools of thought" (*bai jia* 百家) because it was a period in which philosophical debate flourished in China. As Bryan W. Van Norden points out, the influence Kongzi has had on the Chinese tradition and, indeed, on several cultures in Asia is comparable to the combined influence of Jesus and Socrates on the Western tradition.[6] Similar to those of his Western counterparts, we know Kongzi's work and thought only through the writings of his students, followers, and critics.

It is clear that Rawls and Kongzi have had a tremendous influence—Kongzi over East Asian philosophical traditions and Rawls over the fields of Western political philosophy and ethics. In addition, their work reflects important themes and values in the respective cultures from which they come. But a comparison of their thought requires considerable explanation, for as readers will no doubt recognize, the choice is not obvious. Rawls mentions China only in passing in his work, and his writings contain no mention of the work of early Confucian philosophers such as Kongzi, Mengzi 孟子 ("Mencius"), or Xunzi 荀子, or of later Chinese thinkers. Why should we compare the work of these two philosophers on the subject of a sense of justice? Can we not learn enough about their ideas by studying them independently, or in comparison with their contemporaries? My response to this question has two parts. The first addresses the specific question of why we should study the sense of justice in Rawls and the *Analects* comparatively. However, those who raise this type of question often have in mind the more general question of why one should do comparative work, as well as the question of how one ought to go about such work, including one's reasons for selecting the particular thinkers or sources one compares. I will address these more general questions in Chapter 1, but in what follows I focus specifically on the reasons why a comparative study of Rawlsian and Confucian views of a sense of justice is worthwhile.

Why Study a Sense of Justice Comparatively?

This study provides three important answers to the question of why we should study the accounts of a sense of justice in Rawls and the *Analects* comparatively, as opposed to studying them independently: It highlights important features of the two views that might otherwise be neglected, it provides us with a more robust understanding of a sense of justice than we would gain from studying only one of these sources, and it suggests ways in which each of the accounts can be strengthened. Let us consider each of these in turn.

First, I argue that a comparative study can help us to appreciate new and important features of these two views—features that we would be likely to miss otherwise. This work argues that Rawls's moral psychology, particularly his account of the development of a sense of justice, plays a foundational role in his theory of justice and that comparing this neglected aspect of Rawls's thought with the Confucian view can help us to appreciate the emphasis Rawls places on the capacity for a sense of justice—including the role of the family in the development of a just society and the importance of moral cultivation in shaping young citizens' responses to social injustice. It also prompts us to consider more carefully the extent to which a view of human nature informs Rawls's account of social justice. Because Kongzi emphasizes moral psychology more strongly than principles or laws in relation to questions of justice, this comparison can help to remind us of what Rawls says about moral psychology, and the extent to which his theory of justice depends on it.

This work also argues against the view that there is not an understanding of social justice in the Confucian *Analects*. A comparison with Rawls can help us to recognize and appreciate the textual evidence for this view by drawing on Rawls's distinction between a *sense* of justice, the *concept* of justice, and a *conception* or *theory* of justice. This work argues that the absence of a theory of justice, combined with the lack of a single classical Chinese term that uniquely refers to justice, has led many to assume mistakenly that there is not a concept of justice in classical Chinese texts such as the *Analects*. It further argues that Rawls's account of the capacity for a *sense* of justice is a more helpful resource for understanding social justice in the *Analects* than discussions of concepts or theories of justice, because the view of justice in the text is primarily revealed not through theoretical discussions of what justice is but through discussions of how a sense of justice is developed and its role in a harmonious society. The descriptions of some of the moral capacities that exemplary members of society possess, especially the capacity to feel or perceive what is fair, clearly align with Rawls's basic account of a sense of justice, but a variety of deep and important differences exist between the Confucian and Rawlsian senses of justice. These differences—including things that are more strongly emphasized by either Rawls or Kongzi, as well as features of a sense of justice that are absent from one but important to the other—lead us to see why a comparative study of the two views is particularly fruitful. For in addition to highlighting important features of the two views that have been neglected, this comparison provides us with a more robust understanding of the nature of a sense of justice, the different ways it can be manifested, the various ways of understanding its development, and the diverse roles it can have in creating and maintaining a good society. This is my second reason for studying these accounts comparatively: Doing so helps us to better understand a sense of justice. I argue, for example, that studying a sense of justice in the *Analects* broadens our understanding of the wide range of situations in which a sense of justice is important, because Kongzi's discussion is not as narrowly focused as Rawls's. On the other hand, Rawls's detailed theoretical discussion of a sense of justice makes explicit many of the most distinctive features of this capacity.

Third, I argue that a comparative study can help us to see ways in which we might further develop certain aspects of Rawls's and Kongzi's accounts, and to see new ways to apply their insights. For example, the ways in which Kongzi's view was developed by Mengzi and Xunzi can serve as a new resource for developing and strengthening Rawls's account of what it means to possess naturally the capacity for a sense of justice, specifically by highlighting the important differences between incipient, latent, and acquired moral capacities. Examining the challenges that Xunzi's account faces, in particular, can show us ways of strengthening Rawls's account so that it can more ably meet the challenge of explaining the origins of a just society and the initial emergence of "background justice." I also argue that a comparison with early Confucian views can serve as a resource for developing Rawls's account in order to address some of the concerns of communitarian and feminist critics, such as the claim that Rawls neglected areas such as the family. In all of these ways, a comparative study of Kongzi and Rawls sheds light upon the overarching argument of this work, which concerns the value of comparative philosophy.

Although there have been major studies of Confucian concepts like *Ren* 仁 ("humaneness," "benevolence"), *de* 德 ("Virtue," "moral power," "moral charisma"), and *li* 禮 ("rites," "ritual propriety"), there have been no major studies of the sense of justice in the *Analects*, or in classical Confucian-

ism more broadly.[7] I argue in this work that an understanding of the role
a sense of justice plays in the *Analects* leads to a better understanding of
the text as a whole and a more extensive understanding of the concept of
justice itself. In addition, as I have noted, my study shows that important
similarities exist between particular aspects of Rawls's understanding of a
sense of justice and the view found in the *Analects*. This insight not only
serves to correct some previous misunderstandings of both Rawls and the
Analects (a point I will return to later) but also shows that substantial points
of resonance are present between the articulation of a sense of justice by
the most influential American political philosopher of the twentieth century and the most influential thinker in East Asian history. This fact is
both startling and remarkable, and it tells us something about justice and
about ourselves as human beings.

Here we see yet another reason why we ought to study the Rawlsian
and Confucian accounts of a sense of justice comparatively: Doing so
can lead us to notice and appreciate important areas of agreement—and
difference—across different philosophical, cultural, and political traditions. This end can be accomplished only through careful comparative
study across traditions, and it is important for a variety of reasons. Recognizing shared ideas and concerns in different traditions and especially
those that inform societies today can have practical import by helping us
to understand where we can find common ground with other cultures and
societies, while also helping us to understand the nature of our differences
and the origins of those differences. In addition, as I suggested previously,
the shared interest in ideas like a sense of justice can tell us something
important about our nature as human beings by contributing to our knowledge of the ideas and concerns that seem to have been common to human
beings in different times and places. In the case of Rawls's work, this similarity is especially significant because Rawls argues that the capacity for a
sense of justice is a fundamental part of human nature. If Rawls's view is
even close to being right, then we should expect to find examples of a sense
of justice in other cultures. The fact that early Chinese thinkers observed
and described this capacity in their writings lends support to Rawls's view
that the capacity for a sense of justice is something that all human beings
normally possess, even though they develop this capacity to varying degrees and in different ways.

I want to discuss briefly one final reason for studying the accounts of
a sense of justice in Rawls and the *Analects* comparatively. This study—
and my selection of Rawls and the *Analects* in particular as subjects—was
prompted in part by the work of other comparative philosophers who study

the Confucian tradition in comparison with and in contrast to Western philosophy. Although I will discuss this body of work more extensively in the following section, I wish to note here that I believe a comparative study of Rawls and Kongzi is needed partly because it can help to correct some widely held views that have emerged in the literature. I have two views in mind here: first, the view that because there is not a term for "justice" in classical Chinese there is no concept of justice in texts such as the *Analects*; and, second, the view that there are certain essential, mutually exclusive defining characteristics of Confucian and Western liberal thinkers, and as a result they cannot be fruitfully compared.[8] This study aims to show that even though there is not a single term for "justice" in classical Chinese, there is still an understanding of—as well as an appreciation for—justice in the *Analects*. It also aims to show that the similarities and differences between early Confucian thinkers like Kongzi and Western liberal philosophers like Rawls are not as easily characterized as it might seem and that there is much we miss in both accounts when we take them to be as radically different as some scholars suggest. These characterizations have tended to neglect the diversity of views found within both Confucianism and Western liberalism, and they have also sometimes misrepresented the views of both Confucian and liberal philosophers. If one accepts these characterizations, one misses out on a number of interesting and important aspects of the work of these philosophers. In addition, one who accepts these characterizations is likely to dismiss out of hand the possibility of fruitful comparison, and as a result one may miss out on many of the things that can be gained by a comparison of thinkers such as Kongzi and Rawls. I argue that a *comparative* reading of Rawls and the *Analects* can help us to appreciate features of both early Chinese philosophy and Western political philosophy that these views neglect, thus helping us to correct a number of mistaken assumptions. It is important to clarify here that I am *not* claiming that a comparative study of Rawls and the *Analects* is the *only* way to accomplish this goal; rather, my claim is simply that a comparative study *can* help to do this. This constitutes yet another reason why a comparative study of Rawlsian and Confucian accounts of a sense of justice is worthwhile: It can help us to see why there are good reasons to reject certain widely held views about the absence of terms like "justice" in classical Chinese, and about the differences between Chinese and Western political philosophy more generally.

Before turning my attention to a more detailed discussion of these views, I want to say a bit more about why this study focuses on Kongzi and Rawls, in particular. As I indicated previously, my first reason for selecting Kongzi and Rawls as my sources is that these figures have been the subject of much secondary literature, and in my independent study of both Rawls and the *Analects* I came to believe that both of their views were mischaracterized in this literature. My second reason for selecting Kongzi and Rawls is that in examining their work I found that a sense of justice has an important place in each of their views, and comparing and contrasting their accounts of this capacity led me to a more robust understanding of their views and a sense of justice in general. Clearly, my reasons for selecting Kongzi and Rawls highlight some of the key contributions this study makes, including responding to widespread views in the secondary literature and showing how comparative work can deepen our understanding of particular ideas, thinkers, and traditions. In outlining my reasons for choosing Kongzi and Rawls for this book, I am not claiming that comparisons of other Confucian and Western political philosophers could not be fruitful as well; to the contrary, I hope this study prompts others to explore and take seriously other potential comparative studies.

Justice Without "Justice" in the Analects?

Over the past two decades, work concerning human rights and Chinese thought has proliferated.[9] This topic has become an increasingly common focus in comparative philosophy over the past fifteen years, and much of this work has focused on highlighting the areas of agreement and disagreement between modern Western liberalism and Confucianism. Comparative studies in this area can helpfully be divided into three major groups. First are those who maintain that the central tenets of modern Western liberalism are in some important ways compatible with the fundamental ideas of the Confucian tradition.[10] The second and third groups comprise those who maintain that the central tenets of modern Western liberalism are a marked contrast with Confucian views and perhaps even fundamentally incompatible with them. While the second group maintains that the Confucian tradition's failure to address certain liberal concerns represents a shortcoming of Confucian political philosophy,[11] those in the third group argue that Confucianism offers a welcome alternative and potential solution to the problems found within and perhaps even created by modern liberal political philosophy.[12] Many of these studies have helped to highlight the way in which philosophical traditions can offer insight into different cultural and historical concerns, as well as the need to take seriously the role of the family in the basic structure of society. However, several of them have also neglected the diversity of views represented in both the Confucian and Western liberal traditions and have tended to emphasize the differences between Confucian and Western views of political philosophy in ways that are prone to neglecting important features of works in both traditions. My aim here is to provide an introduction to some of these discussions in order to make clear where the contributions of my study lie relative to other important work in this field.

In contrast to the overwhelming body of work concerning human rights, only a handful of essays have explored understandings of justice in Confucianism.[13] In order to begin to understand why studies of Chinese political philosophy have focused more on rights than on justice, it is helpful to examine more closely the basic claims these studies make. A number of scholars of early Chinese thought accept the view that if a philosopher's language lacks a term for "rights" or "justice," this lack is sufficient to demonstrate that the philosopher has no concept of "rights" or "justice."[14] The widely accepted belief that there is no term in classical Chinese that uniquely refers to what we call "justice" is one reason why little attention has been given to the subject of justice in Chinese thought. Although few scholars believe there is a term in classical Chinese that uniquely refers to what we call "rights," many have been more willing to overlook this because the subject of human rights is seen as a pressing area of study.[15] Much of the work in this area is geared toward addressing the need for the protection of human rights in China today, with a special focus on the resources that exist within the Chinese philosophical tradition for constructing a productive dialogue with the Chinese about human rights.[16] There is a tendency in the literature comparing Western liberalism and Confucianism to make a connection between the strategic matter of how to build the strongest case for increased protections of human rights in China and the conceptual question of whether anything like the Western conception of human rights exists in the indigenous philosophies of China.[17]

Stephen Angle and Marina Svensson have noted that the concept of rights found in the Chinese tradition is a normative notion, dependent on, among other things, an understanding of justice.[18] But their work, like many other scholarly discussions of human rights and Chinese thought, focuses on the idea of rights. Quite understandably, there is a tendency in discussions of human rights and Chinese thought to assume that a just society is a good thing and to focus on the question of how best to achieve a just society through understandings of certain rights. As a result of the assumption that human rights protections either help or hinder the establishment of a just society, few who commend the study of Confucian philosophy as a way of better understanding or communicating about the subject of human rights have questioned whether or not the ideal Confucian society *is* just. Later in this section, we will see that most scholars who have explicitly addressed the concept of justice in Confucianism have argued—despite their insistence that there is no term for "justice" in classical Chinese—that the Confucians addressed issues that fall under the rubric of justice "understood broadly" and that the ideal Confucian society was, in some important sense, just.

Despite the fact that many who study human rights in relation to early Confucianism often overlook the absence of a term for "rights" or conclude that its absence is not especially significant, the view that one must produce a term for "justice" in order to show that there was an understanding of justice in early China remains prevalent. A number of scholars have pointed out the absence of a term for "justice" in early China. In the essay "Confucian Justice: Achieving a Humane Society," Randall P. Peerenboom writes that "there is not even a term for 'justice' in the classical lexicon of [Kongzi]." Peerenboom says, "The most likely candidate, *yi*, has been translated in terms associated with justice—righteousness, duty, principle, obligation—though never, to my knowledge, consistently as justice." He concludes that the absence of a term for "justice" should not trouble us because "such Western-influenced language is inappropriate in the Confucian context."[19] A number of other scholars affirm this basic view. In "The Aesthetics of Justice: Harmony and Order in Chinese Thought," Alan Fox writes, "*Yi* as it functions in the Confucian sense is a kind of moral intuition, a sense of right and wrong, which might be described as serving justice, but certainly not as constituting it."[20] Similarly, in "Social Justice: Rawlsian or Confucian?" Ruiping Fan notes that there is no term for "justice" in the Confucian tradition and writes, "Apparently, the classical Confucian literature, although profound in its social concern and rich in its range of topics, does not have a single concept congruent with the Western notion of justice. . . ."[21] Even those who maintain that the concept of justice *is* found in Confucianism usually attempt to identify a term for "justice" in order to show that the concept exists. In the essay "Trying to Do Justice to the Concept of Justice in Confucian Ethics," Yang Xiao argues that the term *yi* can be translated as "justice" in some instances, which "is enough for proving that there is a concept of justice in ancient China."[22] Henry Rosemont Jr. argues that the absence or presence of particular terms is especially significant because it tells us whether there was an understanding of certain concepts. He writes that for the early Confucians, "[t]here are no traditional close semantic equivalents for 'democracy,' 'justice,' or 'rights,'" nor are there "analogous lexical items for most of the modern Western basic vocabulary for developing moral and political theories: 'autonomy,' 'freedom,' 'liberty,'. . . ."[23] As a result of the absence of such terms, Rosemont concludes, there are no such concepts in early Confucianism, because

> the only way it can be maintained that a particular concept was held by an author is to find a term expressing that concept in his text. Thus we cannot say so-and-so had a "theory of X," or that he "espoused X principles," if there is no X in the lexicon of the language in which the author wrote.[24]

Rosemont, then, makes clear why he sees the absence of a term for "justice" as especially noteworthy, for he maintains that without a term for "justice" in classical Chinese, we cannot show that the concept of justice exists in classical Confucian thought.

In addition to the larger question of whether the absence of a term conclusively indicates the absence of a concept, three additional questions must be answered in order to understand fully the position of these scholars. If one thinks there must be a term for "justice" in order for there to be a concept of justice, then one's answer to any one of these questions could lead one to conclude that there is no concept of justice in classical Confucianism. The first question is whether one defines a term as a single lexical item that consistently and uniquely corresponds to the concept it denotes. Second is the question of whether one thinks justice is a part of the semantic range of any classical Chinese characters. The third question is how one understands the concept of justice. I consider these questions in order, before addressing the larger question of whether the absence of a term implies the absence of a concept.

In order to understand why the question of how one defines a term is important for my analysis, it will be helpful to note that Rosemont and Peerenboom both acknowledge their indebtedness to the writings of Alasdair MacIntyre on this set of issues. According to MacIntyre, "[T]here is no expression in any ancient or medieval language correctly translated by our expression 'a right' until near the close of the middle ages: the concept lacks any means of expression in Hebrew, Greek, Latin or Arabic, classical or medieval, before 1400, let alone in Old English, or in Japanese even as late as the mid–nineteenth century."[25] Rosemont and Peerenboom add classical Chinese to MacIntyre's list of languages lacking a term for "a right." Further, they endorse MacIntyre's claim that it follows from the fact that there was no term for "a right" that no one in these cultures had a concept of rights.[26] According to MacIntyre, if a concept "lacks any means of expression" in a given language, then the members of the culture who speak that language have no acquaintance with the said concept. Before discussing the reasons why I think this view is problematic, we should notice that MacIntyre moves quickly from the claim that there is no expression "*correctly translated* by our expression 'a right'" to the conclusion that "the concept [of a right] lacks *any* means of expression" in the languages he mentions.[27] MacIntyre does not specify what he means by a "correct translation" of an expression. Does he mean a *single* lexical item that *uniquely corresponds to* the concept of a right? Or does he allow for multiple lexical items or phrases to serve as translations? Most scholars who note the absence of a term for "justice" in classical Chinese consider only single lexical items (characters) in classical Chinese as possible candidates for translations of the term "justice." That is, they maintain that there is not a term for "justice" in classical Chinese because there is not a single lexical item that uniquely corresponds to the concept of justice on each occasion of its use.

However, it is not a reasonable requirement that a *single* lexical item must uniquely and consistently correspond to a concept in order to serve as a correct translation. As any translator knows, lexical items—especially those denoting concepts rather than discrete objects—simply do not have such narrow semantic ranges. Furthermore, the standard definition of a term is not a single lexical item that uniquely and consistently corresponds to a concept. There are two separate issues here: the matter of whether a term is "a single lexical item" and the matter of whether a term must "uniquely and consistently correspond" to the concept it describes. Regarding the first matter, on the standard definition, a term consists of "a word or phrase used to describe a thing or to express a concept"[28] or, for our purposes, one Chinese character or a group of characters. Some concepts are expressed not by single lexical items but by combinations of them, or phrases.

Philip J. Ivanhoe provides some helpful examples of terms that consist of multiple lexical items. He argues that the larger problem here is the failure to distinguish between a term and a concept, or what he calls a kind of "character fetishism," in which Chinese characters are thought to be identical to the ideas they represent.[29] He points out that this problem sometimes manifests itself in the tendency to neglect the fact that in some cases, multiple words or characters form terms that express concepts. Ivanhoe provides the example of the claim that there was nothing called "Confucianism" at this stage of Chinese history. He writes,

While there was not a single word designating the Confucian tradition at this point in time (the term *ru* 儒 surely did have a much broader and unregulated sense), there was a very clear sense among a certain group of scholars that Kongzi had preserved and codified a particular set of ideas, practices, and related classical texts that embodied the way of the former kings. This was described as "the Way of Kongzi" and was advocated and defended against competing ways.[30]

The terms Ivanhoe mentions appear in *Mengzi* 3B9 and comprise four characters each (*xian sheng zhi dao* 先圣之道 and *Kongzi zhi dao* 孔子之道). These are examples of multiple lexical items used to denote a single concept. As Ivanhoe points out, Kongzi's followers used terms that clearly show they were conscious of themselves as a distinct group dedicated to certain themes, texts, and to the person Kongzi. That is, they had a concept of themselves as a distinct school of thought—which is the concept we denote by the term "Confucianism."[31]

As we can see, the absence of a *single* lexical item designating a concept does not mean that there is not a term for that concept, because a term can consist of multiple lexical items. In addition, though, there is the matter of whether a term must *uniquely and consistently* designate a concept. According to this claim, the term for "justice" must mean *only* justice on *each* occasion of its use. This view, however, excludes terms with a broad semantic range—terms that have different meanings on different occasions of their use and that may in some cases carry more than one meaning on the same occasion of their use.[32] For instance, it might be the case that *yi* 義 ("rightness") is sometimes used in the sense of "appropriateness," while other times it is used to mean "justice," and on still other occasions it is used to describe something that is both appropriate and just.[33] We can see, then, how the view that terms are single lexical items or that they uniquely and consistently correspond to concepts could lead someone to conclude that there is not a term for "justice" at all, when in fact there might be a term that consists of multiple lexical items or has a broad semantic range, or both. Of course, the matter of whether one thinks justice is a part of the semantic range of certain Chinese characters depends on how one understands the concept of justice, and this is an issue that I will address in the following chapters.

The general question of whether the absence of a term implies the absence of a concept is the last and most important issue we need to consider. Bryan W. Van Norden has argued that this view, which he dubs "the lexical fallacy," is based on an erroneous principle, and that there are many examples of authors who have a particular concept or who have a view about something even though they have no term in their lexicon for it. For example, he writes, "[O]utside of crossword puzzle fans and those in the shoelace industry, almost no English speakers know the word 'aglet.' However, I submit that almost all English speakers have the concept of 'the plastic or metal tip on the end of a shoelace.'"[34] Van Norden goes on to point out that in some cases, the absence of particular terms may be significant, while in other cases the absence may not be important at all. As a result, "We have to look at the particulars of the two languages being compared in order to determine whether the presence or absence of a particular term is significant."[35] What Van Norden helps us to see is that even if one could show that there is not *any* term that *ever* means "justice" in classical Chinese, this evidence would still not be sufficient to show that there is no understanding of the concept of justice in classical Chinese thought. Philosophical discussions sometimes reveal an understanding of a concept without a single term designating the concept that is being discussed. There are multiple examples of this in the *Analects*, including the concept of self-cultivation. Although there is a well-developed account of self-cultivation in the *Analects*, a single term does not consistently represent this idea in the text. In Chapter 3 I argue that multiple terms are used to describe self-cultivation and that this is significant in relation to my argument about a sense of justice, but for now I will simply note that throughout the text, the concept of self-cultivation is described through discussions of ideas such as *de* 德 ("Virtue," "moral power," "moral charisma") and the *junzi* 君子 ("exemplary person"). Terms such as *xue* 學 ("learning"), *xiu* 修 ("cultivating"), *si* 思 ("reflecting"), *xing* 省 ("examining"), and *xi* 習 ("reviewing," "practicing") describe some of the activities that constitute the process of self-cultivation. However, no one of these terms alone consistently designates the concept of self-cultivation.[36] Yet despite the fact that no one of these terms is consistently used in all discussions of self-cultivation, few if any scholars of Confucianism would defend the claim that there is no concept of self-cultivation in the *Analects*.[37] Similarly, although the character *xing* 性 ("human nature") appears only twice in the *Analects*, it seems clear that Kongzi has a *view* about human nature, even if it is not an explicitly developed *theory* as in the works of Mengzi and Xunzi.[38] The following claim in *Analects* 1.2 clearly reflects a view of human nature, without using the term *xing* 性: "The *junzi* applies himself to the roots. 'Once the roots are firmly established, the Way will grow.' Might we not say that filiality and respect for elders are the root of *Ren* (humaneness)?"[39]

Here we see one respect in which the text of the *Analects* differs significantly from, say, Socratic dialogues. Socrates and his interlocutors typically search for definitions of terms as a way of understanding certain ideas, meaning that they are likely to use a single term repeatedly as they analyze and reject various definitions of the concept they are discussing. In the *Analects*, Kongzi and his interlocutors engage in discussions that concern a range of interlocking ideas. They provide detailed accounts of these ideas through dialogue and description but not by offering simple definitions to be rejected or affirmed, which means that they are not as likely to use a single term repeatedly in reference to the ideas they are discussing.

In summary, there are a number of reasons why the claim that because there is no term for "justice" in classical Chinese there is no concept of justice is ultimately indefensible. First, this claim is often based on the assumption that a single term must uniquely and consistently represent the concept of justice. Such a view excludes phrases (combinations of multiple lexical items) or lexical items with a broad semantic range from being considered as terms, as well as combinations of different terms used in various discussions that together might express an understanding of justice.[40] In addition, as we have seen, there are abundant counter-examples to the claim that the absence of a term indicates the absence of a concept.[41] As a result, even if there is not a term in classical Chinese that clearly and consistently designates the concept of justice, we should not assume that this means classical Chinese philosophers did not have an understanding of justice, or that they did not write about it.

A small group of scholars have written essays specifically on the subject of justice in early Confucianism, and I want to discuss briefly those essays that deal with justice in the *Analects* in order to highlight the distinctive contribution my study makes to this literature.[42] A review of these studies also helps to underscore the prevalence of the view that there are certain essential, mutually exclusive defining characteristics of Confucian and Western liberal thinkers, and as a result they cannot be fruitfully compared.[43]

Randall Peerenboom (1990), Alan Fox (1995), Xunwu Chen (1997), Yang Xiao (1997), and Ruiping Fan (2003) all argue that we find a distinctive understanding of justice in early Confucianism that differs substantially from Western views of justice.[44] Peerenboom argues that there is no concept of justice in Confucianism that resembles the concept of justice in Western philosophy, because for Kongzi, the ideal of society is social harmony and humaneness instead of justice.[45] Peerenboom goes on to write that a just state is a humane state, one in which each member contributes his or her unique talents to the realization of the highest quality of social harmony achievable. Justice is an aesthetic judgment of quality rather than a deduction from first principles, justice as a harmonization of the disparate interests and potentialities in the creation of a maximally humane state is a matter of degree, and context dependent.[46]

Like Peerenboom, Fan argues that classical Confucian literature "does not have a single concept congruent with the Western notion of justice," either in the sense of "giving everyone their due" or in the sense of "treating people as equals."[47] Fan argues that a society centered on humaneness (*Ren*) constitutes a "Confucian theory of justice" and that in classical Confucianism we find implicit principles of justice.[48] He writes, "[T]he ultimate concern of the Confucian general justice is loving humans by pursuing intrinsic goods rather than distributing instrumental benefits."[49] Chen, too, highlights particular Confucian virtues as constituting a view of justice, writing that "a Confucian conception of justice as a constellation of fairness, harmony, and righteousness" provides "a general intellectual, moral and institutional scheme for a fair society in which individuals can realize themselves as humans in a full sense."[50] Fox, on the other hand, highlights some general functions of a conception of justice: It informs the basic structure of society, leads to social order, is widely agreed upon by members of society, and helps to clarify and prioritize moral considerations. He goes on to argue that some concepts in early Confucianism function in the same way.[51] As a result, he maintains, we can say that there is a conception of justice in early Confucianism.

A shared challenge these accounts face is making clear exactly *why* the qualities they highlight as defining the concept of justice in Confucianism ought to be referred to as "justice." In the case of Peerenboom, Fan, and Chen, it is unclear why we shouldn't simply refer to ideas like humaneness and harmony *instead of* justice, for the values they describe clearly differ in important ways from justice—even if we take justice in the most general sense. In the work of Fox, on the other hand, we find functions that are not unique to justice, for many different kinds of things other than justice often inform the structure of society, lead to social order, create widespread agreement among members of a society, and clarify and prioritize moral considerations. As a result, it remains unclear how these accounts of a distinctive understanding of justice constitute an understanding of justice at all.[52] Fan as well as others whose work I have surveyed here are right to argue against any simple reading of Kongzi as a liberal defender of Rawlsian justice. This is an important point with which I wholly agree. All of the essays I have discussed aim to show that genuine ethical and political views are present in Confucian texts, and that these understandings of human societies are worthy of our consideration. I agree with these claims, as well. These works clearly identify values and ideals that, according to certain Confucian texts, help members of society to get along better. But further work needs to be done in order to clarify why we ought to call these values and ideals "justice."

In contrast with the views I have just discussed, Yang Xiao argues that in the *Analects* and the *Mengzi*, "the concept expressed by the term *yi* [義 ("rightness")] in Confucian ethics is a concept of justice."[53] He also adopts a clear definition of justice: "[T]reat like cases alike and different cases differently," derived from H.L.A. Hart's observation that the leading precept of justice has traditionally been formulated this way. Xiao goes on to offer examples from the *Mengzi* and the *Analects* of the view that "If someone invariably sticks to a general rule, he does not have *yi*."[54] Xiao acknowledges that *yi* does not always refer to treating like cases alike and different cases differently. However, he writes, "The fact that *sometimes* [*yi*] behaves like 'just' is enough for proving that there is a concept of justice in ancient China."[55] Of the various accounts of justice in Confucianism that we have examined, Yang Xiao's account is the only one that offers a definition of justice as a distinct concept that applies to a certain range of cases in a way that other important Confucian concepts do not. Xiao's account is also the only one that offers an understanding of justice which addresses some of the distinct issues that various Western conceptions of justice address. These are distinctive strengths and should not be overlooked. At the same time, I think there is more to the appreciation of justice in the *Analects* than treating like cases alike and different cases differently, but in order to appreciate this we will need to broaden our understanding of these matters beyond the idea of *yi*.

I agree with all of these scholars that there is an understanding of and an appreciation for justice in the *Analects*. I also agree that the understanding of justice seen in the *Analects* has some distinctive features, which are— as many of these scholars note—especially apparent when it is compared with the account of justice found in Rawls. In addition, I agree that ideas such as humaneness (*Ren*) and rightness (*yi*) are central to this understanding of justice, as well as a range of other important virtues and practices. I do think, though, that the understanding of justice found in the *Analects* shares some important features with the views of other thinkers who have written about justice, including Rawls, and that is why I think it is appropriate to call it "justice." Unlike these studies, though, my primary focus in this work is not the concept of justice or a theory of justice; rather, I focus on the capacity for a sense of justice, or the capacity to feel or perceive what is fair. Accordingly, my discussions of the concept of justice and theories of justice concern the relationship between these things and a sense of justice. I argue that there is a shared understanding of and appreciation for this capacity in both Rawls and the *Analects* and that both express an interest in how this capacity is developed. I will thus devote my attention primarily to questions of moral psychology, as opposed to more general questions relating to justice. Nevertheless, as we turn our attention to the Rawlsian and Confucian accounts in the following chapters, we will examine what defines our ordinary understanding of the concept of social justice and, more important, what it means to say that one possesses a sense of justice.

Textual Matters

Before offering an overview of my argument and the issues that are examined in each chapter, I wish to address some important historical and textual matters concerning the way I will proceed with respect to the texts on both sides of my comparative project. It will become apparent in a moment that the work of John Rawls is substantially easier to address than the text of the *Analects*, but nonetheless it will be helpful for the reader to understand the view of Rawls's corpus that informs my argument.

There has been considerable discussion of the relation between Rawls's early work, which culminated in *A Theory of Justice* (1971), and his later *Political Liberalism* (1993). Scholars have speculated about the continuity in Rawls's views and whether certain apparent changes are responses to communitarian critiques of Rawls's early work. I think it is best to consider Rawls's own remarks on this matter first. In his final work, *Justice as Fairness: A Restatement*, Rawls discusses where genuine revisions in his work occur between his earlier and later work and the impact they have on his overall view. He writes that there are three main changes from the view presented in *A Theory of Justice*: ". . . first, changes in the formulation and content of the two principles of justice used in justice as fairness; second, changes in how the argument for those principles from the original position is organized; and third, changes in how justice as fairness itself is to be understood: namely, as a political conception of justice rather than as part of a comprehensive moral doctrine."[56]

The last revision Rawls mentions has been the source of much scholarly discussion.[57] In *Political Liberalism*, Rawls specifies that although the distinction between a comprehensive doctrine and a political conception is absent from *Theory*, and the change from one to the other is a significant shift in the view as a whole, "nearly all the structure and substantive content of justice as fairness" goes unchanged into that conception as a political one.[58] The fact that Rawls acknowledges both fundamental continuity and significant changes in his work allows for a spectrum of positions on how to understand the relationship between his early and later works. Almost all acknowledge a degree of change with respect to the issue of comprehensive versus political liberalism.[59] Some emphasize the continuity, reading *Political Liberalism* as articulating what is implicit in *Theory*, while others emphasize the changes, arguing that the shift in Rawls's view is a response to communitarian criticisms of his work. Rawls's own view does not embrace either of these positions. He says that the distinction between a comprehensive doctrine and a political conception was "unfortunately absent" from *Theory*, but he also maintains that there is not a basis for saying that the changes are replies to criticisms raised by communitarians and others (*PL*, 177n, xixn respectively).

I accept Rawls's own assessment of his work because I think the account he provides is consistent with what we find in his work. Rawls writes that the distinction between a comprehensive doctrine and political liberalism should be seen as

> . . . clarifying how justice as fairness is to be understood . . . . Even though the problems examined in *Theory* in any detail are always the traditional and familiar ones of political and social justice, the reader can reasonably conclude that justice as fairness was set out as part of a comprehensive moral doctrine that might be developed later should success encourage the attempt. This restatement removes that ambiguity: justice as fairness is now presented as a political conception of justice. To carry out this change in how justice as fairness is to be understood forces many other changes and requires a family of further ideas not found in *Theory*, or at least not with the same meaning or significance. (*JF*, xvii)

I view the important changes in Rawls's work as developments rather than as thoroughgoing revisions, primarily because of Rawls's desire to show that his position was not vulnerable to objections raised by his communitarian critics. Although my discussion draws primarily on Rawls's later work, especially *Justice as Fairness* because it is the final formulation of his

view, I think Stephen Mulhall and Adam Swift are correct to point out that
". . . doing justice both to Rawls and to his critics will require us to refer
to both [*Theory* and the later work]. The communitarians were writing in
criticism of the first, but both it and some subsequent writings that were
available to them already provided responses to many of their objections—
responses which a more careful reading might have taken into account."[60]

The textual issues surrounding the *Lunyu* 論語 (the *Analects*) are more
complicated. There is considerable disagreement about the integrity of
the received text of this collection of the teachings of Kongzi and his students. The text compiled by He Yan 何晏 (190–249 C.E.) is divided into
twenty books, which are further divided into chapters that vary in length
from sentence-long quotations to dialogues. Early discussions of the *Analects* mention the existence of three different versions of the *Analects* in the
Western Han, each with a different number of books.[61] Almost all contemporary scholars of the text agree that it was composed by several different
authors from different time periods, and that it may be a synthesis of the
three versions in existence in the Han. Although I follow the view that it
is unlikely that any stratum of the *Analects* was composed after the early
fourth century B.C.E., disagreement among scholars of the *Analects* surfaces
with respect to the question of how many different strata of the text there
are, how they should be dated, and how much weight we should put on the
existence of different strata.[62]

D. C. Lau maintains that the *Analects* can be separated into two strata—
the first fifteen books and the last five. Lau draws on the work of Qing dynasty scholar Cui Shu 崔述 (1740–1816), who demonstrated on linguistic
grounds that the last five books of the *Analects* are significantly later than
the others. Nonetheless, Lau still treats the text as presenting a unified vision.[63] Arthur Waley suggests that books 3–9 represent the oldest stratum
of the text.[64] As Van Norden has pointed out, Waley may be referring to
the thematic or organizational unity of each of these books, which may
indicate that they were edited around the same time.[65] On Waley's view,
then, another distinct stratum of the text exists in addition to Lau's two.

Steven Van Zoeren goes even further in his form-critical approach to
the *Analects*, maintaining that there are four strata: books 3–7, 1–2 and
8–9, 10–15, and 16–20.[66] Van Zoeren argues that these strata represent
not only different time periods but also substantially different viewpoints.
The most extreme position on the stratification of the text, however, is
the view E. Bruce Brooks and A. Taeko Brooks present in their work *The
Original Analects*.[67] Brooks and Brooks argue that each book of the *Analects*
represents a discrete stratum, and they identify a large number of later

interpolations within each book in an attempt to support their claim that the text was composed over a longer period of time than has generally been accepted. They argue, for instance, that the later strata were put together as late as the third century B.C.E. Further, Brooks and Brooks see the text as a heterogeneous collection of different perspectives.[68]

The only agreement among these scholars on the strata, excepting Brooks and Brooks, is that books 16–20 represent a later stratum of the text. But there seems to be a larger disagreement between textual scholars using the form-critical approach, such as Van Zoeren and Brooks and Brooks, and philosophers working on the text. As Van Zoeren notes, textual scholars using the form-critical approach tend to "systematically discount the continuities in a tradition, perhaps unfairly."[69] On the other hand, philosophers have tended to set the textual issues aside based on their view that the influence of the received text alone merits its study. Both sides of this debate make important points, and scholars who study early Chinese texts should work to appreciate how both kinds of work can reveal interesting and important things about texts such as the *Analects*. Philosophers accurately emphasize that the *Analects* in the form we have it is an integral part of the foundation of the Confucian tradition. Roger Ames and Henry Rosemont point out that the accumulation of evidence in favor of any given theory about the composition of the *Analects*, though interesting and important, does not bring into question the enormous influence of the received text. As they argue, "It thus deserves to be read as carefully and as deliberately as it was read by seventy-odd generations of Chinese, in just the form in which it has been handed down to us."[70] I agree with their view, and it is important to recognize that many features of the received text lend support to this position. In addition to the profound influence the received text has had on Chinese culture and on a number of cultures throughout Asia in both pre-modern and modern times, it has generated the rich and extensive commentarial tradition. On the other hand, although this information contributes to the argument for studying the received text, textual scholars are correct to point out that it is not a justification for ignoring the textual issues. Form-critical work and studies of the textual history can reveal a number of interesting features of the text. Unfortunately, those who are narrowly focused on this kind of work often insist on attending exclusively to when particular passages and lines were composed and what the earliest versions of the text may have looked like, while denying that studies of the ideas and themes in the received text also have merit. Obviously, scholars who embrace this type of view will not be interested in this book.

A part of studying the *Analects* as an important philosophical text is considering the extent to which it provides a consistent, unified view on various subjects. Given that the text of the *Analects* is a collection of chapters with interpolations from different eras, written by different authors, we should not be surprised to find a wide range of ideas advocated in the text. However, the existence of distinct and even competing views on certain topics does not preclude the existence of unified themes and ideas. For example, one might find that descriptions of certain virtues are quite consistent throughout the text, while there are different and at times competing accounts of other virtues. In addition, one might find passages that seem to provide different accounts of what constitutes filial conduct or ritual propriety but still find unity in the basic understanding of these ideas and the fact that they are regarded as virtues throughout the text.[71]

In general, I believe the received text of the *Analects* exhibits a high degree of unity and consistency in its themes and ideas. I think that across most of the text, competing accounts of the same concept, or the clearly identifiable presence of multiple and significantly different accounts of the same concept, are the exception rather than the rule. For example, I do not believe there are many different views across the text of what constitutes filial piety. In cases where two or more passages are difficult to square with one another, one usually still finds the same basic vision for human beings and the virtues they should cultivate. Furthermore, it should not surprise us that there would be passages in ancient Chinese texts that are difficult for twenty-first-century Western readers to understand, nor should it surprise us to find some degree of diversity in a text that we know was composed by different authors and that also contains interpolations. As I noted earlier, the *Analects*, like many early Chinese texts, is the product of a family of thinkers associated with a particular founding figure and philosophical vision. All of these issues must be taken into consideration and carefully balanced by readers of the *Analects*.

Although I think the *Analects* presents a reasonably unified and consistent vision for human beings and the societies they live in, my argument regarding a sense of justice in the *Analects* does not *assume* that there is a unified, consistent, and coherent account of this idea. Indeed, it is my responsibility to provide the textual evidence in support of my argument that there is a unified, consistent and coherent account of a sense of justice, and it is also my responsibility to anticipate and answer the objections raised by counter-examples to my view. In Chapter 3, in the course of setting out the defining features of the understanding of a sense of justice found in the *Analects*, I will attempt to do this. I direct the reader to my chapter on the

Analects because my argument that there is a reasonably consistent and coherent account of a sense of justice in the text—as opposed to multiple and
perhaps contradictory senses of justice—can be supported only through
an examination of the textual evidence. In Chapter 3, I examine the passages from the *Analects* that express a sense of justice in comparison with
and in relation to one other, against the background of the broader ethical vision presented in the *Analects*. As readers will see, I believe there *is* a
unified ethical vision in the *Analects*, and I also think there is ample textual
evidence to support this claim.

Thus, my study assumes there are ideas and themes that consistently
surface throughout the text and together reveal a particular vision for human societies. I believe these ideas and themes distinguish the "school of
Kongzi" from the later work of Mengzi and Xunzi, and this is especially
evident in the absence of debates about human nature, more sophisticated
conceptions of the *xin* 心 ("heart-mind"), and discussions of interschool
rivalries that are found in the *Mengzi* and the *Xunzi*. These facts contribute
to the evidence in support of the view that it is unlikely any stratum of the
Analects was composed after the early fourth century B.C.E.

Unlike fields such as Classics, and areas of philosophy such as Kantian
studies, where there are editions of texts that virtually all scholars use as
their standard in making references, there are as yet no universally accepted
standard texts for ancient Chinese works. Chapter divisions within books
of the *Analects* differ slightly from edition to edition. In my references to
the text, I follow the numbering found in the Chinese University of Hong
Kong Institute of Chinese Studies Ancient Chinese Texts Concordance
Series. English-language translations typically follow or approximate this
organization of the text. As indicated, some translations from the *Analects*
in this work are my own while others follow the translation by Edward
Slingerland (2003) with my modifications. In addition, I refer to two traditional commentaries on the *Analects*: the collections of commentaries by
He Yan 何晏 et al., *Lun yu ji jie* 論語集解 (242 C.E.) and Zhu Xi 朱熹, *Si shu
ji zhu* 四書集注 (1177 C.E.). All translations from these two works are my
own, unless otherwise noted.

Overview

This study has two main goals. My first aim, as we have already seen, is to
show the importance and the contemporary relevance of a sense of justice
in Rawls's work and in the *Analects*, thereby helping to show that Rawls's

moral psychology is worthy of sustained study while also helping to correct the view that classical Confucian philosophers were not interested in ideas that are the focus of modern Western political philosophy. My second aim is to address the more general question of what makes comparative studies of works from different ethical, political, religious, and cultural traditions worthwhile. Accordingly, in addition to making important contributions to our understanding of Rawls, Confucianism, a sense of justice, and its contemporary relevance, this work also makes a general contribution to the field of comparative philosophy, both in its explicit discussion of a range of critical issues in comparative work and through its distinctive conclusions concerning Kongzi and Rawls.

My approach is not to compare individual terms or concepts found in Rawls and the *Analects*. Instead, I examine the way certain concepts and themes function together to create a sense of justice that in turn contributes to a larger account of a well-ordered and stable society in Rawls and a harmonious and humane society in the *Analects*. I have chosen this approach for two primary reasons. First and foremost, I maintain that focusing on a set of concepts and themes leads to a more accurate understanding of both of the views under study; it is part of my argument that an understanding of a sense of justice in both Rawls and the *Analects* requires an understanding of the way multiple concepts and themes intersect. In the previous section I discussed some of the reasons why this area of agreement between Rawls and the *Analects* has been neglected, and an important part of my argument concerns the mistaken view that the absence of a term that uniquely refers to justice in the *Analects* is sufficient evidence to show that there is no concept of justice in the *Analects*. I argue that an understanding of a sense of justice emerges from a number of different concepts, even though none of them alone uniquely designates a sense of justice. Likewise, I show how a number of important ideas in Rawls have been neglected in studies that focus on only one or two concepts. Thus, an accurate understanding of a sense of justice in *both* texts under study requires a broader examination of the ideas at work in them.

The second reason I focus on a set of concepts and themes is that I think this approach can help comparative philosophers avoid some of the interpretive problems that other methods sometimes exacerbate—something I explore in detail in the next chapter of this work. In Chapter 1 I focus on methods in comparative work, including the general question of why comparative work is worthwhile. I distinguish between and evaluate the different kinds of answers that have been offered to this question in major studies in comparative and Chinese thought, including those that have influenced my own view. I also discuss the difference between reasons for doing comparative work that focus on what I refer to as "extrinsic value," as opposed to those focused more on "intrinsic value," and I argue that in most cases, the latter will be especially important for philosophers. Chapter 1 also examines the different kinds of issues that can cause difficulties in comparative work. I distinguish between interpretive, thematic, and procedural issues and examine specific examples of different kinds of approaches to comparative work that address these questions in different ways. I also describe my approach to comparative work in relation to these approaches.

In Chapter 2 I offer an account of Rawls's understanding of the capacity for a sense of justice. I begin with an overview of Rawls's basic view, beginning with his claim that humans have an innate capacity for social cooperation. Rawls argues that humans have two moral powers that give them the capacity to be full participants in a fair system of cooperation: the capacity for a sense of justice and the capacity for a conception of the good. I show that for Rawls a sense of justice is the ability to feel or perceive what is fair, and this sense of justice is the primary source of our motivation to act fairly toward other members of society and to act in accordance with the principles or standards that are designed to help establish and preserve a just society, one that addresses circumstances where individuals suffer as a result of the moral arbitrariness of natural or social contingencies. I discuss how a sense of justice is cultivated within the context of the family, community, and society and the contribution it makes to establishing a society that has "stability for the right reasons," on Rawls's view.

In Chapter 3, I provide an account of the sense of justice in the *Analects*. I begin by discussing the larger context of the self-cultivationist account provided in the *Analects*. I then argue that in the *Analects*, members of society, like members of a family, are expected to have a deep and particular concern for the well-being of other members, because they have the capacity for a sense of justice. I discuss the evidence for this view seen in discussions of *de* 德 ("Virtue") and rulership *jun* 均 ("equal distribution"), and *yi* 義 ("rightness"), as well as a number of other important themes and ideas. I then revisit the distinction between a term and a concept that I made earlier in this Introduction and show why this distinction is important for my argument. Finally, I anticipate and respond to some potential objections to my argument, including apparent counter-examples to my view in the *Analects*.

In Chapter 4, I offer a comparative analysis of the senses of justice in Rawls and the *Analects*. After discussing the central features of a sense of justice as they are seen in each view, I discuss some significant differences and similarities between the two accounts, with a special emphasis placed on the contrast between their aims and the general character of their views. I then turn to the question of why these differences and similarities are particularly instructive for philosophers studying Rawls, the *Analects*, or the idea of a sense of justice. I argue that studying the idea of a sense of justice in the *Analects* alongside a Rawlsian sense of justice highlights some important dimensions of Rawls's work that have been neglected, including the role he assigns to the family and the community in his account of how citizens cultivate a sense of justice, as well as the self-cultivationist dimensions of his account. A comparative reading of Rawls and the *Analects* also highlights some areas in which Rawls's views might be further developed or clarified, including his position on questions of human nature in relation to a sense of justice. I then address how an understanding of Rawls's work can help us to better understand certain aspects of the ethical account presented in the *Analects*, especially concerning the importance of non-arbitrary distinctions between members of society, the relationship between the right and the good, and the importance of the judicial virtues. I also argue that Rawls's account helps readers to see how an appreciation for justice can be expressed in a text like the *Analects*, even though there is not a fully developed theory of justice or a single term that consistently designates "justice." Chapter 4 helps to show how my understanding of what makes comparative work worthwhile differs from that of those who see comparative philosophy primarily as an opportunity to show how one philosophical position can serve as a corrective supplement to another or as an enterprise concerned primarily with arguing for the superiority of one philosophical tradition over another.

Chapter 5 examines the contemporary relevance of a sense of justice, arguing that a sense of justice is important for us today. In the first part of the chapter I show how the capacity for a sense of justice is relevant for the kinds of societies that are the focus of Rawls's work—modern liberal democracies. I argue that the emphasis both Rawls and the *Analects* place on the role of the family in cultivating a sense of justice is particularly important for liberal societies today, and I show how the special attention the early Confucians give to the family can serve as a particularly helpful resource in this regard. I argue that the early-childhood intervention program known as the Nurse-Family Partnership offers a clear example of the sort of public policy that the Confucians might envision for a contemporary liberal society, and that the findings of this program also lend support to certain aspects of early Confucian views, giving us good reasons to take them seriously. In the second part of the chapter, I discuss the relevance of a sense of justice for contemporary China. I argue that the liberal value of diversity envisioned in Rawls's account of a sense of justice can contribute to achieving particular Confucian values and practices such as self-cultivation that are still an important part of Chinese culture today. I show how some important aspects of Confucian moral self-cultivation as it is described in the *Analects* can be deepened and enriched in the presence of ethnic and cultural diversity, which expands one's opportunities to cultivate a sense of justice, one's awareness of how much one does not know, one's understanding of why one should work to learn more, one's resolve and dedication to learning more, and one's appreciation for the diversity of good lives that are available to humans—which can enrich one's life in ways that contribute to the process of self-cultivation. In the final part of the chapter, I discuss the relevance of a sense of justice for international justice, arguing that in both Rawls and the *Analects* we find conceptions of moral and political influence that are related to their views of a sense of justice and that offer interesting insights into questions of international justice.

Finally, in my Conclusion, I revisit the question of why a comparative study of a sense of justice is worthwhile, as well as the three different kinds of challenges that are often faced by comparative studies discussed in the first chapter. I discuss the extent to which I have met these challenges, while also noting that my discussion of the aims of comparative work and my discussion of a sense of justice in Rawls and Kongzi depend upon each other in important ways and are mutually enhancing.

Methods in Comparative Work

Although the central argument of this book aims to help readers to more fully understand and appreciate certain aspects of Rawls's and Kongzi's thought, it also aims to show why comparative studies are sometimes helpful. In the Introduction I discussed the reasons why a comparative study of Rawlsian and Confucian understandings of a sense of justice is worthwhile. But although the question of why comparative studies are worthwhile varies considerably depending upon what one is comparing, there are also some more general reasons for doing comparative work. In the first part of this chapter, I take up this more general question of why comparative work is worth doing. After examining some influential answers to this question offered by scholars of comparative and Chinese thought in the disciplines of religious studies and philosophy, I focus on reasons for doing comparative work that will be of particular interest to philosophers.[1] In the second section of the chapter, I discuss the distinctive challenges that comparativists often face, with the aim of showing that different kinds of issues can pose challenges in comparative work—specifically interpretive, thematic, and procedural issues—and that it can be helpful for comparativists and readers of comparative studies to distinguish between them, both in order to sort out the reasons why some comparative studies are more successful than others and also to show how comparative studies might be compelling in certain respects but not in others. In the concluding part of the chapter, I argue that an "anti-method" approach to comparative work seems more promising than specific, single methods for doing comparative work. On the view I describe, the comparativist does not embrace a particular method or approach but rather seeks to address the various sorts of challenges one faces in comparative work carefully and consistently, possibly utilizing different approaches to address different types of issues.

Why Compare?

In recent years the exploration of similarities and differences between Western philosophy and the philosophical traditions of Asia has become the focus of an increasing volume of philosophical work. Within the discipline of philosophy, comparative philosophy is beginning to be accepted by some philosophers as a field of its own, defined by the study of philosophers and texts from non-Western philosophical traditions in comparison and contrast with Anglo-American, European, Greek, and Roman philosophy. But although comparative philosophers have made progress in terms of gaining recognition within the discipline of philosophy, most philosophers still wonder why studying non-Western philosophy is important, and what comparative studies can accomplish. The latter question is also of relevance in the disciplines of religious studies and theology, where scholars of religion continue to raise—and propose answers to—questions about why comparative work is important, and about the nature and possibility of work that aims to put diverse religious, philosophical, and cultural perspectives in dialogue.[2]

In contrast with the discipline of religious studies, where the study of religions from many parts of the world is seen as important, the discipline of philosophy has been slow to recognize the value of studying philosophical traditions that have roots in other cultures. One reason for this is that unlike fields such as religious studies and theology, where there is widespread acceptance of the fact that there are religious traditions outside those of the West, many philosophers remain skeptical about whether there is, in fact, philosophy outside of the West. Philosophers who do acknowledge that there is philosophy outside of the West often remain skeptical about whether there is anything of substance or value in non-Western philosophy. This is why it remains uncommon for philosophy departments to have any course offerings in non-Western philosophy (other than perhaps a token survey course in "Eastern" or Asian philosophy), while for almost all other disciplines in the humanities—including history, literature, religious studies, and art history—it is almost unthinkable not to include the study of other cultures and traditions, and to study them extensively and in a specialized way. It is also the reason why those philosophers who specialize in non-Western traditions are regularly pressed on the question of whether the ideas they study are indeed philosophical and, if so, why we ought to study them. In contrast, scholars of religion tend not to press specialists in, for example, Asian religions on the question of why we should study those traditions. That is not to say that all scholars of religion are interested in studying other religions; rather, my point is to emphasize that most scholars of religion assume that studying other religions has some value. This marks a deep and important difference between the widespread attitudes found within the disciplines of religious studies and philosophy, and this difference is the reason why much of what I have to say in this section is directed toward philosophers. For most philosophers, the question of why we ought to study the views of any non-Western thinkers is an open one.[3]

It is important to recognize this difference between the disciplines of religious studies and philosophy because it helps to show that there are some distinctive reasons why comparativists in each of these fields are often pressed on the question of why comparative studies are worthwhile. Many philosophers who ask this question are really asking why we should study non-Western philosophy. In the case of religious studies, the "why" question can be taken more at face value. Most scholars of religion do not question that studying non-Western religious traditions has value; rather, what they are asking is why we should compare the ideas of religious thinkers from one tradition with those of another. If anything hovers behind this question, it is usually the skepticism that any scholars really possess the necessary expertise to do such work well, as well as the belief that many comparativists do not have an answer to this question, let alone a compelling one. Rather, many scholars of religion simply think comparativists are doing "comparison for the sake of comparison" and that nothing new can be learned from comparing thinkers in different traditions. It is interesting, of course, that comparativists are often held to a different standard here: How many scholars of religion regularly address why their studies of ancient practices or texts are worthwhile? How many of them are able to demonstrate successfully that they are not "studying religion for the sake of studying religion"? What we see here is that in both the disciplines of religion and philosophy it is important to pose the "why" question to one's colleagues who are not comparativists. What makes studying particular ideas, practices, philosophers, or religious thinkers worthwhile? In both disciplines, if comparativists wish to convince their colleagues that comparative work is worthwhile, they will need to give the same kinds of answers that their colleagues working in other areas give to the question of why their work is important.

For those in religious studies and theology, this will mean demonstrating that something new can be learned from comparing thinkers in different traditions, because one of the primary goals of work in the academic study of religion is to help us to better understand various aspects of particular religious traditions and thinkers. Of course, we can press this question even further and ask why we ought to work to understand different religious traditions and thinkers. In response, one can offer two different kinds of reasons, both of which also apply to a variety of works in other disciplines in the academy. On the one hand, the study of religion can be a means to achieving a variety of *extrinsic goods*—that is, goods extrinsic to the study of religion, such as helping us to better understand and get along with others, something we will examine further below in relation to comparative religious studies. However, not all work in the academy readily contributes to the achievement of extrinsic goods. For example, many if not most studies in the history of religions do not contribute to our understanding of other religions or cultures in ways that will genuinely affect our interactions with others. Particularly in these cases, it is important to remember that a part of what it means to be in the academy and the humanities in the particular is to appreciate intellectual inquiry and learning for its own sake—that is, to see reflection and inquiry as an *intrinsic good*, in other words as something that is good in itself and not simply as a means to an end. On this view, it is inherently good for creatures like us to reflect and inquire, even when it does not lead to the achievement of other (extrinsic) goods, such as jobs, money, prestige, or even goods that most of us value deeply, such as more peaceful interactions with others. One who embraces this view sees life as being richer when it includes reflection and inquiry. When we reflect and inquire, we are caring for our minds just as we care for our bodies through nutrition and exercise; doing so helps us to flourish as human beings.[4]

With these things in mind, it will be helpful for us to examine some well-known studies in comparative religion and comparative ethics as resources for helping us to appreciate the distinctive reasons why comparative work is worth doing. One of the best discussions of the advantages of comparative religious studies can be found in Karen L. Carr and Philip J.

Ivanhoe's *The Sense of Antirationalism: The Religious Thought of Zhuangzi and Kierkegaard*. Carr and Ivanhoe outline three reasons why comparative work is worthwhile: "First, it provides a unique opportunity for greater self-understanding. Second, it helps us to understand and appreciate other traditions. Third, it enhances our understanding of the general phenomenon of religion."[5] First, they write, comparative studies provide a unique opportunity for greater understanding of the culture or tradition with which we are familiar,

> for only by stepping outside of one's home tradition can one gain the perspective required for seeing certain of its features. Only after coming to understand and appreciate a fully naturalized form of spirituality such as early Chinese Daoism, one that sees the sacred as an aspect of and lying wholly within the world of everyday experience, can one feel the full force of the role deity plays in a theistic tradition such as Christianity. In the same way, only after having learned another language can one come to appreciate certain features of one's native tongue. Gaining a facility in and feel for the cultural language of another tradition has the power to make the familiar strange; it can raise into consciousness features of one's own life and views that are submerged in familiarity and routine.[6]

The second advantage of comparative study that Carr and Ivanhoe discuss is that it helps us to better see and appreciate other views, "often in ways that are much less likely outside the comparative approach." Even the thin similarities that we observe in comparative studies remind us that we are looking at human systems of belief, which "can help us not only to understand others as objects of study but also to appreciate them as fellow human beings, people providing distinctive and very different answers to a recognizably similar set of human problems."[7] Third, Carr and Ivanhoe argue that comparative religious studies enhance our understanding of the general phenomenon of religion by "forcing us out of our provincial frames of reference." They offer the example of "the broadening of attempts to define religion that occurred when those within the discipline came to appreciate forms of religion that were devoid of notions of deity. The very notion of what a religion is was transformed in this process and we believe that this transformation reflects a clear improvement, even if the result is to leave considerable doubt as to what a fully adequate definition of religion would be."[8] They argue that this helps to show how comparative studies actively discourage cultural hegemony by providing "unique opportunities for broadening our view of the world and deepening our understanding of our own place within it."[9]

It is helpful to consider a potential objection to Carr and Ivanhoe's view. One might argue that these observations concern the value of comparisons generally and are not unique to comparisons across religious or philosophical traditions. For instance, one *could* come to an appreciation of the strengths and weaknesses of various Christian views without comparing them with other religious views. This objection acknowledges that comparisons are valuable and that upon initial introduction to any view alone, one often does not appreciate the complexity of the question or the strengths and weaknesses of the view under study. However, once one learns of an alternative view, she begins to see what is at stake in answering the question and the problems that can arise in the course of answering it. In the process of comparing and contrasting different answers to the same question, one notices issues that are not addressed by one view, precisely because another view addresses them, and as a result one is better able to evaluate the strengths and weaknesses of various views. What this objection questions is whether we need to do comparisons across different traditions in order to benefit from the advantages Carr and Ivanhoe outline. I offer two responses to this objection. First, it is certainly the case that comparisons of many different kinds are advantageous, but views that offer a distinctively different approach, such as many of the views found in other traditions, tend to be *more* helpful for developing a reflective perspective on one's own views. In general, studying the assumptions of those who are significantly different increases our awareness of our own presuppositions.

However, in response to this claim, one could argue that the Christian tradition itself is full of rich diversity, and at the very least we could find Christian views that are *different enough* to help us develop a more reflective perspective but do not involve the hard work of learning about different traditions. The second response to this objection points to the evidence against this sort of view. As Carr and Ivanhoe argue, if one looks to the history of the study of religion, it is simply not the case that the study of one religion *has* produced the same results that have come from careful comparative studies. It is fairly easy to object to a study on the grounds that one *could have* reached certain conclusions without engaging in comparative study, but whether this is true needs to be demonstrated. We ought to base our assessment of the value of comparative study on actual and not merely possible results. It is important to acknowledge that comparative studies which engage other traditions *have* made some novel and important contributions that were not made in other ways, and this precedent gives us good reasons to think that comparative studies across traditions are worthwhile. Of course, that does not mean that all comparative studies will make important contributions, but it does mean that we have good reasons to think that they can make important and distinctive contributions. As a final note, in anticipation of the objection that comparative studies are not the *only* way to reach certain conclusions, in many cases it will be helpful for comparativists to qualify their claims in order to acknowledge that one *can* come to appreciate certain things without engaging in comparative study. For example, as the Introduction to this book makes clear, my argument is *not* that a comparative study of a sense of justice in Kongzi and Rawls is the *only* way to come to appreciate particular features of both views.[10] It is enough for comparativists to show that comparative studies *do* help us to see or appreciate certain things (and to make clear why those things are important or significant); it is unreasonable to expect them to demonstrate that they offer the only way of seeing or appreciating these things in order to be considered valuable.[11] When what is being shown is a novel insight or discovery, surely this is sufficient ground for us to recognize the value of the study in question.

Lee H. Yearley proposes a novel set of answers to the question of why comparative work is worthwhile in his *Mencius and Aquinas: Theories of Virtue and Conceptions of Courage*. Yearley writes that the comparative study of two thinkers can lead us "to recognize features in each thinker [we] had overlooked and to consider again some ideas whose force [we] had barely recognized before—or sometimes missed completely."[12] Many comparativists share this view of comparison, but there is more to Yearley's view than this claim. Martha Nussbaum notes that the central thesis of Yearley's book involves a larger claim about the reasons why we ought to do comparative work, namely that

> this activity of the imagination—probing analogies, looking for sameness in differences and differences in sameness—is at the heart of cross-cultural understanding. These processes are common in all of human life; they underlie our ability "to understand other people in order to help, befriend, or work with them" (Yearley 1990, 200–201). They are present in and are further developed by the reading of literature and the viewing of art (Yearley 1990, 200). But in the encounter with a different culture they play an especially crucial role.[13]

Nussbaum writes that "all too frequently, we refuse to develop and apply habits of analogical thinking and narrative understanding . . . falling back instead on more routinized and simplistic modes of analysis," and she argues that one of the most important things Yearley's work shows is that comparative studies can help us to develop some of the virtues and habits of thought that are necessary for cross-cultural understanding.[14] This is a novel claim, partly because it focuses not so much on what is learned about particular religious thinkers, traditions, or religion generally but on how comparative studies can change us as human beings. Indeed, Yearley and Nussbaum both emphasize that distinctive advantages come not just from the content of comparative studies (although this is certainly important, too) but also from engaging in the activity of comparison. For Nussbaum, one of the most important reasons why comparative studies are worthwhile is that they can aid us in developing virtues and abilities that help us to more effectively understand and engage in dialogue with others, both across cultural boundaries and within our own culture.

Especially because this is an optimistic view of the impact comparative work can have, it is important to note that neither Yearley nor Nussbaum underestimates the difficulties involved in comparative work. Nussbaum notes the opposing vices that are often seen when one engages in comparative study. On the one hand, we find the "hasty assumption of similarity," or the common tendency to re-create others in our own image, "refusing to see their differences from ourselves, making our world homogenous and safe again by erasure," but on the other hand we also find the "excessive dramatization of strangeness and otherness," or the tendency to view other cultures or traditions as "alien and incomparable, seeing them in terms of difference and otherness alone"—a vice that Nussbaum notes is particularly common in contemporary academic life.[15] These are the kinds of vices that comparative studies give us practice in avoiding, for if we do as Yearley suggests and "pursue the ideal of working with similarities in differences and differences in similarities," then we gain experience in the difficult task of working carefully to understand other cultures, which involves, like careful comparative studies, "results that are small and concrete, attended by many qualifications and subtleties, rather than large and easily summarized."[16] Yearley argues that the ability to think carefully about other traditions and make nuanced comparisons between different kinds of views is particularly important in our world today. For Yearley, it is not simply that we must learn about other cultures, but "we must engage in the normative analysis that such comparisons involve if we are to thrive, or perhaps even survive, in the present world."[17]

It not insignificant that Yearley's approach requires normative evaluation and not simply a description of two views and the similarities and differences between them. Indeed, this is a critical part of Yearley's answer to the question of why comparative studies are worthwhile: They can move us closer to achieving—and helping others in our world to achieve—more humane ways of relating to one another. One of the ways we do this is by considering different alternatives and evaluating their comparative merits. Nussbaum agrees that although it has "become common to insist that all attempts to describe a culture from outside—especially attempts in which normative analysis plays any part—must be illicit impositions of power on the culture being described" and that "The only thing one may do is hear the culture's own self-description—and then, hands off on all normative analysis," normative evaluation in comparative study is essential for a number of reasons.[18] For example, it helps to prepare us for coherent and cooperative multicultural dialogues about issues that affect us all, for these conversations often require reflection on which views and approaches are best.[19] Nussbaum further points out that the refusal to engage in normative reflection on the views and practices of other cultures

> can, in fact, be just as condescending as premature evaluation, if not more so: for one is assuming that the people whom one refuses to evaluate are such that no further information about possibilities and no argument would lead them to criticize a form of life that one finds morally and humanely intolerable oneself. It is bad to use one's own way of life as a standard to which the other is expected to measure up, as if there were no way other than one's own of living a reasonable human life, but it is at least as bad to refuse all application of standards, as if one were dealing with an alien form of life that one could not expect to come up to standards that one happens to think terribly important oneself.[20]

Nussbaum goes on to argue that when the challenge of engaging in normative reflection on the views and practices of other cultures is faced well, "it is faced with procedural tools very similar to those Yearley describes in his account of comparison's virtues," including the use of imagination in discerning both similarity and difference, the use of analogical processes of reasoning, and attentiveness to the concrete texture of a form of life.[21] Nussbaum's discussion here is especially important because it shows how the fruits of comparison are not confined to the academy: Skillful comparisons, on the view Yearley and Nussbaum describe, help us to develop virtues and abilities that are important in a wide range of settings and that are especially relevant in today's world.

As we saw previously, Nussbaum notes a common tendency in contemporary academic life to see other traditions "in terms of difference and otherness alone." Indeed, it is not uncommon for comparativists in religious studies to encounter this view in the form of the objection that there are *insurmountable differences* between different religions, and, as a result, we cannot fruitfully compare any aspects of them. In the discipline of philosophy, however, one of the most common objections comparativists encounter is that the views seen in the work of non-Western philosophers are *exactly the same as* those defended by Western philosophers (often at a much later time in history), and as a result, there is no point in studying the views of non-Western philosophers. This is a revealing difference. Although polar opposites, both views are dismissive of the potential value of comparative work and are often held so dogmatically that it is difficult for comparativists to make any headway by arguing against them.[22] The view more commonly found in religious studies emphasizes the distinctiveness of different religious traditions to the exclusion of any possible (or at least significant) similarities, while the view of many philosophers denies the existence of substantive differences between the views found in different traditions. The latter view can help us to appreciate several distinctive features of the discipline of philosophy. The first is the widely held assumption that any views worth studying in the history of philosophy—that is, views that make genuine contributions to our understanding of important philosophical questions—have already been articulated by Western philosophers. What constitutes a "genuine contribution"? For most philosophers, it is not sufficient for a study simply to add to the body of knowledge about a given thinker or tradition, unless it is clear that at least certain aspects of the views under study might be true or valuable, or that they can contribute to helping us understand views that are true or valuable.[23] This is one of the things that help distinguish philosophy from areas such as intellectual history: Philosophical studies are not normally purely descriptive in character but engage in normative analysis.

As we have seen, the reception of comparative work in the discipline of philosophy is considerably different from other disciplines primarily because of the exclusion of non-Western philosophy from most philosophy departments. However, there are some who think the tide will turn in the near future. In a 2002 essay in *The Aristotelian Society*, Graham Priest predicts that philosophy in the twenty-first century will begin to focus more on Asian traditions of thought, because China and India account for nearly half of the world's population and China's economic development is becoming increasingly difficult to ignore. Priest writes, ". . . the group that has economic dominance also has cultural dominance," and he claims that as cultural dominance shifts, so goes "the centre of gravity of the Western philosophical world."[24] Priest predicts that Asian philosophy will become the central focus of the Western philosophical world.[25] Western philosophers, he writes, are already discovering Asia's "rich philosophical traditions, with problems similar enough to those in the West to be recognizable, but with approaches to them that are different enough to be illuminating, often in a very striking fashion" (99). Priest's comments serve as a helpful starting place in our exploration of the reasons why philosophers tend to see particular traditions, movements, and philosophers as worth studying.

Although many philosophers might reject Priest's assessment of the relationships between economic, cultural, and philosophical dominance, comparative philosophers certainly do affirm the claim that Asian approaches to philosophical problems are often illuminating. In addition, some specialists in Chinese and comparative philosophy claim that China's economic growth and large population constitute reasons why philosophers should study Chinese philosophical traditions.[26] Priest's descriptive claim that economic dominance results in philosophical dominance tempts us to make the normative claim that we *should* study Chinese philosophy, because as Priest puts it, once China and India are fully capitalized, "they will swamp the rest of the world, in the way the US has in the second half of the twentieth century."[27] Whether or not one agrees that China will soon become fully capitalized and "swamp" the rest of the world, an interesting question remains: Does China's recent progress constitute a good reason for philosophers to study Chinese philosophy?

I think it is fair to say that a country's economic or political dominance is not the reason why most philosophers study its philosophical traditions. Evidence for this view includes the fact that philosophers still study Greek and Roman philosophy, even though these civilizations no longer hold a dominant economic, political, or military position in the world, nor do they contain a significant percentage of the world's population.[28] It can also be seen from the fact that Eurasian philosophers did not begin studying Mongolian philosophy when Ghengis Khan conquered most of those continents. One might, however, try to defend the claim that a country's economic or political dominance constitutes *one* of the reasons why philosophers study its philosophical traditions. One would then need to explain why philosophical interest in Greek philosophy has not waned since Greek civilization declined in dominance even though philosophers, according to this view, have fewer reasons to study it now. In fact, philosophical interest in Greek philosophy seems to have been relatively unaffected by the economic and political position of Greece. If one rejects the claim that philosophers' interest in Greek philosophy *would* decline with the dominance of Greek civilization if Greek dominance constituted a reason for studying it, then one must acknowledge that the status of Greek civilization was not the primary reason why philosophers studied Greek philosophy.

Here I make a distinction between *primary reasons* for studying philosophical traditions, figures, or ideas, which play a decisive role in motivation, and *supporting reasons*, which provide additional or supplemental reasons for doing something one is already motivated to do.[29] I am interested in identifying the kinds of *primary* reasons why philosophers study philosophical traditions, because this will help us to understand the kinds of reasons we will need to offer philosophers for studying non-Western and comparative philosophy. Clearly, the specifics of these reasons vary to some extent according to each tradition, philosopher, or idea, but we can still identify the kinds of primary reasons philosophers typically accept. Now if the dominance of Greek civilization had been the primary reason why philosophers had studied Greek philosophy, then its decline would have had *some* impact on the amount of attention given to Greek philosophy or the number of philosophers who study it. So it seems clear from the fact that philosophers have continued to study Greek philosophy despite Greek civilization's decline in economic and political status that these things did not represent their primary reason for studying it.

If we wish to identify the primary reason why philosophers normally regard the study of particular philosophical traditions as worthwhile, then it will be helpful to examine the goals of philosophical inquiry. These goals are typically tied to the intrinsic value of truth and goodness, and although I will discuss this matter in greater detail below, for now it will suffice to say that the main goal of philosophy is knowledge of truth and human flourishing, broadly construed. The main reason I reject the claim that philosophers should study certain philosophical traditions because they are tied to economically or politically dominant countries is that economic or political dominance is not the goal of philosophical inquiry. Although it might be the case that many philosophers care about economic and political achievement and sometimes work to show how certain ideas are relevant to these matters, it is not the case that these are the *goals* of philosophical inquiry in general. Philosophers continue to explore a wide range of theoretical and practical matters that are unrelated to economic prosperity and political dominance, because they are interested in questions of truth and value.[30] That is, they are interested in accounts that might lead us to a better understanding of the world and ourselves and that might help us to lead richer lives. Once again, that is not to say that some philosophical discussions cannot be insightfully applied to explorations of economic or political dominance. However, I think it is clear that economic or political dominance—or even achievement—is not the main goal of philosophical inquiry.

Some comparative philosophers, though, have a different position in mind when they suggest that China's economic growth gives us a reason to study Chinese philosophy. According to this view, philosophers should study the philosophies of economically or politically dominant countries as a way of achieving peaceful interactions among nations and citizens. This view is premised on the claim that studying other philosophical traditions helps us to get along better with others in an increasingly pluralistic society and in a world where we are much more likely to encounter those of other cultural traditions. Unlike the previous view of why we should study the philosophical traditions of economically or politically powerful countries, this reason is not premised on the desire to compete more effectively with others or achieve dominance. Instead of marking economic or political dominance as the goal of inquiry, it marks peaceful interactions among nations and citizens as the goal of inquiry. This brings us closer to the goals of philosophical inquiry, for there are good reasons to think that peaceful interactions among nations and citizens are closely tied to human flourishing.

This view provides a noble account of why we should study certain philosophical traditions, and I think it is based on an accurate observation. Most specialists in non-Western philosophy and many other scholars would agree that studying the philosophical underpinnings of other cultures can teach us a great deal about how to interact and engage in dialogue in more culturally sensitive ways with those of other cultural traditions. But it has some of the same difficulties we examined above. To begin with, it only gives us a reason to study philosophical traditions that are tied to cultures we are likely to come in contact with *and* that we have some difficulty understanding. This is what makes Chinese philosophy a candidate for study: China's economic growth seems to guarantee that the West will have more interaction with the Chinese, and Chinese culture is significantly different from Western cultures. European philosophies, however, might not be candidates because they fail to meet the second condition. They have informed Western cultures, including American culture, in important ways. There are also some important differences in the kind of influence that different philosophical traditions have had on their respective cultures. While the influence of Confucianism is pervasive in East Asian cultures and studying Confucian values could certainly prepare one for more effective and meaningful interactions with members of those cultures, one could more easily question whether studying Hegel and Kant would help one to interact and engage in dialogue with Germans in more effective and meaningful ways.[31] Accordingly, this reason for studying philosophical traditions applies to only *some* traditions, which poses a problem: On this view, philosophers have entirely different kinds of goals of inquiry depending upon the philosophical traditions they are studying. Surely, though, there are some goals of inquiry that most philosophers share and that help to define certain inquiries as philosophical.

An additional problem is that this reason for studying certain philosophical traditions is easily undermined. Indeed, it would no longer constitute a reason for studying certain philosophical traditions if one could show that encounters with members of those cultural traditions are not inevitable, or that Westernization is so prevalent and forceful that it will soon no longer be necessary for us to understand other cultural traditions in order to interact and engage in dialogue peacefully. One could also simply reject the claim that philosophers' understanding of Chinese philosophy will ultimately make a noticeable difference in the tenor of the relationship between China and the United States, on the grounds that U.S. politics and foreign relations are driven by economic and political concerns and not by a desire for greater cultural sensitivity and understanding. In addition, although studying the philosophical traditions tied to other cultures can certainly increase our ability to interact with others in a more sensitive manner, it is not the case that it is *necessary* for us to study other philosophical traditions in order to interact with those of other cultures in a sensitive manner. Indeed, one might argue that it is primarily certain traits of character and a broader acquaintance with a culture—as opposed to knowledge of a philosophical tradition—that make one a culturally sensitive person. Although I think there is considerable merit to the claim that a commitment to studying the philosophical underpinnings of some other cultures can move us closer to positive and enduring relations between certain nations, and perhaps among citizens living in a pluralistic society, I nevertheless do not think this constitutes a reason for studying non-Western philosophy that most philosophers would accept.

The important point here is that although some philosophers have offered China's economic prominence and large population as reasons why we should study Chinese philosophy, these are not the primary reasons why professional philosophers normally study philosophical traditions. As we have seen, philosophers do not tend to think they lack a reason to study the philosophies of economically weak countries or those with small populations. Indeed, I think most specialists in Chinese philosophy would maintain that Chinese philosophy was just as worthy of study twenty years ago, prior to the increase in China's economic growth. I think they would also maintain that Chinese thought would be deserving of our attention even if China had not become the world's most populous nation. Why, then, do specialists in Chinese thought or other non-Western philosophies sometimes give economic or political reasons for studying these traditions?

The answer to this question differs when specialists in non-Western philosophy are addressing their colleagues in the field of philosophy as opposed to students and colleagues who are not philosophers. I think it is fair to say that comparative philosophers offer economic and political reasons to philosophers who study the Western tradition primarily out of a desire to show that although professional philosophers have been almost exclusively concerned with the Western philosophical tradition up until this point, there is *now* a reason to study non-Western philosophy. For example, a good number of specialists in Chinese thought have appealed to the rising position of China on the economic and political scene as evidence that philosophers now have a reason to pay attention to the philosophical traditions of China. What is odd about this claim is that it seems to imply that philosophers did not previously have a reason to study Chinese philosophy. But this claim, or any claim that Chinese philosophy is more relevant now than it was before, is strange coming from philosophers who have devoted their lives to understanding the Chinese philosophical tradition, for they clearly do not really think the Chinese philosophical tradition has only *just now* become important. I suspect that when specialists in Chinese and comparative philosophy offer economic or political reasons for studying Chinese philosophy to their fellow philosophers, they do so at least in part in order to avoid insulting their colleagues and predecessors by saying what needs to be said: The systematic exclusion of non-Western philosophical traditions from the discipline of philosophy is an institutionalized form of ethnocentrism.[32] The fact that Western philosophical traditions are considered essential to philosophy and are a central part of how philosophers are educated and evaluated, while non-Western traditions have been excluded in both thought and practice from most philosophy departments, can be understood only as a form of institutionalized prejudice.[33]

It is clear that professional philosophers are trained in a certain range of Western philosophical traditions because certain traditions have been accepted, perhaps uncritically, as essential within the discipline of philosophy. But this still does not tell us anything about philosophers' reasons for studying those philosophical traditions. I have noted that the goals of philosophical inquiry are knowledge of truth and human flourishing, and

I think it is accurate to say that most philosophers study philosophical traditions because they think the ideas and ways of life described by various philosophical traditions might be true and valuable. The exclusion of non-Western philosophies from the discipline of philosophy does not change this fact, but it does indicate the existence of a large body of philosophical work that most philosophers have not even become remotely acquainted with, let alone examined carefully. It also means that if philosophers take their own reasons for doing philosophy seriously, they will work to make these traditions a part of how philosophers are educated and evaluated. What specialists in non-Western philosophies need to say, then, is that the reason why philosophers should study non-Western philosophical traditions is the same reason they study any philosophical tradition: because the ideas found in these traditions might be true or valuable. This is the primary reason why philosophers should study non-Western philosophy, for it reflects the distinctive aims of the discipline of philosophy. In addition, we can now see clearly why comparative philosophy is important: In order to show that the ideas and views found in non-Western philosophies are valuable, one must show that they are not all exactly the same as the views that are articulated in the history of Western philosophy, and that some of the alternative views seen in non-Western traditions are compelling.[34]

As I noted earlier, there is an important difference between intrinsic and extrinsic goods, and it will be helpful at this point to distinguish between reasons that are concerned with intrinsic value and those that are concerned with extrinsic value. Philosophers are typically motivated to study particular philosophers, movements, and traditions because they have good reasons to believe that the ideas and views found in the work of those philosophers, movements, and traditions are intrinsically valuable—that is, there is something about the specific nature of those ideas and views that makes them worth studying. On this view, it is the truth and normative value of particular ideas and views that make them worth studying, and this is a philosophical reason for studying certain philosophers and traditions, for it is uniquely tied to the goals of philosophical inquiry. Now there are obviously other good reasons for studying particular philosophers, movements, and traditions, as well. Many of these reasons highlight the way in which studying certain ideas and practices can help one to achieve certain ends, but it is not the specific nature of those ideas and practices that helps one to achieve those ends. Such reasons highlight the extrinsic value of studying particular philosophical traditions. For example, if one argues that we should study Chinese philosophy because of China's growing dominance in the world, and because an understanding of Confucianism will help us to more effectively understand Chinese responses to issues relating to foreign policy, in turn helping us to negotiate more effectively with China on these issues, one is not appealing to the specific nature of the ideas and views found in the Chinese philosophical tradition. This is made clear by the fact that the very same argument could be made about the philosophies that have informed *any* culture, regardless of the actual ideas or views that are a part of those traditions. The basic point is that understanding the cultural background of a country can help one to more effectively communicate with its people, and this would be true regardless of whether one was dealing with China or India, despite the important differences between the views found in the philosophical traditions of China and India. Accordingly, this is a reason tied to the extrinsic value of studying Chinese philosophy. If, on the other hand, one argued that we should study Chinese philosophy because early Chinese thinkers have valuable insights into the nature of war and how we should deal with other states, then one is arguing that certain ideas and views found in the Chinese tradition are true and valuable. This is a reason tied to the intrinsic value of studying Chinese philosophy. It is significant for comparative philosophers that both kinds of reasons point to the importance of comparative study and not just the study of Chinese philosophy alone. In order for one to utilize effectively what one learns about Confucianism in conversations about foreign policy with the Chinese, one will first need to reflect on how Confucianism has helped to shape views that are different in important ways from our own views in the United States. Likewise, in order to demonstrate that early Chinese thinkers have valuable insights into the nature of war and interstate relations, one must show that these views differ in important ways from those articulated in the Western political tradition. This is precisely the sort of work that comparative philosophers do.

As indicated, the primary reason why most philosophers think studying particular philosophers is worthwhile is that they think some of the ideas and views of those philosophers are true or valuable. Philosophers, then, should be interested in exploring philosophical traditions that have been neglected because the ideas and views found in those traditions might hold insights that we have yet to explore. We have no reason to believe we have exhausted the number of philosophical questions that can be explored, or the ways in which these questions can be addressed. In *On Liberty*, John Stuart Mill points out that ". . . the only way in which a human being can make some approach to knowing the whole of a subject, is by hearing what can be said about it by persons of every variety of opinion, and studying all modes in which it can be looked at by every character of mind."[35] He adds that "the general or prevailing opinion on any subject is rarely or never the whole truth, [and] it is only by the collision of adverse opinions that the remainder of the truth has any chance of being supplied."[36] Mill's point reinforces what I have argued: Philosophers should study different philosophical traditions because they might contain true and valuable ideas.[37] Here we can see that the way one answers the question of why one should study non-Western philosophy is directly related to why one thinks philosophy is worth doing at all.

Reasons having to do with the intrinsic value of studying non-Western philosophy will at first strike many people as overly intellectual and largely irrelevant to the practical concerns of one's daily life. Indeed, this is why specialists in Chinese thought sometimes offer economic or political reasons for studying Chinese philosophy to students and colleagues who are not philosophers, or to those outside of the academy. Most philosophers realize that among those who are unfamiliar with the discipline of philosophy, as well as those who are acquainted with only certain areas or ways of doing philosophy, philosophy is not viewed as a practical discipline. I think philosophers usually appeal to economic or political reasons in an effort to show those who are not in the field of philosophy that the ideas they study are relevant to people's lives. It is important for philosophers to emphasize the many and diverse ways in which an understanding of the traditions and thinkers they study can help to prepare one for life in an increasingly pluralistic world, especially when it comes to the study of non-Western philosophies that have had and continue to have a dramatic impact on cultures in certain parts of the world. The philosophical traditions of China and India also form the core religious traditions of those countries, and their influence spread widely and saturated the cultures of surrounding nations such as Korea and Japan. Despite the turbulent political histories of these nations, the cultural influence of the indigenous traditions of Asia has not been successfully undermined by the entry of Western philosophies like Marxism, even when there have been overt campaigns to do so. Philosophers should be especially aware of the way in which philosophical and religious traditions influence human cultures and shape the thinking of those who dwell in them.

At the same time, it is also important for specialists in comparative and non-Western philosophy to remember that there is another dimension to the practical relevance of the traditions and thinkers they study, seen in the intrinsic value of studying them. Reasons having to do with the intrinsic value of the ideas and views found in these traditions will often be the most personal and compelling reasons for studying them. For example, if one thinks there is truth in the Confucian claim that the early experiences of infants and young children are formative in a special way and that parental caregiving is the most important aspect of these early experiences, one may come to understand one's relationship with one's own children—and one's parents—differently and respond to them differently as a result.[38] In addition, one might also be motivated to work to convince others of the reasons why these claims are worthy of serious consideration, and of the practical impact such views can have on one's life. This helps to show that the way in which philosophy is practically relevant differs significantly from the way in which disciplines driven by current economic and political interests are relevant, but I think it is the case that certain areas of philosophy are much *more* relevant to people's lives if relevance is determined by the things people value most.[39] Although most people are concerned to some degree about matters of global economics and foreign policy, the matter of what values we should instill in our children, what religious beliefs and practices should be a part of our lives, and how we should prioritize the many claims on our time are, in a very real sense, the stuff of our lives. I think it is generally the case that people care a great deal about whether the things they believe are true and whether the things they teach their children to value—and the *way* in which they teach them—will help them to become kind and thoughtful human beings, and to lead better, richer lives overall. In fact, I think most people care a great deal more about these things than about matters of global economics or politics.[40]

I suspect that many philosophers offer a country's economic position, political power, or population as reasons to study its philosophical traditions because these reasons demand less of everyone involved. If one thinks the reason for studying Chinese philosophy is to prevent the Chinese from swamping the rest of the world, or in order to better understand them when they do, then studying Chinese philosophy does not call for us to re-examine our personal beliefs and values, or to evaluate Chinese values. On this view, the goal of studying Chinese philosophy is simply to acquire certain kinds of information that will help us strategically to get along better in the world. If, however, one thinks the reason for studying Chinese and comparative philosophy is that the ideas, views, and practices found in the Chinese tradition might be true and valuable, then something more is required of us, namely a willingness to examine the extent to which our lives might be improved by the ideas and practices we study. Accepting the fact that the ideas and practices advocated by any philosophical tradition could be true and valuable requires a willingness to examine and possibly revise one's beliefs and practices. Economic and political reasons for studying philosophy tend to require less of us because although they may sometimes require us to consider revising our position on an economic or political issue, they normally do not require us to examine and consider revising our personal beliefs and values, nor do they typically lead us to try to convince others to re-examine their beliefs and values.

In sum, I think many philosophers tend not to offer reasons tied to the intrinsic value of particular ideas or views because they are afraid of asking too much of their audience. Indeed, some people might respond by saying or thinking that they are perfectly happy with their lives, and so there is no reason for them to study other approaches. Perhaps it is best to recall Socrates' reply to this kind of response in order to recall just how antithetical it is to the philosophical attitude. In dialogues such as the *Euthyphro*, Socrates does the kind of critical questioning that earned him the reputation of being a "gadfly," picking away at people's confident assertions in order to uncover the truth about what matters most in one's life. This quest for truth and value, which opposes the uncritical acceptance of conventional beliefs, defines philosophy, and it is important to recognize that philosophy is difficult not only because it requires hard thinking but also because it often requires the hard work of getting others to see why the examined life is better than the unexamined life.

According to the view I have argued for, the reason for studying non-Western philosophy that the majority of philosophers in the West would be most willing to accept is that the views of non-Western philosophers might contain ideas and practices that are true and valuable and differ in at least some important ways from those found in the history of Western philosophy. It is not surprising that this reason would most appeal to philosophers, given that philosophers are concerned primarily with evaluating the truth and normative value of certain kinds of claims. The vast majority of philosophers would reject the view that there is a necessary relationship between the truth or normative value of a claim and the number of people who make it, the economic position of the countries where those individuals reside, or the political orientation of their government. And although the increasing economic prominence of China may help to show how studying Chinese culture can be extrinsically valuable, it does not constitute a distinctly philosophical reason for studying Chinese philosophy. Consequently, it is unlikely to convince most philosophers that studying non-Western philosophy is worthwhile.

Three Challenges for the Comparative Philosopher

As the previous section makes clear, comparative studies in different disciplines often face unique challenges in responding to the question of why
comparative work is worthwhile. These differences are sometimes rooted
in the distinctive goals and tendencies that are characteristic of particular
fields of study or the disciplines of which they are a part. Yet despite these
differences, there remain some common challenges that comparativists in
fields such as philosophy and religious studies face. In this section, I argue
that these challenges can be helpfully divided into three main categories,
each of which represents a distinctive set of issues related to the tasks of
comparative work: thematic issues (concerning *what* one compares, including one's choice of topic and texts or thinkers to compare), interpretive issues (concerning one's interpretations of the texts or thinkers under study),
and procedural issues (concerning *how* one conducts one's study, including
particular methods or approaches). I offer examples of these issues from
comparative works and further argue that each of these three kinds of issues represents a different reason why comparative studies sometimes fail
to represent the subjects under study in a fair and accurate manner, or to
deliver fruitful and insightful results.[41] In some cases, there are difficulties
in one or two of these areas that threaten the conclusions of a comparative study, but the other areas of the study are perfectly defensible. For
example, one's choice of thinkers to compare and one's choice of topic,
as well as one's interpretations of the thinkers under study might be well
defended, but the comparison itself might be poorly executed because one
fails to adequately discuss important differences. In this sort of case, naming and distinguishing between thematic, interpretive, and procedural issues can help comparativists and readers of comparative studies alike to
determine a study's strengths and weaknesses so that they can be addressed
more easily and effectively. In other cases, there genuinely may be a problem in one area, but it is not the sort of problem that leads to the complete
rejection of a comparative study's conclusions or even undermines them.
For example, as we will see below, comparativists are sometimes criticized
for the terms they use to refer to shared concepts or practices that are the
focus of a comparative study (a thematic issue), and although one's choice
of terms *could* pose serious problems for one's conclusions, especially if
they reveal problematic aspects of one's interpretations of the two thinkers
under study, in other cases one's choice of terms might just be cumbersome
or awkward for readers. I argue that distinguishing between the different
kinds of issues that are at stake in these kinds of cases helps us to recognize

the significance of particular criticisms and to appreciate where there is room for disagreement without the conclusions of a study being rejected or even undermined.

Although it may seem intuitive to begin by discussing what I call "thematic" issues, I will instead begin by discussing interpretive issues, for two reasons. Interpretive issues concern the initial interpretations comparativists have of the thinkers or texts they are comparing, and specifically whether the study presents a compelling and textually supportable account of the views under study. Sometimes, studies of individual philosophers, religious thinkers, or texts focus almost exclusively on defending a particular interpretation. In comparative studies, the bulk of one's argument typically focuses on a set of comparisons or contrasts between two thinkers, meaning that interpretive questions are not normally the primary focus. But for a comparative study to get off the ground, one must first offer defensible interpretations of the two figures, texts, theories, or concepts being compared. If adequate textual evidence is not available to defend the initial interpretations, then the extent to which other dimensions of the comparison are well done is something of a moot point.[42] This is the first reason why I discuss interpretive issues prior to thematic or procedural issues. The second reason is that one's interpretations of the texts and traditions one studies ultimately determine one's choice of what to compare. As we will see in a moment, there is disagreement in the field of Chinese and comparative philosophy over the question of which philosophers in the Western tradition can be fruitfully compared with early Chinese Confucian thinkers. This is a disagreement over thematic issues, but the reason why scholars in this field disagree over which philosophers should be the subject of comparative study is that they disagree over how to interpret the views of early Confucian, and Western, thinkers.

A number of things can go wrong at the interpretive level of a comparative study, and of course these problems are not unique to comparative work. The challenge of providing responsible and well-supported interpretations is one that all scholars face. One way in which interpretive issues can present unique challenges for comparative studies is simply that comparativists do not always have as much space to present and defend interpretations of the thinkers they discuss. Comparative studies require one not only to present and defend interpretations of the views of two or more thinkers but also to do the constructive work of discussing similarities and differences and the reasons why the comparison is worthwhile. It is difficult to balance these different tasks and find adequate space to complete all of them well, and comparativists are often pressed by critics to focus more on the constructive aspects of their work and to make clear, for example, how they are not "simply" describing two views or "doing comparison for the sake of comparison."[43] These are all reasons why comparativists sometimes devote less space to interpretive issues. As a result, scholars who are familiar with the figures under study may reject the conclusions of a comparison because the initial interpretations of the philosophers under study are insufficiently developed or inadequately defended against an abundance of textual evidence, or because they portray particular thinkers or traditions in a one-dimensional way. Sometimes, the interpretations offered in comparative studies more strongly emphasize features that highlight either the similarities or the differences between the two subjects being compared, leading to the mistaken impression that these features are central to a thinker's view. Normally this is done (either consciously or unconsciously) out of a desire to strengthen the conclusions of the comparative study.

In order to illustrate how interpretive issues can influence comparative studies in especially dramatic ways, I want to examine briefly two different interpretations of early Confucian thought, both of which have shaped a number of influential comparative studies of Chinese and Western philosophy. According to the first of these interpretations, early Confucian ethical views are best understood as forms of virtue ethics.[44] Bryan W. Van Norden offers a detailed and systematic account of this interpretation in his *Virtue Ethics and Consequentialism in Early Chinese Philosophy*, and several features of the view he articulates are shared by others who endorse virtue ethical interpretations of Confucian ethics.[45] Van Norden argues that although Confucians, Aristotelians, Platonists, Augustinians, Thomists, and others who belong to the family of views known as virtue ethics disagree over a wide range of important issues, including what the virtues are, what a good life is, and what the role of the family is in a good life, they are still recognizably forms of virtue ethics because they offer: "(1) an account of what a 'flourishing' human life is like, (2) an account of what virtues contribute to leading such a life, (3) an account of how one acquires those virtues, and (4) a philosophical anthropology that explains what humans are like, such that they can acquire those virtues so as to flourish in that kind of life."[46] Although there are some differences between different virtue ethical accounts of Confucianism on which features are central to virtue ethical views, all of them acknowledge that there are many different forms of virtue ethics and that the best way to interpret Confucian ethics is as a form of virtue ethics. Van Norden also argues that the virtue ethical accounts of Confucian and Western thinkers is a good topic of comparison, because studying Confucian virtue ethics can teach us about new conceptions of the virtues and different ways of living a worthwhile life, and also because Western virtue ethics illuminates many aspects of Confucianism that might go unnoticed otherwise.[47]

On the second view I want to consider, early Confucianism is best interpreted as having substantive affinities with American pragmatism and process philosophy. As a result, on this view the most fruitful comparisons with Western philosophy are those that compare various aspects of Confucianism with pragmatism or process philosophy.[48] David Hall and Roger Ames argue that deep and pervasive differences exist between the views of early Chinese philosophers and the vast majority of views in the history of Western philosophy.[49] However, they argue that Dewey and Whitehead represent notable exceptions. In addition to sharing a number of the most important commitments of early Confucian thinkers and therefore serving as fruitful and interesting comparative subjects, they argue that the language Dewey and Whitehead use in their work can help us to translate Confucian thinking into terms that Western readers will more readily understand. In *Democracy of the Dead*, Hall and Ames write, "In our attempts to translate this thinking into a language that would facilitate a conversation with our Western audience, we have been led away from both the speculative and analytic vocabularies of traditional philosophy to the more concrete and practical modes of American pragmatism."[50] With respect to process philosophy, in *Focusing the Familiar*, they write,

> Our argument is simple and direct: The use of substance language to translate Chinese insights into a world of process and change has led to seriously inappropriate interpretations of the Chinese sensibility. . . . The virtue of the work of A. N. Whitehead and other representatives of the process tradition is that they have attempted to introduce ontological understandings that would allow for the appreciation of the role of true creativity in shaping the processes and events that comprise the world around us.[51]

In addition to providing textual evidence for their interpretations, proponents of both virtue ethical and pragmatic-process interpretations argue that the frameworks these views offer can help us to better make sense of and appreciate important features of Confucian views.[52] It is important to note that embracing a virtue ethical or pragmatic-process interpretation of Chinese thought is very likely to influence one's view of the kinds of Western thinkers with which Confucian thinkers could appropriately or beneficially be compared. Proponents of pragmatic-process interpretations often make stronger claims about this matter than those who ad-

vocate virtue ethical interpretations, because, as we have seen, Hall and
Ames argue that pragmatic and process views are unique among Western
views in having particular affinities with Chinese thought. As a result, they
argue, comparisons with pragmatic or process philosophers not only will
be beneficial to our understanding of Chinese thought; they also will be
the *most* fruitful comparisons we can make with Western thinkers. Van
Norden points out that proponents of this type of view quickly reject the
application of virtue ethics to Confucianism based on the assumption that
the Chinese and Western philosophical traditions are essentially incom-
mensurable.[53] Many of those who embrace a virtue ethical interpretation
of Confucianism have argued against this characterization of both Chinese
and Western philosophy. For example, Stephen Angle has pointed out that
although some philosophers have argued that Confucianism and Western
virtue ethics are "too different to speak significantly to one another," a
number of these claims are based on mistaken premises, "such as collaps-
ing all of Western virtue ethics into Aristotle (and perhaps also reading
Aristotle very narrowly). . . ."[54] An important difference between the virtue
ethical interpretation and the pragmatic-process interpretation is that the
latter view entails the claim that pragmatic and process-oriented views are
unique among Western views in having affinities with Chinese thought,
and that as a result, interpretations of Chinese thought that claim substantial affinities with other Western views (such as virtue ethics) misrepresent
Chinese views. Although most proponents of the virtue ethical interpretation argue that their interpretation of Confucian ethical views is better
than other interpretations, they do not make the exclusivistic claim that
any non-virtue ethical interpretations of Confucian ethics misrepresent
Confucian views. This helps to show not only how one's interpretive commitments can lead to certain judgments about what kinds of comparisons
are fruitful but also how the strength of one's interpretive claims might
lead one to reject other potential comparisons simply on the basis of what
they are comparing.

The second set of issues I wish to examine are thematic issues, which
concern *what* comparative studies compare, including the thinkers or texts
that are the focus of one's study, the particular topic that one focuses on in
those thinkers or texts, and the terminological question of what one should
call that topic. Here we can see clearly the difference between thematic issues, which concern *what* we are comparing (e.g., Confucian philosophers
and Western virtue ethicists, or Chinese philosophers and Western process
philosophers), and the interpretive issues discussed above, which concern
how we interpret what we are comparing (e.g., interpreting certain early

Confucian thinkers as committed to ethical views that share significant affinities with virtue ethical accounts; interpreting Chinese thinkers as committed to a pragmatic and process-oriented view that shares significant affinities with the views of pragmatist and process philosophers). Despite the
fact that one's interpretations can, as we have seen, heavily influence one's
thematic choices in a comparison, these are still different aspects of comparative studies and represent different choices that a comparativist must
make. That is, we can distinguish between the different *kinds* of challenges
that interpretation, as opposed to thematization, poses for comparative
work. For example, one might object to an interpretation of Mengzi that
sees him as offering a virtue ethical view (an interpretive issue), without
objecting to a comparison of Mengzi and Aristotle on the subject of the
virtue of humility (a thematic issue). On the other hand, one might find the
interpretations of Mengzi and Aristotle in a comparative study to be fair
and accurate (an interpretive issue) but object to a comparison of those two
philosophers on the subject of the virtue of humility because it is not particularly illuminating (a thematic issue). In the latter case, for example, one
could object to different aspects of the thematic choices the comparativist
has made: One could argue that the choice to compare Mengzi and Aristotle is not in and of itself problematic but that the virtue of humility is simply
not a good choice of topic, or one could argue that the choice to compare
Mengzi and Aristotle, regardless of the topic one chooses, is a poor one.
One could obviously give a wide variety of reasons for one's objections to
these thematic choices. One who objects to the choice of a topic but not to
the choice of thinkers could argue that Mengzi's and Aristotle's accounts
of humility (unlike some other virtues) have so much in common that a
comparison is not particularly revealing. One who objects to the choice of
thinkers could argue that the differences between Mengzi and Aristotle are
so deep that we can find only extremely thin similarities between them and
that these similarities are not enough to make a comparison worthwhile.
These examples help to show how objections to particular thematic issues in comparative studies are often closely related to one's view of what
makes comparative work worthwhile. In addition, the latter objection in
particular is based on a specific interpretation of Mengzi and Aristotle that
helps to show the relationship between thematic and interpretive issues.
Because there is a close relationship between these different issues, and
because many of the objections to thematic issues in comparative work
concern these relationships, it is especially important for comparativists
to distinguish between the separate issues of interpretation, thematization,
and what makes a comparison worthwhile. This in turn will enable one to

articulate clearly the relationships between, for example, one's thematic choices and the aims of the comparison, and between one's interpretations of the two thinkers under study and one's thematic choices.[55]

Thematic issues, then, include a range of different aspects of a comparison, and thematic questions are often more difficult to address when one compares thinkers or texts from different philosophical, religious, or cultural traditions. For example, one might choose the topic of Heaven (*tian* 天) in a comparison of two early Chinese texts like the *Analects* and the *Mengzi*.[56] In this case, it is not difficult to establish that there is an understanding of Heaven in both texts, even though there are some important differences between the two views, for not only do both texts clearly express an understanding of the concept of Heaven, but they even share a term for it. One will need to defend a particular interpretation of the view of Heaven seen in each text, but we can easily see how the choice of what to compare (including the topic and the texts) is different from the choice of what interpretations to defend and how to go about defending them — even though one's interpretations strongly influence one's thematic choices. Comparative studies that cross traditions often face more challenges in addressing thematic issues, because it is often more difficult to establish that two thinkers from different traditions share a concept, even if it is a thin one.[57] The fact that this tends to be more difficult is partly the result of the genuine differences between different traditions and the importance of taking the time and care to be sure that one is not imposing a concept onto a text or thinker, but it is also partly the result of the widespread failure to distinguish between a *term* and a *concept*, which leads many to assume that there are no shared concepts if there are not shared terms. Of course, philosophical and religious texts written in different languages usually do not share terms, but they share many concepts, regardless of how different their cultures or traditions of origin are. For example, there are texts in early Christianity, Buddhism, and Confucianism that all express the concepts of "woman" and "man," even though they obviously have different terms for them. It is also clear that texts from different traditions express other kinds of shared concepts. For example, Aristotle and Mengzi both clearly had a concept of courage, even though they obviously had different (ancient Greek and ancient Chinese, respectively) terms for it and different theories about the virtue of courage, as well.[58] Indeed, it is the presence of a shared concept like courage in the midst of different theories about why that virtue is important, what it entails, and its role in the good life that normally makes a comparative study worthwhile.

In relation to thematic choices in comparative study, Carr and Ivanhoe outline two requirements: "[A] comparative study must bring together traditions that have enough in common to afford genuine examples of similarity and yet which are distinct enough to reveal deeper differences when studied with care and in detail."[59] The first requirement—that there are genuine similarities—is needed "in order to facilitate communication across the traditions involved."[60] They note that some traditions clearly share more than others, even though there is good evidence to support the view that significant similarities exist between any two religious traditions—and, I might add, philosophical traditions—as we call them religious or philosophical traditions because they fulfill a similar range of functions for human beings. The second requirement they discuss—that there are significant differences—is necessary

> in order for the comparison to offer the distinct perspectives needed to enrich both our understanding of ourselves and our understanding of the general phenomenon of religion. If the traditions compared are too similar, these goals cannot be realized and one runs the risk of drawing the false inference that all religious traditions are really very much like one's own.[61]

They go on to argue that choosing single schools, periods, or thinkers has distinct advantages over comparing entire traditions because, in addition to the fact that the latter sort of comparison is in many ways too complex, a more tightly focused comparison improves one's chances of discovering significant similarities and differences.[62]

What should lead one to choose particular schools, periods, or thinkers over others, though? My reasons for selecting Kongzi and Rawls as subjects, discussed in the Introduction, can help us to note some important issues concerning one's thematic choices, particularly as they relate to other secondary literature on the figures under study and the kind of study and reflection that typically precedes the decision to do comparative work on two figures. First, one's thematic choices should be informed by knowledge of two fields, including areas of neglect and important criticisms of the two figures under study. One must have a sense of what has been said in order to determine what needs to be studied, clarified, or corrected. Obviously, then, one's potential thematic choices are—and should be—narrowed by one's training. Second, one's thematic choices should be rooted in one's own reflection on the figures and traditions in which one is trained. Good thematic choices almost always come from careful textual study, and from noticing and then further exploring genuine features of two views. This means that many comparative projects can and should fizzle out because one's initial investigations show that a comparison is not particularly fruitful. Here we see the close relationship between good thematic choices and having clear and explicit goals in comparative work.

In their comparative study, Carr and Ivanhoe argue that Zhuangzi and Kierkegaard are uniquely suited to fulfill the goals of comparative work because they "share enough genuine points of similarity to allow for significant comparison and yet their similarities reveal deeper areas of disagreement when carefully analyzed."[63] Regarding the topic on which they compare Zhuangzi and Kierkegaard, Carr and Ivanhoe write that they have selected a view they call "antirationalism" that is seen in the work of both thinkers. Antirationalism offers a distinctive position on the relationship between reason and religious experience, and Carr and Ivanhoe argue that this relationship is cast in its fullest relief when these two thinkers are approached comparatively. Their remarks here allow us to make an important observation: A comparativist's thematic choices can and should be explained up front, but ultimately one's comparative study must *demonstrate* why these were appropriate choices. Although in the introduction to their work Carr and Ivanhoe provide an overview of the general and specific reasons why they chose Zhuangzi and Kierkegaard, as well as the topic of antirationalism, their comparative study is dedicated to the task of arguing that Zhuangzi and Kierkegaard indeed share the view they say they do, and that they are different in the ways they outline, as well. One can be fully convinced that their thematic choices were good ones, then, only after one has read their study and seen the evidence they produce to support their view. With this in mind, I want to turn to a specific example of the thematic questions that are sometimes raised by critics of comparative studies.

A recent discussion in the *Journal of the American Academy of Religion* engages the question of why Aaron Stalnaker selected Xunzi and Augustine as the subjects of his comparison in *Overcoming Our Evil: Human Nature and Spiritual Exercises in Xunzi and Augustine*, and also why he chose the topic of spiritual exercises. The criticisms raised in this discussion obviously help to underscore the importance of thematic issues in comparative work. The central criticism is that "Stalnaker cannot seem to give us a reason for choosing Augustine and Xunzi as objects of comparison."[64] In addition, Stalnaker is criticized for not explaining why he did not instead choose other thinkers for his comparison.[65] It is important to note that these are distinct requirements; one can offer clear reasons for why one chose to compare two thinkers without explicitly discussing why one did not choose other thinkers. The latter strikes me as an unreasonable requirement to impose on comparativists, for three reasons. First, this requirement rests on the assumption that comparativists are arguing that their comparisons are the only or most fruitful potential comparisons that can be made on the topics they are studying. It is not clear that most comparativists—let alone Stalnaker—defend this sort of view. If Stalnaker were to claim that a comparative study of Xunzi and Augustine is in some way superior to a comparative study of other potential pairings, then he would certainly need to offer reasons for us to accept this claim, including a discussion of the potential pairings to which he thinks Xunzi and Augustine are superior. But my sense is that Stalnaker does not embrace this type of view; at least, he never indicates that comparative studies of other thinkers on the very topics he discusses could not also yield important results.

The second reason why it is unreasonable to require comparativists to consider other possible subjects in explaining their choices is that the completion of such a task is unrealistic in at least two ways. First, it would require a lengthy survey of other thinkers, and any reasons one offered for where this survey ought to stop would be arbitrary. There are potentially very large numbers of thinkers in different traditions to consider in any given comparison, and if one attempted to discuss them all, the discussion would take up a large amount of space—which would try the patience of one's readers and leave less room for one's actual comparative study.[66] Second, it is unlikely that one could even list all of these different thinkers, let alone describe their views, because no comparativist has adequate training to offer a survey of all of the potential thinkers from different traditions who have discussed one's topic. Like all scholars of religion and historians of philosophy, comparativists are specialists in particular traditions and in particular periods and thinkers within those traditions. This points toward the third reason why it is unreasonable to expect comparativists to discuss why they did not choose other subjects for their comparative studies: The answer to this question would, on a certain level, simply be the uninteresting claim that one is trained in particular traditions and thinkers. It is important to remember that other scholars of religion do not typically explain why they are not writing about other traditions and thinkers. If they did, their answers would likely simply be that they are not trained in those traditions and thinkers. Perhaps, though, comparativists need to articulate what most philosophers and scholars of religion do not articulate, namely that one of the reasons why they are offering comparisons of thinkers in particular traditions is that they are trained in those traditions, and

that they have chosen to specialize in certain traditions and thinkers because they find them interesting.[67] And perhaps, in addition, in cases where
there are particularly obvious alternative choices in the same tradition, one
should simply specify that one is not sufficiently trained to offer a study of
those figures. This objection helps to show why it is especially important
for comparativists to emphasize that they are not claiming that the figures
they have chosen are the only or best possible choices; comparativists need
only offer clear reasons why they have selected particular figures and argue
that such a comparison is worthwhile.

The larger question, of course, is whether Stalnaker makes clear his reasons for discussing Xunzi and Augustine. I think he does, and I think his
discussion indicates that the main impetus for his choice is the theories of
human nature offered by Xunzi and Augustine, and specifically the fact
that they both offer a reasonably pessimistic account of what humans are
like prior to a moral or religious transformation, while also offering an
optimistic account of the potential for real transformation.[68] The similarities and differences between Xunzi's and Augustine's views of human
nature have been noted by other interpreters of Xunzi, which likely also
played a role in Stalnaker's initial decision to investigate these two figures
comparatively.[69] Perhaps one reason Decosimo does not discuss the role of
human nature in relation to Stalnaker's choice is that the majority of his
critique of Stalnaker focuses on the subject of spiritual exercises, which is
what prompts his central question: "Given, as we will see, the paucity of
Augustine's reflection on [*Overcoming Our Evil*]'s key theme of 'spiritual
exercises' in relation to the many others who *have* explicitly, extensively,
and deeply treated that theme," why compare Xunzi and Augustine?[70] In
answering this question, I think it is important to remember that Stalnaker's comparison concerns two main topics—human nature and spiritual exercises—as the title of his work indicates. But Decosimo's focus on
spiritual exercises can help us to better understand where his central criticism really lies. In addition to arguing that Stalnaker should have explained
his choices more clearly, Decosimo offers multiple criticisms of the use
of the category of "spiritual exercises." The main reason why Decosimo
argues that Stalnaker should have explained his choice more clearly is, I
think, made clear in the objection he makes to Stalnaker's use of "spiritual
exercises": He rejects the view that spiritual exercises are an important part
of Augustine's thought.[71] It is important to note that this is an interpretive
issue and not a thematic issue, but it motivates a criticism of Stalnaker's
choice of Augustine and points toward a clear criticism of the selection
of the topic of spiritual exercises, both of which are thematic issues. De-

cosimo goes on to argue that spiritual exercises is interpreted too broadly for it to be a unique category.[72] He writes, "when the concept of 'spiritual exercises' is understood in the way Stalnaker needs for it to apply to Augustine, it becomes hard to think of practically any serious moral thinker who is not a proponent of 'spiritual exercises' so understood."[73] Decosimo adds a terminological objection, raising the question of "why the potentially misleading, heavily freighted, and much narrower language of 'spiritual exercises,' and especially the engagement with, dependence on, and multiple references to Hadot's work[,] is introduced in the first place and used to describe the different, much broader topic of 'moral growth' or 'moral striving.'"[74]

While it is beyond the scope of this study to evaluate and respond to these specific criticisms, it is worth considering how Stalnaker's account might be adapted to meet the latter, terminological objection. Other scholars of Chinese thought have used the more general category of moral self-cultivation—based on the term used by Xunzi as well as his predecessor Mengzi and throughout the history of Chinese thought: *xiu shen* ("self-cultivation")—to describe and analyze these aspects of Xunzi's thought, and this term does not seem to be as problematic as "spiritual exercises" in the ways that Decosimo suggests. Stalnaker writes that self-cultivation is "a serviceable category for analyzing Chinese ethical thought" and says that "spiritual exercises" "is not a radically superior term, sweeping the field of scholarship clear; it is, however, a good way to highlight . . . the specific practices that Xunzi saw as making up the general process of *xiu shen*, thus providing a more nuanced structure for presenting both Xunzi's specific prescriptions for, and general theory of the efficacy of, practices of personal transformation."[75] He mentions three of the models of self-cultivation that have been explored in relation to Chinese thought (the "discovery," "development," and "re-formation" models) and writes that they "will not be particularly helpful in the current comparative study. Augustine and Xunzi are both, in their own ways, examples of a reformation model, so some finer theoretical tool is necessary to bring out the details of each of their views" (39–40).[76] However, I think a term such as "self-cultivation practices" might be a more promising alternative than Stalnaker suggests, especially if we reconsider whether Augustine and Xunzi indeed share the same model of self-cultivation. If we accept Stalnaker's argument, then it seems clear that Augustine, like Xunzi, is a self-cultivationist, but one who believes in a particular conception of God, the self, original sin, and a range of other distinctive ideas. As a result, perhaps Augustine's view will require its own model of self-cultivation. My goal here is simply to suggest there are good reasons to think that various models of self-cultivation do have the resources to bring out the details of Augustine's and Xunzi's views, while avoiding some of the criticisms of "spiritual exercises" seen above.

An overview of these aspects of Stalnaker's work brings to light a number of general issues comparativists face with respect to thematic issues. First, we have seen once again how important interpretive issues are and the impact they can have on one's study as a whole. This particular case serves as a clear example of how a particular interpretation of a thinker (e.g., an interpretation that does not see spiritual exercises as an important part of Augustine's thought) can lead one to reject many other aspects of a comparative study and to judge a comparative study as unsuccessful in many ways. Decosimo's view that spiritual exercises are not important for Augustine leads him to question Stalnaker's choice of Augustine, as well as the topic of spiritual exercises. Some of the questions raised about the choice of "spiritual exercises" as a topic and as a term used to refer to certain kinds of practices highlights the fact that, as noted earlier, in choosing a topic for a comparative study, comparativists also must be attentive to *terminological* questions. Indeed, I think one of the most difficult tasks a comparativist faces is the selection of terms for the ideas being compared. One must try to find terms that are easily recognized and understood and have the least likelihood of being misleading but that will not misrepresent either of the thinkers under study. Perhaps most important, one must be able to distinguish between objections that are solely terminological in character and those that also involve an objection to one's topic. The objection to Stalnaker's work that we have examined involves both types of objections, but one could object to the use of the term "spiritual exercises" without objecting to Stalnaker's conception of spiritual exercises as a topic of comparison. This type of objection is much less serious, because it does not undermine the main conclusions of the study. For example, one could object to Stalnaker's use of the term "spiritual exercises" (e.g., because it brings to mind something other than what he means by it) while still accepting his argument that the moral practices he calls "spiritual exercises" are an important part of both Augustine's and Xunzi's thought and while also accepting his argument that a comparative study of these practices in the work of Augustine and Xunzi is illuminating in some important ways.

Having examined the issue of why one chooses to compare particular figures or texts, and the way in which these choices (as well as criticisms of one's choices) often relate in important ways to interpretive issues, I want to emphasize the wide range of choices comparativists face when it comes to thematic issues. Indeed, one's thematic choices can vary widely in shape and scope. For example, in contrast to the other studies I have mentioned so far, which focus on comparing particular concepts, virtues, practices, or theories, Carr and Ivanhoe compare the philosophical styles of Zhuangzi and Kierkegaard and the way in which those styles—as well as many other features of their work—express different forms of antirationalism. Another way in which one's thematic choices might vary concerns the things one compares. I have so far discussed only examples that compare particular thinkers or texts, but just as one might choose to compare general approaches or styles as opposed to particular virtues or practices, one might also choose not to compare two thinkers or texts. Indeed, some recent works in Chinese and comparative philosophy have departed from the approach of making "one-to-one" comparisons (of single Chinese or Western thinkers or texts) in favor of comparing particular Chinese schools or thinkers with movements or themes within contemporary Western ethics more generally. For example, Stephen Angle's work *Sagehood: The Contemporary Significance of Neo-Confucian Philosophy* argues that Neo-Confucian ethical and political thought can be developed through a critical dialogue with contemporary Western philosophy, and that Western philosophy also can be stimulated by this encounter to develop in new ways. The kind of comparative work done here is different from "one-to-one" comparative studies in two important ways ways: Angle's subjects are Neo-Confucianism and contemporary ethics (with the latter by no means constituting a single thinker or tradition), and he aims to use Neo-Confucianism as a resource for constructing a view that will improve upon certain features of contemporary ethics; the goal is not simply to help his readers understand two views but to improve upon and further develop those views.

Although I think interpretive and thematic issues are both important aspects of one's method or approach to comparative work, the last of the three sets of issues I will discuss, *procedural issues*, are often what we have in mind when we talk about methods or methodology in comparative work. Procedural issues concern such things as how a comparative study unfolds, how it is structured, what it includes, how consistently a comparativist follows her stated or implied method, and, more generally, how carefully a comparative study is conducted. We can clearly distinguish procedural issues from interpretive and thematic issues because one's choice of how to go about conducting a comparative study involves answering a very different set of questions from those one answers when offering and defending an interpretation of a thinker or text, or when choosing texts, thinkers, or topics for comparison. Let us examine some particular examples of approaches to procedural issues in comparative work in order to clarify what procedural questions are and how they are distinctive.

While there are many different kinds of procedural issues, the question of how one proceeds in the comparative process, and in particular the explicit discussion of both similarities and differences in a fair and balanced manner, can determine the success or failure of a comparative study. Indeed, it is probably this aspect of comparative work that has received the most attention in discussions of procedural issues. For example, Lee Yearley's approach of working with "similarities in differences and differences in similarities" has been widely cited by other comparativists.[77] Such an approach involves not simply offering an outline of similarities and differences but going a step further: Once one identifies an area of similarity, one looks for further differences within those similarities; once one identifies differences, one looks for similarities within those differences. The basic goal of such a procedure is to avoid portraying the similarities and differences between thinkers in an overly simplistic or one-dimensional fashion. Through his approach, Yearley cautions us not to accept the conclusion that two traditions, thinkers, or texts are completely different in every way or the conclusion that they are wholly alike; instead, he urges us to move to a higher level of nuance and sophistication in our analyses. It is important that on Yearley's view this process must be a two-way street. For example, one who notes that two thinkers share the view that humans have innate tendencies toward goodness ought to look further in order to note the different understandings of "goodness" in each thinker. But when one notes an important difference, such as the contrast between the claim that life in a monastic community is a necessary condition for the highest form of human flourishing and the claim that life with one's parents, spouse, and children is a necessary condition for the highest form of human flourishing, on Yearley's view one ought to look further in order to note similarities, such as the fact that both views might entail the strong claim that it is *impossible* for humans to flourish in the absence of membership in a certain kind of community or family—both of which entail very specific kinds of relationships with others.[78] Yearley's approach involves a sort of telescoping effect combined with microscopic analysis, because one is constantly pressed to go a step further, to look more carefully and think harder about what one is comparing, and to intentionally look for just the opposite of what one finds: If one finds similarities, one ought to look for differences within those similarities; if one finds differences, one ought to look for similarities. The view behind Yearley's procedure is, of course, that there are both important similarities and differences between any two human thinkers, even though finding them is "a taxing balancing act" because we are often tempted to draw overly strong conclusions about similarity and difference.[79]

Some procedural questions deal more specifically with the way in which one's comparative study is structured, such as the proper order of different discussions. For example, Carr and Ivanhoe reserve the concluding section of each chapter of their work on Zhuangzi and Kierkegaard for a discussion of important differences between the two thinkers. Such a procedure is an intentional way of avoiding the tendency to give too much attention to similarities in chapters that are dedicated to Zhuangzi's and Kierkegaard's views on the same theme or topic, and it is also a way of addressing one of the primary objections any comparativist will face: the claim that one has emphasized only or too strongly the similarities between two thinkers. One could obviously anticipate and address this objection in any number of places in a comparative study, but the choice to *conclude* each chapter with a discussion of important differences ensures that readers will come away from each chapter thinking a bit more about the contrasts, or the differences within the similarities, as Yearley would put it. This is a clear example of how one can build important features of one's approach into the very structure of a comparative study, and when one does so, one makes the most of the different ways of addressing various kinds of challenges in comparative work.

Some comparativists adopt very specific approaches to procedural issues, and an example is seen in Angle's *Sagehood*. His approach has two aspects: "rooted global philosophy" and "constructive engagement," and both aspects emphasize the fundamentally constructive—as opposed to descriptive—approach to comparative work that Angle adopts. Rooted global philosophy means "to work within a particular live philosophical tradition—thus its rootedness—but to do so in a way that is open to stimulus and insights from other philosophical traditions—thus its global nature."[80] The main goal of rooted global philosophy is to *develop* a given philosophical tradition, and so it is important that on this view, one need not give up one's "home" tradition or approach and attempt to take up a third, neutral position when one engages multiple traditions in a comparative project. Rather, one simply must "work to understand other traditions in their own terms, and find grounds on which we can engage one another constructively." Additionally, Angle says, "rooted global philosophy is not premised on our ultimate convergence on some single set of philosophical truths," although "some degree of convergence may be expected."[81] The second part of his approach focuses even more heavily on the comparative dimension of his project: "Constructive engagement means engaging in dialogue with other traditions (by talking, reading and writing, or even through one's own reflection on multiple traditions) in order to learn more through a process of mutual openness, grounded in the belief that no live philosophical tradition has all the answers or is impervious to criticism."[82] The assumption of this approach is that "contemporary, live philosophical traditions can challenge and yet learn from one another" and it emphasizes the possibility of two-way influence (where each tradition influences and shapes the other).[83] Angle's study aims to constructively engage Western philosophers with Neo-Confucian philosophy, and thus the goal is to show how both Neo-Confucian ethics and contemporary Western ethics can be further developed based on challenges from the other perspective.

Another example of a specific and distinctive approach is seen the use of "bridge concepts" in Stalnaker's *Overcoming Our Evil*. I think this work has a number of interesting features, and because we have become familiar with some of the basic aspects of it in the preceding discussion, I want to examine Stalnaker's approach in a bit more detail to see what we might learn about procedural issues, particularly in relation to very specific and distinctive methods. Stalnaker writes that "any comparative ethical study faces two fundamental challenges: It must bring distant ethical statements into interrelation and conversation, and it must simultaneously preserve their distinctiveness within the interrelation" (17). He proposes to bring Augustine's and Xunzi's ethical views "into interrelation and conversation" by means of what he calls "bridge concepts," which he defines as "general ideas . . . which can be given enough content to be meaningful and guide comparative inquiry and yet are still open to greater specification in particular cases" (17). Stalnaker refers to bridge concepts in a variety of ways throughout his study, calling them "organizing themes" (28), "categories of analysis" (33), and "thematic guides" (35). He focuses on two main bridge concepts in his study: "human nature" and "spiritual exercises," with secondary attention given to "person" and the "will" (17).

Bridge concepts are more than simply comparative topics for Stalnaker; they represent his comparative method. He writes that "bridge concepts may be projected into each thinker or text to be compared as a way to thematize their disparate elements and order their details around these anchoring terms. Bridge concepts often work best if near-equivalent terms for the various aspects of the bridge concept can be found in each set of writings to be compared, but this is not necessary" (17). The claim that bridge concepts are "projected into" thinkers or texts being compared seems to imply that bridge concepts are not necessarily concepts that are shared by the two thinkers under study. Stalnaker maintains that bridge concepts differ from "thin concepts" in being designed to bring out particular features of the two systems of thought being compared (17). He writes that "bridge concepts are designed to elicit theoretical formulations in each object compared (i.e., their 'vocabulary'), including questions and basic orientations, but to refrain from reshaping the terms each thinker uses into some fundamentally new form. The analysis of each thinker's vocabulary thus safeguards each side's uniqueness within the comparison" (18). For Stalnaker, bridge concepts help us to avoid the temptation to see too much similarity between two thinkers, and our attention is instead focused on "the way particular ideas fit into larger visions," which allows for "more nuanced comparisons of seemingly similar ideas across traditions" (18).

Stalnaker chooses his words carefully here, referring to "*seemingly similar* ideas across traditions" (italics mine). But while he says "the similarity in the general morphology of [Xunzi's and Augustine's] views is the basis for the bridge concepts used to compare them" (21), which suggests that bridge concepts are similar to the concepts they serve as a bridge for, the bridge concepts themselves appear not to be concepts that are shared by Augustine and Xunzi. This seems to be what makes them "bridge" concepts, as the image of a bridge connotes something that joins two areas *but is not part of either*. This would mean that neither thinker shares *any* part of the bridge concept, and that bridge concepts are a third thing that serves to bridge the gap between different concepts in the work of Xunzi and Augustine. The question, then, is how bridge concepts are related to the concepts they serve as a bridge for, if they do not represent shared concepts.

One of Stalnaker's primary motivations for using "bridge concepts" is his concern to avoid imposing ideas onto Augustine and Xunzi that are not really a part of their thought, or to redescribe one using the language of the other. This is important because it shows once again how comparativists often adopt particular approaches to procedural issues in order to avoid problems that often plague comparative studies. Interestingly, though, Stalnaker intentionally avoids the claim that bridge concepts, at least in Xunzi's and Augustine's cases, might be shared concepts. Now it is important to note that it is not necessarily an imposition to claim that two thinkers have an understanding of the same basic concept. Whether or not this is an imposition, of course, depends upon whether or not it is true. To consider an example from Stalnaker's work, we might consider whether it is really accurate to say that the writings of Augustine and Xunzi do not clearly express an understanding of the concept of human nature. I realize that one of Stalnaker's goals is to uncover "the complexity and tension in frequently used terms such as 'human nature'" (36); he maintains that "talk about 'human nature' is a way of addressing at least four distinct sorts of issues" (36–37) and that human nature "is hardly one thing at all but a family of related concerns that may or may not be seen as aspects of any one postulated theoretical entity" (37).[84] However, what a comparativist might do in this case is specify what she means when she says that both Augustine and Xunzi have an understanding of human nature. For example, one might say that they both believe that all human beings have certain capacities and tendencies, by virtue of being human, which is what we often mean when we say that a thinker has a concept of human nature.

One could, of course, defend this view while also defending the view that these two thinkers have very different *theories* of human nature. Indeed, one of the important things that Stalnaker's work shows is that Augustine and Xunzi, despite certain areas of agreement, ultimately have different *theories* of human nature. Here, I am distinguishing between the *concept* of human nature and a *theory* of human nature.[85] It seems reasonable to claim that although both Augustine and Xunzi express an understanding of the *concept* of human nature (i.e., they both think there are certain capacities and tendencies that all human beings have, by virtue of being human), they have different *theories* of human nature (i.e., they disagree about at least some of the capacities and tendencies that humans have by virtue of being human). My sense is that part of what motivates Stalnaker to use bridge concepts is the concern that the important differences between and the complexity of Augustine's and Xunzi's *theories* of human nature will be neglected if we grant that they both have an understanding of the concept of human nature. However, one could take a different approach and acknowledge that they share a concept while still discussing in detail and emphasizing the differences between their theories. Mengzi and Xunzi serve as a helpful illustration here, as they clearly share a concept of human nature (and even a term), but they have different theories about it.[86]

A key issue here is how easy it is to pick out "thin" concepts that are relevant to comparative studies. In his recent review of Van Norden's *Virtue Ethics and Consequentialism in Early Chinese Philosophy*, Stalnaker claims that Van Norden "glosses over possible difficulties in picking suitable thin concepts" by using the example of the sun, which "elides the difficulties when there is no obvious shared referent for disputed terms."[87] Stalnaker, then, maintains that it is difficult to determine what concept two thinkers share when they are not referring to physical objects. However, even when thin concepts do not refer to physical objects, they often still have clear referents. For example, when Mengzi and Xunzi refer to "human nature," they are referring to human behavior prior to moral cultivation, and they give many examples of these behaviors (e.g., infants' responses to their parents' love and care). I am not, of course, claiming that there is some universal set of shared concepts shared worldwide, trans-historically. The issue of which thin concepts are shared (as well as which theories or thick concepts are shared) must be decided on a case-by-case basis when two thinkers or sources are compared.[88]

There is, though, another reason why Stalnaker is hesitant to claim that Augustine and Xunzi share a basic (thin) concept or understanding of human nature. His work formulates the concern that thinking about human nature as a single thing (e.g., "the concept" of human nature) can be both reductionistic and essentialistic. He writes that most often,

> bridge concepts multiply under comparative scrutiny to cover a cluster of related ideas that can be specified more precisely, but that may or may not cohere in any systematic way; in cases of this sort, comparison serves as a prod to conceptual analysis, and it uncovers the complexity and tension in frequently used terms such as "human nature" and "the will." Such clusters . . . will often but not always seem to share a "family resemblance." (35–36)[89]

Stalnaker writes that "[a]rticulating a manifold bridge concept of human nature allows us to tease out the complexities of their views, going beyond a blinkered focus only on the words previously translated into English as 'human nature' in each figure" (37). Stalnaker seems to be making two basic claims here. (1) Human nature is not a single concept but a cluster of several related concepts.[90] (2) Thinking about human nature in this way has certain methodological benefits in comparative studies, namely that doing so helps us to "tease out the complexities" of the views under study.

These two claims reveal that Stalnaker has two motivations for using bridge concepts. In addition to his methodological concerns as a comparativist, he is working to avoid a certain form of essentialism which motivates the claim that human nature—like other "manifold bridge concepts"—should not be reduced to a single definition. These concerns are related, because for Stalnaker, if we maintain that there is a single "concept" of human nature that Augustine and Xunzi share, then we commit ourselves to talking about only one of the concepts that are a part of the cluster of concepts that is human nature, and as a result we may not fully appreciate the complexity of their views. In considering various kinds of procedural issues in comparative work, it is certainly important to avoid vicious forms of reductionism and essentialism, but at times Stalnaker's approach comes across as being a bit strong. Take, for example, his claims that bridge concepts, like human nature, multiply to cover "a cluster of related ideas . . . that may or may not cohere in any systematic way" and that "may or may not be seen as aspects of any one postulated theoretical entity" and that "often but not always seem to share a 'family resemblance.'" Here, Stalnaker seems to deny that defining features shared by different theories of human nature exist. But in the effort to avoid a strong form of essentialism, we can move too far toward the opposite extreme. To deny that different theories of human nature all have certain things in common seems to be just as misleading as claiming that there is one singular essence to all theories of human nature.

Stalnaker mentions Wittgenstein's notion of "family resemblance" in passing here (36), and I think this would be a good starting place for further examination of these issues. Although many scholars invoke family resemblance as a way of combating essentialism, it is important to remember that Wittgenstein was tackling a particular kind of essentialism in the history of philosophy. With his concept of family resemblance, Wittgenstein offers a response to the claim that there is a *single* defining feature (an essence) of concepts like justice or virtue. However, Wittgenstein by no means claims that no defining features exist at all. Indeed, the very idea of "family resemblance" implies that certain shared features and characteristics define things as part of the same "family," even though not all of the members of a family might display all of these features and characteristics.[91]

These examples help to show why a keen understanding of procedural questions is important in comparative work. One might agree with a scholar's interpretations and also with her thematic choices and yet still disagree with the way she goes about doing a comparative study. A comparative study, then, can be derailed from the outset by indefensible interpretations of the philosophers being compared (interpretive issues), and it can also be derailed by the question of what one compares (thematic issues), or by various aspects of how one goes about conducting a comparative study, such as the failure to discuss both similarities and differences adequately (procedural issues).

On Behalf of an Anti-Method Approach to Comparative Work

One thing our study of the question "Why compare?" as well as interpretive, thematic, and procedural issues in this chapter has shown is that comparativists are often led to embrace certain approaches to comparative work out of a desire to avoid the difficulties commonly encountered in such work. In our examination of interpretive issues we saw that some scholars embrace the view that pragmatism and process philosophy are the only Western philosophies that have genuinely substantive continuities with Chinese philosophy. This position on interpretive issues in Chinese and comparative work is, I think, motivated in part by the desire to show that Chinese philosophy is distinctive and thus worth studying—something that, as we saw in the first part of this chapter, one must demonstrate in order for philosophers to take non-Western philosophy seriously. In relation to thematic issues, we saw that comparativists' choices are often grounded in their awareness of the need to demonstrate both continuity and discontinuity in two thinkers or texts, in order to avoid the difficulties that are sometimes encountered in showing that two thinkers or texts have enough in common to provide the basis for a fruitful comparison. This is true of procedural issues, as well: The desire to avoid certain problems in comparative work is often the primary (or at least a very strong) motivating factor when comparativists embrace very specific methods or ways of going about comparative study. For example, Stalnaker utilizes bridge concepts in part because he sees them as helping to safeguard comparisons against certain pitfalls, such as the tendency to misrepresent two thinkers' views by overemphasizing their similarities.

Based on the foregoing discussion, there are a number of reasons to consider the view that no single method or approach holds the key to successfully addressing the many different challenges one faces when doing comparative work. First, particular methods or approaches tend to be designed for particular aspects of comparative work—or for particular kinds of comparisons—but do not address all of them. For example, Yearley's approach of looking for "differences in similarities and similarities in differences" addresses procedural issues but not interpretive and thematic issues. Similarly, Angle's "constructive engagement" is appropriate for comparisons that seek to challenge and further develop aspects of the views under study, but not for comparisons that have more descriptive aims. Second, the adoption of very specific and distinctive methods or approaches usually creates an additional set of challenges for comparativists. For example, describing and applying a particular theory to one's work requires expanding a study even more in order to explain why and how one is applying that theory, what modifications one is making to it, and why those modifications are appropriate. This can, in some cases, spread a comparativist's energies too thin. Indeed, excessive concern with one's methodological apparatus can distract from the care and attentiveness that good comparative work requires. Of course, this problem is not insurmountable, and one might find that a particular method resolves more difficulties than it creates—which might, of course, be a good reason for using it—but any comparativist who employs a very specific method or theory must guard against this problem, and, as a result, it represents a distinctive challenge. Comparativists who employ distinctive methods or theories must ask themselves why they are doing it. It can be tempting to employ novel and even trendy categories of analysis or theoretical approaches in order to show that one is doing something new and exciting, but along with the employment of new categories and approaches come new challenges and potential objections. Given the complexity of comparative work and the large number of objections comparative studies typically draw from multiple sides, it may be worth considering the possibility that comparative studies are not the best venue for applying distinctive categories and theories. At least in those cases where comparativists do so, they should recognize that this action creates additional challenges and is likely to create an additional set of potential objections, and comparativists will need to evaluate whether the gains outweigh the losses.[92]

A related difficulty is that single methods can sometimes lead a comparativist to think mistakenly that she will not need to worry about particular problems because her method itself will prevent those problems. Although comparativists often embrace particular methods out of the belief that these methods will serve as a safeguard by helping them to avoid certain pitfalls in comparative work, on my view no particular method can replace the effectiveness of continually attending to interpretive, thematic, and procedural issues in the course of a comparative study. It is particularly important for comparativists to recognize this because a comparative study can falter in so many different ways. The worry here is that one will become overly reliant on a particular method out of the mistaken belief that doing so will prevent certain difficulties.

Perhaps most important, very particular, single methods are sometimes adopted out of the belief that one must have a particular methodological apparatus in order for a comparison even to be possible. The idea here is roughly that thinkers from different traditions are so far apart that one must find a way to *facilitate* a comparison. Contrary to this sort of view, I think it is clearly possible to compare thinkers from any two philosophical or religious traditions, based on the similarities between them that lead us to call them philosophers or religious thinkers. As Carr and Ivanhoe point out, these traditions fulfill a similar range of functions for human beings, and that is why we call them philosophical or religious traditions.

Now, even though I accept the view that it is clearly *possible* to compare any number of different thinkers from different traditions, I think the question of whether a comparison is helpful or illuminating is one that must be answered separately. I also think the question of how difficult it is to conduct a comparative study carefully must be answered separately.[93] We should expect a wide range of different answers to these questions given the rich diversity of thinkers and texts in different traditions; a part of what it means to recognize the genuine differences that exist across different traditions is to recognize that not all comparisons will be equally difficult or easy. It is important to recognize that one can reject the view that one needs a special methodological apparatus to make comparative work possible without thinking that "anything goes" in comparative work. While I think it is possible to compare thinkers from any two traditions, I also believe that some comparisons are extremely difficult to carry out and that other comparisons are not particularly illuminating. Indeed, this is precisely why I think it is so important to attend to interpretive, thematic, and procedural issues, for it is by attending carefully to these issues that we will be able to make better choices about which comparisons are worthwhile and where we need to devote more of our energies to working to avoid certain pitfalls.

Now it is important to recognize that one can embrace a very specific approach to some issues without embracing a specific method or approach to *comparative* work as a whole. Here, it is helpful to distinguish procedural issues—which specifically concern how one goes about doing comparative work—from interpretive and thematic issues. For example, Van Norden applies a philosophical perspective to Chinese thought, noting that philosophers use specialized terminologies and are concerned with specialized issues, but also that different philosophers employ different terminologies and focus on different issues, depending upon their particular perspective or approach. Van Norden employs an analytic perspective, by which he means that he is especially concerned with "finding, interpreting, and evaluating arguments in the texts; clarifying the meaning of the texts by spelling out interpretive alternatives and examining whether some make better sense of the text than others; and exploring whether each text is self-consistent."[94] So his approach or method is philosophical and, in particular, analytic. But it is important to remember that Van Norden is describing his general approach; he is not offering a method for doing comparative philosophy in particular. It is also worth noting that Van Norden embraces "methodological pluralism," pointing out that there are "a variety of disciplines and methodologies that can be applied to texts in ways that are illuminating." Indeed, he notes that despite the opposition that often exists between postmodernists and "analytic" philosophers, his approach shares a number of assumptions with postmodern approaches.[95]

Like Van Norden, I endorse methodological pluralism when it comes to the many different scholarly approaches one might take to the study of particular thinkers or texts, for I think that a variety of disciplinary and methodological approaches can be fruitful, even in the study of the very same texts. However, when it comes to procedural issues in comparative work, at least in the disciplines of philosophy and religious studies, I am inclined to endorse what I describe as an "anti-method" approach. It is not that I think comparativists should not have particular methods and ways of proceeding when it comes to addressing, for example, interpretive issues, nor do I deny that comparativists should have clear, well-organized, and systematic approaches. Rather, my argument is that comparativists are usually better off attending carefully to the different kinds of challenges and questions that arise in comparative work than embracing a particular method for doing comparative work.

In light of my view that an "anti-method" approach to comparative work is the most promising, I do not utilize a particular method or approach in my comparison of the *Analects* and Rawls. Rather, in each of the subsequent chapters, I work to give attention to interpretive, thematic, and procedural issues, as well as to the issue of why comparative study is worthwhile. I do, though, address these various kinds of issues in a variety of ways. For example, although I have argued that no thematic approach can in itself prevent interpretive problems in comparative studies, the topic of one's comparison can make one more or less prone to certain difficulties. Focusing on a comparison of the way multiple concepts function together often steers one away from interpretations that misrepresent philosophers and their traditions as exclusively or primarily concerned with single ideas or practices. Especially because there has been much attention given to the absence of a single term that uniquely designates the concept of justice in early Confucianism, and also because there has been a tendency to focus on single concepts such as *yi* and *Ren* in relation to justice, I focus on a variety of different terms and their various uses and roles in the different discussions in the *Analects*. This emphasis on multiple concepts has the added benefit of drawing more attention to the philosophical and cultural contexts in which certain ideas are situated, thereby helping to take account of the bigger picture. However, that is not to say that studies of individual concepts cannot be done carefully, nor is it to say that comparisons of multiple concepts always avoid the pitfalls of other kinds of studies. It is, though, one way in which I aim to address interpretive issues in this book. The interpretive challenge of providing compelling textual evidence for one's reading of both thinkers under study in a comparison and the procedural challenge of discussing similarities and differences explicitly and extensively remain daunting regardless of one's topic. In order to address these issues more carefully, I have made some structural choices. I devote individual chapters to my interpretations of Rawls and the *Analects*, before proceeding with my comparative discussion. In these chapters, I focus intensively on the primary texts under study while also taking account of and responding to important critiques and influential readings of the ideas in question. My comparative discussion opens by describing the defining features of a sense of justice in Rawls and the *Analects*, followed by a specific discussion devoted to the differences between Rawls's view and the view found in the *Analects*, in order to help prevent discussions of the differences between them from being dwarfed by discussions of the similarities. These differences are further developed in a chapter examining the contemporary relevance of both views, providing a further opportunity to develop the deep and remarkable areas of contrast between the two accounts.

CHAPTER 2

The Sense of Justice in Rawls

... [I]f citizens are acting for the right reasons in a constitutional
regime, then regardless of their comprehensive doctrines they want
every other citizen to have justice. So you might say they're all working together to do one thing, namely to make sure every citizen has
justice. Now that's not the only interest they all have, but it's the
single thing they're all trying to do. In my language, they're striving
toward one single end, the end of justice for all citizens.[1]

In recent years there has been a remarkable proliferation of monographs
and introductory texts on Rawls's work, exploring his views on wide-
ranging topics, as well as his life and the legacy of his work.[2] New collections of essays on Rawls's work have also appeared, as well as previously
unpublished work by Rawls such as his *Lectures on the History of Political
Philosophy*.[3] Some of these works even explore the evolution of Rawls's
thought in areas that he never published in, such as *A Brief Inquiry into the
Meaning of Sin and Faith*, which includes Rawls's 1942 Princeton senior
thesis on theological ethics by the same title.[4] Accompanying Rawls's thesis
in this volume is "On My Religion," a short statement he wrote in 1997
describing his religious beliefs and attitudes toward religion, as well as an
accompanying essay by Robert Merrihew Adams examining Rawls's early
religious views. What is especially interesting about this book is that it
shows the depth of interest not just in Rawls's published work but also in
the evolution of his thought as a whole, even on topics that do not pertain
directly to his work in political philosophy. Joshua Cohen and Thomas
Nagel emphasize in the Introduction to this work that it is "a remarkable
resource for understanding the development of his thought," and it should

strike us as remarkable that there is interest in tracing even the early evolution of Rawls's thought in this sort of detail.[5] Given the depth of interest in Rawls and his work, and even in the earliest influences on his thought, it is surprising that no studies have yet provided an in-depth exploration of Rawls's moral psychology.

One place to begin an examination of the account of moral psychology that underpins Rawls's theory of justice is with the fact that Rawls is interested in offering an account of justice that can be understood and accepted by a wide range of people. Rawls offers a conception of justice that is strictly political so that it will be acceptable to citizens committed to a diverse array of comprehensive views. Such diversity is a prominent feature of the modern liberal democracies to which Rawls intends his analysis to apply. Democracy, for Rawls, implies diversity or "reasonable pluralism," which results in part from the freedom to pursue different conceptions of the good—conceptions not dictated by the state. As such, we should expect profound differences in belief and conceptions of the good so that "public agreement on the basic questions of philosophy cannot be obtained without the state's infringement of basic liberties."[6] As a result of this fact, Rawls holds that in order to secure agreement between citizens on political questions of justice in a democracy, we must avoid controversial philosophical, moral, and religious questions.

Still, as the quotation from Rawls that opens this chapter indicates, Rawls maintains that citizens in certain kinds of societies are united in a very important pursuit: "the end of justice for all citizens." This chapter explores Rawls's claim that members of society have both the capacity and the motivation to strive for the end of justice for all members of society. Specifically, I explore the fundamental capacities and motivations Rawls ascribes to human beings in order for his account of justice to work. I focus primarily on Rawls's claim that humans have a *fundamental capacity* for cooperation and a "sense of justice" that leads them to make sacrifices for the least advantaged members of society. I argue that Rawls's definition of the concept of social justice is not tied to a view of isolated autonomous individuals who are alienated from one another but, to the contrary, that Rawls takes an optimistic and socially oriented view of human beings in his account of moral psychology and basic human capacities. I also show that Rawls's account relies heavily on the idea that a sense of justice is a capacity to be cultivated within the context of the family, community, and larger society, and that the fully developed sense of justice resulting from this process of cultivation is the single most important thing in the stability of a just society over time.

My argument in this chapter addresses a common misunderstanding of Rawls's view that has been prevalent not only in discussions comparing Western liberalism and Confucianism but also in communitarian critiques of Rawls's work. One particular communitarian criticism that has served as a resource for a number of comparative studies is Alasdair MacIntyre's claim that Rawls's thought, and his liberalism more generally, fosters a form of asocial individualism. The dimension of Rawls's work that I discuss in this chapter, namely the cultivation of a sense of justice, has been neglected in this literature. I argue that Rawls's understanding of justice rests on his view that members of just societies have the capacity to cultivate certain postures toward other members of society, postures that include emotional and dispositional traits constituted by a sense of justice. Most fundamentally, this posture is characterized by a genuine concern for others and by the desire to advance everyone's position and affirm everyone's good.

Political Liberalism and the Concept of Justice

Early in *A Theory of Justice*, Rawls makes an important distinction between *the concept* of justice and *a conception* of justice. The latter is a technical term for Rawls; a conception of justice comprises "a characteristic set of principles for assigning basic rights and duties and for determining what [members of a society] take to be the proper distribution of the benefits and burdens of social cooperation."[7] Examples of a conception of justice include utilitarianism, perfectionism, and justice as fairness. Rawls goes on to elaborate the distinction between a concept and a conception:

> Thus it seems natural to think of the *concept* of justice as distinct from the various *conceptions* of justice and as being specified by the role which these different sets of principles, these different *conceptions*, have in common. Those who hold different *conceptions* of justice can, then, still agree that institutions are just when no arbitrary distinctions are made between persons in the assigning of basic rights and duties and when the rules determine a proper balance between competing claims to the advantages of social life. Men can agree to this description of just institutions since the notions of an arbitrary distinction and of a proper balance, which are included in the concept of justice, are left open for each to interpret according to the principles of justice that he accepts. These principles single out which similarities and differences among persons are relevant in determining rights and duties and they specify which division of advan-

tages is appropriate. Clearly this distinction between the *concept* and the various *conceptions* of justice settles no important questions. It simply helps to identify the role of the principles of social justice.[8] (*TJ*, 5)

On Rawls's view, then, there is only one *concept* of justice, but there are many different *conceptions* of justice. We should keep in mind here that Rawls's focus is social justice, and so he defines the *concept* of justice in terms of the justice of a society's institutions—its political constitution and the principal economic and social arrangements (*TJ*, 6). A society's institutions are just when they do not make *arbitrary distinctions* between persons in the assigning of basic rights and duties, and when the rules determine *a proper balance* between competing claims to the advantages of social life.[9] Thus, we can see that on Rawls's view, a society exhibits an understanding of the concept of justice when its institutions reflect the view that it is wrong to make arbitrary distinctions between persons in assigning the privileges and obligations they will have as members of society, and when the rules by which society operates address the question of who should be given which advantages of social life, and why.

Different conceptions of justice offer different interpretations of what constitutes a "non-arbitrary" distinction—that is, which similarities and differences are relevant in determining rights and duties. They also have different definitions of what constitutes a "proper balance"—that is, which division of advantages in a society is seen as just. A conception of justice specifies how these terms are understood by formulating principles of justice. As Rawls puts it, a conception of justice is an interpretation of the role of the principles of justice (*TJ*, 9). But in order to have *the concept* of justice, a society's institutions need to reflect only two basic beliefs: (1) arbitrary distinctions between people should not determine what privileges and obligations they have as members of society, and (2) there should be a standard for determining who should enjoy the advantages of social life, and under what conditions. *Conceptions* of justice contain principles that explicitly address these two issues.

It is important to begin our analysis of Rawls with this distinction in mind, because it will be an important distinction throughout this book. There is a profound difference between advancing an explicit theory or conception of justice and presenting a consistent concept of justice expressed by making a cluster of specific claims about human needs, capacities, tendencies, and the like. Much has been written on Rawls's conception or theory of justice, but I focus instead on the *concept* of justice Rawls unveils through the claims he makes about human needs, capacities, and tendencies, as well as through his articulation of the specific conception of justice that is called "justice as fairness." It is important to remember that Rawls confines his analysis to social justice, which specifically concerns a society's institutions—that is, the extent to which its political constitution and principal economic and social arrangements are just. So the question before us is how we are to understand the idea of social justice. Our initial inclination might be to ask what qualities cause us to use the words "just" or "unjust" with respect to different aspects of a society's basic structure, but Rawls makes an important qualification about this sort of question at the beginning of *Theory*. He writes that he is primarily interested in considering a "strict compliance" as opposed to a "partial compliance" theory. Strict compliance studies the principles of justice that regulate a well-ordered society, whereas partial compliance studies principles that govern how we are to deal with injustice, including theories of punishment, just war theory, and civil disobedience (*TJ* §2, p. 8). Rawls maintains that studying the ideal theory—justice in a well-ordered society—is the best place to begin because it is necessary to understand what we are aiming at if we are to provide a basis for addressing the pressing problems of how we are to deal with injustice. A well-ordered society, on Rawls's definition, is a society in which all accept the same publicly agreed-upon principles of justice, have an effective sense of justice that enables them to understand and apply those principles, and act according to the requirements of their position in society (*JF*, 8–9).

Rawls maintains that his understanding of the concept of justice does in fact "tally with tradition" (*TJ* §2, p. 9). That is, he maintains that his understanding of justice does not conflict with the traditional notion of social justice, and he turns to Aristotle's view to show that the two do not conflict. Rawls says that Aristotle's view, from which most familiar formulations of justice derive, is that of refraining from *pleonexia*, or gaining some advantage for ourselves by seizing what belongs to others (e.g., their property, rewards, offices) *or* by denying others that which is due them, (e.g., the fulfillment of a promise, the repayment of a debt, the showing of proper respect).[10] Aristotle's definition is designed to apply to actions, where persons are thought to be just insofar as they have a steady and effective desire to act justly, and Rawls notes that Aristotle's view presupposes "an account of what properly belongs to a person and of what is due to him. Now such entitlements are, I believe, very often derived from social institutions and the legitimate expectations to which they give rise. There is no reason to think that Aristotle would disagree with this, and certainly he has a conception of social justice to account for these claims" (*TJ* §2,

p. 10). Here, Rawls notes that Aristotle's account of just actions and persons depends on an account of social justice.

Even in his earliest work on justice, Rawls maintains that it is important to distinguish between justice as a virtue of particular actions or persons and *social* justice because the meaning of the concept varies according to whether it is applied to particular actions, persons, or institutions. He acknowledges, though, that these meanings are connected.[11] The definition of justice Rawls adopts is designed to apply to the justice of the basic structure, which Rawls considers to be the most important case of justice because it very often serves as a foundation for deriving other sorts of specific accounts of justice. Rawls's account of social justice provides a basis for responding not only to partial compliance and how to deal with questions of societal injustice but also to more specific cases of just actions and dispositions. This is one reason why he says that when the basic structure of a society is just, a society has secured "background justice" (*JF*, 10).

Rawls's theory, then, is offered not as a description of ordinary meanings but as an account of "certain distributive principles for the basic structure of society. I assume that any reasonably complete ethical theory must include principles for this fundamental problem and that these principles, whatever they are, constitute its doctrine of justice" (*TJ* §2, p. 9). He writes that questions of justice and fairness arise when free persons with no authority over one another are participating in their common institutions, and when they are working to settle or acknowledge the rules that define their association and to determine the resulting shares in each person's benefits or burdens.[12] On Rawls's view, the concept of justice is defined by the role of its principles in assigning rights and duties and defining the appropriate division of social advantages. A conception of justice, on the other hand, is an interpretation of this role.

When used within the context of Rawls's definition of *the concept* of justice, "rights and duties" can be understood as the privileges and obligations members of society have because they are members of society. This is particularly important because as we have seen, the idea of "rights" in the technical sense of *human* rights, which "attach equally to all individuals, whatever their sex, race, religion, talents or deserts, and [that] provide a ground for a variety of particular moral stances" is a relatively late development.[13] As we saw in the Introduction, MacIntyre maintains that "those rights which are alleged to belong to human beings as such and which are cited as a reason for holding that people ought not to be interfered with in their pursuit of life, liberty and happiness" had yet to be formulated in the ancient and medieval periods. In using the idea of "rights" to define the concept of justice, Rawls does not mean to imply that Aristotle and other philosophers who expressed an understanding of the concept of justice had developed the idea of human rights in this technical sense. Rather, when Rawls says the concept of justice is defined by the role of its principles in assigning rights and duties, he is talking about basic rights and duties as part of the basic structure of society. By "rights," Rawls means citizens' "opportunities and their ability to take advantage of them," which are specified by a society's basic structure and thus are something citizens have by virtue of having citizenship when they are born in a particular country (*JF*, 10). It is important to remember that the principles of justice which regulate a society's basic structure do not apply directly to or regulate internally institutions and associations within society (e.g., firms, labor unions, religious communities, or families). These institutions and associations are affected by the principles of justice, but "these constraints arise indirectly from just background institutions within which associations and groups exist, and by which the conduct of their members is restricted."[14]

The important point for now is that by "rights" Rawls simply means the opportunities and privileges citizens have *qua* citizens. Similarly, when Rawls discusses "duties" in the context of his definition of the concept of justice, he does not mean moral duties as they are defined in Kantian moral theory. This much is clear from the fact that Rawls's understanding of the concept of justice is sufficiently broad to include a wide range of views, including those of utilitarian and Aristotelian persuasions. In addition, Rawls's goal is to provide a theory of justice that will apply to modern liberal democracies in which reasonable pluralism is a *fact*, which constitutes another reason why Rawls avoids definitions of concepts such as "rights" and "duties" that are specific to certain comprehensive theories, such as the comprehensive liberalisms of Kant or Mill. It is important not to be misled by Rawls's language when he uses terms that we might tend to associate with particular philosophers or theories, including "rights," "duties," "principles," "free," and "equal." Rawls provides specific definitions of all of these terms, and despite the fact that he is deeply influenced by Kant, he does not use all of these terms in the same way Kant does. This should not surprise us given the fact that he clearly distinguishes his view from comprehensive theories. Further, Rawls expects us to remember that even the specific *conception* of justice he calls "justice as fairness" is not a form of comprehensive liberalism. His understanding of the *concept* of justice is of course much broader yet. We will be reminded of just how broad Rawls's definitions are when we examine what Rawls means by "free and equal persons" below.

Now that we have established that Rawls's understanding of the concept of justice concerns the privileges and obligations that members of a society have *qua* members of society, let us turn to the details of Rawls's definition of the concept of justice. For Rawls, the concept of justice is specified by the role played by different sets of principles, or conceptions of justice. The concept of justice is what different conceptions of justice have in common; it is what they are all designed to accomplish. Institutions are just when (1) no *arbitrary* distinctions are made between persons in the assigning of basic rights and duties, and when (2) the rules that govern society determine a *proper balance* between competing claims to the advantages of social life. Different conceptions of justice define what distinctions count as "arbitrary" and what constitutes a "proper balance," but the key is that they formulate principles stating which similarities and differences are relevant and not arbitrary in determining what rights and duties citizens will have, and which division of advantages is appropriate (*TJ* §1, p. 5).

In order to understand exactly what the concept of justice consists of, it will be helpful to note that according to Rawls, the basic structure of society must be the primary subject of justice because its effects are profound, and they are present from the start. Societies are structured in such a way as to contain various social positions. People are born into particular families and thus begin their lives in certain social positions that are not of their own choosing and that do not result from their own actions. These social positions shape one's hopes and expectations, and the opportunities one has to fulfill those hopes and expectations are determined in part by the political system as well as by economic and social circumstances. Rawls writes that

> the institutions of society favor certain starting places over others. These are especially deep inequalities. Not only are they pervasive, but they affect men's initial chances in life; yet they cannot possibly be justified by an appeal to the notions of merit or desert. It is these inequalities, presumably inevitable in the basic structure of any society, to which the principles of social justice must in the first instance apply. (*TJ* §2, p. 7)

Rawls addresses these inequalities by emphasizing that the concept of justice seeks to address arbitrary distinctions between persons in the assigning of basic rights and duties, and also when he speaks of establishing a proper balance of competing claims to the advantages of social life.

Most straightforwardly, the concept of social justice is the idea that citizens should not be automatically penalized for the disadvantages they face through no choice of their own. A regard for justice tells us that arbitrary distinctions should be eliminated and that a proper balance of competing claims in a society means that individuals should have some control over their destinies. When Rawls says that citizens work for the ideal of justice for all, he is positing a good they all value—the good of having choices and control over one's own life and the good of not suffering for the inequalities in their prospects in life that arise from contingencies.

Social justice occurs when a society's institutions include regulations that preserve background justice. Here, society is conceived of in a certain way: A society that values social justice takes as its ideal "the idea of society as a fair system of cooperation between citizens as free and equal" (*JF*, 56). This is Rawls's particular articulation of the concept of justice, and he goes on to formulate a conception in which he specifies what principles of background justice are presupposed by a society that takes this idea of society seriously. Rawls's articulation of "justice as fairness" contains some of his most important remarks about human capacities and motives that create the possibility of achieving a just society. Although my analysis assumes a basic familiarity with Rawls's conception of justice, it will be helpful to review some of the central features of "justice as fairness" as we explore the concept of justice as Rawls understands it. However, it should be remembered that Rawls's particular conception of justice is not our primary concern.

On that note, it is appropriate to turn to the idea of society as a fair system of cooperation between citizens as free and equal. In Rawls's earliest formulation of his view of justice, the 1958 paper "Justice as Fairness," he writes that the fundamental idea in the concept of justice is fairness.[15] In his later work, he retains this idea and develops it at some length, noting that in calling a particular conception of justice "justice as fairness," he does not mean that the concepts of justice and fairness are the same (*TJ* §3, p. 11). Rather, Rawls means that fairness is one aspect of justice, albeit the fundamental aspect. Indeed, fairness is at the heart of Rawls's critique of the classical utilitarian conception of justice, for "it is this aspect of justice as fairness for which utilitarianism, in its classical form, is unable to account."[16] Rawls focuses on "the usual sense of justice in which it is essentially the elimination of arbitrary distinctions and the establishment . . . of a proper balance between competing claims."[17] The concept of fairness, on Rawls's view,

> relates to right dealing between persons who are cooperating with or competing against one another, as when one speaks of fair games, fair competition, and fair bargains. The question of fairness arises when free persons,

who have no authority over one another, are engaging in a joint activity and among themselves settling or acknowledging the rules which define it and which determine the respective shares in its benefits and burdens. A practice will strike the parties as fair if none feels that, by participating in it, they or any of the others are taken advantage of, or forced to give in to claims which they do not regard as legitimate.[18]

On Rawls's view, what makes the concept of fairness fundamental to justice is the possibility of the mutual acknowledgment of principles by free persons who have no authority over one another. Accordingly, the claim that humans have an innate capacity for social cooperation is one of the most basic claims on which Rawls bases his analysis of justice. Fundamental to Rawls's understanding of social justice is "the idea of society as a fair system of social cooperation over time from one generation to the next" (*JF*, 5). The central organizing idea of a fair system of social cooperation is worked out in conjunction with the idea of citizens as free and equal persons, which I return to below, and the idea of a well-ordered society (*JF*, 5; cf. *TJ* §7, §3). On this view, there are three essential features of social cooperation. First, social cooperation is guided by publicly recognized rules and procedures that are accepted as appropriate by those whose conduct they regulate. Second, the idea of cooperation includes the idea of fair terms of interaction. Third, the idea of cooperation includes the idea of each participant's good. For Rawls, citizens' capacities and motivations, especially with respect to their interactions with one another, are integrally connected with the idea of fair terms of cooperation. Fair terms specify "an idea of reciprocity, or mutuality: all who do their part as the recognized rules require are to benefit as specified by a public and agreed-upon standard" (*JF*, 6; cf. *PL*, 16). Rawls maintains that reciprocity is the midpoint between altruism, in which one acts impartially for the interests of others, and mutual advantage, wherein each individual benefits equally.

We can see how reciprocity is distinct from mutual advantage on the one hand, because it does not draw on purely selfish motives. On the other hand, reciprocity is clearly distinct from total altruism because individuals cannot reasonably be expected to support a social arrangement unless they stand to benefit from it in some way. Above all reciprocity is a *relation* among citizens in a well-ordered society, and, according to Rawls, justice as fairness "perches" on this relation (*PL*, 17). When reciprocity characterizes the relations among citizens, they do not desire to preserve the benefits of previous injustices, which means that they do not always benefit equally. In order to overcome previous injustices, benefits must be distributed in such a way as to provide the greatest benefit to the victims of those injustices. These are the individuals Rawls calls the least advantaged members of society. Reciprocity, then, is a relation "expressed by principles of justice that regulate a social world in which everyone benefits judged with respect to an appropriate benchmark of equality defined with respect to that world" (*PL*, 17). According to Rawls, the two principles of justice[19] that define the conception of justice known as "justice as fairness," taken together, formulate an idea of reciprocity among citizens. For Rawls, reciprocity functions (1) in the original position to establish the basic principles of justice and (2) in the well-ordered society for the appropriate application of these principles.

Rawls writes that justice as fairness regards citizens as "free and equal." Citizens are free in that "they conceive of themselves and of one another as having the moral power to have a conception of the good" (*JF*, 19). Rawls understands a conception of the good as "an ordered family of final ends and aims which specifies a person's conception of what is of value in human life or, alternatively, of what is regarded as a fully worthwhile life" (*JF*, 19). Part of what it means for citizens to be free is that they are capable of revising and changing their conception of the good on reasonable and rational grounds, if they choose to (*JF*, 21). A second way in which citizens view themselves as free, according to Rawls, is that they see themselves as "self-authenticating sources of valid claims" (*JF*, 23). This means that they are entitled to make claims on their institutions in order to advance their conception of the good, provided that it falls within the range permitted by the public conception of justice.

Citizens are equal in that "they are all regarded as having to the essential minimum degree the moral powers necessary to engage in social cooperation over a complete life and to take part in society as equal citizens" (*JF*, 20). Here, it is especially important to recognize that "equal" for Rawls does not mean that citizens think of one another as having the same position in life. Rawls's discussion of equality does not concern the number or kinds of responsibilities people have, their economic positions in society, or other features of their particular situations. Indeed, one of the defining features of Rawls's account of justice is that even in just societies, people are *not* equal in these ways. Just societies are committed to responding to some kinds of inequalities in particular ways, but this conception of justice does not imply that we should strive to eliminate all inequalities.

Rather, when Rawls says citizens are equal he means that they have some of the same basic capacities by virtue of being human. According to Rawls, citizens have two moral powers: the capacity for a sense of justice, which includes the capacity to understand, to apply, and to act from principles of justice, and the capacity as just individuals to have, to revise, and to pursue a conception of the good, which I discussed previously. Rawls's discussion of citizens' equality focuses on the way citizens conduct themselves within their individual communities and within the larger well-ordered society. Rawls notes that one's conception of the good is typically situated within and expresses certain comprehensive religious, philosophical, and moral doctrines that exist and are cultivated within individual families and communities. "The members of a community are united in pursuing certain shared values and ends (other than economic) that lead them to support the association and in part bind them to it" (*JF*, 20). Citizens' capacity for a sense of justice, on the other hand, enables them to function in a well-ordered society in which not everyone shares their particular conception of the good. "The citizens of a well-ordered society affirm the constitution and its political values as realized in their institutions, and they share the end of giving one another justice, as society's arrangements require" (*JF*, 20).

In sum, for Rawls "free and equal persons" are free in the sense that they conceive of themselves and others as being able to have a conception of the good that is of their own choosing. They are equal in the sense that they have the basic moral capacity to form, revise, and pursue that conception of the good, as well as the capacity for a sense of justice. This freedom and equality concerns some of the minimal capacities required of a human being for participation in a society, and the idea of free and equal persons belongs to a *political conception* of justice. It is not taken from a psychological or philosophical view of personhood, although it is compatible with one or more of these conceptions. Rawls writes that political conceptions of justice are identifiable by the fact that their principles, standards, and values "are not the result of applying an already elaborated and independent religious, philosophical, or moral doctrine, comprehensive in scope and general in range" (*JF*, 182). Political conceptions of justice instead formulate a family of highly significant moral values that apply to the basic structure of society. These are political values because they arise from two special features of the political relationship. First, it is a relationship of persons within the basic structure of society, which is a structure we normally enter by birth and exit by death; "the power of the government cannot be evaded except by leaving the state's territory" (*JF*, 93, 182). As Rawls points out, "[T]he bonds of society and culture, of history and social place of origin, begin so early to shape our life and are normally so strong that the right of emigration (suitably qualified) does not suffice to make accepting [the state's] authority free, politically speaking, in the way that liberty of conscience suffices to make accepting ecclesiastical authority free, politically speaking" (*JF*, 94). Second, the political relationship is regularly imposed on citizens, some of whom may not agree with the justificatory reasons for the basic structure of political authority (the constitution) or with the grounding of certain laws to which they are subject (*JF*, 182). That is, as citizens we do not and cannot choose to reject the state's authority over us; the acceptance of political authority is not voluntary. Even in cases where we choose to practice civil disobedience or to break laws, we cannot voluntarily free ourselves from the rule of law (e.g., from possible prosecution, imprisonment, etc.).

In short, from a legal and political standpoint, the political relationship is not voluntary in some of the ways that associational, familial, and personal relationships normally are. In modern liberal democracies, these other kinds of relationships usually are not backed by a coercive power such as the state's machinery for enforcing its laws. In the majority of cases, we could, if we wanted to, in principle enter or leave these kinds of relationships (*JF*, 182).[20] Even when individuals are highly unlikely to leave familial or other important relationships because of certain culturally specific values, they still normally have the freedom to leave associational, familial, and personal relationships. It may be the case that they will not exercise that freedom or even reflect on the possibility of exercising it, but clearly whether one is willing or likely to consider certain kinds of actions as real possibilities is different from being *incapable* of considering certain kinds of actions. Being prevented by a coercive power from leaving the political relationship is quite different from being unwilling or unlikely to consider leaving associational, familial, and personal relationships because of one's cultural values.

I want to say a bit more here about Rawls's view of persons and their attachments because this aspect of his view will be important to note when we compare it with the view seen in the *Analects*. Although he has often been misunderstood as claiming that our moral identities are not essential to who we are, Rawls in no way denies the centrality of our commitments, attachments, and relationships to our identities. Indeed, he says, "If we suddenly lost them, we would be disoriented and unable to carry on. In fact, there would be, we might think, no point in carrying on. Our conceptions of the good may and often do change over time, however, usually slowly but sometimes rather suddenly. When these changes are sudden, we are particularly likely to say that we are no longer the same person"

(*JF*, 22). Rawls acknowledges, then, that our commitments, attachments, and relationships are so central to who we are that changes in these areas of our lives constitute a profound and pervasive shift in our moral identities. Rawls's point with respect to free and equal persons, however, is that even when our personal commitments, attachments, and relationships change, we still have the same basic privileges and obligations as citizens. In other words, our public or legal identity is unaffected by changes in our moral identity.[21] Rawls does not mean to minimize the impact or importance of changes in our commitments and attachments. He simply points out that despite these changes, we are still members of society in the same basic sense that we were before (*JF*, 23).

Rawls and the Sense of Justice

As we can see, the meaning and role of the idea of free and equal persons in Rawls's work are grounded in his attribution of two moral powers to human beings (*JF*, 18–19; cf. *TJ* §3–4, pp. 10–19). In what follows, I explore in greater detail the first of these powers: the capacity for a sense of justice, which is the capacity to understand, apply, and act from a public conception of justice that characterizes fair terms of social cooperation. According to Rawls, this capacity, together with the capacity for a conception of the good, gives citizens the capacity to be full participants in a fair system of cooperation.

The capacity for a sense of justice is both the source of citizens' considered judgments about justice and an important part of their motivation to value social justice. It is evident in citizens' attitudes and in their actions. As Rawls puts it, this capacity, combined with the capacity for a conception of the good, enables persons "not only to engage in mutually beneficial social co-operation over a complete life but also to be moved to honor its fair terms for their own sake" (*JF*, 19). It is the latter part of what Rawls says here that is of greatest interest in this analysis, because as we will see, a sense of justice is what *moves* citizens to honor the terms of cooperation that ensure fairness.

Rawls understands a sense of justice as the realization that members of a society need fair terms of social cooperation, and as the reason why they value fair terms. A sense of justice expresses the willingness, if not the desire, to act in relation to others on terms everyone can endorse publicly (*PL*, 19). For Rawls, the very idea of fairness is important from the standpoint of moral psychology. Even in his early discussions of justice, Rawls notes that "acting fairly requires more than simply being able to follow the rules; what is fair must often be felt, or perceived, one wants to say."[22]

The fact that Rawls talks about a sense of justice as the ability to feel and perceive what is fair, and also as what "moves" citizens to act justly, is essential to understanding what it really means to have a sense of justice. We should recall here that in his initial formulation of the concept of justice at the beginning of *Theory*, Rawls acknowledges the reality of injustice in societies. With the source of social injustice in view, it is much easier to see why societies need to address social justice. It is also easier to see how a sense of justice makes us feel about injustices, on Rawls's view. He writes that the basic structure of society needs to be the primary subject of justice because the kind of injustices that result from the structure of society are profound and present in a person's life right from the start. As we saw earlier in this chapter, Rawls tells us that

> the institutions of society favor certain starting places over others. These are especially deep inequalities. Not only are they pervasive, but they affect men's initial chances in life; yet they cannot possibly be justified by an appeal to the notions of merit or desert. It is these inequalities, presumably inevitable in the basic structure of any society, to which the principles of social justice must in the first instance apply. (*TJ* §2, p. 7)

Rawls is specific about the kinds of inequalities he is referring to, and so there should be no confusion about the fact that the inequalities he discusses are tied to those contingencies over which we have no control. His clearest articulation of this is found in his discussion of justice as fairness, and it tells us a great deal about his understanding of a sense of justice and how it works more generally. Rawls writes that inequalities in citizens' life-prospects are affected by three kinds of contingencies:

> (a) their social class of origin: the class into which they are born and develop before the age of reason; (b) their native endowments (as opposed to their realized endowments); and their opportunities to develop these endowments as affected by their social class of origin; (c) their good or ill fortune, or good or bad luck, over the course of life (how they are affected by illness and accident; and, say, by periods of involuntary unemployment and regional economic decline). (*JF*, 55)

Rawls adds that even in a well-ordered society, "our prospects over life are deeply affected by social, natural, and fortuitous contingencies, and by the way the basic structure, by setting up inequalities, uses those contingencies to meet certain social purposes" (*JF*, 55). He goes on to point out that "if we ignore the inequalities in people's prospects in life arising from these contingencies and let those inequalities work themselves out while failing to institute the regulations necessary to preserve background justice, we would not be taking seriously the idea of society as a fair system of cooperation between citizens as free and equal" (*JF*, 56).

Most basically, our sense of justice causes us to feel for those who are born into those stations in life that society does not favor. It is our sense of justice that tells us there is something wrong if children have no real chance to advance in society because they were born, for example, into a family that lacks certain kinds of financial or psychological resources. Here we see most clearly that Rawls is describing a very basic and deep moral sense that human beings have. It is tied to their ability to feel for others, which is one reason why he speaks of citizens' being "moved" by their sense of justice. Another likely reason why Rawls uses the language of citizens' being moved in this way is in order to emphasize just how powerful a sense of justice can be. It moves people to sacrifice some of their own benefits for the sake of others, and citizens with a well-developed sense of justice will not hesitate to say that it is right—and just—to give the child born into a poor family certain compensations that will not be given to a child born into a wealthy family. Here we can see clearly that the sense of justice is most basically the sense that everyone deserves a chance, and that it is wrong to let certain individuals wither away as the result of their circumstances.

Rawls's earliest formulation of this idea is found in the 1963 essay "The Sense of Justice." He takes the idea of a sense of justice from Rousseau's *Emile*, wherein Rousseau asserts that "the sense of justice is a true sentiment of the heart enlightened by reason, the natural outcome of our primitive affections."[23] In this early essay, Rawls develops a psychological construction to illustrate the way in which Rousseau's thesis might be true and to answer some questions about the idea of a sense of justice, including the question of what accounts for people doing what justice requires. Rawls's answer to this question is the capacity for a sense of justice. He maintains that one's sense of justice "may be aroused or assuaged, and it is connected not only with such moral feelings as resentment and indignation but also, as I shall argue, with natural attitudes such as mutual trust and affection."[24] Rawls says that because the ability to do what justice requires is so closely tied to these very important moral feelings, people "would lack certain essential elements of humanity" if they did not have a sense of justice.[25] From the beginning of his work on a sense of justice, then, Rawls ties this capacity to being human.

One of Rawls's most fundamental claims is that a sense of justice is the result of "a certain natural development."[26] He maintains that the psychological construction he offers provides an account of the stages of development by which the sense of justice arises from "our primitive natural attitudes."[27] Rawls does not claim that this psychological construction represents what actually takes place in every human. However, he says he has tried to make it reasonably plausible, including "only those psychological principles which are compatible with our conception of ourselves as moral beings."[28] His goal, then, is not to make an argument that all people develop their natural capacity for a sense of justice in exactly the same way but to show that, indeed, people seem to have a natural capacity for a sense of justice and that certain experiences and environments are particularly conducive to its development.

In "The Sense of Justice," Rawls develops a psychological construction of the way a sense of justice might develop. It consists of three stages representing the development of three forms of guilt feelings: authority guilt, association guilt, and principle guilt.[29] Rawls is influenced by Piaget's work here, noting that he follows the main lines of Piaget's account of the development of a sense of justice, incorporating Piaget's distinction between the morality of authority and the morality of mutual respect.[30] Rawls uses the relationship between parents and children to show how a sense of justice is initially nurtured through the development of authority guilt. Children love, trust, and have faith in their parents, and these natural attitudes are normally not misplaced. Additionally, children tend to be "moved by certain instincts and regulated only (if at all) by rational self-love," and so they come to love their parents and to recognize the love their parents have for them.[31] Rawls notes that while the capacity for love is innate, it requires special circumstances for its development.

> The parents' love for the child, then, may explain a child's love for his parents. . . . He does not love them in order to ensure, say, his security, although he could seem to love them for this reason. That his love of them does not have a rational explanation follows from the concept of love: to love another is to care for him for his own sake as his rational self-love would incline.[32]

Children are not in a position rationally to reject parental injunctions. As a result, if they love and trust their parents, children will accept their parents' precepts, strive to live up to them as worthy objects of esteem, and accept their parents' way of judging them.[33]

In time, children impose these standards on themselves and judge themselves accordingly. That is not to say, of course, that children are not tempted to transgress the parental precepts.[34] However, it does mean that children will manifest what Rawls calls authority guilt when they violate the general precepts or particular injunctions that their parents expect them to obey. "Guilt feelings are shown (among other ways) in the inclination to confess and to ask for forgiveness in order to restore the previous relation; they are part of what defines a relation as one of love and trust."[35] Even in cases in which children have feelings of anger toward their parents, their feelings of love for their parents will in the end prevail, according to this view.

A child's circle widens as she become older, even though the family remains at the center.

> The virtues of a good son or daughter are explained, or at least conveyed.
> . . . Similarly there is the association of the school and the neighborhood, and also such short-term forms of cooperation, though not less important for this, as games and play with peers. Corresponding to these arrangements one learns the virtues of a good student and classmate, and the ideals of a good sport and companion. (*TJ* §71, p. 409)

The second stage in Rawls's psychological construction is association guilt, which involves participation in various joint activities. Rawls says these associations are especially important because this type of moral view extends to the ideals adopted later in life. They help one learn how to interact as a member of different groups, and they also help one learn what it means to be a member of society. "The content of these ideals is given by the various conceptions of a good wife and husband, a good friend and citizen, and so on. Thus the morality of association includes a large number of ideals each defined in ways suitable for the respective status or role. Our moral understanding increases as we move in the course of life through a sequence of positions" (§71, p. 410).

Participants at this stage are bound by ties of friendship and mutual trust, and they rely on one another to do their part. Thus, Rawls is talking only about associations wherein there is a genuine sense of community and caring for one another, and in which the participants know one another personally, or get acquainted over the course of their time together. "So if participants in a joint enterprise regularly act with evident intention in accordance with their duty of fair play, they will tend to acquire ties of friendship and mutual trust."[36] Given these feelings and relations against the background of a scheme of cooperation, persons who fail to do their part will experience feelings of association guilt. Rawls writes that these feelings show themselves in various ways, including the inclination to make good the loss to others when individuals do not fulfill their obligations or play fairly, and to admit what one has done and to apologize to others in the group. Feelings of association guilt are seen in the inclination to ask for reinstatement and to acknowledge and accept reproofs and penalties.

> The absence of such inclinations would betray the absence of ties of friendship and relations of mutual trust. It would manifest a capacity to associate with others in disregard of those principles which one knows would be mutually acknowledged. It would show that one had no qualms about the losses inflicted on others (or gains taken from them) as a consequence of one's own acts, and that one was not troubled by the breaches of mutual confidence by which others are deceived.[37]

Rawls emphasizes the importance of role-specific duties and the abilities one cultivates with respect to thinking about and considering the needs of others at this stage. One learns to apply the principle of reversibility, seeing things from the perspective of others, and as a result it seems plausible that "acquiring a morality of association (represented by some structure of ideals) rests upon the development of the intellectual skills required to regard things from a variety of points of view and to think of these together as aspects of one system of cooperation" (*TJ* §71, p. 412). Familial ties and other close relationships are the basis for the development of such things as one's inclination to make good the harms caused to others, willingness to admit that what one has done is unfair and thus wrong and to apologize for it, and thus for the development of one's sense of justice. "Thus just as in the first stage certain natural attitudes develop toward the parents, so here ties of friendship and confidence grow up among associates. In each case certain natural attitudes underlie the corresponding moral feelings: a lack of these feelings would manifest the absence of these attitudes" (§71, p. 412).

Association guilt, then, involves a genuine sense of what it means to be a participant in a community and to value one's obligations to others. It shows that members of a community have developed moral feelings, leading them to internalize certain practices to the extent that they do not associate with others in a way that completely disregards their feelings and interests. There is a general air of *disregard* in one who does not have association guilt and an extensive sense of *regard* for the well-being of others in one who feels association guilt. It is significant that for Rawls, a sense of justice at this stage is seen most clearly not in one's capacity to associate perfectly without any failures or mistakes but rather in how one feels and responds to those failures or mistakes when one makes them. Of course, one's feelings are likely to affect one's tendency to fail or make mistakes, but Rawls is most concerned with the moral psychology here, namely the question of how one *feels* about what one does and how those emotions and attitudes affect one's actions. This is because, as we will see, a sense of justice is most fundamentally the capacity to feel in certain ways toward others. Rawls notes that the effects of this capacity and the attitudes it generates go a long way toward maintaining stable schemes of cooperation.[38]

The third stage in Rawls's psychological construction concerns principle guilt. In both of the previous stages, Rawls connects the forms of guilt he discusses with "an actual natural attitude toward certain particular persons: with authority guilt these persons are parents, and in association guilt they are fellow-associates. Very often, however, we feel guilty for doing something when those injured or put at a disadvantage are not persons with whom we are tied by any form of particular fellow-feeling."[39] Rawls says these cases form a third type of guilt called principle guilt, which is felt when one does something that violates particular institutions (in this case, principles of justice) one has accepted. He accounts for these kinds of feelings with a third psychological law: "[G]iven that the attitudes of love and trust, friendly feelings and mutual respect, have been generated in accordance with the two previous psychological laws, then, if a person (and his associates) are the beneficiaries of a successful and enduring institution or scheme of cooperation known to satisfy the two principles of justice, he will acquire a sense of justice."[40] Rawls notes that we can determine that a person's sense of justice has been "acquired," or fully developed in two ways. We first see a sense of justice in one's acceptance of just institutions, which "shows itself in feeling guilty for infractions which harm other persons even though these persons are not the objects of any particular fellow-feelings."[41] Second, Rawls says, the sense of justice manifests itself in a willingness to work for (or at least not to oppose) the setting up of just institutions, or for the reform of existing institutions according to the requirements of justice. "Guilt feelings associated with the sense of justice are characterized as principle guilt feelings since in their explanation reference is made to principles, in this case to principles of justice."[42]

When people accept just institutions, they become partly responsible for acting in accord with the standards of those institutions. Principle guilt feelings spring from breaches of institutions accepted as satisfying the principles of justice or from resistance to reforms required by the principles of justice, and individuals feel *guilt* when they violate these principles because of their acceptance of them.[43] According to Rawls, "The acceptance of the principles of justice implies, failing a special explanation, an avoidance of their violation and a recognition that advantages gained in conflict with them are without value; and should such violations nevertheless occur, in cases of temptation, feelings of guilt will tend to restore joint activity."[44]

It is important, too, to see why principle guilt represents the third stage in Rawls's account of how people develop a sense of justice. Rawls actually goes further than simply claiming that principle guilt is a form of guilt. He writes that principle guilt is "guilt proper" because it is "a complete moral feeling" whereas the two previous forms of guilt are not.[45] What Rawls means by a "complete moral feeling" here is that the feeling would be strong enough to move one to interact with others in certain ways even if one did not have a special relationship with them.[46] One who experiences principle guilt feels guilty for having harmed other persons even though they are strangers. So, we know that principle guilt is not felt simply by virtue of emotional and personal ties to particular people. But that is not to say that Rawls thinks family and other special relationships are unimportant, or that we should not feel a greater sense of burden when we have wronged those who are close to us. Indeed, he says that the ability to feel a greater degree of responsibility in cases where we have wronged someone close to us is an important feature of the relationship between principle guilt and association guilt. He writes: "[W]here the ties of natural attitudes are present in the form of friendship and mutual trust, the feelings of guilt will be greater than when they are absent. The transmuted association guilt will reinforce principle guilt."[47]

The need for a commitment to principles of justice is strictly a practical consideration for Rawls. It is simply a fact that members of large societies do not know every other member of their society. Rawls's account is not designed to apply to small villages; in fact, "the institutional scheme in question may be so large that particular bonds never get widely built up. In any case, the citizen body as a whole is not generally bound together by ties of fellow feeling between individuals, but by the acceptance of public principles of justice" (*TJ* §72, p. 415). Rawls's main point here is that an important part of what it means to be moral is to understand that one should treat others with respect, even if they are not a part of one's "inner" circle of family and friends. On most views of moral development, it is not permissible to show respect and consideration for only one's family and friends, while disregarding the interests of others.[48] It is wrong to act unjustly even in cases where it will hurt only those with whom one is unacquainted.

We can see, then, why Rawls maintains that the capacity for a sense of justice is the fundamental aspect of moral personality in the theory of justice.[49] An individual who experiences principle guilt has shown an appreciation for the fact that it is always wrong to violate the principles of justice, regardless of who is harmed. Here we can see clearly that having a sense of justice is about understanding that the principles of justice are designed to protect everyone from injustice, and as a result, we know that people have a well-developed sense of justice when they feel guilty for infractions that harm other persons even though they are not in a personal relationship with them.[50] Again, that is not to say that one does not have additional obligations when one harms those one is close to. But we must remember that Rawls's concern is to address the subject of social justice and not how best to maintain or repair family relationships or friendships. As we have seen from his psychological construction of a sense of justice, he advocates the view that a fully developed sense of justice depends critically on its cultivation within the family and other close relationships.

I highlight this section of *Theory* in part to show that Rawls addresses in considerable detail some issues he has been accused of neglecting. It is not insignificant that Rawls begins with the relationship between parents and children in his psychological construction of a sense of justice. This particular dimension of Rawls's view has been neglected by some of his critics. One of the most significant criticisms feminist philosophers have posed with respect to Rawls's work is rooted in the feminist defense of the centrality of emotions and relationships in ethical and political life. Some feminist philosophers have maintained that Rawls does not give adequate attention to the role of the emotions in moral judgment and moral development.[51] As we have seen, Rawls makes the emotions the most critical factor in his account of children's moral development in the context of the family, which performs the task of caring for children and providing for the initial development of their sense of justice.[52] In a well-ordered society, moral principles actually engage citizens' affections, forming sentiments whose content cannot be described adequately without mentioning the principles of justice. This is why Rawls says "the sense of justice is continuous with the love of mankind" (*TJ* §72, p. 417).[53] Charges that Rawls fails to take the emotions and relationships seriously as contributing to the development of moral and political reasoning or to the bonds of society are significantly undermined by Rawls's discussion of these matters in relation to a sense of justice.[54]

It is also worth pointing out that Rawls's attentiveness to the importance of families and communities does not end with his account of moral development, because his understanding of what the principles of justice allow us to do is bound up in our roles and relationships with others. In *Theory*, Rawls writes that the principles of justice allow one to experience "the realization of self which comes from a skillful and devoted exercise of social duties," and he calls this "one of the main forms of human good" (*TJ*, §14, p. 73). Rawls goes on to claim that the naturally advantaged—with native gifts of, say, intelligence—should not gain merely because they are more gifted,

> but only to cover the costs of training and education and for using
> their endowments in ways that help the less fortunate as well. No one
> deserves his greater natural capacity nor merits a more favorable starting
> place in society. . . . Thus we are led to the difference principle if we
> wish to set up the social system so that no one gains or loses from his ar-
> bitrary place in the distribution of natural assets or his initial position in
> society without giving or receiving compensating advantages in return.
> (*TJ* §17, p. 87)

This passage contains one of the most controversial remarks Rawls ever made: that the difference principle represents, in effect, "an agreement to regard the distribution of natural talents as in some respects a common asset. . . ."[55] As Thomas Nagel points out, though, "not everyone is convinced that there is anything unfair about people's benefiting differentially from the employment of their own natural abilities even though they have done nothing to deserve those abilities."[56] Indeed, this particular remark of Rawls's is at the heart of a disagreement within the liberal tradition between those who, like Rawls, see social justice as the fight against any kind of undeserved inequalities and those who, like many of Rawls's liberal critics, maintain that social justice does not concern natural abilities. On this latter view, as Nagel points out, "it can seem like an assault on the independence of persons to say that they have no right to the benefits which flow from [their] identity, except insofar as this also benefits others."[57]

Obviously, Rawls's account of these matters has drawn criticism from both liberal and communitarian critics. He is unable to pacify his critics in the liberal tradition largely because he acknowledges the role that enduring attachments and loyalties play in the formation and development of our identity. He writes that in addition to affirming the values of political justice and working toward the embodiment of these values in political institutions and social policies, citizens

> often do have at any given time, affections, devotions, and loyalties that
> they believe they would not, indeed could and should not, stand apart

from and evaluate objectively. They may regard it as simply unthinkable to view themselves apart from certain religious, philosophical, and moral convictions, or from certain enduring attachments and loyalties. These two kinds of commitments and attachments—political and non-political—specify moral identity and give shape to a person's way of life, what one sees oneself as doing and trying to accomplish in the social world. If we suddenly lost them, we would be disoriented and unable to carry on. (*JF*, 22)

In *Theory*, Rawls writes that he considers the community absolutely essential to the formation of a person's identity. He acknowledges that the concepts we use to describe our lives often presuppose

a social setting as well as a system of belief and thought that is the outcome of the collective efforts of a long tradition. . . . We need one another as partners in ways of life that are engaged in for their own sake, and the successes and enjoyments of others are necessary for and complementary to our own good. (*TJ* §79, p. 458)

Indeed, one of the reasons Rawls focuses on the basic structure of society is that "the social system shapes the wants and aspirations that its citizens come to have. It determines in part the sort of persons they want to be as well as the sort of persons they are" (*TJ* §41, p. 229). In *Political Liberalism* Rawls develops this idea further by arguing for the full publicity condition, according to which the justificatory grounds of any theory of justice must be publicly available, so that citizens are "in a position to know and to accept the pervasive influences of the basic structures that shape their conception of themselves, their character and ends" (*PL*, 68).[58]

The Cultivation of Justice in Rawls

One of the most interesting dimensions of Rawls's discussion of the capacity for a sense of justice is that he quite clearly conceives of citizens who have a "well-developed" sense of justice, as opposed to those who do not. The psychological construction of how a sense of justice develops makes it clear that Rawls conceives of this capacity as something that one must cultivate. In this section, I want to explore further two questions: (1) What does it mean to say that all human beings have the *capacity* for a sense of justice? (2) Why do certain conditions nourish a sense of justice, and what is missing from those conditions where its development is impeded or prevented entirely?

It is clear that on Rawls's view, the capacity for a sense of justice is something that all healthy, normally raised human beings possess.[59] He writes that

> it seems almost certain that at least the vast majority of mankind has a capacity for a sense of justice and that, for all practical purposes, one may safely assume that all men originally possess it. It is plausible to suppose that any being capable of language is capable of the intellectual performances required to have a sense of justice; and, given these intellectual powers, the capacity for the natural attitudes of love and affection, faith and mutual trust, appears to be universal.[60]

What Rawls appears to mean by "the intellectual performances required to have a sense of justice" are the sorts of abilities we have seen in the psychological construction Rawls provides—the ability to feel guilt, to respond in kind to the love and affection of one's parents, to imagine how it would feel to be in the position of someone else. He associates a sense of justice with the natural attitudes he mentions here—love and affection, faith and mutual trust. And, most important, he says that under normal conditions all human beings originally possess the capacity for a sense of justice.

One might say, though, that Rawls is smuggling in something much more robust than a basic capacity that humans "originally" possess. After all, he says that a sense of justice is "the capacity to understand, to apply, and normally to be moved by an effective desire to act from (and not merely in accordance with) the principles of justice as the fair terms of social cooperation" (*PL*, 302; cf. *JF*, 19).[61] One with a sense of justice *honors* fair terms of cooperation. Rawls also discusses "companion powers" which accompany the two moral powers that enable a person to be a fully cooperating member of a fair system of cooperation. These companion powers are of reason, inference, and judgment. These powers, Rawls says, are required for the exercise of a sense of justice (*JF*, 24). The two moral powers and these three companion powers are, Rawls says, the "minimum essentials to be a fully cooperative member of society" (*JF*, 170). But quite clearly, when human beings are born into this world, they are not yet able to exercise the powers of reason, inference, and judgment.

This difficulty shows why it is important to understand that when Rawls talks about the capacity for a sense of justice, he is describing the capacity *to develop* a sense of justice. At its most advanced stages, one who has a sense of justice can understand principles of justice and act according to them. To put it differently, one is able to understand the rules, and play fairly, and one is also motivated to do so. Those who have a well-developed sense of justice do not break the rules every chance they get. So it is important to understand that Rawls means all humans have the *potential* to be this way, and this is why he speaks of all humans as originally possessing the *capacity* for a sense of justice. He does not say that all humans originally possess a fully or even partially developed sense of justice, nor does he say that the development of a sense of justice is inevitable. For Rawls, a sense of justice is a capacity to be honed, cultivated, and developed, and this process can occur only under certain conditions and circumstances.[62]

Rawls's account of the original position also makes it clear that he thinks the *capacity* for a sense of justice is one of the things all humans begin with, and that one who grows up under just institutions is at least likely to develop that sense of justice. In order to understand the significance of this claim, one must first understand the nature of Rawls's original position. In *A Theory of Justice* Rawls says that the original position is "a purely hypothetical situation" (*TJ*, 104). For Rawls, the original position is not in any sense a theory of human nature or a model of how people really are but a description of a mode of thought or point of view that human beings are capable of adopting. Rawls uses the original position to show that we are capable of making decisions about social justice in the absence of certain biases. The effort to put aside biases is done for the sake of being fair to all *others* affected; individuals are assumed to live in community with others, or else the original position would not serve a purpose. The original position represents a uniquely human capacity, and on Rawls's view it is an important part of what makes us human.

According to Rawls, "the fact that we occupy a particular social position is not a good reason for us to accept, or to expect others to accept, a conception of justice that favors those in this position."[63] Here, Rawls refers to the criterion of reciprocity, according to which humans are both able and willing to establish principles of justice that will benefit others even when they themselves will not benefit in certain ways because their social position is different. In short, we have the ability to reason and act in the best interest of others by considering what reasons for accepting a conception of justice would be convincing to us if we were positioned similarly. Rawls continues:

> To model this conviction in the original position the parties are not allowed to know their social position; and the same idea is extended to other cases. This is expressed *figuratively* by saying that the parties are behind a veil of ignorance. In sum, the original position is simply a device of representation: it describes the parties, each of whom are responsible for

the essential interests of a free and equal person, as fairly situated and as reaching an agreement subject to appropriate restrictions on what are to count as good reasons.[64]

The original position is an "artificial device of representation," and so it does not require a person to abandon her actual roles and relationships (*PL*, 28). Rawls says that the original position does not presuppose a metaphysical conception of self, nor does it have metaphysical implications for the self because our reasoning in the original position does not commit us to a metaphysical doctrine of the self. The idea that the original position presupposes a metaphysical conception of the self—one that sees the essential nature of persons as independent of and prior to their attributes and relationships—is, as Rawls puts it, "an illusion caused by not seeing the original position as a device of representation" (CP, 402).

Further, and perhaps most important, Rawls argues that even as a device of representation, the original position does not give us a picture of individuals who are cut off from other members of society. He tells us in *Theory* that "the persons in the original position are not to view themselves as single isolated individuals. To the contrary, they assume that they have interests which they must protect as best they can and that they have ties with certain members of the next generation who will also make similar claims."[65] Martha Nussbaum has pointed out that the original position gives us "an account of the moral point of view, a point of view we can try to enter in real life at any time. . . . [T]he veil of ignorance is thus a model of one part of a person, the part that is capable of being unselfish and caring for others. . . . In effect, as Rawls insists, the entirety of the original position is a model of benevolence."[66] Why can we not simply model benevolence directly, by imagining the parties as benevolent with full information? Nussbaum reminds us of Rawls's answer. " . . . [T]he original position comes, in effect, to the same thing, but with a superior economy and clarity given by the fact that we do not have to ask questions such as, How intense is the benevolence and toward whom?, What information precisely? And so forth" (*TJ*, 147–49/127–29 rev.).[67]

With the original position, Rawls describes one aspect of the human capacity for moral reasoning; he is not offering a theory of human nature or a description of the extent to which persons are isolated from others or identified by their relationships. However, as we have seen, the capacity for a sense of justice is an important part of the overall view of human nature that Rawls presents, even though he does not give us a theory of human nature, and a well-developed sense of justice is one of the things he accords those behind a veil of ignorance. Rawls writes that "this initial situation is fair between individuals as moral persons, that is, as rational beings with their own ends and capable, I shall assume, of a sense of justice" (*TJ* §3, p. 11). In fact, Rawls says that because "the sense of justice is a necessary part of the dignity of the person," utilitarian conceptions of justice really do not acknowledge it as a basic capacity. "It is because of this dignity that the conception of justice as fairness is correct in viewing each person as an individual sovereign, as it were, none of whose interests are to be sacrificed for the sake of a greater net balance of happiness," but rather only in accordance with principles of justice.[68] Thus, for Rawls, the first and most fundamental error of utilitarianism is that it fails to recognize the inherent dignity of the human person, which consists in our moral capacities. Utilitarians fail to realize that each person has the capacity for a sense of justice, and this shows how Rawls's understanding of justice more adequately addresses the concerns humans actually have. It is important to see that Rawls's conception of a sense of justice does not simply mean that individuals want to get their own fair share. Rather, on Rawls's understanding, human beings have certain feelings when other people are slighted, as well.

> Certainly in the absence of the capacity for a sense of justice no one could complain if the utilitarian principle were applied, and so the possession of a sense of justice is necessary for the conception of justice to hold. But lack of a sense of justice would undermine our capacity to identify ourselves with and to care about a society of such persons. . . . We would not be moved by its injustices, since what they cannot resent and be indignant about among themselves we cannot resent and be indignant about for them. This is not to say that we might not be moved by the cruelties of such a society, but from the standpoint of justice, it would not be a society which aroused our moral feelings.[69]

The contrast with utilitarianism here also shows how Rawls's entire analysis of justice is *based* on the idea that humans have the capacity for a sense of justice. It is not the case, then, that Rawls builds his account strictly on the foundation of Kantian rational principles, because the most basic capacity humans have with respect to justice is the capacity to feel in certain ways toward others. For Rawls it is clear from the natural course of the psychological development of humans that they have the capacity for a sense of justice. This matter simply has to do with the capacities and attitudes humans increasingly display over time when they develop as moral beings. This claim is not uninteresting, because Rawls assumes that in order for humans to develop certain capacities and attitudes, they must be predisposed toward developing them in some sense.[70]

There is some question about what Rawls means by "capacity." At times, he seems to indicate that humans have an initial tendency toward developing a sense of justice, almost as though humans gravitate toward it. This is a stronger view than the position that humans *can* develop a sense of justice but have no initial tendencies to feel and see things in this way. On the first view, humans have an observable, active initial tendency toward a sense of justice regardless of their environment, even though this tendency requires certain conditions for further development. On the second view, however, the capacity for a sense of justice is a latent capacity: It does not begin to develop until it is placed under certain conditions. The question, then, is how much of a "capacity" for a sense of justice humans have prior to being shaped by their environment—that is, what sort of natural tendencies do we have to feel and think that certain situations are right or wrong, just or unjust?[71]

At one point in his discussion of the development of a sense of justice, Rawls mentions "the abilities that we find latent in our nature" (*TJ* 375–76). The fact that he uses the word "latent" to describe the capacity for a sense of justice suggests that although he thinks humans have the potential to develop a sense of justice, he does not think this potential is observable and active at first. Rather, it must be drawn out and encouraged. In other places, though, Rawls describes a sense of justice as the result of "a certain natural development" and says that it arises from our "primitive natural attitudes," which perhaps points toward the view that it is the natural course of development for a capacity that is already observable and active.[72] Despite the lack of clarity here on the nature of our original capacity for a sense of justice, it remains clear that Rawls thinks this capacity is cultivated in the first stage of moral development, which means that the capacity for a sense of justice is observable from a very early age, even though it is not yet fully developed. Perhaps this capacity can be seen when one child grabs a toy away from another child, and the child from whom the toy has been taken insists—through a variety of emotional and linguistic expressions—that something is *not right* about this situation. But consider another example, one that involves a concern for others rather than for oneself: A teacher distributes coloring books and crayons to a group of small children but skips one child, failing to give her what the others have received. The child is likely to object and might even begin to cry, calling her predicament to the attention of the other children, who are *not* likely to simply continue coloring and ignore the child in distress. Rather, they too will become distressed, seeing that something is not right about the situation. They might then notify the teacher that there is a problem, or try to comfort their classmate. Some children might begin to cry as a result of seeing another child in distress. Still others might offer to share their book and crayons. These expressions of the capacity for a sense of justice would certainly be primitive, but they could be counted as observable tendencies toward a sense of justice. The point is that the children in these stories recognize that something is wrong about certain kinds of situations, and their concerns are not simply narrowly egoistic. Of course, one could insist that the children have already been shaped by their environments and learned these behaviors, but living in kin-groups is something we do by nature and share with many related creatures. These kinds of behaviors seem to suggest the existence of basic non-egoistic tendencies to sense that something is wrong or right about a certain kind of situation, and to respond with such behaviors as helping, sharing, and comforting.[73]

As for the question of what conditions help a sense of justice to develop properly and what conditions prevent its proper development, Rawls says a number of things. Clearly, if Rawls takes the position that a sense of justice is an active, visible tendency and not a latent one, then the strength of his account depends significantly on his ability to provide an account of why a sense of justice fails to develop properly in some people. In *Theory*, Rawls says the moral development that occurs during the first stage of his psychological construction fails to take place under certain conditions, such as when a child is made to follow certain precepts that "not only may appear to him largely arbitrary but which in no way appeal to his original inclinations" (*TJ* §70, p. 408). These remarks reconfirm the fact that Rawls thinks a sense of justice is a basic capacity to be developed in humans by appealing to their natural inclinations, rather than a disposition that must be wholly acquired because it is designed to restrain or restrict natural tendencies. Rawls concludes that in the absence of affection, example, and guidance, the process of moral development cannot take place, "and certainly not in loveless relationships maintained by coercive threats and reprisals" (*TJ* §70, p. 408).

Rawls says that native endowments of various kinds require education and training, and "among what affects their realization are social attitudes of encouragement and support, and institutions concerned with their early discipline and use" (*JF*, 57). This is why childhood education should "encourage the political virtues so that they want to honor the fair terms of social cooperation in their relations with the rest of society" (*PL*, 199). By "political virtues," Rawls means "the cooperative virtues of political life:

the virtues of reasonableness and a sense of fairness, and of a spirit of compromise and a readiness to meet others halfway" (*JF*, 116). These virtues,
Rawls tells us, underwrite the desire to cooperate with others on terms
characterized by mutual respect.

Rawls is clear that there are differences between the environments in
which a person's sense of justice might develop, and these differences can
affect its development dramatically. In some cases, individuals' sense of
justice flourishes beyond ordinary expectations.

> For example, the judicial virtues are excellences of the moral power of a
> sense of justice and there is, let's suppose, considerable variation in the
> capacity for those virtues. These powers involve intellect and imagination,
> the capacity to be impartial and to take a wider and more inclusive view,
> as well as a certain sensitivity to the concerns and circumstances of others.
> (*JF*, 170)

Citizens who have a greater capacity for the judicial virtues obviously
have "a greater chance of holding positions of authority with the responsibilities that call for the exercise of those virtues" (170). But Rawls notes
that individuals who have especially highly developed judicial virtues are
those whose sense of justice has been "properly trained and exercised."
His choice of words here indicates the view that a significant amount of
training and shaping of a sense of justice must occur in order for it to be
fully developed. Those who have "highly developed" judicial virtues have
a sense of justice that has been "properly" trained and exercised, which
implies that everyone could, and should, have highly developed judicial
virtues. This claim is an affirmation of Rawls's view that a sense of justice
needs training and exercise in order to be fully developed.

Rawls goes on to say that if a society's basic structure is just, then members of society "have available to them the general all-purpose means to
train and educate their basic capabilities, and a fair opportunity to make
good use of them, provided their capabilities lie within the normal range"
(*JF*, 171). Thus, so long as citizens have the two moral powers and the
companion powers, a just society plays an important role in the *cultivation* of those powers. A just society "trains and educates" one's sense of
justice. Rawls says that when just institutions are established and working well over time, "the cooperative political virtues are encouraged and
sustained. Crucial to this process is that the principles of justice express
an idea of reciprocity that is lacking in the principle of utility" (*JF*, 117).
To put it another way, "citizens' sense of justice, given their character and
interests as formed by living under a just basic structure, is strong enough

to resist the normal tendencies to injustice" (*JF*, 185). When citizens publicly recognize principles of justice, "this public recognition itself not only encourages mutual trust among citizens generally but also nurtures the development of attitudes and habits of mind necessary for willing and fruitful social cooperation" (*JF*, 117). It is clear, then, that a sense of justice must be nurtured throughout its development by a certain kind of environment where certain sorts of commitments are valued. Establishing, maintaining, and reforming reasonably just (though always imperfect) institutions over several generations "is a great social good and appreciated as such. This is shown by the fact that a democratic people esteem it as one of the significant achievements of their history" (*JF*, 201).

Rawls's psychological construction emphasizes the need for a sense of justice to undergo a process of cultivation, beginning within the context of the family and continuing within larger communities. It is important to notice the kinds of words Rawls uses to describe this process. In the passages examined above, he speaks of a sense of justice being "trained," "exercised," "educated," "encouraged," "sustained," "formed," and "nurtured." To be sure, Rawls maintains that a sense of justice requires self-cultivation, and it is clear that within these contexts it is not simply a matter of what others do to and for an individual. As we have seen, children respond in certain ways to the way they are treated, and as they grow older, they begin to make more choices about the sort of person they want to be. These choices are certainly shaped by the environment they have been raised in, but part of what Rawls is saying is that a just society encourages its citizens to cultivate certain virtues, and it also gives them opportunities to exercise those virtues. Eventually, under proper conditions of development where their sense of justice is encouraged, drawn out, and reinforced within the context of the family and the community of which they are a part, individuals develop a concern for those outside of their immediate circle. This is seen in Rawls's account of principle guilt:

> The idea is that, given certain assumptions specifying a reasonable human psychology and the normal conditions of human life . . . citizens' sense of justice, given their character and interests as formed by living under a just basic structure, is strong enough to resist the normal tendencies to injustice. Citizens act willingly to give one another justice over time.
> (*JF*, 185; cf. *PL*, 141)

We should not pass too quickly over Rawls's claim that "the basic structure is arranged to include the requisite institutions of background justice so that citizens *have available to them the general all-purpose means to train and educate their basic capabilities*, and a fair opportunity to *make good use of them*, provided their capabilities lie within the normal range" (*JF*, 171, italics mine). Here Rawls indicates three things: (1) Citizens whose rational capacities function normally from birth have the same capacity for a fully developed sense of justice provided they are given an environment in which it can be cultivated properly. (2) Citizens' capacity for a sense of justice needs to be "trained and educated," just as one's capacity for a conception of the good needs to be—and will inevitably be—developed and shaped by one's family and community. (3) Certain environments contribute to the proper development of a sense of justice more than others. Among other things, the opportunity to exercise one's sense of justice plays an important role in the process of training and educating it.

Some interesting points of resonance between Aristotle and Rawls emerge in the context of Rawls's discussion here. Rawls postulates what he calls "the Aristotelian Principle" as a basic principle of motivation. According to the Aristotelian Principle, "other things equal, human beings enjoy the exercise of their realized capacities (their innate or trained abilities), and this enjoyment increases the more the capacity is realized, or the greater its complexity" (*TJ* §65, p. 374). Rawls notes that in the *Nichomachean Ethics*, Aristotle affirms (1) that many kinds of pleasure and enjoyment arise when we exercise our faculties; and (2) that the exercise of our natural powers is a leading human good (*TJ*, 374 n. 20).[74] One of the ideas expressed by the Aristotelian Principle is that human beings take more pleasure in doing things as they become more proficient at them. It implies that a person's capacities increase over time, and as individuals train these capacities and learn how to exercise them, they will in due course come to prefer more complex activities that call upon their newly realized abilities (*TJ* §65, p. 375).

Rawls notes an additional "companion effect" of the Aristotelian Principle. "As we witness the exercise of well-trained abilities by others, these displays are enjoyed by us and arouse a desire that we should be able to do the same things ourselves" (*TJ* §65, p. 375–76). Now Rawls stresses that this principle formulates only a tendency and not an invariable pattern, but it is important for our purposes because it gives us a better sense of how Rawls thinks a sense of justice develops. Rawls notes that as a consequence of the moral psychology specified by the Aristotelian Principle, the exercise of the two moral powers is experienced as good (*JF*, 200). As citizens develop a sense of justice, they are eager to extend it, use it, and to be challenged in their application of it. In addition, their witnessing others exercising a sense of justice arouses a desire to exercise their own sense of justice.[75]

Some of Rawls's remarks on community, too, resonate with Aristotelian points. He asks how it is possible that moral principles can engage our affections, and one of the answers Rawls offers is that "the sense of justice is continuous with the love of mankind" (*TJ* §72, p. 417). Rawls acknowledges that love goes beyond the moral requirements of justice, "yet clearly the objects of these two sentiments are closely related, being defined in large part by the same conception of justice" (*TJ*, p. 417). He writes that the sense of justice aims very directly at the well-being of persons, and "it supports those arrangements that enable everyone to express his common nature. Indeed, without a common or overlapping sense of justice civic friendship cannot exist" (*TJ*, p. 417).

An outstanding discussion of Aristotle's view of these matters is found in John Cooper's "Political Animals and Civic Friendship."[76] In this essay, Cooper explores Aristotle's claim that human beings are by nature "political animals" or animals that live in cities.[77] This claim is Aristotle's ground for holding the view that "whatever a human being's happiness or flourishing ultimately turns out to consist in, it must be something that suffices not just for his own individual good but also somehow includes the good of his family, his friends and his fellow citizens."[78] For Aristotle, the fact that cities are more than mere conventions but rather contribute to human flourishing means that "cities can demand the abiding respect of independent-minded persons" in a deeper sense.[79] In Aristotle's city, people have a further concern about moral character. As Cooper puts it, "[O]f course they want not to be cheated or otherwise treated unjustly, in business or anywhere else, but they also care what kind of people their fellow citizens are. They want them to be decent, fair-minded, respectable, moral people (anyhow, by their own lights)."[80] Cooper writes that Aristotle

> implies that civic relations among citizens of a single city, since they are not merely commercial, do involve just these concerns. That is, he holds that in cities we find a *general* concern on the part of those living under the constitution of a city and participating in its civic life for the moral characters of all those similarly engaged—a concern that *no one* taking part in civic life *be* unjust or indeed vicious in any way. This is a concern of each citizen for each other citizen, whether or not they know each other personally, and indeed whether or not they have had any direct and personal dealings with one another whatsoever.[81]

Cooper notes that even in twentieth-century liberal states, Aristotle's observation rings true. "There seems to be no denying that ordinary Americans, for example, are characteristically quite a bit concerned about the moral standards of people prominent in government, business and indus-try. . . ."[82] When we hear of corruption in these arenas, "independently of any way one may expect to suffer financial losses or other direct injuries to one's interests from these people's behavior, one feels injured and dimin-ished simply by there being such people in positions like that. Something is wrong with *us*, one feels, that among us that sort of person is found in that sort of place."[83] Cooper points out that even citizens of a modern liberal democracy like our own feel tied to one another "in such a way and to such an extent that they can and do take an interest in what their fellow-citizens quite generally are like as persons; they want to think of them as good, upstanding people, and definitely do not want them to be small-minded, self-absorbed, sleazy."[84] What our fellow-citizens are like matters to us personally, in a way that is tied to our common citizenship in the same country. We are concerned about the personal qualities of our own fellow citizens in a way that we are not concerned about citizens of foreign countries, because we feel "some connection to, some involvement with—almost some responsibility for—the former that [we] do not have for the latter." We feel partly responsible for what our fellow citizens are like in some sense, because doing so somehow reflects on us.[85]

Aristotle grounds the bonds between citizens, which grounds their con-cern for one another's character, on civic friendship.[86] As Cooper puts it, "Each expects his fellow-citizens in their dealings with him (political, eco-nomic, and social) to be motivated not merely by self-interest (or other private particular interests) but also by concern for his good for his own sake (for his qualities of mind and character, as Aristotle emphasizes . . . but also for other elements in his good)."[87] Civic friendship is different from personal friendships in that it does not require any degree of intimacy or personal knowledge of one another. However, Cooper points out that a comparison with the family is instructive, because for Aristotle "the good fortune or success or good character of one member is *experienced* by the others as somehow part of their good as well, and in fact we do think it con-stitutes a contribution to the good of the other family-members."[88] Civic friendship is simply an extension of these kinds of psychological bonds, because it makes citizens like a large extended family in the sense that each member of society participates in the good of the others.[89]

Now these aspects of Aristotle's view are important for the current study because they help us to see the dimensions of Aristotle that are very much present in Rawls, despite the many differences between them—namely, that Rawls thinks citizens care about one another's well-being, and this is an important part of what it means to have a sense of justice. But of course there are important differences between Rawls and Aristotle as well, the most important of which concerns their view of the good. According to Rawls, justice as fairness rejects civic humanism, which is a form of Aristotelianism: "[I]t holds that we are social, even political, beings whose essential nature is most fully achieved in a democratic society in which there is widespread and active participation in political life. This participation is encouraged not merely as possibly necessary for the protection of basic liberties but because it is the privileged locus of our (complete) good" (*JF*, 142).[90] Rawls rejects this view because it is a comprehensive doctrine, evidenced in the fact that it specifies a particular conception of the good. However, Rawls also specifies that civic humanism should not be mistaken for the truism that we must live in a society to achieve our good.[91] "Rather, civic humanism specifies the chief, if not the sole[,] human good as our engaging in political life, often in the form associated historically with the city-state, taking Athens and Florence as exemplars" (*JF*, 143). To reject humanism, Rawls argues, is not to deny that one of the great goods of human life is achieved by citizens through engagement in political life. It is just that the extent to which we make engagement in political life part of our complete good is up to us as individuals to decide, from Rawls's point of view, and it varies from person to person.

Rawls's rejection of civic humanism is tied to the difference between Rawls and Aristotle on the subject of the right and the good. W. D. Ross initially distinguished between the claims of liberty and right, and the good, meaning the desirability of increasing aggregate social welfare.[92] Rawls agrees with the claim that each member of society has an inviolability founded on justice, which even the welfare of everyone else cannot override. "Justice denies that the loss of freedom for some is made right by a greater good shared by others" (*TJ* §6, pp. 24–25). The basic idea of the priority of the right over the good is that one person's freedom should never be sacrificed against her will for the greater good. In Rawls's conception of justice, then, "persons accept in advance a principle of equal liberty. . . . They implicitly agree, therefore, to conform their conceptions of the good to what the principles of justice require, or at least not to press claims which directly violate them" (*TJ* §6, p. 27). As a result, no person's freedom is disregarded and sacrificed in order to benefit others. Certain things are accepted as unacceptable forms of conduct for the members of society from the outset. Thus,

> An individual who finds that he enjoys seeing others in positions of lesser liberty understands that he has no claim whatever to this enjoyment.

ιe pleasure he takes in others' deprivations is wrong in itself. . . . The ρrinciples of right, and so of justice, put limits on which satisfactions have value; they impose restrictions on what are reasonable conceptions of one's good. (p. 27)

The important conclusion from this, for Rawls, is that in justice as fairness, one does not take human propensities and inclinations as a given and then seek the best way to fulfill them. Here Rawls has in mind the utilitarian view, wherein humans are seen as seeking happiness and a society's job is to work for the greatest amount of happiness for the greatest number. Rawls maintains that this view is profoundly unjust because certain people's interests are necessarily sacrificed in the name of the greater good. On Rawls's view, citizens' desires and aspirations are restricted from the outset by the principles of justice, which specify certain boundaries everyone must respect. "We can express this by saying that in justice as fairness the concept of right is prior to that of the good. . . . The priority of justice is accounted for, in part, by holding that the interests requiring the violation of justice have no value" (*TJ* §6, pp. 27–28). The point here is that "initial bounds are placed upon what is good and what forms of character are morally worthy, and so upon what kinds of persons [humans] should be" (p. 28). Unlike the utilitarian view, which sees human propensities as inevitable, Rawls maintains that humans have another set of capabilities that can be cultivated, such as a sense of justice, and that they need not and should not simply give in to following what might be their initial tendencies. That is not to say, however, that Rawls thinks the utilitarian account of natural human tendencies is accurate, because as we have seen, he thinks a sense of justice is a basic capacity all of us possess. The failure to realize the inherent dignity it represents and the fact that this moral capacity can and should be encouraged, cultivated and shaped are among the fundamental mistakes of utilitarianism.[93]

Rawls denies that the priority of the right "implies that justice as fairness can use only very thin, if not purely instrumental, ideas of the good. But to the contrary: the right and the good are complementary; any conception of justice, including a political conception, needs both, and the priority of the right does not deny this" (*JF*, 140). Rawls points out that just institutions and the political virtues serve no purpose unless those institutions and virtues sustain conceptions of the good that citizens affirm as worthy of their allegiance. A political conception of social justice must allow sufficient space, then, for the ways of life citizens embrace. "In a phrase, the just draws the limit, the good shows the point" (*JF*, 141; cf. *PL*, 173–74).

Rawls stresses that the priority of the right does not mean that ideas of the good must be avoided. That, he says, is impossible (*JF*, 201). The priority of the right simply means that the ideas of the good that are used must meet certain requirements.[94] Thus, although Aristotle's view and Rawls's view place different restrictions on what the good can be, both views still consider ideas of the good to be necessary for a conception of justice.

We still may wonder how exactly a sense of justice cashes out in practice. It is thus necessary to discuss the best theoretical instantiation of a sense of justice—that is, Rawls's articulation of a just society. Rawls's clearest formulation of the difference a sense of justice makes in members of a just society is his discussion of a society that has "stability for the right reasons" (*JF*, 185; cf. *PL* xlii).

Stability for the Right Reasons

Social stability, for Rawls, is evident in what happens when a conception of justice is put into practice. Do citizens abide by the principles of justice, and if so, why? A stable society is one in which citizens consistently abide by the principles of justice that govern the institutions of their society. The simple fact that a society has a conception of justice does not mean that people will consistently act justly. The problem of stability arises because a just scheme of cooperation may not be in equilibrium, much less stable, so that "an individual, if he is so inclined, can sometimes win even greater benefits for himself by taking advantage of the cooperative efforts of others" (*TJ* §76, pp. 434–35). By equilibrium, Rawls means that the result of agreements between willing participants is "the best situation that [each person] can reach by free exchange consistent with the right and freedom of others to further their interests in the same way" (*TJ* §20, p. 103). A just scheme of cooperation is in equilibrium when no one has an incentive to alter it. Stability, however, is a step further than equilibrium. Rawls writes, "If a departure from this situation sets in motion tendencies which restore it, the equilibrium is stable" (*TJ*, 103). Social stability, then, occurs when a just scheme of cooperation not only has equilibrium but also safeguards against a departure from the terms of cooperation.

As we have seen, the cultivation of a sense of justice in members of society is an indispensable part of establishing justice in a society. According to Rawls, the conditions that create stability occur when "those taking part in [just] arrangements acquire the corresponding sense of justice and desire to do their part in maintaining them" (*TJ* §69, p. 398). We have seen how ds on citizens' cultivating certain attitudes toward one ortant sense, then, a just society depends on the posture rd one another. Further, Rawls says, social stability has with the posture citizens take toward the principles of tion of justice is more stable when citizens are more will- its requirements. This is why Rawls tells us that stability a balance of motives: the sense of justice that it cultivates lat it encourages must normally win out against propensities ce" (*TJ*, 98).

gness to abide by the requirements of a conception of justice part by a sense of justice. As we have seen, to ensure stability st have a sense of justice, which is characterized by a concern ho would be disadvantaged by the failure of others to abide by ples of justice. The posture citizens have toward the principles must be defined by the belief that the aims that the conception of icourages should consistently take priority over any propensities njustice (*TJ* §69, p. 398).

Rawlsian conception of stability is a notable contrast to Hobbesian y. Both Rawls and Hobbes maintain that when a system of coopera- stable, each person thinks others will do their part and so there is ndency for one not to do one's own part. However, for Rawls, mu- trust that comes from a well-developed sense of justice is responsible his state of affairs, whereas for Hobbes, this role is played by one's fear he sovereign. As Rawls points out, relations of mutual trust are analo- us to the role of the sovereign, except that in the case of the former, "it the consequence of a certain psychological principle of human nature such systems, and the implications of the generated attitudes."[95] Thus for Hobbes, stability comes at the price of justice, because nearly absolute sovereignty is needed to secure stability.[96] Rawls, however, is concerned with only the problem of stability in a *just* society.

As Samuel Freeman indicates, contrasting Rawls with Hobbes distin- guishes a stable society that is just from a stable society that is unjust. An- other important distinction is between a stable society and an unstable one. In a stable society, citizens are satisfied that the existing institutions are just, and as a result they do not desire "either to violate or to renego- tiate the terms of social cooperation" (*JF*, 125). In a democratic regime, "stable social cooperation rests on the fact that most citizens accept the political order as legitimate . . . and hence willingly abide by it" (*JF*, 125). This willingness depends heavily on what Rawls calls the publicity condi- tion: Principles are publicly known and regularly appealed to in deciding and justifying laws and institutions in the society (*TJ* §23, p. 115). The publicity condition allows citizens to see the conception of justice in action and evaluate why it deserves their allegiance. Utilitarian conceptions of justice tend toward instability precisely because of what happens when there is public knowledge of the standard of maximum aggregate utility. When those who are called upon to make sacrifices learn of the standard for determining the distribution of benefits, they resent the arrangement.

> Thus the scheme will not be stable unless those who must make sacrifices strongly identify with interests broader than their own. But this is not easy to bring about. The sacrifices in question are not those asked in times of social emergency when all or some must pitch in for the common good. . . . Even when we are less fortunate, we are to accept the greater advantages of others as a sufficient reason for lower expectations over the whole course of our life. (*TJ* §29, p. 155)

In a stable society, the standard for determining the distribution of benefits must advance *everyone's* position. Fair terms of cooperation specify "an idea of reciprocity, or mutuality: all who do their part as the recognized rules require are to benefit as specified by a public and agreed-upon standard" (*JF*, 6). In turn, unlike utilitarian conceptions, "since everyone's good is affirmed, all acquire inclinations to uphold the scheme" (*TJ* §29, p. 155).

Rawls discusses at length the instability of a compromise. Citizens who abide by a conception of justice as the result of a compromise will likely tire of the arrangement eventually and desire to violate the terms of social cooperation. Rawls uses the term *modus vivendi*, which typically characterizes a treaty between two states whose interests put them at odds, to refer to this scenario. The compromise is honored because it is in the interest of both parties or states to abide by it, "[b]ut in general both states are ready to pursue their goals at the expense of the other, and should conditions change they may do so" (*PL*, 147). The reasons for acting in accordance with the principles of justice are not strong enough in the case of a *modus vivendi* because "its stability is contingent on circumstances remaining such as not to upset the fortunate convergence of interests" (*PL*, 147). For Rawls, the stability achieved by a *modus vivendi* is unreliable because citizens have decided to abide by the terms of cooperation for the wrong reasons.

What, then, are the right reasons for citizens to abide by the terms specified by the principles of justice? This is one of Rawls's central interests when he formulates his conception of social stability. He develops an alternate conception of stability in contrast with a *modus vivendi*, telling us that in the case of stability for the right reasons, "each view supports the political conception [of justice] for its own sake, or on its own merits" (*PL*, 148). Citizens who support the principles of justice for the right reasons will not withdraw their support in the event that their comprehensive view becomes dominant. One test of stability for the right reasons is "whether the consensus is stable with respect to changes in the distribution of power among views. This feature of stability highlights a basic contrast between an overlapping consensus and a modus vivendi, the stability of which does depend on happenstance and a balance of relative forces" (*PL*, 148).

Rawls tells us that stability involves two questions: (1) Will individuals who grow up under just institutions acquire an effective sense of justice, meaning that they will generally comply with the principles of justice that have been adopted by their society? (2) Given the fact of reasonable pluralism in a democracy, will the conception of justice be the focus of an overlapping consensus among a variety of reasonable comprehensive doctrines? (*PL*, 141). These two questions turn out to be closely linked, because as Rawls shows, citizens who acquire an effective sense of justice are those who are prepared and willing to endorse the principles of justice through an overlapping consensus.

Rawls introduces the concept of an overlapping consensus as a way of addressing the diversity of reasonable comprehensive doctrines that characterizes a modern liberal democracy. Rawls is aware that not all citizens of such diverse comprehensive views will desire to abide by the principles of justice for exactly the same reasons. But Rawls also believes there is common ground among these comprehensive views, and this is what makes them "reasonable." Reasonable persons are those who acknowledge that not all citizens share the same comprehensive view, and that this lack of shared ground requires them to moderate their demands out of respect for others. Reasonable persons, then, are ready to discuss terms of cooperation others propose because they desire "for its own sake" a social world in which they can cooperate with other citizens on terms that are acceptable to all and freely pursue their own understanding of the good life (*PL*, 50).

A reasonable society comprises reasonable persons, and so it is one in which "all stand ready to propose fair terms that others may reasonably be expected to accept . . ." (*PL*, 54). In addition, however, stability for the right reasons requires that citizens endorse the conception of justice for reasons rooted in their own comprehensive doctrine. "All those who affirm the political conception start from within their own comprehensive view and draw on the religious, philosophical, and moral grounds it provides" (*PL*, 147). Rawls continues,

> In a democratic society marked by reasonable pluralism, showing that sta-
> bility for the right reasons is at least possible is also part of public justifica-
> tion. The reason is that when citizens affirm reasonable though different
> comprehensive doctrines, seeing whether an overlapping consensus on the
> political conception is possible is a way of checking whether there are suf-
> ficient reasons for proposing justice as fairness (or some other reasonable
> doctrine) which can be sincerely defended before others without criticiz-
> ing or rejecting their deepest religious and philosophical commitments.
> (*PL*, 390)

Just as it is unacceptable for citizens to propose terms of cooperation that
are uniquely associated with one comprehensive view, it is also unacceptable for them to propose terms of cooperation that are a compromise
between their view and the views of other citizens. Instead, citizens must
have reasons for abiding by the principles of justice that are not in conflict with their own comprehensive views or the reasonable comprehensive
views of others. This is the only way stability for the right reasons can
occur.

There is a deep sense in which stability for the right reasons comes
from an overlapping consensus, because the basis of social unity lies here.
If a liberal society is to be stable, its political conception of justice must
be endorsed by an overlapping consensus. Each citizen must see her own
comprehensive doctrine manifested politically in the conception of justice
that governs the basic structure of society. This gives citizens a reason to
uphold its principles regardless of the balance of power among different
comprehensive doctrines. The reasons citizens give for abiding by the conception of justice in the case of an overlapping consensus differ dramatically from those associated with a *modus vivendi* compromise. The stability
of a *modus vivendi* persists only so long as a citizen's favored comprehensive
doctrine is too weak to dominate the others'. A citizen would abandon the
conception of justice if her own view could dominate. Stability, for Rawls,
is a condition in which there is deep-seated agreement on fundamental
questions about the basic structure of society. So in an overlapping consensus, the reasons for abiding by the principles of justice are embedded
in the values of each citizen, as opposed to being a compromise requiring a sacrifice, regardless of how slight, from within these values. Each
citizen believes that abiding by the principles of justice is the best thing
for everyone in the society, and, as a result, they will endorse and abide
by those principles "without being dominated, pressured, or manipulated"
(*PL*, xliv). Social stability emerges when citizens endorse the conception of
justice for these reasons—the right reasons—because these reasons have

roots far deeper than those of the temporary balance of power in society. Regardless of whether one comprehensive view increases and gains dominance, citizens will still abide by the principles of justice, because they are already doing so for the right reasons.

Rawls says the reasons for endorsing the conception of justice include the principles of justice and "an account of the political virtues through which those principles are embodied in human character and expressed in public life" (*PL*, 147). Rawls also maintains that stability for the right reasons "implies that the reasons from which citizens act include those given by the account of justice they affirm" (*PL*, xlii). Stability for the right reasons means that the reasons citizens have for abiding by the principles of justice are connected with the principles of justice themselves. When citizens propose terms that citizens committed to other reasonable comprehensive views would endorse, they are applying a crucial aspect of the principles of justice, namely that the standard for determining the distribution of benefits must advance everyone's position and affirm everyone's good.

A political conception of justice must "generate its own support" and the institutions to which it leads must be "self-enforcing" (*JF*, 124–25). This means that the right reasons for abiding by the principles of justice include reasons given by the principles of justice themselves. The posture citizens take toward their fellow citizens in the process of proposing fair terms of cooperation is one that is specified by the principles of justice. Further, when citizens honor the terms of cooperation specified by the principles of justice, their public recognition of those terms encourages mutual trust among citizens and "nurtures the development of attitudes and habits of mind necessary for willing and fruitful cooperation" (*JF*, 117). When this occurs, the "basis of social unity is the deepest because the fundamental ideas of the political conception are endorsed by the reasonable comprehensive doctrines, and these doctrines represent what citizens regard as their deepest convictions—religious, philosophical, and moral. From this follows stability for the right reasons" (*PL*, 391–92).

What matters is "the kind of stability, the nature of the forces that secure [the conception of justice]. . . . Put another way: citizens' sense of justice . . . is strong enough to resist the normal tendencies to injustice. Citizens act willingly to give one another justice over time. Stability is secured by sufficient motivation of the appropriate kind acquired under just institutions" (*JF*, 185). Despite differences in their comprehensive views, reasonable persons must have a certain posture toward other citizens in their society and toward the principles of justice. This posture is defined by a genuine desire to see everyone benefit from the terms of social cooperation, and as a result to abide by the principles designed to ensure the proper distribution of these benefits. Citizens who have this posture abide by the principles of justice for the right reasons.

Rawls's description of stability for the right reasons is closely related to his description of reasonable persons as desiring a certain sort of social world "for its own sake." Here we should recall that the reasons citizens give for abiding by the principles of justice when there is stability for the right reasons include reasons given by the conception of justice itself. Their reasons, in this sense, go all the way down to the value of justice. Reasonable citizens have a well-developed sense of justice that has been cultivated through the processes discussed earlier in this chapter, and they desire to abide by the principles of justice because they are just. The social world that results from the implementation of the conception of justice is intrinsically good; it is desirable for its own sake.

In sum, a society has stability for the right reasons when its members have inclinations to advance everyone's position and affirm everyone's good. All persons are capable of taking such a posture by virtue of their sense of justice. For Rawls, the best instantiation of a sense of justice is one in which the standard for determining the basic political institutions of society and thereby determining the distribution of benefits in a society advances everyone's position and affirms everyone's good. When a sense of justice works as it should, all are concerned for those who would be disadvantaged by the failure of others to abide by that standard.

For Rawls, a society with fair terms of cooperation produces a strong sense of justice in its members, which in turn produces stability for the right reasons. Those who grow up under just institutions develop an informed allegiance to those institutions sufficient to render them stable. They do not become self-aggrandizing individualists, but good citizens. Growing up in a just society helps to develop and shape citizens' sense of justice, making it strong enough to resist the normal tendencies to injustice. This is why, as we have seen, Rawls points out that citizens "act willingly to give one another justice over time. Stability is secured by sufficient motivation of the appropriate kind acquired under just institutions" (*JF*, 185). In a society whose members count on one another's sense of justice, "a person normally wants to act justly as well as to be recognized by others as someone who can be relied upon as a fully cooperating member of society over a complete life" (*PL*, 306).

Liberal theory is underpinned by concerns about how to achieve a society that functions well. Rawls's account is grounded on the idea that citizens have the capacity for a sense of justice, and when it is cultivated properly the possibility of a just society that is stable for the right reasons exists. However, more than one kind of view makes use of a sense of justice. We will see this clearly in the next chapter, when we turn to the articulation of a sense of justice found in the Confucian *Analects*.

CHAPTER 3

The Sense of Justice in the *Analects*

> I have heard that those who possess a state or noble house are not
> concerned about whether their people are few in number, but rather
> about whether their people are content; they are not concerned [so
> much] about poverty, but about unequal distribution. If wealth is
> equally distributed, there should be no poverty.[1]

As we turn to the *Analects*, we return to the questions raised in the Introduction to this book: Without a term for "justice," how does the text of
the *Analects* reveal an appreciation for a sense of justice? What features, in
particular, help to show that it is appropriate to call it a sense of justice?
This chapter is devoted to showing how an appreciation for a sense of
justice is expressed in the *Analects*. In the first section, I argue that the primary concern of the *Analects* is to advocate the cultivation of a certain set
of virtues in human beings. In the second section, I show that a distinctive
set of concerns emerges in the context of this discussion of self-cultivation,
and that these concerns evince an appreciation for a sense of justice. In
the third section of the chapter I defend my argument against a series of
possible objections, including the view that there is no term for "a sense of
justice" and, therefore, no idea of it in the *Analects*, and the objection that
the term "sense of justice" is a Rawlsian imposition. I also discuss some
passages that could be offered as counter-examples to the view that there is
an appreciation for a sense of justice in the *Analects*, as well as the view that
the history of ancient China does not reflect an appreciation for a sense
of justice.

The Cultivation of the Virtues in the Analects

Although this study focuses on the view we find in the text of the *Ana-lects* as a whole, it will be helpful to begin by getting a sense of Kongzi as his story is presented in the *Analects*. In 4.8, Kongzi says, "Having in the morning heard that the Way was being put into practice, I could die that evening without regret." In passages like this, we get the distinct sense that Kongzi's life is devoted to the propagation of the Way (*Dao* 道) in the world.[2] Most generally, the Way is a path or way of living that comprises the virtues, moral capacities, and rituals that Kongzi advocates. He sees these things as features of traditional Zhou culture, but their origins, for Kongzi, lie beyond the Zhou sage-kings. The *Analects* tells us that Kongzi was called by Heaven (*Tian* 天) to put its plan for human beings—the Way—into practice. In 3.24, we are presented with a scene in which Kongzi and his followers are departing from the state of Lu after he has resigned from his official position as the minister of crime. A border offi-cial says to them, "You disciples, why should you be concerned about your Master's loss of office? The world has been without the Way for a long time now, and Heaven intends to use your Master like the wooden clapper for a bell." On the view that is expressed in this passage, Kongzi's loss of office is somehow part of a grand plan laid out by Heaven, according to which Kongzi is called to spread the teachings of the Way and wake up the world from its fallen state.

In other passages, Kongzi speaks of his sense of vocation and his rela-tionship to Heaven. In 7.23, he says, "It is Heaven itself that has endowed me with virtue," and then he goes on to say that he has nothing to fear in Huan Tui, a military officer from the state of Song who had attempted to harm him. Kongzi makes a similar remark in 9.5, when he is surrounded in Kuang and says, "If Heaven intended this culture to perish, it would not have given it to those of us who live after King Wen's death. Since Heaven did not intend that this culture should perish, what can the people of Kuang do to me?" In both of these passages, it seems clear that Kongzi is not afraid of his destiny in this world because he is following Heaven's plan. In 14.35, Kongzi laments that no one understands him, and when Zigong asks him how he could say this, he replies, "I am not bitter toward Heaven, nor do I blame others. I study what is below in order to compre-hend what is above. If there is anyone who could understand me, perhaps it is Heaven." Together, these passages reflect Kongzi's sense that he has been called to devote his life to the propagation of Heaven's plan for hu-man beings: the Way.

In the *Analects*, the Way (*Dao*) is described in Kongzi's instructions to others, and in his students' remarks and questions. It is also exemplified in the model Kongzi provides in his own life. In 2.11, he says, "Both keeping the past teachings alive and understanding the present—someone able to do this is worthy of being a teacher." Indeed, his calling is tied to his insistence that people should return to the way of life embodied in the earlier part of the Zhou dynasty. In 3.14 Kongzi says, "The Zhou gazes down upon the two dynasties that preceded it. How brilliant in culture it is! I follow the Zhou." Here the image of the Zhou dynasty gazing down upon the Xia and Shang dynasties expresses Kongzi's view that Zhou culture incorporated the best aspects of the cultures that preceded it. He sees the Zhou as a culmination of wisdom, and a clear expression of what the world looks like when people follow the Way. Kongzi says that he is not someone who was born with knowledge; rather, "I simply love antiquity, and diligently look there for knowledge" (7.20). This is why he insists that he transmits instead of innovates (7.1).[3] Further, he says he does not possess the fault of trying to innovate without acquiring knowledge: "I listen widely, and then pick out that which is excellent in order to follow it; I see many things, and then remember them" (7.28). Here again, Kongzi insists that his knowledge comes from learning the Way of the former kings, a well-trodden path to which the world must find its way back.

In a number of places, Kongzi says his mission is tied to encouraging others in their own quest to follow the Way. He is consistently self-deprecating, saying in 7.34, "How could I dare to lay claim to either sageliness or *Ren* 仁 ('humaneness')? What can be said about me is no more than this: I work at it without growing tired and encourage others without growing weary."[4] He says his aspiration is "to bring comfort to the aged, to inspire trust in my friends, and to be cherished by the youth" (5.26). Whenever Kongzi speaks of his life's work, it is tied to his relationships with others and not to some sort of personal reverence or building a personal relationship with Heaven, even though he sees himself as carrying out Heaven's plan for human beings by advocating the Way.

On the view of society presented in the *Analects*, the Way serves as a standard for organizing not only a harmonious life but a harmonious society as well. In 1.12 Master You says, "When it comes to the practice of ritual, it is harmony (*he* 和) that should be valued. It is precisely such harmony that makes the Way of the former kings so beautiful, and in all matters, great and small, we should follow them. Yet if you know enough to value harmony but try to attain it without being regulated by the rites, this will not work."[5] The task of self-cultivation is the key to realizing a harmonious society, and as we shall see, the rites play a pivotal role in this process. The practice of Confucian moral self-cultivation, though, is arduous and involves not only following the rites and promoting harmony but also cultivating a wide variety of different virtues. In 8.7 we are told that for the scholar-official who has devoted his life to the path of self-cultivation, "[T]he burden is heavy and the Way is long. He takes up *Ren* 仁 ('humaneness') as his burden—is it not heavy? His way ends only with death—is it not long?"[6] *Ren* 仁 is the highest of the Confucian virtues, and it carries the sense of humaneness or human-heartedness, benevolence, and highest goodness. As this passage indicates, taking up *Ren* is the task of one who treads the Way.

The Way plays an important part in the unity of the Confucian virtues, which together specify a vision of a certain way of life so that one who embodies these virtues has a life that "hangs together" coherently, which is the weakest sense in which there must be some kind of unity among the virtues. If someone embodies some of the virtues but neglects the others, something is missing and that person's life will not be complete in an important sense. To be sure, it is not that in a given action or on a given occasion one needs to embody all of the virtues in order to have any of them; rather, a life in which some virtues are ignored or in which one cannot realize them is thereby a life that is not as good. On the other hand, each human life is lived in cooperation with and against the backdrop of many other lives, and the Way shows us how to organize and navigate these roles and relationships. Accordingly, the Way serves as a standard for organizing a harmonious life as well as a harmonious society.

In the person of Kongzi, we get a glimpse of what the task of self-cultivation involves, for he not only advocates the Way but also exemplifies what it means to be a self-cultivationist devoted to following the Way. We see this clearly in 7.3: "That I fail to cultivate Virtue (*de* 德), that I fail to inquire into what I have learned, that upon hearing what is right I remain unable to move myself to do it, and that I am unable to reform when I have done something that is not good—these are things I worry about."[7] Self-cultivation, he tells us, concerns the attitude one takes toward learning and not the amount of theoretical knowledge or wisdom one possesses, even though one who is devoted to the path of self-cultivation is likely to acquire the latter. In 9.8, he asks, "Do I possess wisdom? No, I do not. A common fellow asked a question of me, and I came up completely empty. But I discussed the problem with him from beginning to end until we finally got to the bottom of it." Here we see the priority given to intellectual virtues like tenacity, diligence, and intellectual humility.

Indeed, many of the discussions of self-cultivation are related to discussions of learning (*xue* 學) and the attitude one brings to it. In the opening lines of the *Analects* Kongzi asks, "To study and then have occasion to practice what you have learned—is this not a joy?"[8] In 1.7, we are asked to imagine someone who recognizes and admires worthiness and therefore works to eliminate unworthy qualities in herself, who fully exhausts her strength in serving her parents, and who is trustworthy in her interactions with friends and colleagues. The passage insists that "it is precisely such qualities that make one worthy of being called 'learned.'" Throughout the text of the *Analects* are descriptions of the arduous process of "learning" (*xue* 學), "cultivating" (*xiu* 修) Virtue (7.3), "reflecting" (*si* 思) on what one has learned (2.15), "examining" (*xing* 省) one's own conduct (1.4, 12.4), "inspecting" (*xing* 省) the moral conduct of others (2.9), and "going over" (*xi* 習) what one has learned (1.1) and what one has taught (1.4). In 1.15 we catch a glimpse of how rigorous this process is. Kongzi praises Zigong as one who is informed about the past and, thus, one who knows what is to come, after Zigong quotes from the *Book of Odes* (*Shijing*): "As if cut, as if polished; As if carved, as if ground." This passage reflects the difficulty of self-cultivation by using the metaphor of cutting and polishing bone and ivory and carving and grinding jade.

Kongzi insists that "One who is *Ren* 仁 ('humane') sees as his first priority the hardship of self-cultivation, and only afterward thinks about results or rewards. Yes, this is what we might call *Ren*" (6.22).[9] In 8.17 he says, "Learn as if you will never catch up, and as if you feared losing what you have already attained." Kongzi says in 14.42 that the *junzi* 君子 ("exemplary person") cultivates himself in order to achieve *respectfulness* (*jing* 敬), in order to bring peace to others, and in order to bring peace to all of the people. The *junzi*, who serves as a moral exemplar and the ideal to which all should aspire, is the most highly cultivated person in Confucianism. The *junzi* embodies the full range of Confucian virtues, including filiality, trustworthiness, courage, and wisdom. "Cultivating oneself and thereby bringing peace to all of the people is something even a Yao or a Shun would find difficult" (14.42). This passage reflects Kongzi's awareness of the demanding nature of the task at hand, but, more important, the discussion of respectfulness (*jing* 敬) earlier in this passage reflects Kongzi's view that self-cultivation begins with children's learning to show respect for their parents and other elders, then extending that respectfulness to others in their families and communities, and finally to all people. Kongzi encourages his students to demand much of themselves while asking little of others (15.15), and says that "[t]he *junzi* is distressed by his own inability, rather than the failure of others to recognize him" (15.19).[10] In addition, "the *junzi* seeks it in himself; the petty person seeks it in others" (15.21).

We saw earlier that Kongzi is an exemplar of self-cultivation, something that is also seen in 2.4: "At fifteen, I set my mind upon learning; at thirty, I took my place in society; at forty, I became free of doubts; at fifty, I understood Heaven's Mandate; at sixty, my ear was attuned; and at seventy, I could follow my heart's desires without overstepping the bounds of propriety." The *Analects* describes other specific exemplars of self-cultivation as well. One of the clearest and most highly praised is Yan Hui, Kongzi's most exceptional student. Yan Hui died tragically at a young age, and Kongzi's tremendous grief at this loss is described in the *Analects* (11.9–11.10). Kongzi describes Yan Hui as one who truly loved learning, saying, "He never misdirected his anger and never made the same mistake twice" (6.3), which indicates his control over his emotions and his actions. Kongzi also says that Yan Hui embodied the capacity for concentration, attentiveness, and reflection that is most characteristic of a true self-cultivationist. "For three months at a time his heart-mind did not stray from *Ren* ('humaneness'). Others could only sporadically maintain such a state" (6.7).[11] In 9.20, Kongzi says Yan Hui never grows weary in conversation. Yan Hui's own comments also reflect his commitment to self-cultivation and to his teacher, whom he credits with taking the time to encourage and lead him forward on the Way. In 9.11, Yan Hui talks about his pursuit of the Way:

> The more I look up at it the higher it seems; the more I delve into it, the harder it becomes. Catching a glimpse of it before me, I then find it suddenly at my back. The Master is skilled at gradually leading me on, step by step. He broadens me with culture and restrains me with the rites, so that even if I wanted to quit I could not. When I have exhausted my strength, it seems as if there is still something left, looming up ahead of me. Even though I desire to follow it, there seems to be no way through.

It is striking how much humility Kongzi's most outstanding student shows here, and his doing so reflects both the difficulty of the task of self-cultivation and Yan Hui's excellence. A part of his success seems to be his intellectual humility and his realization that he still has a long way to go. Yan Hui says in 5.26 that his aspiration is to avoid being boastful about his own abilities or exaggerating his accomplishments, and indeed, nowhere do we get the sense that he failed to avoid these things. Kongzi says of Yan Hui, "I watched his advance, and never once saw him stop" (9.21). All of this is extraordinary when one considers that Yan Hui came from a very poor background. In 6.11 Kongzi says that Yan Hui lives in an alley, with only a bamboo dish of rice and a gourdful of water to drink. He says that other people could not have endured such hardship in life, but "[I]t never spoiled Hui's joy. Admirable indeed was Hui!"[12]

Yan Hui's attitude toward his low station in life marks an important emphasis in the *Analects*. Kongzi maintains throughout the text that an interest in material gain, fame, or prestige is not the concern of a person following the path of self-cultivation. We will see later in this chapter that the *Analects* describes the virtue of *yi* 義 ("rightness") as directly opposing and guarding against a concern with profit and gain, but this idea is a broad theme running through the text. In 4.9 Kongzi states that one who has set his intentions upon the Way but is still ashamed of his clothing and food is "not worth engaging in discussion." Yan Hui's exemplary attitude serves as an illustration here. Kongzi goes on to say in 4.11, "The *junzi* cherishes Virtue, whereas the petty person cherishes the soil. The *junzi* cherishes [the fairness associated with] punishments, whereas the petty person cherishes exemptions."[13] Ames and Rosemont translate this last line as "Exemplary persons cherish fairness; petty persons cherish the thought of gain," noting that the character *xing* 刑 ("punishments") here carries the sense of the fairness that is associated with just punishments.[14] Here we see that Kongzi associates virtue with an appreciation for the institutions that keep people in line, helping to maintain a harmonious society. On the other hand, he thinks those who are concerned about physical possessions and profit are also likely to be those who are not concerned about the rites and laws and how they maintain a harmonious society. These people have their own self-interest and material gain in mind, rather than their moral character and the character of others.

Kongzi's lack of regard for prestige is related to his disdain for those who are concerned with material gain. In 9.2 we learn of a villager who makes fun of Kongzi, saying sarcastically, "How great is Kongzi! He is so broadly learned, and yet has failed to make a name for himself in any particular endeavor."[15] When Kongzi learns of this cutting remark, he says to his disciples, with equal sarcasm, "What art, then, should I take up? Charioteering? Archery? I think I shall take up charioteering." Here Kongzi shows his contempt for mere technical skills, but he clearly thinks there is nothing more important—indeed, more practical—than the matter of what sort of person one should be. *Analects* 9.6 accords well with this theme. The prime minister says to Zigong, "Your Master is a sage, is he not? How is it, then, that he is skilled at so many menial tasks?" Later, hearing of this, Kongzi says, "How well the Prime Minister knows me! In my youth, I was of humble status, so I became proficient in many menial tasks. Is the *junzi* broadly skilled in trivial matters? No, he is not." Here Kongzi asserts that his technical skills come from his humble background and not from his commitment to the path of self-cultivation, continuing to insist that there is a distinction between the origins of technical skills and moral character, even though, as in his case, we may find some people who possess both.

As I noted briefly above, the capacity to feel and act in certain ways toward others in a society grows out of self-cultivation that begins in the context of familial relationships. In 1.2 Master You says,

> A young person who is filial and respectful of his elders rarely becomes the kind of person who is inclined to defy his superiors, and there has never been a case of one who is disinclined to defy his superiors stirring up rebellion. The *junzi* applies himself to the roots. "Once the roots are firmly established, the Way will grow." Might we not say that filial piety and respect for elders constitute the root of *Ren* ("humaneness")?

The quotation from the *Book of Odes* in this passage indicates a connection between the cultivation of filial piety as the "roots" of one's moral character and the ability to follow the Way throughout one's life. One who cultivates the virtue of filial piety tends to develop a moral sense, learning to embody the other virtues that are part of the Way.

In particular, we should notice that 1.2 mentions that one who is filial does not stir up a rebellion. The idea that filial piety constitutes the roots of political order prevails in the *Analects*. One of the clearest formulations of this idea is found in 2.21, where Kongzi responds to questions about why he is not involved in government with a quotation from the *Book of Documents* (*Shujing* 書經): "Filial, oh so filial, Friendly to one's elders and juniors; Exerting influence upon those who govern." After quoting this passage, Kongzi says, "Thus, in being a filial son and good brother one is already taking part in government. What need is there, then, to speak of 'participating in government'?" It is difficult to imagine a clearer indication of the connection Kongzi sees between the cultivation of filial piety and political order. He thinks that the government alone cannot bring about a stable and harmonious society; rather, such stability must be initially cultivated in the context of the family. Members of society must develop certain dispositions, learning to think and feel for others in certain ways, if there is to be political order. The family serves as the model for the ideal state in this regard.

In 14.43, Kongzi gives us a sense of what he thinks happens when this process of self-cultivation does not occur. Upon observing a young man who is waiting for him sitting with his legs sprawled out, which is a breach of the proper posture and attitude for receiving an honored guest, Kongzi says, "A young man devoid of humility and respect for his elders will grow into an adult who contributes nothing to his community. Growing older and older without dignity to pass away, he becomes a burden on society." This remark accords well with the other passages we have been examining, because it shows that Kongzi does not endorse the view that children will simply "grow up" and automatically take responsibility at a certain point in their lives. Rather, poor behavior at a young age, and in particular the failure to show respect for one's elders, grows into a larger problem and actually obstructs one's moral progress as one gets older. Kongzi thinks this young man will grow up to be someone who has no sense of responsibility to others and as such will be nothing but a burden on society. One learns to think of others in certain ways and feel the responsibility to contribute at a very young age.

When we examine the remarks about filial piety in the *Analects*, we see that one's accordance with the Way has just as much to do with feelings and attitudes as it does with actions. *Analects* 2.7 says, "Nowadays 'filial' means simply being able to provide one's parents with nourishment. But even dogs and horses are provided with nourishment. If you are not respectful, wherein lies the difference?" This passage sees respect (*jing* 敬) as constituting an emotional attitude and not simply actions.[16] In 2.8 Kongzi points out, "It is the demeanor that is difficult. If there is work to be done, disciples shoulder the burden, and when wine and food are served, elders are given precedence, but surely filial piety consists of more than this." Demeanor or face (*se* 色) refers to the outward manifestation of one's inner reflections and feelings about one's conduct. In the context of self-cultivation, Kongzi describes a particular conception of the capacities humans have in relation to one another—both with respect to their feelings and attitudes and with respect to their conduct.

In a number of other places Kongzi discusses the importance of cultivating certain emotional attitudes. When Kongzi is asked about "the roots of ritual," he responds by saying, "What a noble question! When it comes to ritual, it is better to be spare than extravagant. When it comes to mourning, it is better to be excessively sorrowful than fastidious" (3.4). The rites (*li* 禮) are an integral part of the Way, and a cultivated person embodies the virtue of ritual propriety. The rites include a rich variety of social rituals and practices, including matters of etiquette, social customs, and religious ritual. They also play a special role in self-cultivation, for they help to cultivate as well as express the virtues that partly constitute the Way. In 3.4,

Kongzi tells us that the roots of ritual are actually the emotions that inform and motivate the rites. We should be reminded here of the claim that filial piety is the root of *Ren* ("humaneness"). In 3.4 Kongzi indicates that one's feelings about what one is doing are the roots of ritual. One way to understand these claims about roots is to see them as evidence for the view that one's feelings toward others are where moral cultivation begins and also what provides the enlivening force sustaining self-cultivation. Thus one's filial love and respect for one's parents and elders, and one's sorrow when one performs a mourning ritual, are the foundation of filial piety and ritual propriety. We begin with the feelings, and it is the feelings to which we must return when there is a problem. We should err on the side of showing our feelings rather than going through the motions, although of course we must balance proper feelings with proper actions.

Additional evidence in 3.26 supports this view: "Someone who lacks magnanimity when occupying high office, who is not respectful when performing ritual, and who remains unmoved by sorrow when overseeing mourning rites—how could I bear to look upon such a person?" Kongzi's own performance of the rites as it is described in the *Analects* also indicates the importance of emotional attitudes. Although many passages describe for us Kongzi's careful performance of ritually specific behavior, other passages describe behaviors that are significant because they concern his emotional attitudes. *Analects* 7.9 and 7.10 note that "when the Master dined in the company of one who was in mourning, he never ate his fill" and "the Master would never sing on a day when he had wept." As Slingerland points out in his summary of the accompanying commentaries, these passages show that Kongzi *felt* the rituals and "was profoundly affected by the emotions they evoked. Understood this way, the point is not that [Kongzi] consciously refrained from eating his fill or singing, but that he was actually rendered unable to eat a full meal or engage in light-hearted activities."[17] These passages all indicate that being a cultivated person involves having certain virtues that are constituted by both emotional attitudes and actions.

The *Analects* presents a novel view of how it is that a variety of different individuals engaging in self-cultivation can add up to the sum total of a stable, harmonious society. To begin with, Kongzi maintains that it is through the conduct of others that we learn how to become good ourselves. In 4.1 he says, "To live in the neighborhood of those who are *Ren* ('humane') is fine. If one does not choose to dwell among those who are *Ren*, how will one obtain wisdom?"[18] In 5.3 he remarks that Zijian is truly a *junzi* and asks, "If [the state of] Lu were really without *junzi*, where did he learn how to be like that?" The *Analects* expresses the idea that it is simply a basic tendency of human beings to gravitate toward those who are good and that cultivated individuals increasingly feel a particular affection for those who are *Ren* ("humane") (1.6). This view naturally reinforces the view I have presented above, that our feelings are of the utmost importance when it comes to moral character. I will discuss in a moment the origins of the view that we are drawn to good people and its relationship to the concept of *de* 德 ("Virtue"), but first I want to examine more carefully how this idea manifests itself in the *Analects*. To begin, we find Kongzi instructing his students not to accept as friends those who are not their equals (1.8, 9.25). He maintains that individuals are more successful in the process of self-cultivation when they surround themselves with those who are similarly committed to following the Way. In 15.10, he compares this dimension of self-cultivation to a craft: "Any craftsman who wishes to do his job well must first sharpen his tools. In the same way, when living in a given state, one must serve those ministers who are worthy and befriend those scholar-officials who are *Ren* ('humane')."

Kongzi repeatedly indicates that we should surround ourselves with good people, "drawing near to those who possess the Way in order to be set straight by them" (1.14). The *Analects* also asserts that those who are *Ren* ("humane") help others to cultivate themselves: "[W]anting to realize himself, [one who is *Ren*] helps others to realize themselves" (6.30). Kongzi says in 12.16, "The *junzi* helps others to realize their good qualities, rather than their bad. A petty person does just the opposite."[19] On a related note, Zengzi says in 12.24, "The *junzi* acquires friends by means of cultural refinement, and then relies upon his friends for support in becoming *Ren* ('humane')."

This is not to say that we cannot learn from those who are not good, for a real self-cultivationist seizes these opportunities for further reflection. Kongzi says in 4.17, "When you see someone who is worthy, concentrate upon becoming their equal; when you see someone who is unworthy, use this as an opportunity to look within yourself." Similarly, he says in 7.22, "When walking with two other people, I will always find a teacher among them. I pick out their good points and emulate them; I pick out their bad points and correct these things in myself."[20] Kongzi also thinks we should try to help those who are erring, but Kongzi's remarks about whom we should expend our efforts on are restricted only to those individuals who show a genuine desire to improve. In 15.8, he says, "If someone is open to what you have to say, but you do not speak to them, this is letting the person go to waste; if, however, someone is not open to what you have to say, but you speak to them anyway, this is letting your words go to waste. The wise person does not let people go to waste, but he also does not waste his words." Similarly, when Zigong asks Kongzi about friendship in 12.23, he replies, "Reprove your friend when dutifulness requires, but do so gently. If your words are not accepted then desist, lest you incur insult." This passage reflects a similar view to Kongzi's remarks concerning remonstration with one's parents in 4.18: "In serving your parents, you may gently remonstrate with them. However, once it becomes apparent that they have not taken your criticism to heart you should be respectful and not oppose them, and follow their lead diligently without resentment." The disposition that is cultivated in the context of one's relationship with one's parents serves as a basis for interacting with others. One learns virtues like patience and good judgment, and one also learns what real respect demands of us in a relationship.

The *Analects* also warns us about the dangers of becoming too closely involved with those who are not following the Way. In 8.13, Kongzi advises against entering a state that is endangered and against living in a state that is disordered. He goes on to say, "If the Way is being realized in the world then show yourself; if it is not, then go into reclusion."[21] Here Kongzi is concerned that individuals might be derailed in their efforts to follow the Way if they live in an environment in which no one else is committed to it. Similarly, in 15.40 he says, "Do not take counsel with those who follow a different Way." In 16.4 there is a discussion of beneficial and harmful friendships that clearly distinguishes between genuine friendships and deceptive people who may disguise themselves as friends: "Befriending the upright, those who are true to their word, or those of broad learning—these are the beneficial types of friendship. Befriending clever flatterers, skillful dissemblers, or the smoothly glib—these are the harmful types of friendship."

The idea that we gravitate toward those who are good is related to the traditional Chinese understanding of *de* 德 ("Virtue") that preceded Kongzi.[22] This idea is retained and quite prominent in the *Analects*. As David S. Nivison's influential study shows, an early form of *de* 德 is found on oracle bones and bronze vessels from the Shang dynasty (ca. twelfth century B.C.E.).[23] In these early uses, the character appears to be related to its cognate *de* 得 ("to get") phonetically, graphically, and semantically, in that one who has *de* 德 ("Virtue") has a hold on or "gets" others. Philip J. Ivanhoe has developed this line of argument, showing that *de* 德 ("Virtue") was a kind of power that accrued to and resided within individuals—especially rulers—who acted favorably toward the spirits or toward other people.[24] One who has Virtue receives the favor of the spirits and also the allegiance of other people. "Across the different meanings this character has, *de* 德 retains the sense of an inherent, spontaneously functioning power to affect others."[25]

In the *Analects*, a person's *de* ("Virtue") is his inherent power and natural effect on others, and *de* retains its ties to the ideal of rulership in this usage. In 2.1, Kongzi says, "One who rules through the power of *de* ('Virtue') is analogous to the Pole Star: it simply remains in its place and receives the homage of the myriad lesser stars." In 13.4, Kongzi says that the mere existence of a ruler who loves ritual propriety, rightness, and trustworthiness would "cause the common people throughout the world to bundle their children on their backs and seek him out." Both of these passages emphasize the sense in which the ruler with *de* attracts others, who are then inclined to respond to him as an exemplar, paying him homage. The tendency of others to be attracted to and respond in kind to the ruler is one reason why Kongzi says in 4.25, "Virtue is never solitary; it always has neighbors." The good ruler guides the people with Virtue and keeps them in line with the rites, ordering society with his virtuous example instead of with regulations and punishments (2.3).

The idea that a ruler leads the people with Virtue is found throughout the *Analects* in other discussions of rulership and also in discussions of the *junzi*'s influence. In 8.2, Kongzi says, "If the *junzi* is kind to his relatives, the common people will be inspired toward goodness; if he does not neglect his old acquaintances, the people will honor their obligations to others." Kongzi also maintains that when the ruler is correct, he does not even need to issue official orders—his will is put into effect immediately (13.6). Likewise, when a ruler is not correct, the people will not do what he says even if he issues official orders. In all of these passages we see the power that virtuous individuals have.[26] Even though *de* ("Virtue") is not explicitly referenced in these passages, the concept influences the descriptions of the remarkable influence that good rulers and *junzi* have over those around them.

It is evident even from this cursory review of some of the central themes in the *Analects* that the task of self-cultivation involves cultivating a particular posture toward other members of society. Kongzi maintains that through self-cultivation, one's dispositions are harmonized with one's roles in the family and community, and the larger society is characterized by a concern for the well-being of each of its members. The key to a harmoniously functioning society is not found in governmental policies and techniques. Rather, members of a society must cultivate dispositions like filiality in concert with practices such as following the rites in the appropriate way. Self-cultivation does not remain in the context of one's own immediate roles; the *Analects* indicates that it should have an outward movement. As we have seen, the concept of *de* ("Virtue") can help us understand why the fruits of self-cultivation are seen as spreading outward from one's own roles and relationships, having an impact on other members of society.

Kongzi and the Sense of Justice

Now that we have established the central theme of self-cultivation, it is time to turn our attention to whether those qualities that are associated with a sense of justice are discussed in the *Analects*. We have already seen that according to the view presented in the *Analects*, having the proper feelings toward others is an essential part of self-cultivation and that the cultivation of feelings in the context of filial relationships and practices such as the rites is believed to lead to the cultivation of feelings in wider settings. This account is mirrored in the description of *de* ("Virtue") and governing.

The *Analects* has a robust view of governing that reflects the important relationship between Virtue and the larger question of how to organize a harmoniously functioning society. *Analects* 2.20 and a series of passages in Book Twelve recount a series of exchanges between Kongzi and Ji Kangzi, the head of the most powerful of the three ruling families in the state of Lu. The exchanges are significant because we find Ji Kangzi—a powerful political figure of the time—seeking Kongzi's advice about how to be an effective ruler. In response to his question about how to get the people to be respectful, dutiful, and industrious, Kongzi says, "Oversee them with dignity, and the people will be respectful; oversee them with filiality and kindness, and the people will be dutiful; oversee them by raising up the accomplished and instructing those who are unable, and the people will be industrious" (2.20). In 12.17, Kongzi again advises Ji Kangzi that the most effective way to govern is to exemplify those qualities he wishes to see in the people: "If you set an example by being correct yourself, who will dare to be incorrect?" Similarly, in order to address the problem of stealing, Kongzi says, "If you could just get rid of your own excessive desires, the people would not steal even if you rewarded them for it" (12.18).

Here we see clearly the understanding of Virtue we have been discussing. Kongzi says the ruler will get back from the people the Virtue that he gives them. Perhaps the clearest formulation of this idea is in 12.19, where Ji Kangzi asks Kongzi, "If I were to execute those who lacked the Way in order to advance those who possessed the Way, how would that be?" Kongzi remains unshaken in his reply, saying, "In your governing, Sir, what need is there for executions? If you desire goodness, then the common people will be good. The Virtue of a *junzi* is like the wind, and the Virtue of a petty person is like the grass—when the wind moves over the grass, the grass is sure to bend." In this passage, it is not especially surprising that Kongzi disapproves of the idea of executing those who lack the Way, given his own calling to propagate the Way in a world that has strayed from it. Rather, he places the responsibility at the feet of the ruler, maintaining that it is fully possible for a good ruler to inspire goodness in the people. Here, it seems clear that Virtue is indeed a power one has to affect others.

Discussions of governing in the *Analects* consistently emphasize the importance of the posture a ruler takes toward the people. In 12.7, Zigong asks about governing and Kongzi tells him, "Simply make sure there is sufficient food, sufficient armaments, and that you have the confidence of the common people." Zigong then presses Kongzi to prioritize these three things, and Kongzi says he would first sacrifice the armaments, and then the food, because "death has always been with us, but a state cannot stand once it has lost the confidence of the people." Here Kongzi prizes the relationship a ruler has with his people and the posture he takes toward them over material gain or military success.

However, we should not think that questions of fair distribution are considered unimportant. In 16.1, Kongzi says that good rulers

> are not concerned [so much] about poverty, but about unequal distribution. If wealth is equally distributed, there should be no poverty . . . and if your people are content, there should be no instability. This being the case, if those who are distant will not submit, then enhance your culture and Virtue in order to attract them. Once you have attracted them, make them content.[27]

This passage reflects a deep interest in the quality of life members of society have and recognizes how the distribution of wealth contributes to that quality. The term *jun* 均 means even, equal, adjusted, or uniform, and it carries the sense of keeping in order or in balance and dividing equitably, evenly, or impartially.[28] This is the clearest passage where Kongzi indicates how he thinks society should be ordered with respect to questions of fair distribution, and although this passage does not formulate a policy or theory concerning distribution, it is important to note the concern that is shown with questions of fairness in relation to distribution here, as well as the fact that this concern suggests a sense of justice. The larger worry Kongzi expresses in this passage is that distributive inequalities can lead to poverty when there is not enough to go around. He exhibits a high degree of confidence that all of the people can be provided for, so long as the ruler does not become fixated on immediate problems like poverty. Instead, a ruler or government must look for the source of the poverty in order to find a solution to it, and distributive justice is a part of that process.

It is not the case, then, that the *Analects* simply does not show a concern with basic matters such as the distribution of food and taxation, and 16.1 is not the only passage where this concern is apparent. In 12.9, Duke Ai expresses his concern about the poor harvest and his inability to meet his own needs. When Master You suggests that he try taxing the people by the traditional ten percent, Duke Ai says, "I am currently taxing them twenty percent, and even so I cannot satisfy my needs. How could reducing the tax to ten percent help?" Master You then replies, "If the common people's needs are satisfied, how can their ruler be lacking? If the common people's needs are not satisfied, how can their ruler be content?"[29] A good ruler considers the common people's needs as if they are his own. *Analects* 12.11 can be seen as providing additional explication of how this process works. Duke Jing asks Kongzi about governing, and he replies, "Let the ruler be a ruler, let the ministers be ministers, let the fathers be fathers, and the sons, sons."[30] The Duke, seeing what Kongzi meant, then said, "Well put! Certainly if the ruler is not a ruler, the ministers not ministers, the fathers not fathers, and the sons not sons, even if there is sufficient grain, will I ever get to eat it?" In 1.5, Kongzi again emphasizes the importance of being aware of role-specific duties, saying that in order to guide a state of 1,000 chariots, a leader must be respectful in his handling of affairs and display trustworthiness while being frugal in his expenditures and cherishing others. Finally, Kongzi says that one must employ the common people only at the proper times, meaning that the use of peasant farmers in public works projects should be timed so that it will not interfere with their livelihood. A ruler must, for example, pay attention to the times of planting and harvest and keep in mind the demands on the time of those who work the land.

Trustworthiness (*xin* 信) is mentioned throughout the text as a quality of the cultivated person and as an important feature of a harmoniously functioning society. The basis of any society is cooperation, and trust is one of the primary factors that make cooperation possible. When members of society trust one another, things are both more efficient and more satisfying. Julia Tao has explored the importance of trust (*xin*) in the political philosophy of the *Analects*. Tao writes,

> What motivates and sustains the following of *li* ["procedures"] and *de* ["Virtue"] in the making of a covenant is mutual trust that others will share the same concern to achieve the common good, the same respect for mutual interests, and the same commitment to good faith (*xin*) or sincerity. The contemporary significance of the traditional Chinese approach to politics is that it reminds us that it is this spirit or value of sincerity shared by citizens of a polity that makes political decisions binding. . . . In the absence of the spirit of sincerity or *xin*, there is no ground for any trust in the reciprocal good faith of others. . . .[31]

Indeed, as we will see below, an important part of the ability to judge a situation fairly is one's ability to perceive untrustworthiness in others (14.31). The cultivated person not only exemplifies qualities like trustworthiness but also has a heightened awareness of these qualities in others, which is of course one way in which individuals continually cultivate virtues like trustworthiness.

One of the things that Tao's discussion of trust highlights is that according to the *Analects*, people have good reasons to put their trust in one another and in their leaders because they share a concern for the common good. In his work *Centrality and Commonality: An Essay on Confucian Religiousness*, Tu Weiming discusses the idea of society as a "fiduciary community," which he contrasts with the idea of society as an "adversary system."[32] He writes that

> politics seeks not just to achieve a high level of social solidarity but also to lay the foundation of a fiduciary community. . . . According to this line of thinking, a person without a strong moral commitment can never become a truly exemplary teacher and exert a long-lasting influence upon society; a political system without a firm ethical basis can hardly provide creative leadership for the establishment of a durable pattern of social intercourse.[33]

Tu's discussion of the idea of trust within Confucian political society appears to make use of a distinction that is made in theological accounts of trust in God. A fiduciary community is a kind of moral community that is distinct from mere law and order by virtue of the fact that individuals put their trust in God strictly as an act of faith. They are not thought to have *reasons* for this commitment. Theologians traditionally have distinguished between this Protestant idea of *fiducia* and the Catholic idea of *assensus*.

Whereas *fiducia* is a commitment based strictly on faith, *assensus* requires reason's assent to evidence and argument.

Tu's understanding of Confucian political society as a community of trust offers insight into a variety of important features of Confucianism, and we might extend this view even further. Although Tu uses *fiducia* as a way of describing the Confucian idea of trust, the idea of *assensus* is in many respects closer to the view that is presented in the *Analects*.[34] On this view, members of society are not asked to put their trust in things unseen based on faith alone; rather, they have good reasons for trusting and caring for others, and their feelings of mutual trust grow out of feelings and dispositions that have been grounded on family relationships in which they have experienced reciprocity and filial love. Unlike *fiducia*, which is based on faith alone, people have reasons to trust one another in this sort of society. Like *assensus*, which requires individuals to have *reasons* for assenting to views that point toward God, members of a Confucian society have something on which to ground their commitment to other members of society.

The idea of trust within a political society in the *Analects* is partly revealed through discussions of roles and practical matters like the distribution of food. In several passages Kongzi indicates that a society in which everyone's needs are met involves something much deeper than governmental policies that are designed to ensure enough grain for everyone. If all do not serve conscientiously in their roles as rulers, ministers, fathers, and sons, the grain will never be distributed properly. It is worth noting, too, that the ruler's role with respect to the people is grouped together with family responsibilities in 12.11. The *Analects* seems to present the view that rulers must consider their responsibilities to the people on the analogy of parental responsibilities. Indeed, if we consider Duke Ai's difficulties in 12.9, we can easily see that if children's needs are lacking, their parents should not be content. The expectation that rulers should feel for their people in ways that are *to some degree* analogous to how parents feel for their children is significant because it suggests that even the ruler, who cannot possibly know each person in his state personally, has special feelings for them.

The *Analects* emphasizes the importance of all people, and not just rulers, cultivating caring feelings for other members of society. Kongzi says in 1.6, "A young person should be filial when at home and when going out, respectful of his elders. Conscientious and trustworthy, he should care widely for the multitudes but have affection for those who are *Ren* ('humane')."[35] Here, we should notice that Kongzi first describes filiality at home; second, respect for elders in the community; and third, care for

others who are not in one's immediate circle. Zhu Xi notes that the connotations here are of caring widely, as in the rush or overflow of water. Legge
follows Zhu Xi's reading and translates this line as "He should overflow in
love to all."[36] For Kongzi, one who cultivates filiality and respect in one's
relationships will not have an impoverishment of caring feelings for others but, to the contrary, will have a strong, almost unstoppable, tendency
toward such feelings and actions.

Other passages emphasize the cultivation of one's ability to care for "the
multitudes," or members of society who are further removed from one's
own circumstances. Kongzi tells us in 1.16 to be concerned about not knowing others instead of worrying about being known by others, a statement
that reflects a concern with the ability to have moral feelings for others.
In 12.22, Kongzi is asked about *Ren* (humaneness), and he admonishes his
interlocutor to "Care for others," and "Know others." In 6.30, Zigong asks
Kongzi, "If there were one able to broadly extend his benevolence to the
common people and his assistance to the multitudes, what would you make
of him? Could we call him *Ren* ('humane')?"[37] Kongzi responds by telling
Zigong that such a person could be considered more than *Ren*: "Such a
person is surely a sage." This response reflects a concern with extending
one's moral feelings beyond one's own family and community. The *Analects*
also gives us specific examples of people who have their priorities in order,
which for Kongzi concerns the extent to which, in addition to avoiding
an obsession with material goods and showing reverence and diligence in
one's religious practices, one cares about the multitudes. An example is
seen in Kongzi's praise of sage-king Yu in 8:21: "He subsisted on meager
food and drink, and yet showed the utmost filiality in his offerings to the
spirits. His ordinary clothes were poor, but his ceremonial headdress and
cap were of utmost beauty. He lived in the humblest of dwellings, expend-
ing all of his strength on the construction of drainage ditches and canals. I
can find no fault with Yu."[38] In the latter part of this passage, Kongzi refers
to Yu's legendary devotion to taming the floodwaters and making China
habitable for people. One of the reasons why Kongzi finds no fault with Yu
is that he put the needs of the people over his own personal needs.

In 12.5, we find a similar attitude, where Zixia says that the *junzi* ("exemplary person") is respectful to others and observes the rites properly,
and "in this way, everyone within the Four Seas is his brother."[39] In 8.6,
we are told that the *junzi* is someone who can be entrusted both with the
care of a young orphan *and* the command of a large state, and that he
remains unshaken in the midst of all of these challenges. This passage is
interesting because it emphasizes that the *junzi* is a person of enormous

sensitivity—the kind of sensitivity required to care for a young orphan—
and who also has the rare ability to lead a large group of people. Additionally, we learn from 12.5 and 8.6 that the *junzi* treats others as though they
were his family.[40] Of course, when the *Analects* says that a cultivated person
thinks of everyone as his brother or could be entrusted with the care of a
young orphan, it does not mean that he thinks of everyone in *exactly* the
same way as a brother or as his own children. Rather, a cultivated person
feels a moral responsibility toward others. Cultivated individuals are also
able to respond appropriately to the demands of different people. They
have certain emotional responses to other human beings, and these are
cultivated responses that begin with and are clearly seen in our responses
to family members.

Thus we see in the text an emphasis on caring for other members of
society. This is one of the ideas seen in discussions of *shu* 恕 ("reciprocity"). A person who cultivates a sense of reciprocity regularly employs the
principle of reversibility, imagining herself in the place of others as a way
of sympathetically understanding and responding to them. In 12.2, Kongzi
responds to a question about *Ren* ("humaneness") by saying, "When in
public, conduct yourself as though you were hosting an important guest;
when managing the common people, conduct yourself as though you were
in charge of a great sacrifice. Do not do to others, what you do not want
done to yourself. In this way, you will encounter no resentment in the state
or in the family."[41] The teaching that one should not do to others what one
does not want done to oneself is repeated in 5.12, and in 15.24 Kongzi uses
it to define *shu*.

The idea of *shu* ("reciprocity") and the principle of reversibility it specifies are important because we are not always initially inclined to feel for the
plights of those who are far removed from us. However, Kongzi thinks all
humans possess the capacity to feel for others, and part of the process of
self-cultivation as it is described in the *Analects* is exercising this capacity
regularly so that we become more inclined to feel for others in this way.
Now I do not mean to say that one who imagines herself in the place of
others and works at sympathetically understanding their situations will *ap-
prove* of the actions others perform. It is important to see that one can feel
for others and respond in a way that reflects sympathetic understanding
and a sense of reciprocity and still have a keen sense of rightness that informs and accompanies one's feelings for others. There are two dimensions
of this sense of rightness. If a hurricane devastated an especially poor area
of a city where citizens were unable to evacuate because they did not have
transportation, other citizens would feel for them because they were disad-

vantaged by their position in society, which they did not choose. Questions would be raised about why the government failed to assist these citizens during the evacuation process, and other citizens would express outrage at the fact that they were not given the assistance they needed. One's sympathetic understanding for these individuals, then, would be tied to the view that they suffered an injustice and thus to a sense that they were wronged. On the other hand, one might still disapprove of desperate actions these citizens took in response to the situation they found themselves in (e.g., stealing, looting). Disapproving of certain kinds of actions because they wrong others and because they conflict with one's obligations as a member of society comes from a moral sense.

The concept of *yi* 義 ("rightness") is one of several ideas that express this sort of concern in the *Analects*, and the best way to understand this idea is to examine the passages where it is discussed.[42] In the first set of passages I want to examine, *yi* is paired with the opposing vice of an excessive concern for profit (*li* 利). *Li* 利 indicates all of the things that provide material wealth, and the Confucians use it primarily in a negative sense. In passages where it is paired with *yi*, we can see clearly that even in an ethical tradition that is context-sensitive, some things—such as an excessive concern for profit or material wealth—are always considered wrong.[43] In 4.16, Kongzi says, "The *junzi* is conversant with *yi* 義, whereas the petty person is conversant with profit (*li* 利)."[44] In 14.12, he says that when complete persons see an opportunity for profit, they think of *yi* (*jian li si yi* 見利思義). Similarly, in 16.10 Kongzi says that when the *junzi* sees an opportunity for gain (*de* 得), he thinks of *yi* (*jian de si yi* 見得思義).[45] In each of these passages *yi* is contrasted with the desire for profit or material gain. Furthermore, when virtuous people see an opportunity for profit or gain, they think of *yi*. This claim is especially significant, because it indicates that an appreciation for *yi* is what keeps good people from simply taking whatever they can get. So a sense of *yi* is what keeps people from stealing or cheating, or from taking more than they need. Here *yi* reflects a sense of rightness, fairness, and honesty. *Analects* 1.13 tells us that "trustworthiness comes close to *yi*, in that your word can be counted on," which reinforces the connotations of honesty seen here.

In these passages, *yi* keeps people from becoming excessively concerned with material wealth, from becoming greedy or taking more than their fair share. Perhaps most accurately, then, in these passages *yi* seems to mean a sense of fairness, although it does not concern fairness in the sense of a disposition to adhere to the law or in regard to distribution and retribution. Rather, it means something more like fair-mindedness or the tendency to make balanced judgments about persons or situations. This understanding of *yi* is also seen in 4.10, where having a sense of *yi* is contrasted with being partial and holding grudges. Kongzi says, "In the world, the *junzi* is not for or against anything. What is *yi—this* is what he accords with."[46] The *junzi* does not simply side with someone he is partial to, or hold a grudge against someone he does not like. Rather, he judges a situation based on *yi*. This passage resonates with the passages above, where *yi* indicates a sense of fairness and good judgment.

The second set of passages I want to consider relate *yi* to public service. In 17.23, Kongzi is asked whether the *junzi* esteems courage, and he says, "The *junzi* esteems *yi* above all else. A *junzi* who has courage but lacks *yi* will create chaos (*luan* 亂); a petty person who has courage but lacks *yi* will commit robbery (*dao* 盜)."[47] To begin with, Kongzi distinguishes between esteeming courage (*shang yong* 尚勇) and esteeming *yi* above all else (*yi zhi wei shang* 義之為上). The term meaning "to esteem" or "to place a high value on" (*shang* 尚) here is a cognate of the term used for "the highest" (*shang* 上), indicating that Kongzi draws an important distinction between placing a high value on courage and placing the *highest* value on *yi*. The idea here is that too much courage and too little *yi* results in chaos or political disorder in the *junzi*'s case, whereas in the case of petty persons it results in their becoming thieves. The latter case is close to the passages we saw before, where *yi* carries a sense of fairness that keeps one from pursuing profit and material gain. The former case, however, is interesting because it indicates that the *junzi*, as an exemplar and sometimes as a ruler, can throw a state into utter disarray if he doesn't value *yi* above all, but still places a high value on courage. One must understand that *yi* takes priority over courage and must guide, inform, and shape it.

In 5.16, Kongzi describes the exemplary rulership of Zichan, a minister from the state of Zheng, saying that "[I]n the way he cared for the common people, he displayed benevolence; and in the way he employed the people, he displayed *yi*." Here Kongzi indicates that Zichan's actions showed that he had a sense of *yi*, and *yi* here is used to characterize the way he employed the people. Based on the passages we have already examined, we can conclude that he did not overtax them or lead them into needless conflicts with other states. He displayed a sense of honesty and fairness, genuinely seeming to have the well-being of the people in mind. This sense of *yi* bears an interesting relationship to 18.7, where Zilu says,

To avoid public service is to be without a sense of what is *yi*. Proper relations between elders and juniors cannot be discarded—how, then, can one discard the ruler's and minister's *yi*? To do so is to wish to keep one's hands from getting dirty at the expense of throwing the great social order into chaos. The *junzi* takes office and does what is *yi*, even though he already knows that the Way will not be followed.[48]

Here *yi* is again credited with the *junzi*'s sense of political responsibility. In both 12.10 and 18.7, *yi* is in good part responsible for the *junzi*'s diligent fulfillment of his political role and his sense of fairness with respect to the needs of the people.

The virtue of fair-mindedness that is seen in one who has a sense of *yi* is reinforced in a number of other discussions in the *Analects*. Kongzi tells us in 2.14 that the *junzi* associates openly with others (*zhou* 周) and is not partial (*bu bi* 不比), whereas the petty person is. This passage reinforces a claim we have already seen with respect to *yi*—the avoidance of judging situations based on personal biases or grudges. The *junzi* does not rely on partisan connections to get things done. Rather, he associates with different kinds of people, examining each person's moral character for himself according to the standard provided by the Way. The He Yan commentary emphasizes the close connection between the virtues of conscientiousness (*zhong* 忠), trustworthiness (*xin* 信), and *zhou*.[49] Literally, "associating openly" (*zhou* 周) implies wide association and keeping the public good in mind. Slingerland notes that some commentators take this to imply that the *junzi* understands the broad, overarching vision that is the Way and does not become mired down in trivial details or personal biases.[50] Here it is important to recognize that when we talk about one's ability to set aside grudges or biases and judge a person or a situation on its own merits, we are describing the judicial virtues. We normally say that such a person has a well-developed sense of justice or that she is fair-minded. We might also praise her in a more general sense, but it seems that we are really pointing to a spirit of fairness and good judgment, and, indeed, these are among the capacities we associate with a sense of justice.

Earlier in this chapter we looked briefly at 4.11 with its emphasis on profit. In the second half of this passage, Kongzi indicates that the *junzi* thinks about punishments, whereas the petty person thinks about exemptions or personal favors that will prevent him from being punished if he is caught. Now this passage is interesting because it requires us to interpret what it means for the *junzi* to "cherish [the fairness associated with] punishments" (*huan xing* 懽刑). It seems clear from the passages we have seen about governing, such as 12.19, wherein Kongzi indicates his view that the *junzi* leads by virtue *instead of* by punishments, that he does not mean that the *junzi* literally cherishes—in the sense of *enjoys*—punishments. Zhu Xi maintains that this passage concerns the *junzi*'s public, impartial orientation as opposed to the petty person's interest in personal gain at any cost.[51] On this reading, what Kongzi means when he says the *junzi* "cherishes punishments" is that the *junzi* thinks about the importance of a judicial system that judges people fairly and punishes people when punishment is called for, protecting other members of society and the values they uphold. Given the contrast with the petty person's concern for exemptions or favors in this passage, we can also conclude that the *junzi* cares about a fair trial and officials who do not forgive transgressions because they owe someone a favor. The *junzi* realizes that a good society relies on its members' having and acting on a sense of justice—a moral sense that calls them to act in a spirit of fairness rather than on personal interests, biases, or grudges.

The seriousness with which Kongzi takes those who do not judge situations fairly is evident in 15.14. He criticizes Zang Wenzhong, a former minister in Lu, for refusing to recognize a virtuous minister, saying that Zang failed to give a person of exceptional moral character a position. Here he makes clear that intentionally denying a qualified person the position he deserves is reprehensible. In Kongzi's view, Zang took what one person had rightfully earned and gave it to someone else. Kongzi also criticizes Zang's lack of good judgment in 5.18, and what is interesting about his criticism of Zang in this particular area is that Zang Wenzhong was formerly the minister of justice in Lu.[52] Thus, Kongzi's criticism may be indicative of his view that Zang was especially unfit for his official position. In all of these passages, Kongzi emphasizes the need for members of society to cultivate the ability to judge a situation fairly, and he does not hesitate to criticize someone who fails to do so. He expresses disapproval of situations in which cases are judged in a biased manner or where someone is denied the position he has rightfully earned. Kongzi is not content to let these kinds of situations pass by so long as things seem to be functioning smoothly, because he is concerned for those who are treated unfairly and also for the moral character of those who treat them unfairly.

Among the passages that even more obviously reflect a sense of justice in the *Analects* are those that explicitly mention the justice system. In 19.19, Zengzi says, "When you uncover the truth in a criminal case, proceed with sorrow and compassion. Do not be pleased with yourself." Here, one of Kongzi's students describes the feelings individuals should experience upon learning of and examining a case of injustice. They should feel sorrow and compassion upon seeing that there has been injustice, rather than be elated at their own ability to discover the truth. These feelings should outweigh anyone's desire for fame or success.

As with a number of other ideas in the *Analects*, Kongzi's own behavior illustrates this aspect of a sense of justice. In 5.1, we are told that Kongzi gave his daughter in marriage to Gongye Chang, a man who had been wrongly imprisoned for a crime: "The Master said of Gongye Chang, 'He deserves a wife. Although he was bound and imprisoned, he was guilty of no crime.'" The fact that Kongzi not only declares Gongye Chang's innocence but also gives his daughter to him in marriage is significant because of the social stigma that was attached to former criminals in ancient China. At times, criminals were even marked physically when they were found guilty, sometimes in the form of tattoos. In such circumstances, one who was wrongly convicted could not simply be "cleared" and go on to live as he previously did. By accepting someone who was wrongly imprisoned as his son-in-law, Kongzi makes a powerful statement about the priority of justice over social stigmas. Kongzi is surely aware that his daughter, and eventually his grandchildren, may be stigmatized. However, he values Gongye Chang's innocence and the justice that is exemplified in his being cleared and going on with his life *over and above* the difficulties that doing so may cause his family. This passage shows that Kongzi cares more about Gongye Chang's being treated fairly than social stigmas.[53]

The appreciation for justice in this passage, and in the other passages discussed above, concerns the fact that having a sense of justice involves judging a situation for oneself and not simply following one's biases, grudges, or the erroneous judgments of others. Although we have already discussed the concern to combat biases or grudges in the *Analects*, the issue of not simply going along with the judgments of others is significant because on an initial reading of the *Analects*, one might mistakenly think that harmony is valued above all else. But harmony as a value does not necessarily mean agreeing with everyone else in order to keep the peace. Although there are instances in which it is certainly easier to go along with the judgments of others, Kongzi does not advocate doing so, nor does he think this sort of response achieves harmony. In 13.23, Kongzi says, "The *junzi* harmonizes (*he* 和) and does not merely agree (*tong* 同). The petty person agrees, but he does not harmonize." This passage shows Kongzi's awareness that an unwillingness to stand up and raise objections to the unfair judgments of others does not produce a harmoniously functioning society in the long run, even though it may temporarily prevent a conflict.

The *Analects* does not call for us to defer continually to others just to keep the peace. To the contrary, in 15.28 Kongzi says, "When the multitude hate a person, you must examine them and judge them for yourself. The same holds true for someone whom the multitude love." Kongzi thinks a good society requires its citizens to judge situations in a fair and balanced way, even when their judgment goes against the majority. This view is also significant because it shows that Kongzi does not think we should simply favor those to whom we are closest; rather, we must judge a situation apart from any biases or grudges we may have for or against those who are involved.

On this note one might argue that on Kongzi's view, it is not so much that harmony is not still the ultimate goal but rather that citizens' having good judgment is conducive to harmony. On this view, judging a situation fairly is the way to achieve the end of a harmonious society. The problem, however, is that it simply does not seem to be the case that judging situations in a fair and balanced manner and defending one's judgments against the objections of others always *is* a means to harmony, unless one thinks of harmony as a long-term goal that can be achieved only by challenging norms and standards and encouraging certain virtues in members of society despite their resistance to it. The point, though, is that harmony in these cases is not achieved immediately. As we have seen, *in spite of* the social stigma, Kongzi gives his daughter in marriage to someone who was convicted of a crime. In 15.28 he tells us to judge a person's character for ourselves *in spite of* the fact that others already hate them or love them. In these cases he calls us to go against the grain, rather than to accede to the judgments of others. This implies that he values fairness and good judgment even when they do not help to preserve harmony. Indeed, harmony could be attained fairly easily in some cases simply by going along with the judgment of the majority. But what Kongzi indicates in these passages is that he thinks it is wrong to sacrifice one person for the sake of harmony. Or, perhaps more accurately, if one person's well-being is sacrificed in the name of preserving harmony among the majority, then the state of affairs is not really harmonious at all. Kongzi thinks it is more important to act fairly, treating people as they deserve based on their innocence or guilt. We should base our judgments on what people have actually done and who they really are.

It seems clear that in these cases, Kongzi advocates acting on one's own sense of what is right and fair as an alternative to going along with the court of public opinion. These passages emphasize one's ability to perceive situations accurately and clearly. In 14.31 Kongzi says, "Not anticipating betrayal, nor expecting untrustworthiness, yet still being the first to perceive it—this is a worthy person indeed." This passage calls us to set aside our preconceived ideas and expectations in order to give others a fair hearing, but it also speaks of a certain kind of perceptiveness. A cultivated person is able to see people and situations for what they really are. They see things in a fair and balanced manner. In 12.20 Kongzi notes that cultivated persons carefully examine the words and demeanor of others and always take the interests of their inferiors into account when considering matters, regardless of whether they are serving the state or a noble family. Interestingly, he mentions two qualities together here: first, the ability to examine carefully the conduct of others and judge it fairly, and, second, the ability to consider one's inferiors rather than simply proceed with the interests of one's superiors, or oneself, in mind.

In 4.5, too, Kongzi acknowledges the importance of considering the situation of the least advantaged members of society, while acknowledging that we should notice more than just one's economic status. He says,

> Wealth and honors are things that all people desire, but unless they are acquired by following the Way they are not worth having. Poverty and disgrace are things that all people hate, and yet unless they are avoided by following the Way they are not worth avoiding. If the *junzi* abandons *Ren* ("humaneness"), how can he merit the name? The *junzi* does not go against *Ren* even for the amount of time required to finish a meal. Even in times of urgency or distress, he necessarily accords with it.[54]

In this passage, Kongzi presents the Way not simply as an end worth having but as the right way of doing things. He is most interested in the *way* in which poverty is avoided, which resonates with his remark in 16.1 that good rulers "are not concerned [so much] about poverty, but about unequal distribution. If wealth is equally distributed, there should be no poverty." These remarks support the overall view that the *Analects* does not articulate a picture that is focused on achieving certain ends such as eliminating poverty at any cost. Rather, Kongzi thinks there is a specific way in which poverty must be eliminated. As we saw earlier, the concern with unequal distribution in 16.1 reflects a larger concern seen in other passages that there may not be enough to go around if some individuals have a large share of the resources. This is why it is deemed appropriate in places like 6.4 to offer assistance to some but not others; here, Kongzi makes clear that the *junzi* provides for the needy but does not help the rich to become richer. However, Kongzi says that the end of making sure everyone is provided for must be achieved in the right way, namely in a way that is *Ren* ("humane"). In 8.10 Kongzi says that a person who is fond of courage but who despises poverty will become rebellious, which similarly indicates that

there is a right way and a wrong way to go about addressing the problem
of poverty. He even goes so far as to say that poverty is not worth avoiding
unless it is avoided by following the Way (4.5). If poverty is not eliminated
in the right way, then the elimination of poverty is not an end worth having, in Kongzi's view. These remarks seem to be consistent with the view
we have been discussing—that no individual should be sacrificed in the
name of the greater good.

In 8.13 Kongzi says,

> Be sincerely trustworthy and love learning, and hold fast to the good Way
> until death. Do not enter a state that is endangered, and do not reside in a
> state that is disordered. If the Way is being realized in the world then show
> yourself; if it is not, then go into reclusion. In a state that has the Way, to
> be poor and of low status is a cause for shame; in a state that is without the
> Way, to be wealthy and honored is equally a cause for shame.

Several things should be noticed here. First, Kongzi speaks of following
the Way in a fairly literal sense. It is clear that following the Way means
avoiding those places where one does not see the Way in practice. Second,
Kongzi is concerned about good people being derailed when they are surrounded by corruption and a lack of virtue. This idea can help us to understand 5.2, where Kongzi gives his niece to Nan Rong in marriage after
noting that when the state possesses the Way, Nan will not be dismissed
from office and when the state is without the Way he will avoid punishment or execution.[55] Kongzi thinks highly of Nan, and as such he believes
that when the state is following the Way, Nan will continue to hold office,
but when the Way is no longer followed, he will extricate himself from a
prominent position and thus will not become involved in corruption or
find himself unjustly accused. Kongzi's instruction in 8.13 indicates that
withdrawing from those places where the Way is not in practice is the right
thing to do, at least for most of us.[56]

Kongzi also remarks on poverty and wealth in 8.13, saying that being
poor in a state that has the Way is a cause for shame, and being wealthy in
a state that is without the Way is a cause for shame. The idea here is that in
a good state, virtuous persons will rise to positions of authority, and they
should pursue and accept these positions willingly when a state has the
Way. The implication also seems to be that those who live in obscurity or
in low positions are either virtuous persons who are not fulfilling their responsibilities, or they are persons who are not virtuous. Thus it seems that
on Kongzi's view, criminals suffer poverty as a result of their own actions
in a state that has the Way. The latter part of this remark indicates that only

those who are corrupt will be prosperous in a state that lacks the Way. In an ideal state, then, no one suffers from poverty unjustly.

In 14.9 and 14.10 we find an interesting illustration of the idea of just poverty. The latter part of 14.9 mentions the story of Guan Zhong, a seventh-century B.C.E. statesman and the leader of the Bo clan, who evidently committed a crime. When Kongzi is asked about Guan Zhong, he says that Guan Zhong "seized the city of Pian, with its three hundred families, from the head of the Bo clan, who was reduced to the most humble circumstances and yet did not utter a single word of resentment to the end of his life."[57] The passage refers to the fact that Guan Zhong seized the Bo family fiefdom as punishment for a crime committed by the leader of the family. In 14.10, Kongzi says, "It is difficult to be poor and still free of resentment, but relatively easy to be rich without being arrogant." If we read 14.9 and 14.10 together, as some commentators do, then 14.10 seems to praise the head of the Bo family for accepting his punishment—poverty— without resentment.[58] On this reading, 14.10 commends the leader of the Bo family for accepting his punishment without resentfulness, because it is hard to avoid feeling resentful when you are reduced to abject poverty, even when one legitimately is being punished for a crime. In relation to 8.13, it seems that the state has the Way in this case, because those who are reduced to poverty here are those who are guilty of a crime.

There is, however, an additional complexity, because 14.10 also seems to reprimand Guan Zhong, who was wealthy and whom Kongzi criticizes in *Analects* 3.22 for living lavishly and for ritual improprieties.[59] When we read 14.10 as the last line of 14.9, we must remember that the original question was about Guan Zhong's character. So, when Kongzi says that it is easy to be rich without being arrogant, this comment seems to be about Guan, who we know tended to flaunt his wealth. On this reading, 14.10 is an especially harsh critique of Guan Zhong, because he first points out how honorable the Bo family was in the midst of abject poverty, and then he goes on to say that Guan did not even try to cultivate himself. Indeed, when we read 14.9 and 14.10 together, the text seems to praise the head of the Bo family above Guan Zhong.

Regardless of whether it is considered in relation to 14.9, in 14.10 Kongzi calls our attention to how difficult the task of self-cultivation is, and it is a passage that is worthy of careful examination because it shows that Kongzi was acutely aware of how hard it is to be poor. In his commentary to 14.10, He Yan says, "Dwelling in poverty is difficult, and enjoying wealth is easy—this is the constant nature of human beings. However, people should work diligently at difficult things, and yet not grow careless with regard to things that are easy."[60] Legge notices that in 14.10 Kongzi remarks about self-cultivation when he compares the level of difficulty involved in a poor person's avoiding resentfulness with a rich person's avoiding arrogance. In fact, he notes a relationship between what Kongzi says in 14.10 and *Analects* 1.15.[61] In 1.15, Zigong says, "Poor without being obsequious, rich without being arrogant—what would you say about someone like that?" Kongzi replies, "That is acceptable, but it is still not as good as being poor and yet joyful, rich and yet loving ritual." Zigong goes on to quote the passage from the *Book of Odes* concerning self-cultivation that we examined earlier: "As if cut, as if polished; As if carved, as if ground." By linking these passages, Legge seems to be pointing out that 1.15 is an appropriate remark to consider in relation to Guan Zhong, because Kongzi says it is better to be rich and love ritual than to be rich and not arrogant, and in 3.22 Kongzi criticizes Guan Zhong for being rich and not understanding ritual.

One of the things this passage shows us is just how seriously Kongzi takes being a self-cultivationist. Despite the transgressions of the leader of the Bo clan, he is praiseworthy because he works at not developing resentful feelings about his punishment, whereas Guan Zhong is not as admirable for Kongzi because he lives in luxury but does not work to avoid arrogance. From a self-cultivationist point of view, avoiding arrogance in the midst of wealth is a relatively easy task compared with avoiding resentfulness in the midst of poverty. What matters most about Guan Zhong and the leader of the Bo clan is not their past transgressions but what they do with their lives in the present and whether they work at being virtuous in the midst of the very different circumstances they face.

We can be fairly certain, then, that Kongzi was aware of the different levels of difficulty involved in cultivating different virtues under very different circumstances. In general, Kongzi's judgment is that it is harder to avoid feeling resentment when one is poor—even when one must endure poverty as the direct result of having committed a crime—than it is to work at avoiding arrogance when one is wealthy. Further, if Kongzi has the Bo family in mind when he says this, then it is interesting that he says it is difficult to be *poor* and still free of resentment, instead of saying that it is difficult to be *punished for one's crime by being reduced to poverty* and still free of resentment. Thus, he emphasizes one's economic position, as opposed to how one attained that position, as the critical factor in deciding whether it will be difficult or easy to cultivate a good disposition. Kongzi does not remark on how Guan Zhong attained his wealth but says only that it is easy to be wealthy and not arrogant. Kongzi may be referring to the fact that wealthy people can take active steps to avoid arrogance, like involving themselves in activities that keep them in touch with the needs of others and allow them to express and reinforce their sense of responsibility to others, which is certainly what Kongzi expected of rulers. In contrast, poor people generally do not have the same number of options, or the luxury of time, that wealthy people have, which can make working on their disposition in certain ways much more difficult.[62]

Although these passages highlight Kongzi's continual emphasis on self-cultivation, they also show that Kongzi does not think a society that has the Way decides poverty or wealth arbitrarily. Indeed, the *Analects* repeatedly indicates that arbitrariness is not a good thing. In 9.4, Kongzi is said to have never made foregone conclusions or arbitrary predeterminations, and he was not rigid or selfish. These are all qualities of a person with the ability to judge a situation fairly. The He Yan commentary suggests that according to this passage, Kongzi took the Way as his standard, as opposed to simply relying on personal opinion (*yi* 意).[63] In this case, arbitrariness arises from valuing one's personal opinion over the Way, because, like flipping a coin or following whatever norm happens to be accepted in a given place or time, one's personal opinion does not involve judging situations according to a well-established standard. The Way, in contrast, specifies a reliable standard that is to be met when judging situations. In other places, too, the *Analects* takes a clear stance against arbitrariness and carelessness, which is significant in relation to justice because principles of justice are a codified attempt to ensure that decisions about a society's organization are not arbitrary.

Within the context of the larger ethical vision of society presented in the *Analects*, the passages I have discussed in this section reveal an appreciation for a basic sense of justice. From our examination of *shu* 恕 ("reciprocity"), we can see the manner in which a morally cultivated person acts on a genuine concern for all members of society, based on her ability to imagine herself in another's place. In 6.30, we see that being able to imagine oneself in another's place is integrally tied to the concept of *Ren* 仁 ("humaneness"): "Desiring to take his stand, one who is *Ren* helps others to take their stand; wanting to realize himself, he helps others to realize themselves. Being able to take what is near at hand as an analogy could perhaps be called the method of *Ren*." We have seen that cultivated persons, for Kongzi, rely on an internal moral sense instead of social prejudice when they judge a situation. The *Analects* also makes clear that the exemplary person is interested not in personal profit but in *de* 德 ("Virtue") and *yi* 義 ("rightness"). This view is evidenced further by the fact that the exemplary person aids the needy but does not help the rich to become richer.

Additionally, we have seen that a good leader is discontent when his people are in need. His sole concern is their welfare and not his own personal profit. In 12.20 Kongzi tells us that the accomplished person "examines other people's words and observes their demeanor, and always takes the interests of his inferiors into account when considering something—no matter whether serving the state or a noble family." These themes in the *Analects* reveal an interest not only in the well-being of all members of society but also in their well-being with respect to a certain range of issues that we would call basic questions of social justice. The discussion of ideas like *yi* ("rightness"), *shu* ("reciprocity"), and *Ren* ("humaneness") together reveals a commitment to cultivating a sense of justice in members of society.

Before moving on to the next section, in which I discuss and respond to some possible objections to my argument, I want to address my use of the *Analects* with respect to questions of stratification. In the Introduction, I set aside some questions about the stratification of the text and reserved them for this chapter. I think it is clear from my presentation of the textual evidence on this particular set of issues that there is a consistent view presented throughout the text of how members of society should treat one another. It is not that I deny that there are multiple strata or interpolations, and I do not intend to minimize the importance of text-critical work. In fact, I avoid tying my argument to specific terms that may appear only in one or two passages in the text because I appreciate the implications of some of these studies. Instead, I focus on ideas that are found throughout the text, because I am interested in identifying a set of ideas that are advocated in the text. Based on the textual evidence examined above, I think that regardless of the different periods during which various parts of the *Analects* may have been written, an abiding interest in the cultivation of a sense of justice prevails.

Justice without "Justice" in the Analects

Now I want to stress a couple of things with respect to my claim that the *Analects* speaks to the importance of cultivating a sense of justice. To begin with, I am not claiming that a term meaning "justice" or "sense of justice" is used throughout the text. Rather, my claim is that when one examines the various discussions of how members of society are to treat one another, one finds a concern with treating members of society justly and fairly. More important, there is a concern with the feelings and attitudes one cultivates toward others, and these attitudes reflect a sense of justice. I will return in a moment to the question of how these concerns are revealed in the absence of a term for "justice" or "sense of justice," though it should be clear that I do not think one has to use the word "justice" to show that one thinks justice is important. I am also not defending the view that "justice" is a part of the semantic range of certain characters I have discussed. Although "fairness" is pretty clearly a part of the semantic range of *yi* 義 ("rightness"), fairness is not the same thing as justice, even though it is an important part of the idea of justice.

I also want to stress that although I think in the *Analects* it is clearly considered important for members of society to cultivate a sense of justice, I do not think there is a full-fledged *theory* of justice in the *Analects*. The reason I discuss a *sense* of justice is that according to the *Analects*, what is most important is that members of society work to develop certain feelings and abilities as a part of their disposition. The *Analects* does not provide any clear and specific criteria for how one should balance questions of justice in a legal system or in a constitution. In other words, the *Analects* does not give us anything like rules or principles of justice. Indeed, this omission is one of the things that most concerned the Mohists about Confucianism, and the degree of concern we find with the need for establishing specific policies and principles for addressing questions of justice is one of the things that distinguish the *Analects* from the *Mengzi* and the *Xunzi*.[64]

However, that is not to say that questions of justice are wholly neglected in the *Analects*. Rather, these questions and concerns are addressed in some very different ways. One important difference is that they are tied to a concern with self-cultivation, and as I indicated in the Introduction, the discussion of self-cultivation can help us to understand why the absence of a term for "justice" does not necessarily mean that the idea of cultivating a "sense of justice" is absent from the *Analects*. As we saw in the first part of this chapter, a cluster of different terms are used in the *Analects* to describe the various activities and processes involved in the task of self-cultivation. These terms include *xue* 學 ("learning"), *xiu* 修 ("cultivating"), *si* 思 ("reflecting"), *xing* 省 ("examining"), and *xi* 習 ("reviewing," "practicing"). Only two passages use the term that means "cultivate" (*xiu* 修) in the *Analects*. In 7.3 Kongzi mentions failing to cultivate Virtue (*de zhi bu xiu* 德之不修), and in 14.42 he says that the *junzi* cultivates himself (*xiu ji* 修己) with respect to a number of different virtues.[65] Obviously, only one of these two passages literally mentions "self-cultivation" by combining the term for "cultivate" (*xiu* 修) with a term for "oneself" (*ji* 己).[66] But many passages clearly describe the process of self-cultivation, even though they do not use *xiu ji* or another term that specifically means "self-cultivation." Furthermore, it seems reasonable to say that if we did not have 14.42, or if textual scholars concluded that 14.42 was an interpolation from a later date, it would still be clear from the other descriptions of self-cultivation in the *Analects* that it is an important idea in the text.

Nevertheless, one might object to my comparison of the case of self-cultivation and a sense of justice precisely because a term for "self-cultivation" *does* exist in the *Analects*, even if it appears in only one passage. But if one grants that without the one passage where this term is used we would still be able to see the importance of self-cultivation in the *Analects*, then one grants that without a term for "self-cultivation" we can still tell that there is an understanding of self-cultivation presented in the text. In other words, the fact that the term *xiu ji* ("cultivate oneself") exists is not particularly important, because many other characters describe the process of self-cultivation and what it involves. One might, of course, object to calling it "self-cultivation," because this term is not an exact translation of the terms in question, but one must then specify what we should call it. Should we simply refer to "learning," "cultivating," "reflecting," "examining," "inspecting," "reviewing," and "practicing" separately, or list all of these terms each time we want to talk about this range of ideas? This approach seems to imply that nothing in particular unites these ideas, when in fact it seems clear that they are all part of a larger picture. It is important to acknowledge that genuine themes, ideas, and virtues constitute a rich picture of human lives in the *Analects*, as opposed to claiming that there is merely a series of fragmented ideas that are not particularly united in any way. The latter view is unfaithful to the view presented in the *Analects* itself, and it strongly deviates from the commentarial tradition, as well. My view is that it is helpful to use a term to refer to a cluster of ideas we find in the text, when that term points to what unites those ideas, to what they all have in common, or to what they are all designed to be a part of in the larger scheme of things. To put it another way, a term like "self-cultivation" here points to the family resemblance between ideas like learning, reflecting, examining, inspecting, reviewing, and practicing. This interpretation is in line with traditional Confucian commentators, who saw these activities as together specifying a distinctive conception of self-cultivation.

The idea of a sense of justice in the *Analects* presents a similar case. In describing a cultivated person who behaves in an exemplary way toward other members of society, the text uses terms like *yi* 義 ("rightness"), *shu* 恕

("reciprocity"), *Ren* 仁 ("humaneness"), *xin* 信 ("trustworthiness"), *bu bi* 不
比 ("not partial or biased"), *zhou* 周 ("associates widely, keeping the public
good in mind"), and *xing* 刑 ("punishments and the sense of fairness that
is associated with them"). But it is not enough just to pay attention to the
terms that are used; one must pay attention to the way in which they are
used and the broader discussion of which they are a part. In other words,
we must pay attention to what Kongzi tells us about the ideas in question
and the fact that he praises certain qualities over others when it comes to
judging certain kinds of situations. Simply presenting a list of terms does
not take proper account of the many themes and ideas that are important
in the *Analects*. This is evident in passages like 5.1, where Kongzi gives his
daughter in marriage to Gongye Chang, saying that he is innocent of any
crime. We can point to terms like "not guilty" (*fei qi zui* 非其罪) as expressions of Kongzi's sense of justice, but in fact Kongzi's sense of justice is
seen not only in the fact that he openly declares Gongye Chang's innocence but in the fact that he also gives his daughter in marriage to him. The
circumstances surrounding this situation show that Kongzi has a sense of
justice, and the fact that this story was written down and included in the
Analects shows that a sense of justice was important to the early Confucians. *Analects* 5.1 is but one of many such illustrations.

One could still argue that "justice" is included in the semantic range
of some of the characters I have mentioned, because some of these characters include fairness in their semantic range, and fairness is one aspect
of justice.[67] This argument would emphasize the fact that the semantic
range of certain characters in early China was seen as coherent and unified,
whereas to us the semantic range appears fragmented because we don't
have a matching concept whose semantic range fully overlaps with that of
the character. What this means is that characters carried what we would
call multiple meanings but were understood as a unified whole. An example is seen in the term *li* 禮, which is used to designate a set of traditional
moral and religious practices—including what we would call rites or rituals, social customs, rules of etiquette, and sacrificial offerings. Although
I have just employed multiple English words in my description of what
this term means, *li* 禮 is a single term that includes all of these meanings.
When Kongzi refers to the *li* in the *Analects*, he means a set of practices that
constitute a *unified* code of conduct—not a *combination* of different kinds
of practices like rituals, social customs, and rules of etiquette. The frag-
mentation reflected in this list is not a part of the understanding of the *li* in
the *Analects*, even though what we mean by this list encompasses the same
kinds of practices that are designated by the term *li*. A great deal is implied

by one single character; by our standards, several meanings are implied by it. So according to this argument, the idea of justice could be included in the semantic range of terms like *yi* and *zhou* because their semantic range includes fairness.

Although I think some significant evidence supports this sort of argument about the semantic range of certain Chinese terms, this is not the view I am defending here. Rather, I am interested in the specific nature of the disposition that members of society should cultivate with respect to one another, according to the view presented in the *Analects*. One might say that what the foregoing discussion shows is that capacities like a sense of justice tend to slip through the cracks if all we pay attention to are the terms in translation. The philosophical task involved in interpreting a text like the *Analects* involves not only understanding the semantic range of specific terms and the best way to translate them, but also—and more important—understanding the ideas that are advocated in the course of various discussions. We face the same task when we read a Western philosopher like Rawls. One could open *A Theory of Justice* and not find the word "justice" used anywhere on a certain page, even though that page provides a robust description of what justice is through a discussion of the least advantaged members of society, the obligations that members of a society have to make certain sacrifices for one another, and the role that guilt feelings play in helping us to realize these obligations. Even though the word "justice" may not be used, there is no reason to doubt that Rawls is discussing the idea of justice.

Similarly, when I say there is an understanding of justice in the *Analects*, I do not mean that what constitutes a just or unjust state of affairs is exactly the same as what Rawls thinks constitutes these things. There are many different theories about what constitutes social justice, and when we attribute an appreciation for social justice to different philosophers or cultures, we do not mean that they all agree on what is just. Rather, we mean that they all think a certain range of issues is important. Here the distinction between the concept of justice and specific conceptions or theories of justice is important. In a moment I will turn to the question of whether the understanding of justice in ancient China was instantiated in the form of a specific conception of justice, but for now I wish to point out only that there is, indeed, an understanding of justice in the *Analects*. This means that evidence of the concept of social justice exists in the *Analects*. By "social justice" here I mean the idea that the distribution of privileges, obligations, and advantages in a society should not be arbitrary. Based on the textual evidence examined in this chapter, the *Analects* does not present the view that these things should be decided arbitrarily; it consistently advocates certain standards for assigning privileges and obligations to members of society and also for the distribution of advantages. But, more notably, the evidence shows that according to the view presented in the *Analects*, cultivating a sense of justice is important. One's sense of justice indicates, among other things, that it is wrong for people to suffer the consequences of certain kinds of circumstances that are beyond their control, and that it is important for people to recognize the aspects of their lives over which they *do* have control.

But what is distinctive about a sense of justice? What distinguishes it from other kinds of moral sensibilities? Individuals with a sense of justice have cultivated virtues like reciprocity (*shu*), and rightness (*yi*) that exercise their intellect and imagination, their capacity to be fair and to take a wider and more inclusive view, as well as a certain sensitivity to the concerns and circumstances of others. A sense of justice is often reflected in the feelings one has when other members of society are harmed because the structure of society has failed to meet their needs or ensure fairness. Those who have a sense of justice identify themselves with and care about other members of society. They are moved by injustices, which means that they have feelings of resentment and are indignant when, for example, someone is punished for a crime he did not commit or when someone does not get an official position she clearly deserved because of a grudge or a bias. A strong sense of moral accountability is implied by a sense of justice.

As the passages from the *Analects* discussed in the preceding section indicate, members of the society Kongzi envisions are expected to feel and care about one another in these ways. Cultivated persons recognize when something is unfair or unjust. They feel bad about the injustice and try to rectify the situation whenever possible. The *Analects* makes clear that our behavior is not to stop with filial piety; rather, filial piety should *grow into* something that directs our relationships with those outside of our families, as well. The understanding of *Ren* ("humaneness") seen throughout the text helps to show that although the *Analects* clearly supports the view that a society should be strictly just in terms of the distribution of food and meeting other basic needs, it also emphasizes that a society should be humane. Further, the claims we find in the *Analects* indicate that societies cannot sustain any version of strict justice unless individuals are humane, meaning that they exemplify certain virtues or traits of character. A sense of justice is part of what constitutes humaneness because it is characterized by the ability to judge a situation fairly and justly and to feel for those who are disadvantaged by injustices.

For all of these reasons, it seems clear that an understanding of a sense of justice exists in the *Analects*. Nevertheless, one might object that in using the term "sense of justice," I am imposing a Rawlsian category on the *Analects*. One might mean two different things by this claim. One could be raising a terminological objection—that is, an objection to my choice of what to call this capacity in the *Analects*, without denying that this capacity is, indeed, a part of Kongzi's view. On the other hand, one might be objecting to my argument that an idea of a sense of justice exists in the *Analects*. It is important to distinguish between these claims for the reasons I discussed in Chapter 1, in relation to thematic issues. I will discuss the terminological objection in a moment, but I want to begin by responding to the denial that an understanding of a sense of justice is present in the *Analects*. Such a claim can be defended only by constructing an argument which demonstrates that the textual evidence I discuss in this chapter does not reflect an understanding of what I am calling a sense of justice. I suspect, though, that some who might make this claim are relying on the relativistic assumption that there are no shared concepts across different traditions, and that as a result, it is impossible for Kongzi and Rawls both to have an understanding of a sense of justice. I discuss my view of this position in Chapter 1, but even if one could produce substantial evidence in favor of this general view (which I think is doubtful), one would still need to demonstrate that the textual evidence I present here does not show that there is an understanding of a sense of justice in the *Analects*. Ultimately, I think this is a question that can be settled only through an examination of the textual evidence, and not *a priori*.

A terminological objection is, as we saw in Chapter 1, considerably less serious, unless of course it is simply a thin disguise for the view I have described above. One might object to my use of the term "sense of justice" in relation to the *Analects* because of the worry that using this term will lead us to impose Rawlsian ideas onto the *Analects*. Let me, then, make a few points in defense of my terminological choice. First, I think referring to a "sense of justice" is the most sensible choice because an established term for this capacity exists in English, and no single term for it exists in classical Chinese. But even if there were a Chinese term for a "sense of justice," using different terms for this capacity would likely mislead readers into thinking that I deny that the same capacity is being described. In fact, I do think the basic capacity being described in the *Analects* clearly is the same as the capacity Rawls uses this term to describe—despite the fact that this capacity plays a different role and is cultivated in different ways. In considering these matters, we must remember that minimizing or denying the genuine similarities between two views is just as unfaithful to the views under study as minimizing the genuine differences between them. Second, "sense of justice" is not a highly specialized term for Rawls, as terms such as "justice as fairness" and "the original position" are. As we saw earlier in this work, Rawls was not the first to use this term or to discuss the idea of a sense of justice. Because it refers to a general capacity that has been discussed by others and is not a distinctive term that is narrowly associated with Rawls's theory of justice, it is less likely that by using this term we will impose particular features of Rawls's theory onto the *Analects*. Third, in comparative work the differences between two views must ultimately be emphasized through a detailed discussion, and although terminological choices can sometimes influence the tendency to see more similarities than differences, one's terminology cannot replace this task. In this work, I accomplish the task of emphasizing the important differences between the Confucian and Rawlsian senses of justice not through the use of different terms but through a detailed comparative discussion of the two accounts in the following chapters.

Another objection one might make to my argument concerns the fact that some passages in the *Analects* raise the question of whether the text consistently expresses an appreciation for justice, and how the capacity for a sense of justice is related to the family. In 13.18, Kongzi is conversing with the Duke of She, who says, "Among my people there is one we call *zhi gong* 直躬 ('upright one'). When his father stole a sheep, he reported him to the authorities." Kongzi replies, "Among my people, those who we consider 'upright' are different from this: fathers cover for their sons, and sons cover for their fathers. 'Uprightness' is to be found in this."[68] Upon an initial reading of this passage, it seems that Kongzi values parental loyalty over justice. Kongzi seems to advocate circumventing the legal system by "covering" for one's father, regardless of his wrongdoing. However, a closer look at the text reveals that more is going on in this passage than at first meets the eye. Indeed, this passage can tell us some important things about the relationship between filial piety, the family, and the development of a sense of justice.[69]

First, we should notice that 13.18 does not necessarily undermine the view that developing a sense of justice is considered an important part of self-cultivation in the *Analects*. Instead, according to the reading presented above, it shows only that legal justice is considered secondary to parental loyalty or filial piety. Further, it is quite reasonable to think that part of what it means to have a sense of justice is to have a sense of when it is appropriate to report someone to the authorities for breaking a law. The acknowledgment that there are cases in which it is appropriate to "cover" for someone does not mean there is little or no understanding of (or appreciation for) justice. In fact, there would be no need to comment on this purported event if Kongzi had not been interested in justice. The fact that he did comment on it and that his remarks are reported in the *Analects* shows that this was an issue he took seriously, and it may indicate that this kind of issue was being debated at the time. It is also significant that Kongzi and the Duke of She seem to share a *common sense of justice*: They both know that stealing a sheep is wrong. What they disagree about is how to respond to this event when it involves one's father.

It also is not clear that Kongzi is offering a universal principle that applies to all fathers and sons. According to the view presented in the *Analects*, one must first cultivate filial piety in order to develop other virtues and moral sensibilities like a sense of justice, but nowhere in the text does Kongzi indicate that filial piety and a sense of justice are incompatible, or even that the latter must be suspended in favor of the former. *Analects* 13.18 seems to be the only passage that can be read in this way, and the fact that it stands alone in this regard should encourage us to explore other possible readings to see if we can find an interpretation that is more consistent with the rest of the text.[70] Indeed, as I argue below, a number of matters must be considered before we can conclude that this passage undermines the appreciation for a sense of justice in the *Analects*.

To begin, the term used for "stealing" (*rang* 攘) in 13.18 is not the same as the term used throughout the *Analects* for habitual stealing, robbery, or thievery (*dao* 盗).[71] According to the Zhu Xi commentary, the term *rang* 攘 is used here instead of *dao* 盗 to indicate that the father had a reason for stealing beyond mere avarice.[72] Legge notes that *rang* means "'to steal on occasion,' i.e. on some temptation, as when another person's animal comes into my grounds, and I appropriate it." If this is how one reads the passage, it takes on a significantly different tone. To *not return* a sheep that wanders onto one's property is to fail to be wholly honest, but it is not the same as the crime of stealing. One who seeks to turn his father in for this omission surely has an overly scrupulous sense of rightness. Indeed, *rang* has the connotations of seizing or plundering, rather than professional or habitual robbery or thievery.[73] The passage, then, does not say that the father was a thief (*dao* 盗), which is significant because it may indicate that the passage refers to a case in which extenuating circumstances caused the father to act out of character. The question, of course, is what exactly these circumstances were, and in a moment I will consider some options. For now, we should note that Kongzi's response is not necessarily the same response he would give to someone whose father was a thief or robber (*dao* 盜) but rather a response to someone whose father stole (*rang* 攘) in a single, particular instance, apparently for a reason. Additionally, it is important to keep in mind that Kongzi is reacting to the fact that the son is *praised and considered a moral exemplar* for having reported his father to the authorities, apparently without even talking to his father about what happened. Moral exemplars play a critical role in self-cultivation, especially in the Confucian tradition, and so it should not surprise us that Kongzi has a strong reaction against this son's being heralded as a moral exemplar. It is possible that Kongzi would not have responded as strongly if the son's behavior were not being praised as exemplary. If, for example, he had simply not been reprimanded for reporting his father, or if others had overlooked his behavior, then Kongzi might not have been as alarmed by the situation.

Now one might argue that stealing is stealing, and that it is wrong regardless of the circumstances under which it is done, and that accepting such a view is central to having an appreciation for justice. But there are at least two problems with this claim. First, clearly, stealing was not always stealing in ancient China. A wide range of characters in classical Chinese are used to describe different cases of taking something that does not belong to you; the difference I cite above and the characters I reference are representative of a wider range of distinctions that were made between different kinds of stealing or different circumstances under which one takes things from others. Second, it is simply not true that most people—even in Western cultures—believe that "stealing is stealing." We distinguish between those who take food and water to sustain their families during a natural disaster, and those who steal in other circumstances. Most of us would say that stealing is morally reprehensible, and our justice system reflects this view, but we do not find those who take food and water for their families in order to survive in an emergency to be morally blameworthy.[74] We would not be inclined to call them thieves, and we might not even say they "stole" food. Rather, we are inclined to say that they "took" what they needed, even though it was not theirs, and we should notice how this language is laden with a lesser degree of moral blame, perhaps like the term (*rang* 攘) used to describe the father's actions in the case of the stolen sheep. The fact that we distinguish between different kinds of crimes, even when they involve the same action, is also reflected in our legal system's consideration of things like pre-meditation and intent, and the way in which the law distinguishes between first-, second-, third-, and fourth-degree crimes.

I now wish to return to the subject of the extenuating circumstances that apparently surround the case of the "upright one's" father. If Zhu Xi is correct, and *rang* 攘 means to steal when one has a reason, then the father may have stolen because he needed food, in which case the passage is not really about whether it is just for fathers and sons to report each other's offenses. Instead, it concerns the fulfillment of filial responsibilities. At this time in China's history, and even today in China, most people would think that a son in this sort of situation is at least partially if not fully responsible for what occurred, because he neglected his father's needs. Not only did he not provide for his father in the sense of meeting his basic needs, but he apparently alienated his father to the point where his father did not even feel that he could ask his son for assistance in dire straits. It is important to see how backward this son's response really is, even by contemporary Western standards. Most of us would feel that we had failed our parents if they felt that their only option was to steal when they needed food, and our culture does not take filial piety and responsibility for one's parents as seriously as East Asian cultures do. Furthermore, even if one did not feel *responsible* for what had happened, it would still be considered callous—in both Western and East Asian cultures—to report one's parents to the authorities under such circumstances, without even trying to work the situation out with them first.[75]

If indeed the "upright one's" father was in need, then his actions in reporting his father show a complete and utter lack of understanding of his moral responsibilities or, worse, intentional neglect of his responsibilities. According to this reading, Kongzi is responding to an extreme case of moral bankruptcy. If the son had covered for his father, he would have in fact been covering his own moral ineptitude in failing to care for his father as he should have. The fact that he is not ashamed that his father felt his only option was to steal, and that he is considered a *moral exemplar* by his community, is reprehensible from a Confucian point of view. We can see, then, why Kongzi begins his response to the Duke of She with the words "Among my people . . . ." Surely this case looks to him like the product of a foreign moral culture.

Even if the father did not take the sheep in order to meet his needs, we can still assume that some exceptional circumstances motivated his actions. At any rate, it seems that he is not a habitual thief. The real problem, then, is that the son apparently did not even attempt to understand the circumstances before he reported his father to the authorities. In the *Analects*, Kongzi emphasizes that children should work to understand their parents' positions, regardless of whether they agree with their parents' actions. Children should "gently remonstrate" with their parents but also be respectful and not oppose them regardless of how they respond to the criticism (4.18). As we have seen, the relationship between parent and child is the basis for other relationships in the *Analects*. In the context of our relationship with our parents we learn how to resolve conflicts and deal with people who do things we do not like. By cultivating filial piety in the midst of the tensions that are an inevitable part of parent–child relationships, we begin to develop the ability to respond to others in a thoughtful, sensitive, fair, and respectful manner.

Indeed, the ability to feel for others and to try to understand their situations in a fair and charitable way, even in the worst of circumstances, is a crucial part of what it means to have a sense of justice. One of the first things a person with a sense of justice—and notice here the emphasis we have seen throughout the *Analects* on cultivating good judgment and being fair-minded—would notice about this situation is the fact that the father is not a habitual thief. A particular set of circumstances motivated him in this instance to take what did not belong to him. These circumstances do not make his actions right, but they certainly call for a closer examination of the situation. On the Confucian account of what constitutes a sense of justice—which involves the ability to judge a situation carefully, attentively, and fairly—the son did *not* exemplify a sense of justice when he reported his father. He seems to lack both filial piety *and* a sense of justice, which is consistent with the view that filial piety and respect for elders are the root of *Ren*. Someone who does not develop a sense of filial piety, in Kongzi's view, is unlikely to properly develop other moral sensibilities, including a sense of justice.

According to this reading, the "upright one's" actions betray not only a lack of filial piety but also a lack of a sense of justice. It is significant that Kongzi re-defines "uprightness" (*zhi* 直) in this passage rather than simply say that he does not value uprightness. It is not that he thinks uprightness is unimportant; rather, he thinks that what counts as being upright is different. The Duke of She's account of uprightness is based solely on the rightness of actions according to the law. On his view, an upright person is one who feels accountable first and foremost to the rule of law and who strictly enforces it in all situations.[76] Kongzi's account of uprightness, in contrast, is based on a particular understanding of what it means to fulfill one's moral responsibilities, according to which the responsibilities between parents and children have a special status. So even if one interprets Kongzi as calling for a son to take active steps to cover up his father's wrongdoing, it is still not the case that this passage shows a disregard for a sense of justice. For Kongzi, a sense of justice is inextricably bound up with filial piety. Parent–child responsibilities go both ways, and the son failed his father both by not providing for him and by not cultivating an honest, reciprocal relationship with him. As a result, in an important sense he is responsible for his father's stealing, at least on Kongzi's view. Thus, it is appropriate for a son to "cover" for his father in this situation by taking steps to make sure his father will not be punished. We can be sure that for Kongzi, much else is required of the son as well, such as mending the broken relationship with his father and perhaps taking legal responsibility for the crime. Nothing in the passage would lead one to think that Kongzi does not think a son who "covers" for his father should make things right with the owner of the sheep. On Kongzi's view, "covering" for one's father might entail taking responsibility for the theft; indeed, that is what we often mean when we say one person "covered" for another person.

I want to offer a final piece of evidence in support of my claim that this passage does not imply a lack of concern for justice in the *Analects*. In any given passage from the *Analects*, it is worth considering the matter of whom Kongzi is talking to, because Kongzi sometimes gives different people different advice, based on his knowledge of the individual's character and situation.[77] The Duke of She is a minister to the king of the powerful state of Chu, in the walled city of She. He is discussed in two other passages in the *Analects*. In 7.19, the Duke of She asks Zilu about Kongzi, but Zilu does not reply. Then, later, when Zilu returns to Kongzi's side and recounts what happened, Kongzi says, "Why didn't you tell him that he's the kind of person who in bursts of enthusiasm forgets to eat, in his delight forgets to worry, and doesn't even realize that old age is coming on?"[78] Early commentators think the Duke of She was a power-hungry minister who had been trying to lure Kongzi into his service, and that Zilu was afraid to answer because he did not want to say something that would encourage the Duke. Kongzi's words to Zilu after the fact, then, indicate his lack of interest in the prestige and material rewards associated with an official position, and that he does not possess the traits the Duke of She would want in an official.

Although Zhu Xi and other later commentators see the Duke more sympathetically and take Zilu's lack of a response as a reflection of the fact that he is in awe of Kongzi, the earlier reading is worth considering based on what we learn about the Duke in other passages. In addition to the backward view of the Duke that is presented in 13.18, in 13.16 the Duke asks Kongzi about governing, and Kongzi tells him, "When those close by are happy, those from far away gather around." In this passage Kongzi appears to be instructing the Duke about the importance of ruling in such a way that both those near to you, such as your family, are pleased, and in such a way that those one does not have daily contact with, such as the masses, are drawn closer. Kongzi's instructions here are somewhat unusual because as we saw earlier in this chapter, in talking about ruling he often emphasizes the need to display *de* ("virtuous power") in one's daily conduct in order to evoke good conduct from the people. So it may be the case that the Duke of She is especially deficient in his sense of how to interact with those who are closest to him, and this is why Kongzi advises him to govern in such a way that those near to him are pleased and that those who are far away from him are drawn closer. This passage may suggest, then, that he needs to use filial piety as a model of how to interact with others.

Regardless of whether we consider these other passages, it is still the case that in 13.18, the Duke of She disregards the value of filial piety. Given that Kongzi is talking to the Duke of She, it is quite possible that Kongzi's remarks are not intended to be a general rule for everyone to adopt but are instead intended to call to the Duke of She's attention his own short-sightedness and neglect of filial duties. One reason for thinking that Kongzi does not intend this to be a general rule is that the claim that sons and fathers should cover for each other seems to be inconsistent with what Kongzi says about the need for remonstrance as opposed to automatic compliance or approval. Although Kongzi says that if one's parents do not listen when one remonstrates with them, one should desist, it is still clear that a filial son would not *just* cover up for his father. Rather, he would see many more responsibilities implied in this scenario. It is likely, then, that Kongzi responds to the Duke of She in part to make a point to the Duke about his own neglect of filial piety. Along similar lines, Legge maintains that the last line of the passage, *zhi zai qi zhong* 直在其中 ("uprightness is to be found in this"), "does not absolutely affirm that this [sons and fathers covering up for each other] is upright, but that in this there is a better principle than in the other conduct."[79] It is also worth noting that as Han Feizi points out, the Duke's preferred response serves *the Duke* well, because people will report crimes in his kingdom. Kongzi's response could be understood as insisting that the Duke's primary concern should instead be the welfare of his subjects.

As I pointed out earlier, the very fact that this case is discussed in the *Analects* shows that early Confucians were concerned to address what constitutes a sense of justice and how it is related to filial responsibilities. Other passages reflect an understanding of how a sense of justice works out in a society, as well. For example, in 16.2 Kongzi says, "When the Way

prevails in the world, commoners do not debate matters of government,"
which reflects the view that when a government is ordered properly, the
people will not need to debate about and criticize government policies. In
this passage, Kongzi makes clear that when the Way is put into practice,
members of society will no longer have to struggle with questions of justice and fairness and the extent to which their government ensures these
things in its policies. In 12.13 Kongzi says, "When it comes to hearing civil
litigation, I am as good as anyone else. What we must strive for, though, is
for there to be no civil litigation."[80] Both of these passages reflect Kongzi's
concern with the goal of bringing about a certain sort of society, and they
seem to minimize the practices that are used to ensure justice in liberal
democracies (e.g., a fair justice system, open discussion and debate about
political issues). We should notice, however, that even liberal democratic
political philosophers typically do not see the establishment and use of a
fair justice system as the end for which they are striving. Most Western
judicial scholars, political philosophers, and ethicists would agree that it
would be good to have a society without civil litigation. Most of them
would also acknowledge that human societies inevitably involve conflicts
that need to be resolved, and that is where justice comes in. However, this
does not make them pessimists about achieving well-ordered, harmonious societies. In fact, as we have seen, Rawls remains optimistic about the
possibility of achieving a just society, which is why he says we are striving
toward the end of justice for all citizens.[81] And although 16.2 and 12.13
indicate that Kongzi is concerned with the goal of achieving a humane and
harmoniously functioning society, we also know from passages like 16.1
and 4.5 that he thinks that end must be achieved in the right way.

Some other passages that might trouble a reader who is interested in
justice are those that, like 16.2, appear to discourage the open discussion of
government policies. In 8.14, Kongzi says, "Do not discuss matters of government policy that do not fall within the scope of your official duties." In
terms of social justice, we often tend to see free discussion of governmental policies as crucial to making sure the needs of everyone are met and that
everyone gets a fair hearing. Thus, one might also be troubled by Kongzi's
claim that the *junzi* is concerned about the Way and not about poverty
(15.32). The commentarial tradition can provide some assistance in understanding why Kongzi might have made such claims. Some commentators
think 8.14 is a criticism of some specific contemporaries of Kongzi who
tended to involve themselves in matters that did not concern them. Others
think Kongzi is giving an explanation for why he is not involved in governmental affairs, namely that he considers his calling to be that of a moral

teacher and not an administrative official or advisor.[82] *Analects* 15.32 is a reflection of Kongzi's refusal to embrace material goods over Virtue, and also the belief that people should focus on things they can change, such as their own conduct, as opposed to things they have no control over, such as how well the crops do in any given year as a result of the weather patterns. Kongzi maintains throughout the *Analects* that meeting the needs of the people cannot be achieved simply by having all of the right policies, which are of course subject to things we do not control, like floods and droughts. Rather, a ruler must lead through the power of Virtue, setting an example for the people through his conduct.

A number of other passages in the *Analects* encourage remonstration with leaders, and several report Kongzi doing this as well, so it is not the case that all free discussion or criticism of policies is discouraged in the text. In 13.15, Kongzi says that the only saying which can come close to causing a state to perish is, "I take no joy in being a ruler, except that no one dares to oppose what I say." Kongzi then remarks that if what the ruler says is good, and no one opposes him, then this policy is fine. "On the other hand, if what he says is not good, and no one opposes him, does this not come close to being a single saying that can cause a state to perish?" In both 14.21 and 14.22, Kongzi emphasizes the importance of opposing one's superiors openly. All of these passages indicate that Kongzi does not think silent compliance when one disagrees with a policy or with a leader's actions is consistent with following the Way. Additionally, these passages confirm the connection Kongzi sees between the way one interacts with one's parents and the way one interacts with other members of society, including one's superiors. One develops the skills that will be necessary to be a good member of society first by learning how to remonstrate with one's parents. As we have seen, this is how a sense of justice is initially cultivated.

I want to consider one final potential objection to my argument that the *Analects* expresses the importance of cultivating a sense of justice. One might object to my argument on the historical grounds that the early Chinese did not establish a system that valued fair distribution and argue that their failure to do so undermines the view that they valued a sense of justice. However, the view presented in the *Analects did*, in fact, create an interest in addressing concerns about distributive justice in China. The ideas and themes that are central to the *Analects* were an important part of what motivated the civil service examinations, the institution that most clearly sought to establish distributive justice.[83] Kongzi's view, as we have seen, is that although a hierarchy is necessary, all of the people should be provided for equitably (e.g., 16.1, 6.4), and the individuals who evidence the highest state of moral cultivation should rule (e.g., 2.3, 13.4). This is where the practice of distributing advantages in the form of governmental positions according to one's performance on a civil service examination seems to have originated. According to this system, individuals who hold governmental positions have access to a wide range of privileges. The recruitment of exceptional individuals into governmental service—as opposed to those who had hereditary or other privileges not based on merit—began in the Warring States Period, and institutions began to implement an official system for selecting meritorious individuals for government service in the second century B.C.E., under the Han government.[84] This system was the forerunner of the elaborate civil examination system of the Tang and Song dynasties.[85] The idea behind the examinations was essentially to measure one's virtue, as well as one's abilities in a range of different areas, and although the difficulty in doing this resulted in ongoing revisions to the examination process, one thing that remained constant was an emphasis on knowledge of the Confucian classics. In relation to a sense of justice, what is particularly important about these examinations is the belief that privileges should be awarded by merit. This belief, as we have seen, has Confucian origins.[86]

Of course, the later development of the civil service examination system does not demonstrate that there was an understanding of justice in the *Analects*. Such demonstration can be accomplished only through a discussion of the sort of textual evidence that has been the focus of this chapter. My point in discussing the examination system here is to emphasize that subsequent Confucians understood the *Analects*, as well as other early Confucian texts, as showing an appreciation for a sense of justice. The fact that traditional Confucians read the *Analects* in this way helps to show that it is not simply a modern imposition to say that the text expresses an interest in a sense of justice. Indeed, the idea that political offices should be awarded based on merit, which is determined by public examination rather than by lineage or the like, contributes to the argument that traditional Confucians had a highly developed sense of justice. It also shows that their sense of justice informed a central feature of their social and political practices. Such offices played a major role in the distribution of goods such as money, power, and prestige, and they also had a fundamental role in determining one's own sense of worth. As we saw earlier in this book, according to Rawls, "the sense of justice is a necessary part of the dignity of the person."[87] It is indeed the case that the examination system created an opportunity for upward social mobility that had not existed before. Although the process of safeguarding a certain degree of impartiality by trying to make sure a wider range of people competed for governmental positions became increasingly difficult, an interest in justice is apparent in these efforts. A quota system gave poorer areas more generous allotments of successful candidates on the examinations at the local level, so that more people who were not from elite families were allowed to compete in the secondary examinations. Despite the controversy that the quota system created and its failure to make upward mobility possible for many members of the lower classes, as Thomas H.C. Lee notes, the examination system nevertheless in many ways "embodied the very ideal of social justice."[88]

It is important to recognize that the civil service examinations did not seek to establish the same sort of distributive justice that Rawls seeks to establish. Additionally, the civil service exams did not entirely realize what they were designed to achieve, which is why there was a continual effort to revise them and create a more effective measure of moral worthiness. But we should recall that Rawls's standard for what constitutes having a sense of justice, the concept of justice, or even having a conception of justice is not dependent on having the same standard for fair distribution that he establishes in justice as fairness. Justice functions broadly to guard against indiscriminate distribution, manipulation, or monopoly of a range of fundamental social goods. Arbitrarily taking away one's land and not acknowledging one's contributions are injustices. The examination system provides strong evidence that traditional Confucians acknowledged the importance of working to establish justice, and the textual evidence presented in this chapter helps to show why they understood this task as an expression of the values described in early Confucian texts such as the *Analects*. This observation brings us to the heart of this comparative project, and it is the comparison of Rawls and the *Analects* to which I turn my attention in Chapter 4.

Two Senses of Justice

The Way of Heaven, is it not like the stretching of a bow?
What is high it presses down;
What is low it lifts up.
It takes from what has excess;
It augments what is deficient.
The Way of Heaven takes from what has excess and augments what
   is deficient.
The Way of human beings is not like this.
It takes from the deficient and offers it up to those with excess.
Who is able to offer what they have in excess to the world?
Only one who has the Way![1]

One of the distinctive features of the *Daodejing* 道德經 is its conception of what it means for rulers to act in accordance with the Way, and how human societies should be arranged in order to meet the needs of the people. Although the authors of the *Daodejing* and the *Analects* articulate very different conceptions of the ideal society, both texts address the problems of excess and deficiency in human societies. They also share the view that rulers play a critical role in correcting these and other problems relating to establishing justice. And despite the deep and important differences between their accounts of the ideal ruler and their conceptions of the Way, the *Daodejing* and the *Analects* agree that working to establish social justice is a part of following the Way. As chapter 77 of the *Daodejing* says, those who have the Way offer what they have in excess to those in need; in *Analects* 6.4 Kongzi says that those who are dedicated to the Way give to the needy but do not make the rich richer.

In Chapter 3 I argued that the *Analects* provides an account of a sense of justice, which is one of many capacities individuals must cultivate in order to live in accordance with the Way. Social justice and fair distribution are among the central concerns of Rawls's work as well, and as we saw in Chapter 2, Rawls grounds the claim that citizens can cultivate both the capacity and the inclination to work toward these goals on his account of a sense of justice. In this chapter, I explore these two accounts of a sense of justice comparatively. In the first section I describe the defining features of a sense of justice in Rawls and the *Analects* before focusing on some significant differences between them. I go on to compare some of the details of their views of a sense of justice, highlighting both similarities and differences between them. Then, in the next two sections I show why a comparative study of their views is particularly instructive for philosophers studying Rawls, the *Analects*, or the idea of a sense of justice. I discuss how a comparative reading of Rawls and the *Analects* highlights the importance of Rawls's position on questions of human nature, while helping us to better understand the self-cultivationist dimensions of his account. I then address how an understanding of Rawls's work can help us to better understand certain aspects of the ethical and political view presented in the *Analects*, especially concerning the importance of non-arbitrary distinctions between members of society, the relationship between the right and the good, and the importance of the judicial virtues.

Comparing Senses of Justice

What is a sense of justice? Although we've examined this question independently in Rawls and the *Analects*, one question that this comparative study has yet to consider is the extent to which it is clear that these two sources are describing the same basic capacity in human beings. After all, Rawls's work and the *Analects* represent dramatically different projects. Rawls provides an account of a conception of justice that is designed to accommodate the fact of reasonable pluralism in modern liberal democracies, while the *Analects* describes Kongzi's account of the Way, which he has been called to reveal to his ancient and troubled culture. A sense of justice is but one of many important ideas that are discussed in these larger accounts. In this section I show that despite the many differences between their historical and philosophical contexts, Rawls and the *Analects* describe the same basic moral capacity, which I have called a sense of justice. I begin by discussing the respective answers Rawls and the *Analects* give to three questions about a sense of justice: (1) What is the basic nature of this moral capacity? (2) What circumstances arouse or assuage it? (3) Why is a sense of justice an important capacity for members of society to have?

According to Rawls's general definition, a sense of justice is the ability to feel or perceive what is fair, and it is the primary source of our motivation to act fairly toward other members of society and to act in accordance with the principles or standards that are designed to help establish and preserve a just society. But Rawls carefully notes that a sense of justice is much more than simply being able to follow the rules. At bottom, it is a feeling or sense of right and wrong. In particular, a sense of justice is what causes us to value fairness; it makes us not want to take advantage of others and it is the source of our feelings of indignation toward those who do take advantage of others, as well as our feelings of sympathy for those who are taken advantage of. A sense of justice is the moral compass telling us that there is something wrong about a certain range of circumstances, and so it leads us to *feel for* those who are victims of these circumstances. This is why Rawls tells us that a sense of justice "may be aroused or assuaged, and it is connected not only with such moral feelings as resentment and indignation but also . . . with natural attitudes such as mutual trust and affection."[2] Here we see the answer to the first question: A sense of justice is a basic moral sense that something is wrong about certain kinds of situations. It is something all humans are born with the capacity for, meaning that it is a very basic moral sense that can be developed and cultivated, and it is situated within and closely related to other moral feelings.

This remark brings us to our second question: What circumstances arouse or assuage a sense of justice? I have already stated that a sense of justice leads us to feel that certain states of affairs are right or wrong, but what makes it a sense of *justice*, as opposed to a more general sense of morality? Rawls notes above that although a sense of justice is connected with certain moral feelings and attitudes such as indignation and affection, it is not identical to them. A sense of justice leads us to value fairness generally, but because Rawls's analysis concerns *social* justice, he focuses primarily on circumstances in which individuals suffer as a result of the moral arbitrariness of natural or social contingencies—in other words, things over which they could not possibly have control. Rawls is interested in what causes us to feel in certain ways toward those who are the victims of arbitrary distinctions that cannot be justified by an appeal to merit or desert, including social contingencies such as one's social class of origin, natural contingencies such as one's native endowments of intelligence or special talents, and the opportunities one has to develop these endowments based on one's social class of origin. A sense of justice, according to Rawls's analysis of social justice, leads us to feel contempt for institutions, practices, and attitudes that exacerbate and deepen these kinds of inequalities. Correspondingly, it motivates us to support institutions, practices, and attitudes that help to prevent or correct these inequalities. Here we can see how a sense of justice differs from feelings of compassion, which often stem simply from seeing others in pain, regardless of the cause. A sense of justice, in contrast, tells us that something is wrong about situations in which individuals suffer *as a result of* circumstances they never had any control over: the moral arbitrariness of certain contingencies. It is not aroused by human suffering per se but by moral contingencies that cause human suffering.

It will be helpful at this juncture to examine the historical circumstances Rawls has in mind as he formulates his account of a sense of justice. Modern liberal democracies reject the feudal idea that birth into a particular social class should determine a person's opportunities. The first alternative to be embraced, best seen in the form of anti-discrimination legislation, was the principle of "careers open to talents," or the idea that positions and offices should be awarded according to a person's actual talents and skills, instead of traits such as class background, race, gender, sexual orientation, or family connections (*TJ*, 57ff). However, it is difficult for societies that have a history of class or caste discrimination, racism, or sexism to eliminate social practices that lead to the underdevelopment of talents, skills, and expectations, even after they have enacted laws to eliminate institutional forms of discrimination.[3] Accordingly, morally arbitrary social contingencies can be the source of especially deep and pervasive inequalities, even in societies in which certain forms of discrimination are illegal.

In addition to social contingencies tied to the particular circumstances into which one is born, such as class or race position, natural contingencies can also determine our opportunities in life or at least shape our prospects, such as natural talents, skills, and abilities, which vary widely from person to person. Natural contingencies can help to offset social contingencies, or they can make them worse. For example, children born into economically disadvantaged families might have exceptional natural aptitudes in areas such as music or mathematics. When these children are given the opportunity to cultivate their natural talents and receive encouragement to do so, they may have access to opportunities that will help to counteract the disadvantages of their socioeconomic starting place. However, other children might have learning disabilities that, combined with their disadvantageous socioeconomic starting place, will at least severely limit their success in many if not most areas. Children born into families with a more advantageous socioeconomic status tend to have greater access to educational resources and opportunities, and this advantage will likely affect the outcome of their natural talents or disabilities. Of course, not all natural or social contingencies begin at birth; adults are sometimes faced with sudden and debilitating changes in their circumstances caused by illnesses, accidents, natural disasters, or other events beyond their control. The point is that the combined results of natural and social contingencies are not things we choose or deserve; which family one is born into and the talents or disabilities one has can be seen as social and natural lotteries.

This observation is what arouses a sense of justice, leading us to say that it is unjust to leave the victims of these contingencies to fend for themselves. We want to say there is something *unfair* about the fact that people are pushed to the fringes of society by no choice of their own, and we think that a good society would do something to help its members if they are so placed. This sentiment lies at the heart of a sense of justice. It is worth noting here that Rawls's account depends heavily on the view that it is important for humans to be able to make choices about their lives. A sort of *arbitrariness* is what many of the situations we call unjust or unfair have in common. It was by no choice of their own that these individuals are in their present position, and this is what causes us to say that it is unfair for them to suffer. Again, we can see how a sense of justice is distinguishable from feelings such as compassion and sympathy that we might feel for anyone who is marginalized or otherwise suffering. Although people who have a highly developed sense of justice often are compassionate, benevolent, and humane, and although instances that arouse a person's sense of justice also sometimes create opportunities to act benevolently and humanely, we should be clear on the difference between these ideas. Benevolence and humaneness describe caring attitudes, actions, and people, whereas a sense of justice in part describes a person's ability to perceive what is fair or unfair.

The third question I want to consider with respect to Rawls's account is why a sense of justice is an important capacity for members of society to have. Rawls thinks that a sense of justice, when it is cultivated and developed properly, results in the realization that we are bound to others in an important way. It causes us to feel a sense of responsibility to and for our fellow members of society, and so it prevents us from walking away when others are being marginalized and harmed in circumstances that are unfair. But on Rawls's account of social justice, a sense of justice tells us not only that it is wrong that certain people suffer as a result of the deep and pervasive inequalities that affect their chances in life; it also tells us it is wrong not to do anything about it. As a result, a properly cultivated sense of justice moves citizens to sacrifice some of the things they have in order to help those individuals who are the victims of these injustices. It also motivates them to fulfill their societal obligations in order to avoid putting others into marginalized positions. A sense of justice causes members of society to take offense at certain states of affairs, and it motivates them to act in certain ways as a result.

On Rawls's view, a sense of justice is seen clearly in citizens' understanding of what society's institutions should do. Part of having a sense of justice is supporting the idea that a society owes something to those who are suffering from morally arbitrary contingencies. On this view, a society's institutions should work to ensure that its members have choices and opportunities in life, in order to minimize the possibility that their futures will be thoroughly or primarily determined by their circumstances. A sense of justice keeps us from ignoring the inequalities in people's prospects that arise from natural and social contingencies. It also motivates us to work toward establishing and maintaining institutions that will help people in these kinds of situations.

Like Rawls, the *Analects* maintains that humans have a basic capacity to sense or perceive that something is wrong about certain situations, and that people can hone and cultivate this capacity. One of the important differences between a sense of justice as Rawls understands it and the moral sense discussed in the *Analects* is that while Rawls confines his discussion to social justice, the *Analects* discusses a moral sense that guides humans in a wide range of situations.[4] In fact, the best way to understand the development of a moral sense in the *Analects* is through the development of a set of virtues. The unity among these virtues is seen in Kongzi's conception of the Way and in some of his remarks about *Ren* ("humaneness"), which also indicate that he thinks humans can cultivate an internal moral sense. For example, Kongzi says that the key to achieving *Ren* lies within (12.1), and that if one desires it, one will find that "it is right here" (7.30). It is clear that on the view found in the *Analects*, cultivated persons are guided by an internal moral sense, regardless of whether this moral sense is the result of a cultivated innate capacity for morality or the product of the transformation of one's original nature.[5] The *Analects* does not present a theory of human nature or a clear view of whether a sense of justice originates from an innate capacity. However, in claiming that people can cultivate and eventually possess a wide range of virtues and moral capacities, the *Analects* makes clear that humans have certain basic capacities, including the capacity to cultivate and possess a range of moral sensibilities. These sensibilities include a sense of justice, but it is important to remember that a sense of justice is just one among many different virtues and moral sensibilities that cultivated persons possess. As Kongzi points out, cultivated individuals "always move in the direction of what is right" (12.10), taking rightness (*yi* 義) as their substance (15.18), thinking about what is right and relying on their moral sense even in the midst of the distractions of the world (4.16, 14.12).

Although cultivated individuals rely on their sense of rightness to guide them in a broad range of situations, some of the situations used to describe the importance of one's moral sense involve what are properly called the judicial virtues. In these passages, a person with a cultivated moral sense is a person with a highly developed sense of fairness. They do not base their actions on slander or accusations but rather judge situations based on what is right (12.6). Although they do not anticipate betrayal or expect untrustworthiness, they are still the first to perceive it (14.31). In addition to their perceptiveness and fair-mindedness, these individuals are also resolute, decisive, and straightforward, but they are not *too* quick to speak or act and are reticent at just the right times (13.27). Repeatedly, Kongzi describes individuals who are able to judge situations fairly, examining people for themselves rather than simply believing what others say about them or what people say about themselves (15.28, 15.23). They judge situations based on their sense of what is right, as opposed to personal grudges or biases (4.10, 15.22). These passages, among others, show that the moral sense described in the *Analects* includes a sense of right and wrong when it comes to scenarios we would describe as unfair or unjust. Cultivated persons have a sense of justice: They feel or perceive what is fair, and this moral sense leads them to act fairly toward other members of society.

In the *Analects*, fairness is a part of the Way, and a sense of justice is one of the many cultivated capacities that help individuals to act in accordance with the Way. I want to focus on two discussions in the *Analects* that clearly show the importance of having a sense of justice. First, the *Analects* says in a number of places that a good society helps those who are marginalized; it is not simply the responsibility of individual families to take care of their own members. Rather, society itself is viewed as a kind of family, and the ruler has special obligations as the head of that family to make sure his people are cared for. For example, in 12.9, the people under Duke Ai's rulership are suffering from a natural contingency—a poor harvest—and Master You expresses his disapproval of the fact that Duke Ai is taxing them heavily while complaining that his own needs are not being met. This passage addresses a fundamental injustice—heavily taxing those who are suffering as a result of circumstances beyond their control. According to the *Analects*, a cultivated person should immediately recognize that there is something wrong with this situation, as Master You does. Further, for a ruler to respond by reducing the taxes on people suffering from natural contingencies is a basic matter of justice. Of course, we can praise such a ruler for exemplifying a number of other virtues, but a sense of justice is one of the capacities he has shown through his actions.

The *Analects* also presents an account of how a sense of justice motivates individuals to work toward establishing and preserving shared standards and practices that are dedicated to fairness. In 6.4 Kongzi says the *junzi* ("exemplary person") provides for the needy but does not help the rich to become richer, and in 16.1 Kongzi tells us that the good ruler is concerned about unequal distribution. These passages show a concern with making sure everyone is provided for, and they even provide some specific ways in which economic inequalities should be addressed. In *Analects* 4.5 Kongzi says, "Wealth and honors are things that all people desire, but unless they are acquired by following the Way they are not worth having. Poverty and disgrace are things that all people hate, and yet unless they are avoided by following the Way they are not worth avoiding." This passage clearly shows that Kongzi understands both that there are different reasons why people fail to achieve a certain economic status and that the nature of these reasons is morally significant. Kongzi goes on to say that the *junzi* always accords with *Ren* ("humaneness"), even in times of urgency or distress. Here, as with several of the passages we have examined, it seems that acting in accordance with a sense of justice is one part of what it means to accord with *Ren*.

The second discussion that shows the importance of having a sense of justice concerns the importance of taking responsibility for one's actions, attempts, and omissions. In the *Analects*, a sense of justice indicates that it is wrong for people to suffer the consequences of circumstances beyond their control, but it also indicates that it is important for people to recognize the aspects of their lives over which they do have control. This emphasis is a natural outgrowth of a concern with moral self-cultivation. Accordingly, the *Analects* discusses instances in which individuals are reduced to poverty or are otherwise rejected as a result of their own moral failings. Kongzi praises the leader of the Bo clan for accepting his punishment of poverty without resentment (14.10), indicating that it is appropriate for this man to accept a low position in society as a result of his criminal activity. Kongzi's behavior toward his students is also illuminating on this matter. He rejects students like Zai Wo and Ran Qiu for choosing not to cultivate themselves (5.10, 6.12), and in Ran Qiu's case, the Master's rejection of him is tied to a matter of social justice. In 11.17 Kongzi says, "The head of the Ji Family is wealthier than even the Duke of Zhou ever was, and yet Ran Qiu collects taxes on his behalf to further increase his already excessive wealth. Ran Qiu is no disciple of mine. If you disciples were to sound the drums and attack him, I would not disapprove."[6] In contrast, Kongzi praises Yan Hui for never complaining about the hardship he endured being poor (6.11).[7]

In these and other passages, Kongzi makes clear that he thinks individuals are fully capable of cultivating themselves, regardless of their economic circumstances. It is not that he fails to realize that things are harder for the poor; it is clear that part of his praise for Yan Hui is tied to the fact that he knows things *were* harder for Hui. This is an interesting view in part because it shows that Kongzi does not regard one's socioeconomic status as something that determines a person's future, and this represents a contrast to Rawls, who at least thinks that individuals' futures *can* be determined by their position in society. The *Analects* does not accept poverty as an excuse for moral failure. As 14.43 suggests, and as we will see later in this chapter, Kongzi thinks a lack of filial piety is the primary reason why most individuals become a burden on society, because filial piety is the foundation for one's moral development. Interestingly, both Rawls and the *Analects* maintain that it is important to work for greater economic equality, which for both of them means providing assistance to the poor and not the wealthy.[8] But Rawls focuses strictly on the fact that a sense of justice leads us to address those aspects of our lives that we cannot control, while Kongzi also discusses the fact that a sense of justice leads us to address those aspects of our lives that we can control. Even in the case of the leader of the Bo clan, Kongzi sees that he had a choice in how he responded to his punishment, which is why he notes that the Bo leader accepted his punishment willingly and that this is not an easy thing to do. A sense of justice, for Kongzi, helps us to see that it *is* just for people to be pushed to the fringes of their communities when they intentionally violate the rules in serious ways. The leader of the Bo clan deserves his punishment because he acted freely, and he remains free to respond to his punishment in whatever way he chooses.

In general, Kongzi is much more optimistic than Rawls about the degree of control people have over their lives as a result of their capacity for self-cultivation. At the same time, Kongzi maintains that families and societies have obligations to their members, and he expresses an understanding of social justice that addresses a number of the same concerns Rawls addresses. The *Analects* makes it clear, though, that Kongzi does not excuse individuals who do not do their part to cultivate themselves.[9] According to Kongzi's view, it is both the case that people are affected by natural and social contingencies *and* that they can choose to cultivate themselves even in the midst of the most difficult circumstances. In the *Analects*, a sense of justice leads one to recognize the need to respond humanely to those who are affected by moral contingencies *and* the importance of holding people responsible for the choices they make.

It seems clear that Rawls and the *Analects* each describes a sense of justice that has three central features. First, a sense of justice is a moral sense or feeling that something is wrong about a certain range of situations, and all humans have the capacity to cultivate and develop it. Second, this moral sense is aroused in situations that are fair or unfair, including situations in which people are harmed by morally arbitrary contingencies and those circumstances in which they harm themselves through their own choices. Here we can see two different understandings of justice: justice as fairness and justice as desert. While Rawls is concerned strictly with the former, we find examples of both in the *Analects*. The third feature of a sense of justice is that when it is properly cultivated, it motivates people to work for the good of other members of society and results in the establishment of just institutions. A sense of justice causes us to identify with one another, and the feelings that result from this identification are sufficient to motivate individuals to abide by certain terms of cooperation that will result in the rectification of injustices and that will also help to preserve just conditions.

We have now seen the basic shared idea in Rawls and the *Analects* concerning a sense of justice that moves individuals to cooperate with other members of society in ways that are considered fair by all. However, the shared understanding of a sense of justice in each case is situated in a larger account of human societies. Whereas Rawls's account is based on liberal ideas such as the view that each person has the same claim to a fully adequate scheme of equal basic liberties, the view found in the *Analects* is rooted in a moral self-cultivationist perspective that is devoted to helping individuals embody a set of virtues over the course of their lives.[10] The most pervasive difference between these accounts is the fact that the Confucian understanding of a sense of justice is but one part of a larger ethical account found in the *Analects*, whereas the Rawlsian analysis of a sense of justice is designed to show how a political conception of justice, as opposed to a conception of justice that is derived from a comprehensive moral doctrine, is possible. This speaks to the different philosophical projects that are undertaken in the *Analects* and in Rawls. While Rawls is outlining principles of justice that could be affirmed by citizens in a modern liberal democracy who are committed to a diverse range of religious, philosophical, and moral doctrines, Kongzi is outlining and defending one particular view of what human societies should look like. Additionally, Rawls is addressing only the principles of justice by which a modern liberal democracy's institutions are to operate in light of the fact of reasonable pluralism, whereas Kongzi is outlining an entire way of life that includes certain kinds of religious rituals and family relationships, in addition to matters of fair distribution among people from very different economic circumstances. The contrast between Rawls's concern with principles of justice in a pluralistic liberal democracy and Kongzi's concern with the virtues, rituals, and relationships that help to define the Way is particularly striking.[11]

One of the well-known changes in Rawls's work between *A Theory of Justice* and *Political Liberalism* was his self-conscious attempt to move away from providing a comprehensive theory of justice. Rawls writes that the dualism between the point of view of the political conception of justice and the many comprehensive points of view "originates in the special nature of democratic political culture as marked by reasonable pluralism" (*PL*, xxiii). In other words, it originates not in philosophy but rather as a result of a particular set of historical and cultural circumstances. Rawls says that according to his view, the fact of reasonable pluralism is a product of "the different problems of political philosophy in the modern as compared with the ancient world" (*PL*, xxiii). He conjectures that when moral philosophy began with figures like Socrates,

> . . . ancient religion was a civic religion of public social practice, of civic festivals and public celebrations. Moreover, this civic religious culture was not based on a sacred work like the Bible, or the Koran, or the Vedas of Hinduism. The Greeks celebrated Homer and the Homeric poems were a basic part of their education, but the Iliad and the Odyssey were never sacred texts. As long as one participated in the expected way and recognized the proprieties, the details of what one believed were not of great importance. It was a matter of doing the done thing and being a trustworthy member of society, always ready to carry out one's civic duties as a good citizen—to serve on juries or to row in the fleet in war—when called upon to do so. (*PL*, xxiii)

The ideas of immortality and eternal salvation did not have a central place in classical Greek culture, and Greek moral philosophy began with the historical and cultural context of a civic religion of a *polis*, which contained no idea of the highest good that served as an alternative to that expressed by the Homeric gods and heroes. In rejecting the Homeric ideals, Greek philosophy had to work out for itself ideas of the highest good. Rawls notes that Greek moral philosophy "was not based on religion, much less on revelation, as civic religion was neither a guide nor a rival to it. Its focus was the idea of the highest good as an attractive ideal, as the reasonable pursuit of our true happiness. . . ." (*PL*, xxiv).

Against this background, Rawls points out the enormous consequences of the Reformation in the sixteenth century, the subsequent development of the modern state, and the development of modern science in the seventeenth century. The Reformation alone fragmented the religious unity of the Middle Ages and led to religious pluralism. Medieval Christianity was an authoritarian religion of salvation, doctrines, and priests. It was also an expansionist religion of conversion, which in turn led to intolerance (*PL*, xxv). The question that emerged was, "How is society even possible between those of different faiths? What can conceivably be the basis of religious tolerance?" (*PL*, xxvi). Rawls's discussion of these matters is important because he acknowledges that the fact of reasonable pluralism is the product of certain historical developments in Western philosophy and religion. He is not attempting to impose his account of a political conception of justice on all societies, nor is he even suggesting that that would be a viable option for all societies. Rawls does, however, maintain that to think "that social unity and concord requires agreement on a general and comprehensive religious, philosophical, or moral doctrine" is to accept intolerance as a condition of social order and stability (*PL*, xxvii). As Rawls points out, "The weakening of that belief helps to clear the way for liberal institutions" (*PL*, xxvii). Hence, we have the problem of political liberalism, which serves as Rawls's central question in his later work: "How is it possible that there may exist over time a stable and just society of free and equal citizens profoundly divided by reasonable religious, philosophical, and moral doctrines?" (*PL*, xxvii).

This review of the historical circumstances surrounding Rawls's work makes it even clearer that there are deep and important differences between both the nature and content of the accounts of human societies found in Rawls and in the *Analects*. One of the most important of these is the fact that Rawls clearly does not intend his account of how justice is achieved in a pluralistic society to apply to the sort of societies found in the ancient world in either Greece or China. Acknowledging this feature of Rawls's view can help us to appreciate more fully the contrast between Rawls's theory of justice, which is designed to accommodate the fact of reasonable pluralism, and Kongzi's view, which is meant to promote social harmony. Especially in light of these very different aims, it is important to remember that my aim in this book is not to compare Rawls's *theory* of justice with the view we find in the *Analects*. Rather, my study concerns the two understandings of a *sense* of justice—the moral sense on which Rawls and the *Analects* ground the claim that all humans have the capacity to understand and act in accordance with standards (or, in Rawls's case, principles) that are designed to help establish and maintain social justice. My comparative project is not focused exclusively or primarily on the specific content of those standards but rather on the capacity and motivation humans have to abide by them.

An even more interesting area of contrast between Rawls and the *Analects* concerns the way in which a sense of justice is developed and extended to the whole of society. According to Rawls, a sense of justice must first and foremost be cultivated within each individual family and then within individual communities. Only after these initial stages of cultivation is one able to fully develop a sense of justice that extends to members of society that are not a part of one's family or immediate community. This view represents an area of agreement with the *Analects*, which maintains that one's capacity to be a good member of society spreads outward from filial relationships with one's parents to one's relationships with elders in the community and finally to one's posture toward other members of society.[12] According to the *Analects*, however, in addition to each member of society developing certain capacities and virtues, it is also necessary to have an exemplary ruler. A sense of justice first must be cultivated in parent–child relationships, then in the community, finally extending to one's behavior toward other members of society, but the *Analects* also maintains that societies must have virtuous rulers who care for the members of their societies.

The understanding of the relationship between *de* 德 ("Virtue") and rulership that we examined in Chapter 3 obviously is not a part of the cultivation of a sense of justice in Rawls. As we have seen, the idea that the most virtuous individuals should rule is at the heart of the emergence of the civil service examination system, which allows one's moral character and scholarly abilities to determine one's share of wealth and power. On this view, it is understood that the ruler and other officials may be wealthier than others, and this is seen as proper and fair because these individuals are the most virtuous. According to the *Analects*, if a virtuous ruler is in charge, then the fact that the ruler is wealthier than the people will not be a problem because virtuous rulers are not satisfied until their people are all provided for. The *Analects* tells us that good rulers do not even worry about meeting their own needs until their people have all been taken care of. So, a part of choosing the most virtuous rulers and allowing them to have the greatest share of the wealth and power is the fact that if they *are* virtuous rulers, they will not simply hoard their wealth and disregard the needs of the people. Rather, they will ensure that food and other forms of wealth are fairly distributed so that everyone's needs are met.

Rawls's model is an obvious contrast to this kind of view because it depends on just institutions—as opposed to virtuous leaders—to ensure things like fair distribution. Thus, on Rawls's view, "when everyone follows the publicly recognized rules of cooperation, and honors the claims the rules specify, the particular distribution of goods that result are acceptable as just (or at least as not unjust) whatever these distributions turn out to be" (*JF*, 50). Institutions are what keep property and wealth "evenly enough shared over time to preserve the fair value of the political liberties and fair equality of opportunity over generations. They do this by laws regulating bequest and inheritance of property, and other devices such as taxes, to prevent excessive concentrations of private power" (*JF*, 51). This view depends heavily on each individual's having a cultivated sense of justice, meaning that each individual is properly motivated to establish and sustain these institutions.

It is important to note a couple of things here. First, Rawls's view works to prevent excessive concentrations of private power and relies on institutions and the citizens who support them to establish and preserve justice, whereas the view seen in the *Analects* obviously accords the ruler a great deal of power and relies on him to use it humanely. But this dichotomy is not quite as sharp as it may appear at first blush. The *Analects* clearly presents a view wherein institutions, which include practices such as taxation as well as other laws and policies, are a part of governance. Although Kongzi says that an ideal society would not need *certain* kinds of institutions (2.3), it is not the case that he simply favors a powerful ruler *instead of* institutions for establishing justice. Rather, Kongzi maintains that the standards represented by the rites should be used to order society, and he maintains that members of society should adhere to these standards (4.13).[13] Similarly, Rawls does not deny that a society needs strong leaders to guide the formation, revision, and preservation of its institutions. Indeed, he affirms the view that some individuals are more qualified than others for leadership positions, and that what makes them qualified are certain excellences of character, many of which are also a part of what makes for a virtuous ruler on the account provided by the *Analects*.

Focusing strictly on Rawls's concern with just institutions and the *Analects'* insistence on virtuous rulers also neglects the emphasis both of these views place on the role played by members of society in achieving a just and humane society. According to the *Analects*, there should be a general improvement in people's moral character as a result of their having a virtuous ruler, and a part of what this means is that people will act in accordance with certain standards, including those specified by the rites, as well as the laws and policies that have been put into place by good rulers. For Rawls, citizens with an effective sense of justice must take an active role in the institutions designed to establish and maintain justice, and this means that some citizens will assume positions that allow them considerably more influence than others. So long as these offices are open to all, however, Rawls does not consider the power associated with them to be problematic.

So although Rawls's view depends on establishing just institutions, and also on the commitment that individual citizens make to those institutions, whereas the Confucian view depends more on having a virtuous leader and on the influence of his *de* ("Virtue") on the people, there are some important similarities between these accounts as well. On both views, individuals cultivate a sense of justice in the context of the family and community, and without this foundation they are unlikely to develop into good members of society. This is perhaps the most important and substantive area of agreement between the two views: A good society can never be achieved unless its members care about one another's well-being and feel a responsibility for one another's welfare. Ultimately, according to both Rawls and the *Analects*, parents are responsible for helping their children to cultivate a sense of justice. Parents are responsible for helping their children come to see how others are harmed by injustices, and for helping them learn how to avoid perpetuating social injustice. This foundation leads citizens, on Rawls's view, to endorse principles of justice which "make it likely that economic and social inequalities contribute in an effective way to the general good or, more exactly, to the benefit of the least-advantaged members of society" (*JF*, 52). The posture that members of society take toward one another based on a highly cultivated sense of justice is also a part of what leads members of society in the *Analects* to support rulers who advocate policies of equal distribution and who do not make the rich richer but work to help the poor.

Now that we have in view these two accounts of how a sense of justice functions in a society, we can ask what difficulties might emerge within each model. For the Confucian view, there is the question of how to ensure that the most virtuous people—and not just members of the elite class or especially intelligent or well-educated individuals—become rulers and officials. The examination system attempted to systematize this process, and it underwent a continual process of revision, expansion, and reorganization throughout its existence both in order to address the privileged access that members of elite and educated classes had to official positions and in order to find more effective ways of selecting virtuous leaders. Although it is possible to measure one's knowledge of the Confucian classics, the Confucians realized that there is more to moral character and being a virtuous leader than this dimension of learning. In addition to the challenge of determining who the most virtuous individuals are, there is the matter of defending the view that *de* ("Virtue") actually works in the way the *Analects* says it does, namely that virtuous people have an attractive power and a profound influence on those around them. The Confucian account of achieving a society that embodies the Way—a society that is just, among other things—depends partly on members of society developing a sense of justice, but it also depends on this account of the ruler's impact being accurate.

For Rawls, one of the most serious lingering questions is how just institutions are established in order to provide the kind of background justice he envisions. Rawls's account of moral psychology and how a sense of justice develops includes the claim that "given certain assumptions specifying a reasonable human psychology and the normal conditions of human life, those who grow up under just basic institutions—institutions that justice as fairness itself enjoins—acquire a reasoned and informed allegiance to those institutions sufficient to render them stable" (*JF*, 185). However, the question that remains is how just basic institutions are established in the first place, if citizens must grow up under them in order for their sense of justice to be fully developed, and in order to render their just institutions stable. Here Rawls faces something much like "Xunzi's Dilemma," which I mentioned briefly in Chapter 2 and will further discuss in the next section of this chapter. But first it will be helpful to review Rawls's dilemma, which takes the following form: If citizens must grow up under just basic institutions in order to fully develop a sense of justice, then where do just institutions come from in the first place? An illustration of this problem can be further seen in Rawls's remark that

> the basic structure is arranged to include the requisite institutions of background justice so that citizens have available to them the general all-purpose means to train and educate their basic capabilities, and a fair opportunity to make good use of them, provided their capabilities lie within the normal range. It is left to citizens as free and equal persons, secure in their basic rights and liberties and able to take charge of their own life, to avail themselves of the opportunities guaranteed to all on a fair basis. (*JF*, 171)

Another difficulty with Rawls's account is seen in his subsequent claim that "those with a greater capacity for the judicial virtues have, other things equal, a greater chance of holding positions of authority with the responsibilities that call for the exercise of those virtues" (*JF*, 171). Here we see some important areas of resonance with the *Analects*: On Rawls's view, too, virtuous persons are at least in some ways uniquely suited for positions of authority. Concerning the judicial virtues, for example, most of us would agree that it would be ideal to have Supreme Court justices who have cultivated these virtues to a higher degree than have others. We tend to think that someone who has a highly cultivated sense of fairness and good judgment should be the person who takes a position on the High Court. The problem, however, is the fact that in our current system, only a narrow range of candidates will have a realistic chance at serving on the Supreme Court. This is not necessarily because they are the most highly skilled judges but partly because they are the candidates who have the right pedigrees, including Ivy League degrees and clerkships with the right justices. It is well and good to say that once just institutions are in place and functioning properly it is up to all citizens to "take charge of their own [lives]" and "avail themselves of the opportunities guaranteed to all on a fair basis." But Rawls has already stressed to us the degree to which individuals can be determined by the social and natural contingencies that are a part of their lives and the way in which social practices often continue to perpetuate the problems associated with these inequalities even after institutions become just. There is a tension here between Rawls's initial claims about the problems posed by moral contingencies and the self-cultivationist language he sometimes uses to describe the capacities human beings have. On the one hand, he indicates that people are often determined by their circumstances, while on the other he clearly thinks that people have the capacity to cultivate their moral powers.[14]

Given Rawls's account of the way in which moral contingencies often determine the course of human lives, his claim that anyone can "avail [him- or herself] of the opportunities guaranteed to all on a fair basis" leaves us wondering how to achieve a society in which opportunities *are* guaranteed to all on a fair basis. Is it realistic to think that a society can attain this ideal? Here we see another important area of resonance between Rawls and the *Analects*: Both accounts are ideal theories. Rawls continually reminds his readers of this fact:

> We ask in effect what a perfectly just, or nearly just, constitutional regime might be like, and whether it may come about and be made stable under the circumstances of justice, and so under realistic, though reasonably

favorable, conditions. In this way, justice as fairness is realistically utopian: it probes the limits of the realistically practicable, that is, how far in our world (given its laws and tendencies) a democratic regime can attain complete realization of its appropriate political values—democratic perfection, if you like. (*JF*, 13)

In the *Analects*, Kongzi wonders at times whether he will ever see the Way put into practice (4.8, 5.27). It is clear at many junctures that his account may be considered an ideal theory. For example, *Analects* 4.5 says that the *junzi* 君子 ("exemplary person") does not go against *Ren* 仁 ("humaneness") even for the amount of time required to finish a meal, or in times of urgency or distress. In *Analects* 4.6 Kongzi goes on to say that he has never met a person who truly loved *Ren* and hated a lack of *Ren*: "Is there a person who can, for the space of a single day, simply devote his efforts to *Ren*? I have never met anyone whose strength was insufficient for this task. Perhaps such a person exists, but I have yet to meet him." So although Kongzi articulates his vision of the Way in practice, he is aware that his own society is far from embodying it.

As a result of the fact that both the *Analects* and Rawls present ideal theories, both accounts face the question of how an ideal theory can serve as a realistic guide when at times it seems unattainable. As we have seen, Rawls maintains that his theory is "realistically utopian" (*JF*, 13). He also says that studying the ideal theory should "provide some guidance in thinking about nonideal theory, and so about difficult cases of how to deal with existing injustices. It should also help to clarify the goal of reform and to identify which wrongs are more grievous and hence more urgent to correct" (*JF*, 13). So on Rawls's view, this vision of society is attainable, but he does not deny that it calls for difficult and extensive degrees of reform.[15]

The *Analects* confronts the question of how an ideal theory can serve as a realistic guide by praising those who struggle with the difficult task of self-cultivation, keeping the ideal vision of the Way in mind, while admonishing those who simply give up because they think their strength is insufficient for attaining the Way. When Ran Qiu says in 6.12 that he delights in the Way but his strength is insufficient to follow it, Kongzi objects to his response, saying, "Someone whose strength is genuinely insufficient collapses somewhere along the Way. As for you, you deliberately draw the line." He points out that Ran Qiu is not even *trying* to follow the Way, which once again makes him a contrast to Yan Hui, who as Kongzi notes in 6.7 did not stray from *Ren* for three months at a time. Kongzi's remarks about Ran Qiu and Yan Hui provide a sense of what his response might be to someone who objected that the ideal of a society which follows the Way is simply out of reach. As a self-cultivationist, Kongzi thinks our task is to pursue the Way even when we doubt that we, or the societies we live in, will ever succeed in following it perfectly. That is not to say, however, that Kongzi thinks the Way is unattainable, for he clearly believes that past societies have succeeded in following the Way. Like Rawls, he thinks we must use the ideal theory—and the model provided by societies that followed the Way—to take steps toward improving ourselves and our societies. This is why Kongzi compares the task of self-cultivation to building a mountain: ". . . if I stop even one basketful of earth short of completion, then I have stopped completely. It might also be compared to the task of leveling ground: even if I have only dumped a single basketful of earth, at least I am moving forward" (9.19).

The response of both Rawls and the *Analects* to someone who has difficulty believing that their accounts are attainable is that ideal theories tell us a great deal about the steps we need to take toward improving our societies; they provide a good starting place for a long and arduous journey *and* they serve as a guide throughout that journey. Both Rawls and the *Analects* maintain that the reason their accounts are ultimately achievable is that human beings can cultivate their moral capacities, and these capacities enable them to feel for and think about their fellow human beings in humane and compassionate ways. On both views, humans have the capacity for a sense of justice, among other capacities, and their ability to refine and cultivate that capacity is one of the most important sources of a stable society for Rawls, and a society that pursues the Way in the *Analects*.

Comparative studies can help us to understand ideas like a sense of justice because we have the opportunity to examine the manner in which it is understood within very different frameworks, and thus comparative work enables us to learn more about the way an idea like a sense of justice works in relation to other important ideas, practices, and institutions. The next two sections of this chapter focus on how this comparative study can help us to understand and evaluate the two views under study and thus how it makes a contribution to the larger body of knowledge within the discipline and practice of philosophy through the comparative process.

Justice and Self-Cultivation in Rawls

An important shared feature of a sense of justice in Rawls and the *Analects* is the idea that, as Rawls puts it, people "would lack certain essential elements of humanity" if they did not have a sense of justice.[16] In the *Analects*, *Ren* is the fullest realization of one's capacities as a human being, and as passages like 4.5 and 6.30 make clear, Kongzi sees having a sense of justice as part of being *Ren* ("humane"). In both Rawls and the *Analects*, having a sense of justice is something that makes us human. We have seen that both Rawls and the *Analects* maintain that a sense of justice is initially cultivated in the context of parent–child relationships, and then in one's relationships with other elders and friends in one's community. These are the contexts that lay the ground for a fully developed sense of justice that shapes one's responses to other members of society.

In Chapter 2 I highlighted the self-cultivationist dimension of Rawls's account, and this is perhaps the most important feature of Rawls's work that is brought to the forefront by a comparative study with the *Analects*. In this section, I explore the question of why it is important to understand this dimension of Rawls's work—that is, what we gain by examining this theme in Rawls, and in what ways a self-cultivationist analysis deepens our understanding of the strengths and weaknesses of Rawls's account. In Chapter 2 I argued that studying this side of Rawls's work helps to highlight the resources in his work that offer a defense against some of the criticisms raised by communitarian and feminist critics. I argue here that in addition, the self-cultivationist dimension of Rawls's work can serve as a resource for interpreting Rawls's account in a way that will allow him to meet the challenge posed by the problem that resembles "Xunzi's Dilemma." It can also help to resolve the tension between his claim that moral contingencies can determine the course of human lives and the claim that all humans have the capacity to cultivate their moral powers. In the course of my argument I will highlight some dimensions of Mengzi's account of human nature that resonate with some of Rawls's remarks and that might be used to augment and extend his account in certain ways, in the same way that Mengzi's account augmented and extended Kongzi's ethical view in ways that helped defend it against various critics.[17]

A serious concern that emerges with any attempt to associate Rawls's account with a theory of human nature is that Rawls explicitly denies that his account includes a theory of human nature. Rawls writes that although political liberalism differs from comprehensive liberalism because it does not *take a general position* on certain questions, it does *affirm a certain range of answers* to those questions with respect to a political conception of justice for a constitutional democratic regime. In this respect Rawls says his account resonates with the work of Hume and Kant (*PL*, xxix). The three basic questions of moral epistemology and psychology that Rawls is talking about here are: (1) Is the knowledge or awareness of how we are to act directly accessible only to some, or is it accessible to every person who is normally reasonable and conscientious? (2) Is the moral order required of us derived from an external source—say, from an order of values in God's intellect—or does it arise in some way from human nature itself (either from reason or feeling or from a union of both), together with the requirements of our living together in society? (3) Must we be persuaded or compelled to bring ourselves in line with the requirements of our duties and obligations by some external motivation—say, by divine sanctions or by those of the state—or are we so constituted that we have in our nature sufficient motives to lead us to act as we ought without the need of external threats and inducements?

Rawls writes that political liberalism affirms the second alternative in each of these cases: It sees the moral order as arising "in some way from human nature itself, as reason or as feeling, and from the conditions of our life in society" (*PL*, xxix). It also sees the knowledge or awareness of how we are to act as "directly accessible to every person who is normally reasonable and conscientious." Finally, it sees human beings as constituted so that "we have in our nature sufficient motives to lead us to act as we ought without the need of external sanctions, at least in the form of rewards and punishments imposed by God or the state." So although Rawls says that political liberalism "does not take a general position on the three questions above" because it leaves them to be answered in different ways by different comprehensive views, he maintains that "political liberalism does affirm the second alternative in each case with respect to a political conception of justice for a constitutional democratic regime" (*PL*, xxix).

How are we to interpret Rawls's remarks here? This is something of a challenge, as Rawls denies that political liberalism takes a general position on these three questions while still maintaining that it affirms the second alternative in each case with respect to a political conception of justice for a constitutional democratic regime. How is it possible for political liberalism to avoid taking a general position and yet affirm one of the two possible answers to each question? What Rawls seems to mean is that political liberalism does not endorse a fully developed *theory* of human nature; however, it does consider certain *kinds* of answers to questions about human nature to be correct. Specifically, one must believe that most citizens have the resources to act justly. Here we see clearly Rawls's acknowledgment that his account is dependent on the idea that humans have a basic moral sense by virtue of being human.

Rawls writes that all humans originally possess the capacity to develop a sense of justice.[18] But as we have seen, there is some question about what Rawls means by "capacity" here: Do humans have an initial *tendency* to develop a sense of justice, or do they simply have the *ability* to develop it? That is, does Rawls think humans have initial, observable, active tendencies toward a sense of justice, or does he think only that they have a latent or hidden capacity for a sense of justice? Although Rawls says he is discussing "the abilities we find latent in our nature," he sometimes indicates that he takes a stronger view of how active and visible this capacity is initially (*TJ*, 375–76). For example, consider his account of how the capacity for a sense of justice is observable from an early age in a child's response to her parents. In this discussion, Rawls seems to be describing not a hidden moral sense that must undergo certain forms of cultivation before it is noticeable but rather a moral sense that is already observable and active from the earliest stages of childhood. Thus, Rawls's account does not always appear to be entirely consistent with his claim that a sense of justice is a *latent* part of our nature.

In order to understand why this question is important, and in order to better understand the difference between an observable, active moral sense and a latent one, I want to turn to the discussion of this subject in the early Confucian tradition. As we have already seen, the *Analects* does not present a systematic account or theory of human nature, but the debate between Mengzi and Xunzi on this subject, specifically concerning the question of what moral capacities humans have simply by virtue of being human, provides a clear picture of what is at stake in the distinction between latent and observable, active moral capacities. Mengzi was the first Confucian thinker to discuss explicitly the relationship between human nature and self-cultivation, maintaining that self-cultivation is a process of developing our original inclinations toward goodness.[19] According to Mengzi, all human beings are born with four observable, active moral senses or "sprouts" (*duan* 端) that are already in their initial stages of development. He uses the metaphor of sprouts to express and develop this idea by describing how these four moral senses, if properly nourished and protected from harm, eventually grow into the virtues of benevolence (*Ren* 仁), righteousness (*yi* 義), propriety (*li* 禮), and wisdom (*zhi* 智).[20] The *Mengzi* says, "People having these four sprouts is like their having four limbs. To have these four sprouts but say of oneself that one is unable to be virtuous is to steal from oneself . . . . In general, having these four sprouts within oneself, if one knows to fill them all out, it will be like a fire starting up, a spring breaking through!"[21]

Mengzi's choice of a metaphor here is telling. As Ivanhoe points out, "[L]ike sprouts, our moral sense is a *visible and active*, not *hidden or latent*, part of the self."[22] Ivanhoe notes that Mengzi uses a number of different terms for "sprout" throughout the text, including *meng* 萌, *nie* 蘖 ("buds"), and *miao* 苗 ("sprouts of grain"). He does not, however, use the term for "seed," which would have illustrated a tendency that is hidden, unlike the active, visible moral senses Mengzi envisions. As Ivanhoe shows, Mengzi seems to have been aware of the fact that in order for his program of self-cultivation to work, people must already possess an active and visible moral capacity that can be developed.[23] In support of the claim that all humans have moral sprouts, Mengzi offers examples of people with visible and active moral tendencies. Mengzi argues that human moral capacities are rooted in the *xin* 心 ("heart-mind"), which contains cognitive and affective faculties, including the four moral "sprouts," as well as volitional abilities.[24] Because the moral sprouts reside in the *xin*, humans use their moral sense when they think and reflect about things: "The function of the mind is to reflect. When it reflects, it gets things right; if it does not reflect, it cannot get things right."[25]

So, according to the *Mengzi*, all human beings are the same in having an active, visible moral sense, and those who use it "follow their greater part." He further expounds on this claim with the parable of the barley sprouts: "The soil is the same and the time of planting is also the same. They grow rapidly, and by the time of summer solstice they have all ripened. Although there are some differences, these are due to the richness in the soil, and to unevenness in the rain and in human effort."[26] Mengzi emphasizes that everyone starts out with moral sprouts, and while some aspects of the sprouts' environment are the same, others are different. In the parable of Ox Mountain, we learn that although the trees on the mountain were once beautiful, they were not protected from a variety of harms. Similarly, moral sprouts need a safe and nourishing environment in order to flourish. Mengzi notes that in the case of Ox Mountain, "[I]t was not that there were no sprouts or shoots growing there. But oxen and sheep then came and grazed on them. Hence, it was as if it were barren."[27] He tells us in the parable of the man from Song, who tugged on his sprouts of grain in an effort to make them grow more quickly and inadvertently uprooted them, that humans must neither neglect their moral sense nor try to force it to grow. These passages show clearly that Mengzi did not think humans were born with fully developed moral capacities; rather, they were born with an initial inclination toward goodness. Mengzi stresses that we can see these moral capacities in action simply by observing human behavior. But although one's moral "sprouts" are visible and active right from the start, they are in need of considerable encouragement and growth in order for one to develop into a moral person.

Although Mengzi and Xunzi agree on many aspects of moral self-cultivation, including the qualities of the cultivated person, Xunzi rejects Mengzi's claim that humans are initially inclined toward goodness. As a result, he also maintains that moral cultivation necessarily involves something much more difficult and heavy-handed than reflection and personal effort combined with the proper conditions for growth and development. According to the Xunzian account of human nature and self-cultivation, persons become moral not as the result of original inclinations toward morality but because of how teachers and traditions shape them. Xunzi maintains that humans are morally blind at birth, led only by their physical desires, which lead inevitably to destruction and harm.[28] Accordingly, humans must be stamped with the shape of morality. Ivanhoe points to the difference between Mengzi's "developmental model" of moral self-cultivation, evident in Mengzi's claim that we must develop the moral "sprouts" we are born with, and Xunzi's "re-formation model," expressed in his metaphors for humans, including warped boards that are re-formed with steam and pressure to fit the Confucian design.[29] Xunzi writes, "Through steaming and bending, you can make wood straight as a plumb line into a wheel. And after its curve conforms to the compass, even when parched under the sun it will not become straight again, because the steaming and bending have made it a certain way."[30]

Xunzi maintains that rituals and social obligations "are produced from the deliberate effort of the sage; they are not produced from people's nature. Thus, when the potter mixes clay and makes vessels, the vessels are produced from the deliberate efforts of the craftsman; they are not produced from people's nature."[31] As Ivanhoe points out, Xunzi sees morality *itself* as artificial.[32] He does not think human beings have active, visible tendencies toward morality, nor does he think they are guided by an innate moral sense. Rather, through a long and arduous process of self-cultivation humans acquire moral capacities and the ability to judge situations properly. Xunzi, then, maintains that humans acquire a sensibility they never had before instead of developing a moral sense they are born with, and he is explicit in his disagreement with Mengzi's view. He makes a point of rejecting Mengzi's claim that *si* 思 ("reflection") is the key to allowing our moral sense to lead us. Rather, Xunzi says, "I once spent a whole day in *si* 思 'reflection,' but it wasn't as good as a moment's worth of *xue* 學 'learning.'"[33] Mengzi's and Xunzi's remarks on reflection and learning serve to remind us of the fact that they both consider themselves interpreters and defenders of Kongzi's account of moral self-cultivation.[34]

"Xunzi's Dilemma" stems from Xunzi's apparent failure to explain the origins of the sages' moral capacities, as well as exactly how people with the sort of nature he describes were both willing and able to commit themselves to the rituals and standards of righteousness that the sages offered, prior to the establishment of society.[35] In order to understand how this constitutes a dilemma, we will need to review what Xunzi says about what normal humans are like when they are born, as well as his account of the origins of society:

> People's nature is bad. Their goodness is a matter of deliberate effort. Now people's nature is such that they are born with a fondness for profit. If they follow along with this, then struggle and contention arise, and yielding and deference will perish therein. They are born with feelings of hate and dislike. If they follow along with these, then cruelty and villainy will arise, and loyalty and trustworthiness will perish therein. They are born with desires of the eyes and ears, a fondness for beautiful sights and sounds. If they follow along with these, then lasciviousness and chaos will arise, and ritual and standards of righteousness, proper form and good order, will perish therein. Thus, if people follow along with their inborn nature and dispositions, they are sure to come to struggle and contention, turn to disrupting social divisions and disorder, and end up in violence. So, it is necessary to await the transforming influence of teachers and models and the guidance of ritual and the standards of righteousness, and only then will they come to yielding and deference, turn to culture and order, and end up under control.[36]

It is important to note that Xunzi is absolutely clear on what humans are like prior to these transforming influences, namely that "without teachers or proper models for people, they will be deviant, dangerous, and incorrect in their behavior. Without ritual and the standards of righteousness, they will be unruly, chaotic, and not well ordered."[37] Where, then, did these teachers, models, rituals, and standards emerge from initially? Xunzi offers the following answer to this question:

> In ancient times, the sage-kings saw that because people's nature is bad, they were deviant, dangerous and not correct in their behavior, and they were unruly, chaotic, and not well-ordered. Therefore, for their sake they set up ritual and standards of righteousness, and established proper models and measures. They did this in order to straighten out and beautify people's nature and inborn dispositions and thereby correct them, and in order to train and transform people's nature and inborn dispositions and

thereby guide them. Then for the first time they were well ordered and conformed to the Way.[38]

Xunzi also addresses this set of issues in response to the question "From what did ritual arise?" He responds,

> I say: Humans are born having desires. When they have desires but do not get the objects of their desires, then they cannot but seek some means of satisfaction. If there is no measure or limit to their seeking, then they cannot help but struggle with each other. If they struggle with each other then there will be chaos, and if there is chaos then they will be impoverished. The former kings hated such chaos, and so they established rituals and the standards of righteousness in order to allot things to people, to nurture their desires, and to satisfy their seeking. They caused desires never to exhaust material goods, and material goods never to be depleted by desires, so that the two support each other and prosper. This is how ritual arose.[39]

Now, Xunzi is clearly aware of the point that can be pressed here, namely "From what are ritual and the standards of righteousness produced?" He responds, "In every case, ritual and the standards of righteousness are produced from the deliberate effort of the sage; they are not produced from people's nature." He goes on to write, "The sage accumulates reflections and deliberations and practices deliberate efforts and reasoned activities in order to produce ritual and standards of righteousness and to establish proper models and measures."[40]

Putting all of this together, we can see that Xunzi argues that the morality and order seen in society comes from the accumulated deliberate efforts of sages and not from human nature. He also argues that the former kings hated the chaos that resulted from human nature and that this dislike motivated them to produce the rituals and standards of righteousness, all for the sake of the people. These claims suggest that on Xunzi's view, the sages were fundamentally different from other people in at least two important ways: First, they hated the chaos, and second, they knew how to put an end to it. The first of these differences is primarily affective: The sages had different *feelings* about the chaos that existed in society. The second difference is mainly cognitive: The sages had *knowledge* of how to put a stop to the chaos. Here, we must take note of the fact that Xunzi does *not* argue that all people hated the chaos and over time worked to put a stop to it; rather, Xunzi distinguishes between the people and the sage-kings, making it clear that this chaos came to an end only through the actions of the sage-kings. This suggests that on Xunzi's view, the people were not capable of doing what the sages did; at least, it seems reasonable to assume this, given that they did not do what the sages did. He also notes that as a result of the fundamental character of human nature, change is *impossible* without the work of the sages: "*[I]t is necessary to await* the transforming influence of teachers and models and the guidance of ritual and the standards of righteousness, and *only then* will they come to yielding and deference, turn to culture and order, and end up under control."[41] The fact that Xunzi uses such strong language is important because it shows that people *cannot* transform themselves; they have no natural resources with which to do so.

Given the crucial differences—both affective and cognitive—between the sages and the people, the key questions that pose difficulties for Xunzi are: (1) If the sages started out with the same nature as other humans, how did they turn themselves into beings who not only recognized morality but also loved and delighted in it? If they did not possess the same nature, why and in precisely what ways were the sages different from everyone else? (2) What initially *motivated* people to embrace the rituals and the standards of righteousness offered by the sages? (3) If they were so motivated, what accounts for their *ability* to commit themselves to following the models and standards provided by the sages? A number of interpreters have suggested potential answers to these questions, and I am not claiming that it is impossible to construct a response that is faithful to at least some aspects of Xunzi's view.[42] There is an important distinction, though, between describing what Xunzi actually said on these matters and constructing a solution to "Xunzi's Dilemma" based on what he said elsewhere or based on our own reflections on his view. To acknowledge "Xunzi's Dilemma" is simply to recognize that there is an apparent inconsistency in what Xunzi says on these matters, and that its resolution has important consequences for Xunzi's view.[43] Whether or not we can find the resources to address these questions elsewhere in Xunzi's thought, it is important to note that that these questions are not directly answered in Xunzi's account of the origins of ritual and society. People's desires, Xunzi makes clear, are originally geared solely toward the fulfillment of their physical desires. Prior to the establishment of society, were people originally motivated to follow the sages by the impression that the Way would lead to the fulfillment of their physical desires? Did they make a purely rational calculation based on the likelihood of survival or fear of punishment?[44] Even if one maintains that people were driven to follow the Way largely out of fear of the chaotic and dangerous life they knew, one still must explain how people with the capacities Xunzi describes were *able* to commit themselves to following the Way, particularly in light of how difficult Xunzi thinks the path of self-cultivation is. The idea that the people would be able to set themselves on the path of self-cultivation and remain on it long enough to begin to experience real change implies that they were able to restrain their desires in at least some basic ways, and yet Xunzi's account suggests that it was only *after* they had experienced the transforming influence of teachers and traditions that this type of restraint was possible. Here we see clearly "Xunzi's Dilemma": In order for people to even begin to follow the new ways created by the sages, it seems that they must have had some sort of natural response to the Way when they saw it (such as a natural tendency to follow it), but this would clearly be a natural moral tendency, and Xunzi's account of human nature explicitly denies the existence of such tendencies. In order to offer a compelling explanation of the origins of morality, it seems likely that Xunzi's account will need to be modified in order to show why and how people would respond positively to the Way presented by the sages.[45] Additionally, because Xunzi makes clear that the sages were, indeed, different from other humans in some important respects, it seems that Xunzi did not think the sages possessed the same nature as other humans, by virtue of their heightened capacities in certain areas—something that, in itself, raises further questions about Xunzi's view.[46] To be clear, in recognizing "Xunzi's Dilemma" I am not claiming that it is not possible to resolve these issues by drawing upon or developing other aspects of Xunzi's thought. I do think, though, that addressing these issues in a truly satisfying way requires some revision of Xunzi's theory of human nature.[47]

In addition to "Xunzi's Dilemma," another feature of Xunzi's account that is important for our purposes is that despite his pessimism about what humans are like prior to cultivation, he still maintains that human beings have the *capacity* for morality, because they have the capacity to cultivate themselves. We can see here how Mengzi and Xunzi mean very different things when they say that humans have the capacity for morality. For Xunzi, this capacity is hidden or latent, and it becomes visible only after a great deal of training and hard work, whereas for Mengzi it is visible and active from the start, needing the proper environment combined with personal effort and reflection in order to grow. The question, then, is which view Rawls is closer to when he discusses the capacity for a sense of justice. Is the capacity for a sense of justice a hidden moral potential, or is it a visible and active tendency toward morality? I do not think Rawls exhibits an awareness of this distinction or its importance for his view, but looking at the sort of language he uses in describing the cultivation of a sense of justice can help us determine which view seems to be more consistent with his account.

In *Theory* Rawls says that the success of a child's development of a sense of justice depends on precepts that "appeal to his original inclinations," which suggests that the process of cultivating a sense of justice engages our natural, pro-social inclinations (*TJ* §70, p. 408). Rawls provides a three-stage account of how a sense of justice develops that gives us a picture of a moral sense being drawn out and extended initially within the context of parent–child relationships and then cultivated in relationships with family and friends. Finally, it is cultivated and expressed in one's relationships with fellow citizens. We can understand this as a process of learning to see oneself and understand one's different roles and obligations—first, as a son or daughter; next, as a sister or brother, niece or nephew, friend, and student; and, finally, the role of a citizen in relation to other citizens. Each role has responsibilities and obligations tied to it, and one's understanding of those responsibilities as well as one's motivation to fulfill them is tied to one's sense of justice—the feelings one has toward others by virtue of their common membership in a family, community, or society. Rawls talks about one's ability to relate to others as something that *spreads outward*, a dynamic movement that occurs when one's moral development is on track. This description is very close to Mengzi's account of how moral sprouts develop. In 2A6, as we saw earlier, the *Mengzi* says that "if one knows to broaden and fill them all out, it will be like a fire starting up, a spring breaking through!" Mengzi also says that moral development proceeds by nourishing (7A1) and extending (7A15) one's natural moral impulses.

Rawls writes that a sense of justice needs to be "properly trained and exercised." A just society "trains and educates" one's sense of justice (*JF*, 171). Throughout his analysis, Rawls uses a list of self-cultivationist terms to describe how a sense of justice must be "trained," "exercised," "educated," "encouraged," "sustained," "formed," and "nurtured." Rawls seems to be closer to Mengzi than to Xunzi in thinking that a sense of justice is an original inclination toward morality that all humans are born with and that develops under the proper circumstances and in the proper environment. None of the words he uses to describe the cultivation of a sense of justice resonate with Xunzi's harsh metaphors of re-forming a difficult substance or of uncovering a hidden, dormant capacity.

Interestingly, the points of resonance between Rawls's account and Mengzi's account extend further than their basic accounts of human nature and self-cultivation. We have seen that Rawls postulates "the Aristotelian Principle," according to which "human beings enjoy the exercise of their realized capacities (their innate or trained abilities), and this enjoyment increases the more the capacity is realized, or the greater its complexity"

(*TJ* §65, p. 374). Here Rawls follows Aristotle's view that various kinds of pleasure and enjoyment arise when we exercise our faculties, but we should recall that Rawls also postulates a "companion effect" of the Aristotelian Principle, namely the fact that as we witness the exercise of well-trained abilities by others, "these displays are enjoyed by us and arouse a desire that we should be able to do the same things ourselves" (*TJ* §65, pp. 375–76).

This account represents a deep and interesting area of agreement with Mengzi, who maintains that reflecting on good conduct produces a special feeling of joy that reinforces our moral sense and gives us moral courage. Mengzi says that if we delight in our moral sprouts, "then they grow. If they grow then how can they be stopped? If they cannot be stopped, then without realizing it one's feet begin to step in time to them and one's hands dance according to their rhythms."[48] The joy that is produced by performing good actions or seeing others perform good actions, and by reflecting on those actions, produces "flood-like" *qi* 氣 or energy, which then nourishes our moral sprouts and promotes moral growth. According to Mengzi, when our moral sprouts are nourished, we are able to perform more difficult moral tasks than before; our moral character is strengthened. Mengzi writes that flood-like *qi* is

> supremely great and supremely unyielding. If one cultivates it with uprightness and does not harm it, it will fill up the space between Heaven and earth. It is a *qi* that unites righteousness with the Way. Without these, it starves. It is produced by accumulated righteousness. It cannot be obtained by a seizure of righteousness. If some of one's actions leave one's heart unsatisfied, it will starve.[49]

The two areas of agreement I wish to focus on here are, first, the idea that using one's moral sense to do good actions produces a kind of joy that leads to moral development; and, second, the idea that seeing the moral conduct of others also produces joy that furthers our own moral motivation. On Rawls's view, living in a just society is critical for one's development of a sense of justice because one sees just institutions at work and wishes to take part in them. Actions that accord with principles of justice help to strengthen one's sense of justice. According to the companion effect of the Aristotelian Principle, the more cases one sees of justice at work, the more one's sense of justice grows and develops, and the more one wishes to stand up to instances of injustice. One's sense of justice becomes a meter which not only indicates that something is wrong but also helps to motivate one to act. On Mengzi's view, actions that accord with the Way produce a special kind of joy, which in turn produces *qi* that nourishes the moral sprouts of those who perform the actions *and* those who witness them. What is especially important about Mengzi's account is that one must have the proper emotional comportment to accompany one's actions. Experiencing the joy of moral thoughts and actions causes our native moral sense to grow, strengthening our moral character. An important part of this process is seeing others perform good actions, because our moral feelings are reinforced and extended when we witness moral exemplars in action.

These similarities between Rawls's and Mengzi's accounts are important because they help to show that additional reasons exist for interpreting Rawls's claims about a sense of justice in Mengzian as opposed to Xunzian terms. It seems clear that Rawls's description of the initial capacity for a sense of justice is more Mengzian than Xunzian in the sense that he describes a tendency in human beings that is related to our natural, pro-social inclinations and that is cultivated through a process which sounds more like encouraging a natural course of development as opposed to engaging in a difficult process of re-formation. Interpreting Rawls in this way not only extends and makes explicit what seems to be implied in his account; it also strengthens Rawls's account by making clear how he can avoid a dilemma like Xunzi's. On a Mengzian-style interpretation of Rawls, it is clear that background justice is a natural outgrowth of the basic human capacity for a sense of justice. This is not insignificant, for as David Wong has noted, this kind of dilemma is by no means unique to Xunzi:

> The problem is a general one. Theories that explain the presence of genuine moral virtue on the basis of transformation of a recalcitrant human nature have difficulty explaining how the conditions favorable to such a transformation are ever effected. The temptation is to illicitly presuppose the presence of those conditions.[50]

If we interpret Rawls as making a Mengzian kind of claim, namely that humans have an initial tendency to develop a sense of justice—as opposed to merely having a latent capacity for a sense of justice or one that is visible only after one's nature is re-formed and cultivated—then Rawls can avoid this problem and account for the initial emergence of the just institutions that shape and cultivate citizens' sense of justice.

In addition to helping Rawls avoid a dilemma like Xunzi's, a Mengzian-style interpretation also helps to resolve the tension that initially emerged between Rawls's claim that humans can be determined by moral contingencies and his claim that they have the capacity for self-cultivation. On a Mengzian view, it is both the case that one's environment plays a critical role in one's chances in life and that one has extraordinary capacities for self-cultivation. In order to understand Rawls's claim that all humans are able to exercise and cultivate their sense of justice—despite the fact that they may suffer from a variety of contingencies and that a society has a responsibility to try to address those inequalities—we must assume that their initial resources are sufficiently strong to allow them to overcome certain deficiencies in their environment. Here we can see how the Confucian view presented in the *Analects* offers an account of justice that balances the concerns of moral arbitrariness with the importance of self-cultivation, because a sense of justice is connected to the recognition that societies have a responsibility to address the disadvantages people have no control over *and* to hold individuals responsible for the things they do have control over.

This observation brings us back to the question of why it is important to understand the self-cultivationist dimension of Rawls's work, and what we gain by examining this theme in Rawls. One response, seen here, is that it helps us to better understand the strengths and weaknesses of his view. A comparative study such as this can also help us to understand his general account more completely and accurately by showing how important Rawls's self-cultivationist account is for the rest of his work. As we saw earlier in this chapter, one of the most serious objections one might raise to Rawls's account and to the Confucian account is that they present ideal theories in which members of society all cooperate well and are willing to make sacrifices for one another. As a result, their accounts at times appear to simply describe something that seems unattainable. However, the self-cultivationist dimensions of each account show exactly *how* their ideal societies are to be attained, and this is one reason why it is important to understand this aspect of their views.

Both Rawls and the Confucian tradition devote a considerable amount of attention to moral psychology and specifically to the question of why and how members of a society who do not even know one another are motivated to make sacrifices for one another. As we have seen, there are good reasons to think that both Rawls and Mengzi maintain that this capacity originates with the moral inclinations with which all human beings are born. Here we can see yet another important contrast between Rawls and the *Analects*: While we have a textual basis for interpreting Rawls in this way, Kongzi does not articulate a position on the original character of human nature, as Mengzi does. Additionally, interpreting Rawls as presenting a Mengzian-style view of a sense of justice—and clarifying and extending his account on this matter—strengthens his overall account by helping to explain the emergence of background justice, whereas there is no similarly pressing need to extend or augment Kongzi's view of human nature in relation to a sense of justice. This points toward a further difference between the two senses of justice: Rawls articulates an account of the relationship between background justice and the development of a sense of justice, while Kongzi does not.

Now, it is important to remember that Rawls and Mengzi each maintain that our natural moral inclinations must be cultivated and developed, even though they may be active and visible from the earliest stages of our lives. Here we can begin to see further shared ground with the *Analects*. On Rawls's view, a sense of justice must be drawn out and extended over the course of a person's life as she forms different kinds of relationships. For Rawls this amounts to a three-stage process of self-cultivation within the family, community, and society. In the *Mengzi* and in the *Analects*, the development of capacities such as a sense of justice begins with the development of filial piety in the context of parent–child relationships; for Mengzi, it also begins in the initial cultivation of our four natural moral tendencies. According to both Kongzi and Mengzi, our moral sensibilities continue to grow in the development of virtues like rightness and humaneness, as well as filial piety, in our relationships with other elders and family members. These virtues eventually lead us to feel for and interact with other members of society in ways that are characterized by a spirit of fairness and reciprocity, among other things.

Perhaps most important, uncovering the self-cultivationist dimensions of Rawls shows how self-cultivationist approaches to morality can take many different forms. Although self-cultivation has primarily been discussed in relation to Confucian ethics and other virtue theories, it is an important part of the ethical writings of many philosophers, even those who, like Rawls, are usually associated with deontological theories. Highlighting the self-cultivationist side of Rawls's work and showing how it contributes to an understanding of the project Rawls is engaged in can help to show Western ethicists how important self-cultivation is for a wide range of ethical approaches.[51] This is one way in which comparative studies can help philosophers recognize areas within their own field that are in need of study. Using the framework of self-cultivation, we can more fruitfully understand how human beings become good citizens, which shows why philosophers should study moral self-cultivation. It also commends the study of Chinese philosophy to Western ethicists, because Confucian philosophers are responsible for many of the most sophisticated accounts of moral self-cultivation in the history of philosophy. Thus, an understanding of the various models of self-cultivation found in Confucianism can assist Western ethicists in uncovering and developing these dimensions of Western moral philosophy.

Political Philosophy in the Analects

Now that we have seen some of the contributions this comparative study can make to our understanding of Rawls's work, it is time to examine the way in which this study contributes to our understanding of the *Analects*. In this section I address three main areas: the avoidance of arbitrariness, the relationship between the right and the good, and the importance of the judicial virtues.

Earlier in this work, we saw that for Rawls, in order to have *the concept* of justice, a society's institutions need to reflect only two basic beliefs: (1) Arbitrary distinctions between people should not determine what privileges and obligations they have as members of society, and (2) There should be a standard for determining who should enjoy the advantages of social life, and under what conditions. *Conceptions* of justice contain principles that explicitly address these two issues. Accordingly, a society can articulate an appreciation for the concept of justice without having a fully formed conception of justice. This is important for our purposes because in order to have a sense of justice, one must have a concept of justice. My discussion of what constitutes a sense of justice makes this clear, because in all of those cases in which one exhibits a sense of justice, one senses that something is wrong about those cases in which distinctions between persons have been determined arbitrarily. When we say that something is unfair, we are referring to these kinds of circumstances. Similarly, when we say that something is fair, we refer to circumstances that have *not* been determined arbitrarily. This lack of arbitrariness is one of the central features of fairness. One who has a sense of justice, as we have seen, thinks that those who are suffering through no choice of their own—arbitrarily—should be helped in some way. In other words, such individuals deserve certain privileges, and other members of society have certain obligations to them. This makes clear how a sense of justice implies an understanding of the concept of justice.

In the *Analects*, an understanding of the concept of justice is implied in the discussions of the role a sense of justice plays in a humane and harmoniously functioning society. According to Kongzi's vision of society, privileges and obligations should not be assigned arbitrarily; rather, standards should exist for determining who enjoys advantages under certain conditions. Many of these standards have to do with age and relationships, but the *Analects* also indicates that one's economic status and, perhaps more important, one's virtue, should play a role in the assigning of privileges and obligations. For example, 6.4 says that cultivated persons provide for the needy but do not help the rich to become richer. This passage invokes a non-arbitrary distinction between those who are in need and those who are not. Further, it indicates that individuals with exceptional moral character should play a critical role in the distribution of privileges. This is just one of many places where the *Analects* clearly expresses the idea that privileges and obligations should not be assigned arbitrarily.

According to Rawls, however, a society's *institutions* should reflect a concern with addressing arbitrariness if its members have a sense of social justice. By "institutions," Rawls means public systems of rules that define offices and positions and the rights, duties, powers, and immunities associated with those offices. Rawls says, "These rules specify certain forms of action as permissible, others as forbidden; and they provide for certain penalties and defenses, and so on, when violations occur. As examples of institutions, or more generally social practices, we may think of games and rituals, trials and parliaments, markets and systems of property" (*TJ* §10, pp. 47–48). Those who take part in institutions know what the rules demand of them and of others, because, as Rawls points out, "The basic structure is the background social framework within which the activities of associations and individuals take place" (*JF*, 10). We should notice that Rawls's definition of political and social institutions is sufficiently broad to include a wide range of practices and organizations. In fact, Rawls says that his characterization of the basic structure "does not provide a sharp definition, or criterion, from which we can tell what social arrangements, or aspects thereof, belong to it" (*JF*, 12).

A number of institutions play an important role in the basic structure of society in the *Analects*. Examples include legally recognized forms of property, seen in the case of the father who stole a sheep; the distribution of food and wealth, seen in 16.1; and taxation, seen in 12.9. But two other institutions in the *Analects* play an especially critical role in addressing issues of arbitrariness and the advantages associated with social justice: the family and the rites. Rawls writes that the family in some form belongs to the basic structure of society,

> the reason being that one of its essential roles is to establish the orderly
> production and reproduction of society and of its culture from one
> generation to the next. . . . [E]ssential to the role of the family is the ar-
> rangement in a reasonable and effective way of the raising and caring for

children, ensuring their moral development and education into the wider culture. Citizens must have a sense of justice and the political virtues that support just political institutions. (*JF*, 162–63)

Here Rawls acknowledges one of the central concerns of this study: the critical role that the family plays in the development of a sense of justice. Although Rawls defines the family broadly enough to accommodate many different kinds of families, he says that one of the defining features of the family is the critical role played by elders, writing that "as children we grow up in a small intimate group in which elders (normally our parents) have a certain moral and social authority" (*JF*, 163). We might say, then, that intergenerational relationships are a defining feature of the family as a basic institution, for Rawls.

The family is one of the primary institutions we see at work in the *Analects*. Indeed, it is especially important to take account of the family because one of the most distinctive features of Kongzi's view—and of Confucian views in general—is the view that life with one's family is not simply a means to some higher goal but has tremendous value in itself and represents the central feature of the good life.[52] Although I emphasize here the way in which a sense of justice is related to this larger conception of the family, it is important to remember that this is one small part of the larger view of the family seen in thinkers like Kongzi. Specifically with respect to a sense of justice and institutions, in the context of the family we see an emphasis placed on non-arbitrary distinctions in the obligations that filial piety (*xiao* 孝) specifies for children in relation to their parents and other elders. The *Analects* also specifies what advantages parents and elders are to receive under certain conditions, from giving them precedence when serving wine and food (2.8) and not traveling far from one's parents (4.19), to serving them in accordance with the rites while they are alive, burying them in accordance with the rites after they have passed away, and sacrificing to them in accordance with the rites when they are gone (2.5).

Clearly, the rites (*li* 禮) are also an important consideration when it comes to the basic structure of society in the *Analects*, and although some might expect Rawls to exclude rituals from his definition of basic institutions, in fact he notes that rituals can serve as institutions because they can involve in some way the allocation of certain kinds of privileges and obligations. Accordingly, Rawls says that rituals sometimes, in some systems, "assume the role of justice" (*TJ*, 50). The *Analects* offers a good illustration of such a system, because as we have already seen, the idea of *li* 禮 includes more than the standard examples of rituals as they are understood in most

Western cultures. One of the many functions of the rites is to ensure that privileges, obligations, and advantages are not arbitrarily assigned. Rituals, though, are not exclusively concerned with restricting behavior; they also work to connect people with one another, unify society, and provide for a greater sense of oneself as part of more extensive and enduring institutions. In the *Analects*, the rites provide public standards to which all members of society adhere, and these standards specify which individuals are to enjoy certain privileges and when they are bound by obligations to others. Some of these standards concern matters of etiquette, while others concern matters of religious reverence. Still others describe practices that give us an account of non-arbitrary privileges and obligations that bind members of society. In these cases, we see a basic institution of society assuming the role of justice in that it assigns privileges and obligations in a non-arbitrary fashion. Some of these privileges and obligations specify inequalities in certain relationships and situations, while others specify the need for equal treatment of different individuals despite their place in society. For example, *Analects* 10.18 describes Kongzi's fulfillment of his ritual duty as a minister to taste the food of his lord before giving it to him to eat, which clearly specifies one of the obligations of a minister and one of the privileges of a lord. The rites specify certain inequalities in this case; one enjoys a privilege or fulfills an obligation depending on his position. On the other hand, in 10.25 Kongzi acts in accordance with the rites by bowing down and grasping the crossbar of his chariot when he passes someone dressed for a funeral, "even when the mourner is a lowly peddler." This passage specifies a rite that accords *all* mourners equal respect, specifying a non-arbitrary privilege assigned to those in mourning. Those who are not in mourning are obligated to observe this rite with respect to everyone who is in mourning, regardless of their rank or position in society.

My argument here is not that the *Analects* articulates a *conception* of justice, or explicit principles for determining precisely who is to receive certain benefits under certain conditions. This is why Rawls's discussion of social justice is especially helpful for examining the concern with social justice in the *Analects*: He distinguishes between a conception of justice, which specifies principles of justice, and the basic concept of social justice. His account, then, allows us to see that the *Analects* clearly reflects an understanding of the concept of justice and a sense of justice, without having a fully developed theory of justice. As I noted in Chapter 3, the *Analects* does not offer precise rules or principles of justice, and we have no reason to think that Kongzi wished to impose such principles, even though he expresses a clear view on questions of justice in places like 16.1, where he describes the connection between inequitable distribution and poverty. Here, again, we can see the critical differences between the kind of account offered by Rawls and the view found in the *Analects*. At the same time, passages like 16.1 remind us that despite the remarkable differences between their overall aims, both Rawls and the *Analects* exhibit a concern with questions in political philosophy in general, and with social justice in particular. They both maintain—amidst many other claims—that parent–child relationships play a critical role in the cultivation of a sense of justice and that a sense of justice contributes in important ways to the foundation of a stable and harmonious society. According to Rawls, justice is conducive to stability, while for Kongzi justice is conducive to harmony; and harmony is seen as one reliable way to achieve stability.

I now want to turn to the second area where I think a comparative study with Rawls's account helps us to learn more about political philosophy in the *Analects*. The distinction between the right and the good, and the idea that one must be prior to the other in all accounts of morality, emerges in response to the difference between deontological and utilitarian ethics in Western philosophy. It is a distinctive historical fixture in the development of Western ethics, and it is strongly associated with the view that there are two basic kinds of ethical theories. It is also a dichotomy that in many ways excludes the insights of virtue ethics, and this is one of the reasons why we should be cautious about attributing the priority of either the right or the good to classical Confucian ethics. Virtue ethical views, which take a wide variety of forms, all have in common the fact that they evaluate virtues and vices, which are seen as stable dispositions to feel and act in certain ways, as the primary way of understanding whether actions are right or wrong and whether lives are good or bad. The Confucian tradition tends to focus more on an assessment of moral character than on the rightness of individual actions or the value of the consequences of actions, and as a result Confucian ethics has more in common with virtue ethics than the various forms of either deontology or utilitarianism.[53]

As virtue ethics has become an increasingly significant force in contemporary ethics, philosophers have begun to realize that certain approaches and dichotomies that were previously viewed as central to ethical inquiry are not, in fact, necessary or even helpful. These discussions in virtue ethics and moral psychology may in part account for the fact that in his later work Rawls makes some additional remarks about the right and the good. His remarks can be seen as either clarifications or revisions of his earlier position, but in any event they make it clear that his position is more complex than it appears to be in his early work. As we saw in Chapter 2, Rawls's work offers an alternative to utilitarian accounts of justice that define the good independently from the right and define the right as maximizing the good. According to the classical version of utilitarianism, this means that society is just when its major institutions are arranged so as to achieve the greatest net balance of satisfaction summed over all the individuals who belong to it (*TJ*, 20). On the principle of average utility, society is just when its major institutions are arranged so that society maximizes not the total but the average utility (*TJ*, 140). Despite these differences, classical and average forms of utilitarianism often have similar consequences. For example, according to both views, if a radically inegalitarian distribution will result in the greatest satisfaction, then the inequality of the distribution is no reason to avoid it. According to this view of justice, it is legitimate to ask some people to make sacrifices in order to achieve greater advantages for others, because the greater gains that some members of society will experience are believed to outweigh the losses of others. Here, the good is seen as prior to the right.

As we have seen, Rawls rejects this view, maintaining to the contrary that justice "denies that the loss of freedom for some is made right by a greater good shared by others" (*TJ* §6, pp. 24–25). Rawls's principles of justice require that social institutions be arranged in such a way as to protect the capacity of each person to lead a life of her own choosing, according to her own conception of the good. But Rawls's commitment to the priority of the right means that there are certain boundaries on what can count as the good and what forms of character are considered morally worthy. Certain kinds of circumstances, even if they appear to achieve a good end, are considered unacceptable because of the sacrifices that are made in the process. Additionally, the priority of the right does not allow for the good of some individuals to be sacrificed in order to achieve the good of others. So we can see that the priority of the right is opposed to the idea that the good of the majority necessarily justifies sacrificing some citizens' good. As Rawls puts it, "The principles of right, and so of justice, put limits on which satisfactions have value; they impose restrictions on what are reasonable conceptions of one's good" (*TJ*, 27). In Rawls's later work, he writes that the priority of the right does not imply that only thin or instrumental ideas of the good are a part of his conception of justice. Rather, he says, "[T]he right and the good are complementary; any conception of justice, including a political conception, needs both" (*JF*, 140). For Rawls, when we talk about the priority of the right over the good, we do not mean that the good is unimportant. The priority of the right over

the good simply means that ideas of the good must meet certain deontological requirements.

Rawls's view can help us to understand why it would be wrong to conclude that the good is considered prior to the right in the *Analects*. Kongzi
indicates in many places that it is unacceptable for good ends to be attained
at the expense of certain individuals or values. In 4.5 he says, "Poverty and
disgrace are things that all people hate, and yet unless they are avoided by
following the Way they are not worth avoiding." In 8.7 he says that the
junzi does what is right even when he knows the Way will not be achieved.
In these passages, Kongzi indicates that doing the right thing and going
about things in the right way are, at least in some cases, more important
than achieving certain ends. In 16.1 Kongzi says that good rulers are not
focused on the problems of poverty, scarcity, and instability but rather on
avoiding those things in the proper way: through equitable distribution,
creating harmony in the state or house, and making the people content.
Interestingly, Kongzi offers the latter not as ends but rather as the right
way of achieving certain ends. In these and other places, Kongzi shows
that he is concerned with not simply achieving good ends but rather with
achieving them in the right way. Furthermore, he indicates clearly in 4.5
that unless those ends are achieved in the right way, he does not consider
them to be worth achieving at all.

Accordingly, it seems clear that in the *Analects*, the good must meet certain requirements. But it is not clearly the case that the right is prior to the
good in the *Analects*. As Rawls's later remarks suggest, this way of describing moral theories may not always be the most helpful one. In Rawls's early
work, he speaks more freely of the priority of the right without specifying
that the right and the good are *both* required for any conception of justice. And on his later view, he indicates that the right partly constitutes the
good, which seems to be closer to the view we find in the *Analects*, where
the Way is seen as constitutive of both the right and the good. It is both
the Confucian account of human flourishing and the way in which it is
achieved.[54] Here we do not see the sharp separation between the right and
the good or the requirement that one must be prior to the other, and this
view is a feature of many forms of virtue ethics. In the case of individual
virtues, fairness serves as a helpful illustration. According to the view outlined above, playing fairly is partly constitutive of what makes winning
valuable. If one wins unfairly, one cannot enjoy victory fully.[55]

Rawls's view and the utilitarian view both maintain that the justice of
any particular assignment of benefits depends on the justice of the larger

distribution of benefits in a society. In other words, even though Rawls defends the view that the right is prior to the good, whereas the utilitarian maintains that the good is prior to the right, they both agree that the life prospects of different people are inevitably interrelated by virtue of their shared participation in certain institutions. Accordingly, they both acknowledge that the benefits given to one person have morally relevant implications for others; it is not possible to assess the justice of an assignment of benefits to any one person without considering the larger distributive context of that assignment.[56] This view would certainly be compatible with the account found in the *Analects*. Confucian accounts of virtue typically are not exclusively or even primarily person-focused. Part of what makes something a virtue is that it contributes to social and not just individual welfare. One sees hints of this in certain Western accounts of virtue, but it is central in Confucian accounts.

The increasing influence of virtue ethics may or may not have played a role in Rawls's later remarks on the right and the good, but his discussion of the virtues in his later work resonates strongly with virtue ethical accounts. Rawls's discussion of the judicial virtues represents the third area I want to discuss in relation to the *Analects*. He defines the judicial virtues as "excellences of the moral power of a sense of justice" (*JF*, 170). They are those virtues which specifically stem from a highly developed sense of justice, and according to Rawls they "involve intellect and imagination, the capacity to be impartial and to take a wider and more inclusive view, as well as a certain sensitivity to the concerns and circumstances of others" (*JF*, 170). The judicial virtues reflect one's sense of justice, fairness, and the ability to maintain a balanced perspective when judging a situation.

In the history of Western studies of the *Analects*, the judicial virtues have been neglected for a variety of reasons, one of which is that they are typically discussed within the context of the larger account of the Way, in which ideas like *Ren* ("humaneness") and filial piety play a much more prominent role. To Western ethicists, the judicial virtues also may appear less interesting than concepts such as *Ren* because they are more familiar. Virtues like fair-mindedness might seem prosaic by comparison with some of the other ideas found in early Confucian thought. Another reason why the judicial virtues have been neglected in discussions of the *Analects* is that a number of scholars have observed that the *Analects* represents a different approach to organizing society from many contemporary Western approaches and as a result have surmised that the *Analects* does not have much to contribute in the way of political philosophy. But although the *Analects* provides an account that is primarily ethical in nature, we should remember that Rawls's own political liberalism is based on an account of moral development, as this study has shown through its discussion of how a sense of justice is cultivated, on Rawls's view. Even Western philosophers like Rawls realize that moral and political philosophy are closely related; indeed, Rawls is explicit about the fact that social and political institutions are built upon more basic moral institutions like the family and that they depend upon basic moral powers. So, it should not surprise us to find a discussion of the political virtues within ethical accounts, such as the account found in the *Analects*.

Rawls explicitly outlines the way in which a well-developed sense of justice manifests itself in the judicial virtues. Rawls's account, then, provides a model of how the judicial virtues fit into a larger program of moral development and what capacities they involve. Examining Rawls's view on these matters allows us to see why the judicial virtues are important and how they might hang together with a larger ethical account. As we saw earlier in this chapter, discussions of the judicial virtues are one of the primary ways in which we can see that a sense of justice is important in the *Analects*. In addition to the passages we have already examined in this chapter, the judicial virtues play an important role in the discussion of Virtue (*de*) and its relationship to effective rulership. In places like 2.14 we see that the *junzi* ("exemplary person") embodies the judicial virtues by associating openly with others while keeping the public good in mind. As I noted previously, Rawls says the judicial virtues deal with one's ability to take a wider, more inclusive view and to be impartial when judging a situation. In the *Analects*, when the multitudes hate a person, the *junzi* examines and judges the case for himself (15.28). Rawls notes that the judicial virtues also involve using one's intellect and imagination and having sensitivity toward the circumstances of others. In the *Analects* we see an emphasis on these capacities in places like 19.19, which says that one should "proceed with sorrow and compassion" when uncovering the truth in a criminal case.

Clearly, the *Analects*, like Rawls, assigns an important place to the judicial virtues in a good society. In addition, both the *Analects* and Rawls maintain that those who exhibit these virtues in an exceptional way should hold positions of authority. The *Analects* tells us that the judicial virtues are among many virtues that good leaders embody. In fact, good leaders are able to order the people by providing a virtuous example for them to follow, instead of using regulations and punishments (2.3). Virtuous leaders carefully examine the words and demeanor of others and take the interests of their inferiors into account (12.20). They also harmonize instead of merely agreeing (13.23) and do not anticipate betrayal or expect untrustworthiness but are still the first to perceive these things (14.31). Similarly, Rawls maintains that individuals with an exceptional sense of justice exhibit a greater capacity for the judicial virtues, thereby giving them a greater chance of holding positions of authority that require the exercise of those virtues. One of the reasons why Rawls goes to such lengths to ensure that his sense of justice will allow all citizens, regardless of their economic or social position, to have a fair opportunity to hold public office is that he considers it important for the individuals who exemplify the virtues of a just society to have a hand in shaping just institutions. As we have seen, a society with just institutions is much more likely to produce members who have a strong sense of justice.

In this chapter I have shown that there are important resources in the Confucian *Analects*, and in other early Confucian texts as well, that should be of interest to contemporary ethicists and political philosophers. I have also explored ways in which self-cultivationist approaches can offer a powerful tool for understanding and appreciating a variety of aspects of contemporary Western political philosophy. Additionally, by bringing Rawls and the *Analects* into dialogue, I have sketched a useful approach to comparative philosophy. In the next chapter, I turn to the question of how these two accounts of a sense of justice are relevant to us today. This will allow for a more extensive and detailed discussion of the way in which this comparison contributes not only to our understanding of Rawls and the *Analects* but also to our understanding of the capacity for a sense of justice and moral development more generally.

CHAPTER 5

The Contemporary Relevance
of a Sense of Justice

One of the main goals of this work has been to uncover the sense of justice in the *Analects* and to argue that an understanding of a sense of justice deepens our understanding of the *Analects* as a whole. This chapter aims to show that this ancient idea is important for us today as well and that the different views of a sense of justice found in the *Analects* and in Rawls help to show why. In *Virtue Ethics and Consequentialism in Early Chinese Philosophy*, Bryan W. Van Norden draws upon Lee Yearley's work to point out that if we are to retrieve historical views—such as the view of a sense of justice found in the *Analects*—and apply them in a contemporary setting, certain criteria should be met. According to Yearley, early philosophical views must be "credible," "appropriate," and "inspiring."[1] Van Norden writes, "A credible appropriation of an earlier philosophical view is one that is a 'live option' for contemporary thinkers, given our knowledge of cultural diversity, historical change, modern science, and at least some of the values and institutional forms that have been emphasized as a result of the Western Enlightenment."[2] For the present purposes, this would mean that the idea of a sense of justice must be plausible for us today—that is, it must be something that we could reasonably learn from or apply in a contemporary setting. This is something that the comparative dimension of this study has helped to establish, and although many challenges are involved in comparing an ancient text with the work of a contemporary philosopher, one of the outcomes of this type of comparative study is that the potential contemporary application of the ideas under study, at least in some cases, becomes more readily accessible. Because we have already seen that the idea of a sense of justice is found not only in the *Analects* but also in Rawls's work, the credibility criterion seems clearly to have been met. Substantial evidence shows that a sense of justice functions in a wide range of settings—although in diverse and remarkably different ways—in both the ancient society discussed in the *Analects* and in the modern liberal democratic societies that are the focus of Rawls's work. As far as Yearley's credibility criterion is concerned, the important feature of a sense of justice in this case is that it is not an ancient practice or idea that could not plausibly be recovered and accepted or implemented in the contemporary societies we are concerned with in this chapter. Indeed, we have good reasons to think that it is not merely an ancient idea but a basic human capacity.

In addition to being credible, according to Yearley, the position that is outlined for a contemporary setting based on the retrieval of ancient philosophical views should be "appropriate" in that it should be "*faithful* to the philosophy that inspires it. It must be recognizable as being, at some fundamental level, a version of the original philosophy."[3] If this chapter is to meet the appropriateness criterion in its discussion of the sense of justice in the *Analects*, then the sense of justice that is described as having contemporary relevance must be faithful to the view presented in the *Analects*. At the same time, this project is constructive and not purely descriptive, because my aim is to take the sense of justice as it is seen in the *Analects*—as well as the sense of justice in Rawls's work—and use it as a starting place or resource for recognizing, understanding, and developing potential solutions to some of the challenges facing Chinese and Western societies today. A critical aspect of this work is that its aim is not to suggest how the views presented in these two texts can be appropriated in their entirety and implemented or to argue for a return to the sort of society described in the *Analects* but rather to suggest that at least some aspects of these two senses of justice can be helpful to us today.

The third criterion discussed by Van Norden is that the resulting position should be "inspiring." This means that it should be clear "why the reconstructed position offers something distinctive and valuable to ongoing philosophical debates."[4] Indeed, the main argument of this chapter is that a sense of justice, both as it is seen in the *Analects* and as it is outlined in Rawls, can—in some distinctive and valuable ways—help us to better understand and develop responses to particular issues facing contemporary Chinese society and Western democratic societies. The main goal, then, is to show that a sense of justice in the two sources examined in this work has contemporary relevance for different societies today.

It is important to specify what sort of contemporary relevance I will be arguing for in this chapter, and I want to make two points here. In his work *Beyond Liberal Democracy*, Daniel A. Bell draws an important distinction between different kinds of proposals for social and political change, noting that in order to be realistic, short- to medium-term proposals should not deviate dramatically from existing social practices and should draw more upon detailed knowledge of relevant contemporary political and economic issues than on philosophical traditions. In the case of medium- to long-term proposals, however, "the constraint of feasibility is relaxed somewhat and there is more room to seek inspiration from traditional philosophical resources."[5] As Bell puts it, "Part of the point of putting forward medium- to long-term proposals is the expectation (hope) that they can shape the future, though not necessarily the foreseeable future."[6] My arguments in this chapter are of the latter type. Given the nature of this study and the fact that it focuses on moral psychology and political philosophy and not on, for example, applied ethics or public policy, I will draw more from philosophical resources than contemporary political issues in constructing my argument. My aim is not to propose public policy changes but to argue that quite robust resources are present in both the *Analects* and Rawls for thinking through the options for future changes and that attending to the idea of a sense of justice—and studying it comparatively in these two sources—can be particularly fruitful in this endeavor because doing so can help us to recognize and consider a wider range of possibilities than we might have otherwise considered.

The second point I want to make concerning the type of contemporary relevance I will be focusing on here is that, as noted above, my project is constructive and not purely descriptive in nature. My basic aim in this chapter is to show how early Chinese thought can help us to think about some important issues of contemporary relevance, but we should not expect to find ready-made answers to complex modern problems in early Chinese texts. As Philip J. Ivanhoe has argued, ancient thinkers can still have important things to tell us about modern problems even if they did not think about these problems because they were not problems in their historical time and place. Our ability to address modern problems, after all, depends not just on the information we have about those problems in particular but on the way in which we approach these and other challenges. Ivanhoe maintains that "the form of ethics practiced by Confucians and by many other traditional cultures may well point the way toward the most fruitful approach to such problems," for only in light of a more general conception of what humans can be, and what they would like to be, is it possible to decide many of these questions.[7] If we take the early Confucians as articulating an account of the kinds of lives that are most satisfying for creatures like us, then we can appreciate how they might point the way toward answers to a number of contemporary problems despite the fact that they did not discuss and do not provide ready-made answers to them.[8]

In the first part of this chapter, I consider the question of how the idea of a sense of justice is relevant for the kinds of societies that are the focus of Rawls's work—modern liberal democracies. I argue that the emphasis both Rawls and the *Analects* place on the role of the family in cultivating a sense of justice is particularly important for liberal societies today. I further argue that the special attention the early Confucians give to the family can serve as an especially helpful resource in this regard. In the second section, I discuss the relevance of a sense of justice for contemporary China. I argue that some of the liberal values which play a key role in Rawls's account of a sense of justice represent goods that can contribute in important ways to achieving particular Confucian values in a contemporary setting. In the final part of the chapter, I discuss the relevance of a sense of justice for international justice, arguing that in both Rawls and the *Analects* we find conceptions of moral influence that are related to their views of a sense of justice and that offer some interesting insights into questions of international justice.

The Relevance of a Sense of Justice for Modern Liberal Democratic Societies

One thing this study makes clear is that if Rawls is right about a sense of justice, then we should expect to find it in other cultures, because the sense of justice is, for Rawls, a basic part of our humanity. Indeed, we have seen that an understanding of a sense of justice is present in the *Analects*, but because Rawls's account of a sense of justice evolved independently of early Confucian views, it should not surprise us that the two views of a sense of justice, including how it is developed and sustained and the nature of its role in a good society, differ in substantial ways. By virtue of these differences, the Confucian view has the potential to serve as a resource for augmenting, extending, and deepening our understanding of a sense of justice in modern liberal democracies in new ways. By no means will I argue that the Confucian alternative is a remedy that should or even can be taken off the shelf; rather, my claim is that the view presented in the *Analects* can prompt us to think in some new ways about familiar problems, and the shared ground of a sense of justice can help to facilitate this process.

Most members of modern liberal democracies would surely agree that although we regularly see evidence of citizens actively exercising a sense of justice, we still ought to look for ways to improve the opportunities for cultivating, refining, and strengthening a sense of justice. For regardless of one's position on the political spectrum, we all encounter situations in which we wish that some of our fellow citizens had a keener sense of justice. Now much will depend on what one takes to be just and unjust and there is clearly room for considerable disagreement on these matters, but if we focus on cases of social justice, we can begin to see a shared concern that members of one's society perceive that something is wrong when citizens are marginalized through no fault of their own and that they feel a sense of moral urgency over this sort of unfairness. As we have seen in both Rawls and the *Analects*, one must possess considerable moral capacities in order to have a well-developed sense of justice. This is something we can appreciate more fully when we reflect on specific examples of cases in which a sense of justice leads one to judge that something is unfair. For example, a sense of justice would likely lead one to say that racial profiling is wrong because this practice marginalizes some citizens for reasons that are not their fault, namely their apparent race or ethnicity and the belief that significant numbers of certain racial or ethnic groups are associated with particular kinds of problems. What leads one to feel or perceive that racial profiling is unfair? It seems clear that one will be more likely to perceive the injustice in these cases if one is able to imagine oneself and one's family and friends being a part of a targeted group (or a group whose members might easily be mistaken for members of a targeted group). If one is descended from Japanese Americans, Italian Americans, or Irish Americans, for example, one might reflect on the way one's ancestors were treated in America during certain periods and consider whether one would consider it to be a fair practice if all those who looked Japanese, Italian, or Irish today were routinely stopped and searched, taken into police custody, or required to produce proof of citizenship on a whim. In addition, in order to recognize fully what is unfair in such cases, it will usually—or at least in many cases—not be enough for one simply to imagine, at a general level, being a part of a targeted group. One will need to imagine *with considerable specificity* what it would be like, and often it will be important for one to consider the implications for one's family members and close friends. How would one feel if one's elderly parents, children, or grandchildren were treated in these ways simply because of their physical characteristics? Even if one wants to maintain that we must endure various security measures as a result of the choices of others, in which case one might advocate for all members of society being searched or subjected to random searches, one surely does not want to maintain that it is fair for individuals who have clearly not done anything wrong to be searched simply because they in some way resemble individuals who are suspected of certain crimes.[9]

This example shows the extent to which the principle of reversibility, or the ability to imagine oneself in another person's place and identify the appropriate moral response on that basis, is a basic component of the moral reasoning that is a part of having a sense of justice. As a result, as we think through ways of strengthening citizens' sense of justice, it is worth considering how we learn to apply the principle of reversibility regularly and with considerable dependability. As Rawls and the *Analects* both point out, the earliest stages of our moral development normally occur in the context of our interactions with our parents. One of the distinctive features of Rawls's moral psychology is that he drew on some of the best science available to him in constructing his account, which distinguishes him from a number of his predecessors and contemporaries. Of course, Rawls's work in this area can also be updated and strengthened in light of more recent studies in psychology.[10] The psychologist Martin Hoffman's work on moral development is a good example of a potential resource. Hoffman's research shows that the most constructive and important types of disciplinary encounters for children in cases of transgression are parental "inductions," wherein parents "highlight the other's perspective, point up the other's distress, and make it clear that the child's action caused it."[11] In such cases, parents appeal to their children's moral sensibilities by directing children's attention to the pain they caused and asking them how they would feel if someone treated them in that way. This type of discipline, Hoffman shows, has better long-term consequences than other disciplinary approaches, such as "power assertion" or "love withdrawal," evidenced by the fact that children are more motivated to avoid transgressions in the future and to make reparations when they fail. It is not insignificant that according to Hoffman's research, parents' efforts to awaken and extend certain responses in their children are largely successful. Among other things, this helps to show that children *do* normally have feelings of sympathy for others and they feel bad when they realize that they have hurt others. It is extremely significant that efforts to appeal to these sensibilities in children are *more effective* ways of educating children about how to interact with others than other forms of discipline.

Hoffman's work on parental induction can be used to augment Rawls's moral psychology, as well as our general understanding of a sense of justice and how it develops, especially seeing as a sense of justice is bound up with the ability to apply the principle of reversibility. But one of the important things to which Hoffman's work draws our attention is the extent to which moral capacities like a sense of justice have their roots in the early interactions between parents and children. This is something about which the early Confucians, of course, had much to say and that will be the main focus of my argument here.

Two of the most distinctive features of early Confucian philosophy are the emphasis placed on the primacy of parent–child relationships in human moral development and the nature and possibility of moral self-cultivation. Early Confucian philosophy is further characterized by the view that the key to a flourishing society, politically, lies most fundamentally in these two concerns. As we have seen, though, the account of parent–child relationships offered by early Confucian thinkers entails an even more specific claim, for they discussed the importance of the virtue of filial piety in family relationships more than did other schools of thought, and beginning with Kongzi they explicitly argued for the distinctive claim that filial piety is the root of other ethical sensibilities.[12] Kongzi sees other virtues as springing from the feelings and capacities that one develops in response to one's parents and older siblings. As Ivanhoe points out, for Kongzi "[t]he strongest feelings are originally and forever those within the family. The virtues of 'filial piety' (*xiao* 孝) and 'respect for an elder brother' (*ti* 悌) are the source from which one draws in extending and developing such feelings for others and are the most profound examples of the type of concern that characterizes those who are *ren* ["humane"]."[13] As we have seen, for Kongzi the government cannot establish and preserve a good society by relying exclusively or even primarily on laws and policies enforced from the top down; rather, the basis of a good society is nurtured within and is an extension of the family. In the context of our relationships with our parents and siblings, we learn to feel for others and respond to them in ways that will prove essential if we are to become active, contributing participants in a larger community and society. For Kongzi, such participation is part of a good life; it is good for us and for others to be a part of a family, a community, *and* a society. Through our relationships with our parents in particular, we make our initial and most important strides toward developing the traits of character that will enable us to be contributing members of a community and a society; and when all or most members of a society possess these virtues, a society can flourish. This is one of the ways in which Kongzi's account of moral capacities like a sense of justice is bound up with his account of filial piety.

The view that emerges in the *Analects* is extended and developed in new and significant ways by Mengzi. For Mengzi the process of developing natural moral tendencies begins within the context of family relationships, and it can be derailed if parents do not provide the right sort of nurturance. Mengzi clearly sees filial piety as having a key role in this process and as having political implications as well: "The Way lies in what is near, but people seek it in what is distant; one's task lies in what is easy but people seek it in what is difficult. If everyone would treat their kin as kin, and their elders as elders, the world would be at peace."[14] Here Mengzi tells us that the path of self-cultivation begins (and continues) with those who are closest to us—our families—but people tend to look toward what is distant or further away as the key to change. Given that our focus in this chapter is the contemporary relevance of these views, it is important to recognize that the type of view Mengzi is criticizing here is not confined to ancient societies. Indeed, certain expressions of this view are quite prevalent in modern liberal democracies today. One expression of this view is the tendency to reserve special admiration for those who prioritize the needs of the many (or work to achieve "the greatest good for the greatest number") over the needs of their special relations, particularly their families. Although many would agree that good mothers and fathers and caring sons and daughters deserve more praise than they typically get, there is not a widespread tendency to reserve special admiration for—and seek moral inspiration from—the stories of good mothers and fathers. Consider, for example, the reasons why Gandhi, Mother Teresa, Martin Luther King Jr., and Dr. Albert Schweitzer are widely considered sources of moral inspiration. Another example is the degree of interest in books written by or about humanitarians, many of whom have made and continue to make significant personal sacrifices—including time with their own families—in order to serve the greater good.[15] Another liberal expression of the view that we should look toward what is distant as the key to change is the insistence that conceptions of the good, along with the family, ought to be seen as private matters. Interestingly, citizens on opposite ends of the political spectrum have defended this position in the United States. For some conservatives, concerns about excessive governmental involvement in personal matters are rooted in worries about the government's becoming too large and overtaxing citizens to fund programs that they feel should be managed by individual families. Some liberals express the concern that governmental involvement in the family will restrict personal freedom and result in the imposition of one set of values. While both conservatives and liberals often are willing to support government intervention at the level of the family when it converges with their position on particular social issues, it is still the case that issues of national and global political significance are often prioritized, and positions like Mengzi's are frequently viewed as being overly concerned with "personal morality" or as expressing values that ought to be pursued within individual families and not by the state.

Both Kongzi and Mengzi maintained that genuine, far-reaching change in a society is possible only when we recognize the unique relationship that obtains between parents and children and the importance of "treating our kin as kin, our elders as elders." In 4A5, Mengzi again emphasizes the connection between families and the larger society in which we live: "People have a common saying: 'The world, the state, the family.' The root of the world lies in the state; the root of the state lies in the family; the root of the family lies in oneself."[16] In the last line of this passage, Mengzi reiterates his view that the beginnings of filial piety and other virtues are implanted in us; they are a part of our nature, and our task is to extend these basic inclinations within the family and then within the expanding concentric circles of our community and society.[17] For Mengzi, as for Kongzi, the relationship between parents and children is the foundation of a good society, and the quality of the relationships between parents and children in a society has a direct and observable impact on its members and their willingness to make sacrifices for one another.

What relevance can this account have in a modern liberal democracy? Specifically, how might the account of a sense of justice in the *Analects*, with its strong emphasis on the role of parent–child relationships, inform our attempts to strengthen citizens' sense of justice? While Rawls maintains that the capacity for a sense of justice needs to be developed and that the family has a critical role in that process, one of the additional and most distinctive features of the Confucian view is the claim that parent–child relationships generally and filial piety in particular *provide the foundation for* a person's moral development, including the development of a sense of justice. There are reasons to suggest that this type of view should be of interest to those seeking to revise and refine public policy in modern liberal societies. In recent years there has been an increasing recognition that brain development is most rapid during a child's first three years of life and that opportunities to influence the course of a child's life are greatest during those years. As a result, policymakers have been increasingly pressured to fund early-childhood intervention programs that focus on the first three years of life.[18] Early-childhood intervention programs share the assumption that "children's earliest experiences play a fundamental role in shaping their life opportunities and that parental care-giving is the most important of these earliest experiences."[19] Although these programs have a wide range of goals and service elements, many are home-visiting programs that aim to reach high-risk families with young children by bringing services to them. Indeed, early findings in studies of a program of home visitation by nurses, now known as the Nurse-Family Partnership, intensified interest in this type of service and prompted a proliferation of home-visiting programs, although few have rivaled the success of this one.[20] I will argue that this program can help us to appreciate the contemporary relevance of views such as those found in the *Analects* and the *Mengzi* by providing an example of how one might instantiate, in the form of public policy, a view that takes seriously the role of parent–child relationships in creating and sustaining a good society while also providing evidence that our public policies ought to conform to this type of view.

The Nurse-Family Partnership (NFP) is a thirty-five-year program of research that aims to achieve long-term improvements in the lives of at-risk families through intensive efforts aimed at children's early years and the pivotal role that parents play in shaping children's lives. The program provides first-time, low-income mothers with home visits from public health nurses beginning early in pregnancy and continuing through the first two years of the child's life. NFP nurses are trained to engage clients in activities associated with (1) improving pregnancy outcomes by helping women to improve prenatal health, (2) improving child health and development by helping parents provide sensitive and competent caregiving, (3) improving parental life-course and economic self-sufficiency by helping parents to develop plans for the future, including completing their education, finding work, and engaging in family planning.[21] The program has been tested in three separate large-scale, randomized controlled trials that began in Elmira, New York, in 1977; Memphis, Tennessee, in 1987; and Denver, Colorado, in 1994. Follow-up studies of the long-term outcomes for mothers and children in the three trials continue today, and since 1997 the NFP has helped new communities develop the program outside of research contexts so that today the program is operating in 250 counties nationally from 170 local operating sites.[22]

The NFP shows remarkable promise for reducing some of the most damaging and widespread problems faced by low-income children and

families in American society today, many of which have far-reaching consequences for other members of society as well. Consistent program effects
include improvements in a range of areas for nurse-visited mothers and
children compared with mothers and children randomly assigned not to
receive the program. These effects include improved prenatal health, fewer
childhood injuries, fewer unintended subsequent pregnancies, increased
intervals between births, increased paternal involvement, increased maternal employment, reductions in families' use of welfare and food stamps,
better infant emotional and language development, and improved school
readiness for children born to mothers with low psychological resources.
Fifteen-year follow-up studies found fewer arrests, convictions, and days
in jail for mothers and reduced child abuse and neglect as well as reduced
arrests and convictions among the fifteen-year-olds.[23]

During home visits following the birth of the child, in addition to assessing and providing education on issues that relate more centrally to
physical health such as infant/toddler nutrition, health, and environmental
safety, nurses assess parent–child interaction, model activities that promote sensitive parent–child interactions that in turn facilitate developmental progress, and guide parents in fostering social support networks.
These activities are all focused on promoting the distinctive kind of parental caring that, on the view of early Confucians like Kongzi and Mengzi, is
a source of filial piety. Indeed, short-term outcomes of the studies (changes
that occur by completion of the program) report substantial improvements
in sensitive and competent parental caregiving for infants and toddlers,
including decreases in childrearing beliefs associated with child maltreat-
ment, increases in stimulating home environments, and increased paternal
involvement in child care and support. Intermediate outcomes (changes
that are measured within two to six years of program completion) include
continued improvements in stimulating home environments, higher rates
of fathers living with the mother and child, and higher rates of marriage.
Long-term outcomes (changes that require a greater time to measure, often ten or more years following program completion) include a decrease
in arrests and adjudication for incorrigible behavior involving the children
(e.g., truancy, destruction of property) and fewer arrests, convictions, and
days in jail for the parents.[24] These latter findings show that the impact
of the program is seen far beyond the home, illustrating the Confucian
belief that better childrearing practices have direct consequences for society, including the idea that a sense of justice nurtured within families
naturally "extends" to society. In addition to decreased involvement with
the criminal justice system for both mothers and children, low-income,

unmarried nurse-visited women are more likely to participate in the work force than their counterparts in the control groups.[25] An economic evaluation of the NFP by the RAND Corporation that extrapolated the results of the fifteen-year follow-up study found that the savings to government and society for serving families in which the mother was low-income and unmarried at registration exceeded the cost of the program by a factor of four over the life of the child.[26] The return on the investment was realized before the child's fourth birthday, with primary savings found in reduced welfare and criminal justice expenditures and increases in tax revenues.

One of the premises of early-childhood preventive interventions is summarized appropriately by Mengzi's claim that "the root of the state lies in the family." The NFP offers a clear example of a contemporary family-based approach to sustaining and strengthening a good society, seen within the context of a modern liberal democracy. Kongzi and Mengzi both thought that many if not most societal problems have their deepest origins in the family and more particularly in parent–child relationships. The NFP is based partly upon—and provides evidence for—this type of view. When Mengzi distinguishes between "treating our elders as elders" and "treating our young ones as young ones," he exhibits an awareness that the way we interact with and care for our children is unique, as is the response of children to their parents. As we have seen, textual evidence suggests that for both Kongzi and Mengzi, the interactions we have with our parents early in life form the roots of the moral sensibilities we will need later in life.[27] The NFP is grounded in the evidence-based view that a child's early experiences are formative in a special way and that parental caregiving is the most important of these experiences. Early-childhood interventions like the NFP are obviously based on much more specific (and evidence-based) claims than those of Kongzi and Mengzi, seen for example in their particular focus on the prenatal period through the beginning of school because of its special potential for change. However, these programs share with the early Confucians the more general view that the early interactions between parents and children represent "a unique developmental period that serves as a foundation for behavior, well-being, and success later in life."[28]

Another feature of the NFP that has a clear link to important features of early Confucian views is its emphasis on holistic approaches to problem solving, or approaches that emphasize the importance of families and communities. This emphasis on families and communities is something we noted earlier in this work as a distinctive feature of the account of a sense of justice in the *Analects*, and in the NFP it is seen in the degree of attention given to the role of families in helping the mothers to become good parents. Nurses spend considerable time working with mothers on the roles and responsibilities of fathers and encouraging paternal involvement in all aspects of the program, so long as the mother wants the father to be involved and there is a constructive basis for the relationship.[29] Rates of marriage are higher among nurse-visited women in the program, as are rates of paternal involvement, which is significant because marriage has been shown to increase the likelihood of economic self-sufficiency and lower children's risk for a range of different problems.[30] The NFP also works to involve other family members, including grandparents. In the Elmira study, by the end of the fourth year after the delivery of the children, other family members played a greater role in the care of the children than did family members in the control group.[31] This aspect of the program is especially interesting from a Confucian point of view, because the program aims to help not by focusing on individuals but by addressing them in relationship to others and primarily to family members. Without question, one of the distinctive features of Confucian ethics is the amount of emphasis it places on the cultivation of a range of virtues that enable one to flourish within a family and community, as well as an emphasis on the good of the family, community, and society—though always with a special emphasis placed on the good of families—in contrast with a narrower concern with the good of individuals.[32]

Of course, holistic approaches to problem solving are made possible by relationships of care and trust, and one way in which the NFP works to cultivate these kinds of relationships within families is through the close relationship formed between mothers and the nurses. In each of the studies conducted, a sizable number of mothers reported that they had never before experienced the sort of consistent care and support they received from the nurse-visitor.[33] These relationships help to show the mothers that "positive, caring relationships are possible. The parent begins to see herself as someone who deserves support and attention, and by extension sees her child as deserving the same."[34] The nurses serve not only as teachers but offer models or paradigms for how to care; they offer the mothers a sense of being cared for, and this elicits a sense of gratitude. Like the actions of good parents, the nurses' actions express the priority of care over power and prerogative. Accordingly, the nurses constitute the kind of relationship they seek to elicit from the mothers and others. The nurse–mother relationship is unique in these ways; it cannot be understood as simply a medical relationship and should be understood in ethical terms rather than in a solely medical way. In addition to working to strengthen supportive relationships within families explicitly by including fathers and other family members in various decisions and activities, the nurses exemplify care and concern, and their impact on the families demonstrates that caring for others produces tangible, quantifiable benefits that are seen in the mothers as well as in their children.[35]

The findings of the NFP undermine the view that protecting individual rights and autonomy should be our sole or even primary concern when dealing with high-risk families.[36] This point is worthy of our attention because such a view tends to prevail in the political culture of modern liberal democracies. For example, advocates of abortion rights have tended to emphasize that choices having to do with a woman's body are hers alone, a view that in some circumstances can further isolate women in need of support and care by too strongly emphasizing their individual rights and autonomy.[37] The NFP, in contrast, is explicitly designed to reduce social isolation and promote supportive and engaged families and communities that ideally participate together with women in caregiving and decision making.[38] What I wish to highlight here are two contrasting ways of thinking about and treating pregnant women—many of them in the same high-risk groups—in our society. Although women often become more confident and effective agents through the NFP program—something that is seen in such areas as economic self-sufficiency—this is primarily achieved not by helping them to recognize their individual rights or autonomy but through relationships of care and trust and through a carefully designed program of self-cultivation.[39] As we have seen, one of the strengths of the program is that it enlists family and friends in a common cause; rather than highlight the individual alone with her rights, it embeds her in a supportive community.

The NFP not only helps to illustrate the sort of public policy that Confucian views of the family would commend; it also provides evidence showing why we should embrace particular aspects of the Confucian view, namely that the early experiences of children are formative in a special way, that parental caregiving is the most important aspect of these early experiences, and that working to cultivate the right kinds of parent–child relationships is the most effective way of bringing about societal change, at least in some key areas. Program founder David Olds emphasizes that because home visiting for parents of young children has been studied in randomized controlled trials to a greater extent than many other child health services, we are able to evaluate the effectiveness of home-visiting programs and dedicate our resources to those programs that reliably achieve their goals.[40] Ethical and political theories, as well as public policies, must not only be able to account for what our best science tells us; they should be constructed and revised through a careful examination of this sort of evidence.[41] Ethical accounts should be influenced by the evidence showing that some ways of life lead to greater human flourishing than others, as well as evidence showing that certain contexts and practices are more conducive than others to the development of particular virtues. These approaches are clearly value laden, and although not all ethical matters can be decided through an examination of empirical evidence, ethical accounts should at least be informed by our best science on those matters where we have significant evidence. The NFP represents an excellent example of studies that can and should inform work in ethics and political philosophy by showing us that we have good reasons to endorse certain kinds of views.

To illustrate this point, let us consider a couple of specific examples of how work in ethics might be informed by taking seriously the Confucian claim that we ought to invest more in parent–child relationships—a claim that NFP studies give us good reasons to accept, while also providing a model of how such changes can be implemented. First, considering the research on the impact on children of having married parents, statistically, children from homes with unmarried parents do not tend to flourish in the same ways and to the same degree that children from homes with married parents tend to flourish. Those working in ethics might take this into account by naming, describing, and offering detailed studies of the virtues associated with good spouses and the relationship between these virtues and the virtues of good parents, including the ways in which these virtues are cultivated. Ethicists might also examine the impact on the process of moral education and self-cultivation in children of having married parents.[42] It is worth noting that if philosophers take into account evidence of this sort, it should lead them to place less emphasis on certain kinds of abstract issues. For example, a concern with the issue of necessity might lead a philosopher to point out that it is not *necessary* for a child to have married parents in order to flourish. While this claim is true, it ignores the force of the empirical evidence, which shows that the *probability* of a child's flourishing is greater with married parents because marriage lowers certain risk factors to a statistically significant degree. As a result, issues such as necessity are substantially less important for philosophers who are interested in ethical claims that reflect and inform actual practice.[43]

Another example concerns the effectiveness of more holistic, indeed collective, approaches to problem solving. The evidence shows that this approach more effectively brings about change in the lives of high-risk families than simply providing financial support or focusing on the individual rights of pregnant women and mothers. In order to take this into account, ethicists and political philosophers might examine the extent to which their analyses tend to focus on the welfare and rights of individuals in ways that are prone to neglect, as opposed to drawing upon, the role of relationships of care and support within families. The impact of the involvement of fathers and other family members in the NFP calls into question certain liberal presuppositions that are often held uncritically. This data warns us against one widespread understanding of autonomy in our society, in particular, according to which individuals should practice "self-reliance" or "go it alone" when making moral decisions. This is particularly important when decisions will affect not only the individual but also those around her. The evidence shows that it is often helpful for us to have support and guidance when making important decisions and that we need support in order to successfully bring about change in ourselves. This same evidence also shows that the family is uniquely positioned to provide this type of support. Those working in ethics and political philosophy might explore ways of focusing more on the good of families as a way of strengthening and working for the welfare of individuals. In early Confucian philosophy, we find a sketch of and some of the resources for developing this type of account.

Scientific studies, in turn, also can be augmented in different ways by philosophical accounts in ethics and political philosophy. In the case of the NFP, philosophers can provide analyses of program outcomes that differ in significant ways from the kinds of analyses offered by those working in the sciences and public policy. For example, one of the central tasks of those working in virtue ethics is to provide theoretical and practical discussions of the virtues that help us to understand the moral transformations we observe in others or experience ourselves. These kinds of discussions can enable us to more effectively encourage this sort of change in others. One example of how a virtue ethical account might contribute to our understanding of the work of the NFP is through a study of the virtues associated with good nurses.[44] Because the hiring of nurses as home visitors was one of the major distinguishing factors between the NFP and other less successful home-visiting programs, a study was conducted to evaluate whether nurses are more effective than paraprofessionals (those with no formal training in the helping professions) as home visitors.[45] Both nurses and paraprofessionals in the study received the same home-visit guidelines, training, and supportive supervision in the NFP program model. For most outcomes on which either paraprofessional visitors or nurse visitors produced significant effects, including mother–infant responsive interaction, paraprofessionals typically produced effects that were approximately half the size of those produced by the nurses. Indeed, nurses produced more significant effects on a wide range of maternal and child outcomes, had lower dropout rates among families visited, and had a lower number of attempted visits in which women were not at home.[46] Discussing the reasons for the nurses' effectiveness, the NFP cites nurses' clinical experience, the fact that their nurses are viewed as authorities because of their formal training in women's and children's health, as well as the public's rating of nurses as having the highest standards of honesty and ethics of all professionals.[47] This explanation, however, could be augmented by a discussion of the virtues that are distinctively associated with nursing. An account of the traits of character that help nurses to succeed in their profession, as well as the traits that nursing provides unique opportunities to cultivate, might help us to more fully understand the things that enable nurses to help bring about change in the lives of high-risk mothers and potentially other groups as well. Such a discussion might also shed light on how to more effectively cultivate these virtues in others.

How can Confucian views augment efforts to bring about positive change at the level of public policy? To be sure, the quantitative data provided by programs like the NFP can and should help policymakers make informed decisions about worthwhile investments of societal resources; but social change is incredibly difficult to bring about, for it involves not just policy change but also changing citizens' ways of thinking and acting. The humanities can be of considerable assistance here. We need citizens to reconsider their views on how important the earliest years of a child's life are and the dramatic and tangible ways in which the right kinds of parental caregiving can shape the entire course of a person's life during these early stages. Presenting scientific evidence from the NFP ought to have an important role in convincing citizens that social change is necessary, but the kinds of stories, anecdotes, and specific approaches that we find in the texts of early Confucianism can make an important contribution to this process, as well. Because our views and practices are not solely based on science but are heavily shaped by culture, we will likely need to make use of resources in both the sciences and the humanities in order to bring about change that encompasses not only our public policies but the views and practices within individual families as well.

One reason why early Confucian sources can play an important role in helping citizens to reconsider their views and practices is that they can help us recognize and appreciate the *qualitative* improvements that attending to parent–child relationships during the earliest years of a child's life bring about. While citizens certainly care about the way in which their tax dollars are spent, most of us care a great deal more about the *quality* of the society in which we live. In addition to areas such as improved physical health, economic benefits, and lower rates of incarceration, individuals who have benefited from the NFP experience remarkable changes of a qualitative nature: They are living more satisfying, happier, and ethically better lives.[48] The Confucians would focus on the fact that these outcomes define a more humane form of existence. Here we see the qualitative dimension of the discussion—including our deepest values and ideals—that philosophers can remind us of and help us to better understand. So in addition to helping us to recognize and more fully understand things such as the virtues of good nurses, spouses, and parents, as I suggest above, the work and goals of the NFP—from a public policy standpoint—can be supported by philosophical accounts in ethics through a discussion of qualitative issues. Jurists and legislators, as well as our fellow citizens, need to see that programs like the NFP are worth investing in. Discussions of the kinds of qualitative issues on which early Confucian thinkers focus can further strengthen efforts to convey the value of the program. Here, we see one example of how the humanities and the sciences can work together in mutually reinforcing ways to address some of the problems facing societies like that of the United States today, and to bring about social change.

Now one might argue in response to this claim that we do not *need* early Confucian accounts to help us recognize the importance of parent–child relationships in addressing social problems because we already know that the family is critical in this regard. One might offer the very existence of programs such as the NFP in the United States as evidence that at least some Americans recognize the fundamental role of the family and have already devised solutions to societal problems based on this recognition. In response to the objection that early Confucian accounts cannot contribute substantively to our understanding of the importance of addressing parent–child relationships because these accounts do not tell us anything new, I want to make three basic points. First, my aim is not to show that early Confucian accounts are the *only* way to bring the importance of parent–child relationships to our attention; rather, my aim is simply to show that there *are* productive, helpful resources in Confucianism for helping us to think through the role of parent–child relationships in a good society and that the stories and anecdotes the Confucian tradition brings have the potential to engage people's hearts and minds in a way that is conducive to social change. Confucian resources might reinforce reasons we already have and thereby provide added strength to our views. A range of other resources may help us with this process as well, and the research findings of programs such as the NFP are among them, as is the work of ethicists who have written about the important role of the family in relation to social policy.[49]

That does not mean, however, that there are not some unique features of Confucianism that support such a policy, and this is my second point. There is much more to the Confucian view than simply the claim that the family, and parent–child relationships in particular, are important; and to misrepresent Confucian discussions of the family as constituting nothing more than these sorts of general claims is to miss most of what is valuable about them. I have argued that early Confucian thinkers make a range of distinctive and nuanced claims about the specific role of parent–child relationships in moral development and in the development of a good society. The early Confucians assign family relationships and moral cultivation— and the relationship between these two—much greater weight and importance than do other schools of thought. Indeed, only the Confucians argue that the general ethical sensibilities we develop within the context of parent–child relationships are the basis for nearly every virtue and that the family is the ideal model for the state. No other tradition sees filial piety as playing such a foundational role in ethics and politics. The Confucians are the only ones to link virtue in general directly with the early experiences within families, and they are the only ones for whom these experiences play a central role in ethics and political philosophy. As we have seen, the early Confucians maintained that relationships within the family have a *direct bearing* on the quality of a society. This means that the Confucians offer us a powerful theoretical explanation for programs like the NFP. Further, as I have noted, the Confucian tradition brings a unique, particularly poignant and powerful set of stories, anecdotes, and approaches (including specific practices) to reinforce and encourage an ethical understanding of the family and its role in moral development. These illustrations show how families perform this role in our ethical and political lives, and these themes are found not only in well-known stories such as those about Mengzi's mother but in texts such as the *Classic of Filial Piety*, *The Twenty-four Filial Exemplars*, and in philosophy, religion, art, and literature throughout the Chinese tradition. Such resources offer a practical source of inspiration and guidance.[50]

Finally, and perhaps more important, one who objects to my account on the grounds that Americans already sufficiently recognize the role of parent–child relationships in moral development must explain why the

United States does not devote a greater share of its resources to this area. Numerous examples show that the critical role of parent–child relationships is not something that is fully recognized or taken seriously in laws and public policy, not to mention studies in ethics. The bulk of public spending on children in the United States presently occurs during the school-age years, in the form of expenditures on primary and secondary schools, criminal justice, youth employment, and other youth programs.[51] Federal law requires employers to offer only up to twelve weeks of unpaid leave to new parents.[52] Unfortunately, it is simply not the case that U.S. public policy reflects anything like the view that parent–child relationships are the foundation of a good society, and as a result, there is little support for the claim that we have little to nothing to learn from the early Confucian view. Perhaps it is true that most of us already know "deep down" that something like the Confucian view is true, but it is also clear that our public policies are radically out of line with this intuition. If this is true, then the contemporary relevance of the early Confucian view may be that it can help us to recognize what our own moral sensibilities implicitly are and prompt us to work toward ensuring that our public policies reflect those sensibilities more accurately and effectively. As I have argued, one who takes seriously the view presented by the early Confucians and works to apply it in a contemporary setting will maintain that we ought to devote a greater share of our resources and attention not only to expenditures on children but also to preventive interventions focused specifically on parent–child relationships in the earliest years of a child's life and even during the prenatal period. The NFP represents an example of a highly effective program of this sort.

The Relevance of a Sense of Justice for Contemporary China

In this work, one of the clear differences we have seen between the sense of justice in the *Analects* and the sense of justice in Rawls is the tendency in the *Analects* to prioritize cultivating a set of virtues and moral capacities (of which a sense of justice is a part) over and above laws, policies, or procedural justice. In contrast, despite Rawls's insistence that a sense of justice is a part of the necessary foundation for his theory of justice, the principles of justice and issues surrounding them in many ways represent the heart of his work. To be sure, both moral psychology and laws (in the case of the *Analects*) or principles of justice (in the case of Rawls) are recognized as important by both sources, and this is something I have discussed. However, we have also seen that there remains a pervasive difference in the weight or priority assigned to these areas. In the *Analects*, it is more important for members of a society to engage in moral self-cultivation than to institute the right sorts of laws or principles, because self-cultivation is seen as having a more fundamental role in creating and preserving a harmonious, flourishing society. Rawls, on the other hand, is primarily concerned with the task of establishing principles of justice that will guarantee a basic level of justice in a society. As we have seen, many important differences between these accounts help to explain their orientations. For now, though, I want to focus on how this key difference between the sense of justice as it is seen in the *Analects* and in Rawls might help us to appreciate some of the ways in which a sense of justice is relevant for Chinese society today.

One might ask, based on the difference outlined above, why we need both virtue and procedural justice. Someone who is more sympathetic to the early Confucian view seen in the *Analects* might suggest (as the *Analects* does) that if one had a society of virtuous individuals—who possessed, among other things, a strong sense of justice—then there would be little or no need for laws or principles of justice. Similarly, one who is more sympathetic to Rawls's theory of justice—perhaps while also being skeptical of the importance of his moral psychology—might argue that if one had the right laws and principles of justice in place, then the possession of virtues and capacities like a sense of justice would become at least significantly less important and perhaps not important at all. To the proponent of the former view, one might respond that without laws or principles of justice, one is simply left with a utopian view that is ultimately unattainable. We simply don't have good reasons to think that large-scale human societies can flourish in the complete absence of laws or principles of justice. Even if many or most members of a society are virtuous and have a strong sense of justice, it seems likely that there will always be exceptions. As a result, we need checks on individuals who might become power-hungry or corrupt, have lapses in judgment, or acquire power but lack important moral sensibilities. In addition, laws and principles sometimes help to shape citizens' sense of justice in important ways, helping to promote social change and making it clear that they are not just important for individuals who have lapses in judgment or lack certain moral sensibilities. In these cases laws and principles of justice can encourage the development in citizens of particular virtues and moral capacities. So the process of cultivating a sense of justice in members of a society should not be seen as entirely separate from having laws or principles of justice, for the two are surely mutually reinforcing.

Those who would question whether a sense of justice is really important, maintaining that laws and principles can do at least most of the work should remember that even if we have good laws and principles, we still depend on humans to follow, enforce, and apply them. Additionally, even nondemocratic societies depend on at least some members of society to institute and amend laws and policies. As a result, it seems clear that because principles of justice entail certain procedures and processes that must be followed by humans, and because humans have a role in choosing the laws and policies that will play a key role in sustaining justice in a society, the moral capacities possessed by members of a society remain critical even with the right sorts of laws and principles of justice in place. As Van Norden puts it, "procedural justice requires at least minimal virtue to operate."[53] He argues that procedural justice is an institutional good that has been underemphasized by Confucians historically, and he points out that although having certain kinds of procedural rules can be worse than having none at all, many procedural rules

> provide individuals with *some* protection against the arbitrary use of authority. It is easy to underestimate the value of procedural justice, emphasizing that it not infrequently fails in one of two ways. Sometimes procedural justice fails when, precisely because it *is* followed, it fails to achieve either efficiency or substantive justice or both.[54]

Other times, he points out, procedural justice fails because there are no minimally virtuous individuals to implement it.[55] Rawls and Kongzi share this last concern, yet it also highlights a critical difference. Specifically, while Rawls's account strongly emphasizes the importance of procedural justice and the role that a sense of justice plays in creating, preserving, and maintaining principles of justice in a stable society, the *Analects* places a greater emphasis on how people acquire a sense of justice and the important role that individuals with a sense of justice—as well as many other virtues and moral capacities—have in creating, preserving, and maintaining a good society. In addition, Rawls's sense of justice is bound up with certain goods, and some of these goods differ substantially from those outlined in the *Analects*. This difference is important, because it can help us to identify ways in which traditional Chinese views such as those found in the *Analects* might be augmented by Rawls's account.

Before proceeding, it is worth considering a potential objection. One might press the question of why we should look for ways to augment Chinese views with Rawls's view, and whether it isn't more appropriate, when discussing the relevance of a sense of justice in contemporary China, to draw upon the account of a sense of justice found in the *Analects*. This is an important question: Why should we look to Rawls when discussing the relevance of a sense of justice in contemporary China? I will argue that we should turn to Rawls's work because certain goods have an important role in Rawls's sense of justice and are seen in particular liberal values that are not a part of the sense of justice in the *Analects*. Some of these values are not incompatible with traditional Chinese values; to the contrary, I will argue that they can even be used to help sustain and support certain traditional values and practices—such as the emphasis placed on moral self-cultivation—that are central to the view presented in the *Analects* but that need to be updated and adapted for a contemporary setting. It is important to note that I am *not* arguing that Rawls is the only helpful resource here or that Rawls's work provides the only way to reach these conclusions, nor am I arguing that helpful resources are not present within the Chinese tradition itself; to the contrary, in what follows I will show how certain aspects of Rawls's account can prompt us to think in some innovative ways about how the view of self-cultivation presented in the *Analects* might be amended in a contemporary setting. Accordingly, I follow the same procedure here that I followed in the previous section, where I argued that certain aspects of early Confucian views of the family can help us to think in new ways about some familiar problems in modern liberal democracies. In both cases, one of my aims is to show how the resources of other philosophical traditions can sometimes be helpful because they push us to consider a wider range of approaches and perspectives.

One way of approaching the question of how Rawls's sense of justice might be relevant to contemporary Chinese society is to examine the appeal of some of the liberal democratic values that play a key role in Rawls's account. Specifically, I will focus on values that have an important role in Rawls's sense of justice but that do not play a similar role in the sense of justice in the *Analects*. In some cases, these values also distinguish modern liberal democratic societies like that of the United States from other kinds of societies. Ethnic and cultural diversity is one example, and I have chosen to focus on this value in particular because, as I will argue, I think it represents a good that has relevance for contemporary China for several reasons. First, dealing with ethnic and cultural diversity in a constructive way is becoming increasingly important for China both domestically and in relation to the international community. This is something that has been documented quite extensively and so I will not go into further detail here, except to say that the challenges facing China today include the needs and concerns of ethnic minorities as well as the way in which China responds to other cultural influences and seeks to influence others as its presence grows internationally.[56] In addition, as I will argue below, ethnic and cultural diversity can more easily be seen as a good in Chinese culture than a number of other liberal values, in part because it can serve as a constructive resource for Confucian moral self-cultivation in a contemporary setting. As I will show, Confucian accounts of self-cultivation continue to shape Chinese cultural perspectives and practices in deep and remarkable ways. To be clear, my aim is not to propose solutions to social problems in China today based on the liberal values associated with Rawls's account of a sense of justice. Rather, my aim is to show that some liberal values—and in what follows I will examine diversity as an example—are goods worth having and goods that not only are compatible with certain traditional Chinese values but can contribute to the achievement of those traditional values in Chinese society today. My claim here is not simply that accepting and working to integrate particular liberal values can help to *preserve* certain traditional values, but that doing so can, in some cases, *augment* or *strengthen* traditional values by showing how they can be realized in new ways. This helps to show how both traditional and liberal values have relevance and can serve as constructive resources in a contemporary setting.[57]

Although it will seem obvious to those who study China, as well as to many who have spent time there, that Chinese culture continues to be deeply informed by Confucianism, I want nevertheless to address the question of how and in what ways Confucian views of self-cultivation, in particular, continue to influence Chinese culture today. Substantial resources in cross-cultural psychology show that an emphasis on self-cultivation continues to be a distinctive feature of Chinese culture, especially with respect to views about learning. These sources also demonstrate that this feature of Chinese culture distinguishes it sharply from American culture. Multiple studies support the claim that Chinese students have a more adaptive view of intelligence, emphasizing effort-related notions like hard work and persistence, as opposed to mental processes and natural intelligence, which are strongly emphasized by American students. As a result, Chinese students tend to understand extraordinary abilities possessed by good students and scholars *as an achievement* and not as a *cause for achievement*, like their U.S. counterparts.[58] This difference is significant in part because it helps to highlight the more general Chinese cultural tendency to view intelligence "not as an inherent quality of a person but something that one can increase through learning," whereas the American cultural tendency is to see various kinds of intelligence (e.g., being "book smart") as characteristics already possessed by the learner.[59] For example, in one study of U.S. and Chinese college students that sought to examine what learning means to people in these two cultures, common words and phrases related to learning were examined. The terms used by American students to describe learning primarily concerned thinking, mental processes, and inquiry. Chinese students, in contrast, used few of these terms. Most striking of all, however, was the near-absence of references to hard work, effort, and persistence by American students, whereas such concepts were used in abundance by the Chinese students. Another significant difference is that the Chinese students more strongly emphasized the importance of a strong desire and passion for learning, compared with a relative lack of such affect in the accounts of the American students.[60] Chinese students also saw learning as something that heavily informed and enriched other areas of their lives, as opposed to seeing it as a purely or primarily academic endeavor, and this marked another key contrast with American students.

In another study, which examined cultural influences on conceptual orientations of learning in U.S. and Chinese preschoolers between four and six years old, children provided responses to two stories about the learning behavior of two protagonists, one who worked hard and one who gave up. Almost all of the U.S. children liked both protagonists, and a majority of U.S. children gave personal attraction reasons for liking both of them (e.g., "I like the bear because she is cute"), though in the case of the protagonist who worked hard, a significant number of children (30 percent) also gave task-oriented reasons for liking the protagonist (e.g., "I like Little Birdie because she can fly good"). In contrast, more than half of the Chinese children did not like the protagonist who gave up, and when asked why, 77 percent of them gave virtue reasons or reasons related to diligence, persistence, or concentration (e.g., "I don't like Little Bear because she doesn't practice," "I don't like Little Bear because she doesn't put her heart into learning how to catch fish"). The Chinese children overwhelmingly liked the hardworking protagonist, though, and also overwhelmingly gave virtue reasons for this (e.g., "I like Little Birdie because she didn't give up").[61] Not only were the Chinese children strongly focused on qualities such as diligence, persistence, and concentration, but the possession or lack of these virtues was the basis on which most Chinese children evaluated the protagonists in each story. One of the things these findings help to show is that the Chinese cultural focus on learning as a process of cultivating personal virtue is internalized very early in life. Virtues like diligence and persistence "are held as highly positive dispositions to be acquired by children and therefore are actively fostered by parents, teachers, and children themselves." Indeed, they constitute a set of qualities that characterize the ideal learner in Chinese culture, and "even though this pursuit of learning was first articulated by Confucius, it still holds a strong appeal to Chinese learners today."[62]

For our purposes, what is important about this research is that it helps to show how Confucian understandings of self-cultivation continue to shape and influence Chinese culture, and especially cultural attitudes about learning. It also helps us to identify some of the distinctive features of Confucian self-cultivation that remain an important part of Chinese culture today, including an emphasis on certain virtues and attitudes such as persistence and a willingness to work hard, the importance of one's feelings and desires about learning, and the insistence that learning is continuous with other areas of one's life and development. Many of the views expressed by the Chinese students in these studies have distinctively Confucian features. In elaborating on what leads to success in learning, the American college students focused on the learner's mental functioning and the related learning processes, while the Chinese college students emphasized personal virtues, attitudes, and action principles in learning and especially those that underscore the importance of effort such as hard work and persistence. Similarly, Chinese preschoolers tended to like or dislike protagonists based on their possession or lack of diligence, persistence, and concentration, while U.S. preschoolers tended to like or dislike them primarily on the basis of personal attraction or the possession of certain skills (e.g., being able to fly well). One of the shared features of Confucian views of self-cultivation is the idea that learning is an achievement and not something one possesses simply by virtue of a natural ability or native endowment of intelligence.[63] Even Kongzi emphasizes that he was not born with knowledge but diligently searches for it (7.20). Confucian self-cultivationists emphasize that the process of coming to possess certain virtues is long and difficult, for it involves a continuous commitment to working to improve one's abilities, attentiveness to one's strengths and shortcomings, and a willingness to try new things while continuing to practice the things one has mastered. *Analects* 1.15 reminds us of how rigorous this process is by stressing the difficulty of self-cultivation but also the potential for transformation: "As if cut, as if polished; As if carved, as if ground."

The particular virtues, attitudes, and action principles Chinese students emphasized in these studies were also heavily informed by the Confucian tradition, including the view that virtues like humility are central to learning and that action principles described in sayings such as "gain new insights by reviewing old materials" offer important guidance.[64] As this last example shows, in some cases the connection between the students' views and Confucianism was quite explicit. When asked to give examples of learning-related activities and goals, while American college students tended to use single and regular words (e.g., "study," "books"), Chinese college students frequently used idiomatic expressions including proverbs and sayings—many of which come from Confucian texts. The importance of one's feelings and desires in learning is another important feature of Confucian self-cultivation seen in these studies. One of the typical reasons Chinese preschoolers gave for not liking the protagonist who gave up ("Little Bear") was that she "didn't put her heart into learning how to catch fish."[65] The importance of loving learning (*hao xue* 好學) is emphasized in many places in the *Analects* (e.g., 1.14, 6.3), and Kongzi says that he will not waste his time instructing students who are not eager to learn (7.8). In China, proper learning still is primarily a moral and not an epistemological issue. The tendency of Chinese college students to see learning as intimately connected to their emotional, spiritual, or moral lives is fundamental to the Confucian tradition of self-cultivation and the role of learning within it, a view that researchers have noted "is consistent with the age-old Confucian understanding of learning. Knowledge, accordingly, includes not only the externally existing body but also social and moral knowing."[66] *Analects* 1.7 is explicit about this:

> Imagine someone who recognizes and admires worthiness and therefore changes his lustful nature, who is able to fully exhaust his strength in serving his parents and extend himself to the utmost in serving his lord, and who is trustworthy in speech when interacting with his friends and associates. Even if you said of such a person, "Oh, but he is not learned (*xue*)," I would still insist that it is precisely such qualities that make one worthy of being called "learned."[67]

Now that we have seen some of the ways in which Confucian understandings of self-cultivation continue to shape and influence Chinese culture, we are in a better position to ask what might make ethnic and cultural diversity a good in a culture in which beliefs and attitudes about learning are heavily informed by Confucian understandings of self-cultivation. Although one might offer many reasons here, I want to focus on three things that underscore the nature of Confucian self-cultivation but that also relate in significant ways to the account of a sense of justice offered by Rawls. First, ethnic and cultural diversity can provide unique opportunities to cultivate and strengthen a sense of justice by giving us practice in relating to and feeling for those who are different from us. Second, it provides us with the unique opportunity to cultivate some of the virtues that early Confucian thinkers like Kongzi envisioned, because working to understand other cultures represents a distinctive and highly effective way of developing virtues like learning. Third, it can lead us to appreciate the rich and diverse variety of good lives and ways of being that exist for humans by exposing us to a wider range of virtues, practices, and capacities and the different ways in which they can be a meaningful part of human lives. This unique sort of appreciation plays a special role in self-cultivation, as well. I will now consider each of these in turn.

One of the first things that Rawls's work can help us to appreciate about ethnic and cultural diversity is the way in which it provides an opportunity to become acquainted with those who are different from us in significant ways. This experience can have a number of important moral consequences, including providing critical opportunities to develop the capacity for a sense of justice. The willingness of citizens to make sacrifices for those who are differently positioned in society, and specifically for those who are among the least advantaged members of society, is basic to Rawls's account of social justice. It is clear that in order for members of a society to be willing to make these kinds of sacrifices, they must have the capacity to feel or perceive what is fair, and in order to possess this sense of justice, they must have the capacity to feel for those who are severely marginalized. As we have seen and as Rawls makes clear, the capacity to feel for others in these ways begins early in our lives, within the context of our relationships with family and friends. Eventually, though, in order to fully develop a sense of justice, these feelings must be extended to other members of society with whom we are not directly acquainted, so that citizens are willing to support principles of justice that will help even those they do not know.

For example, in both China and the United States today, there are significant challenges relating to migrant workers. In China, some 120 million migrant workers, who make up China's "floating population," are deprived of equal access to health care, education, work, and residence as a result of the household registration system (*hukou* 戶口).[68] Those seeking to improve the well-being of migrant workers must also deal with the substantial challenges concerning their social standing, especially the fact that they are viewed with considerable contempt by many Chinese citizens and are often suspected of criminal activity.[69] In order to improve both the legal status and the social standing of migrant workers, social reformers will need other Chinese citizens to have a sense of justice when considering the migrant workers' plight. That is, other citizens will need to develop an appreciation for what it might be like to be born into an impoverished rural part of China and migrate to an urban area in search of better work opportunities in order to provide a better life for—and in many cases, simply in order to support—one's family, including one's children and one's parents. Having a strong sense of justice here means understanding that although we do not choose where we are born, these circumstances have dramatic consequences for our opportunities in life, and that there is something fundamentally unfair about the fact that some individuals not only are marginalized by these circumstances, but they are further marginalized by a societal structure that severely limits their opportunities to improve these circumstances.[70] Having firsthand experiences with those of different backgrounds, such as migrant workers, can, at least in some cases, help one to develop and extend one's sense of justice so that one is able to more fully understand and work to address an issue like this.[71]

There are good reasons to think that this final stage of cultivating a sense of justice could potentially be enriched if individuals had regular exposure to those of different ethnic and cultural backgrounds. Now one might, of course, have ethnic and cultural diversity within one's own family and community, which might give one additional opportunities at earlier stages of cultivation to develop an attentiveness to and appreciation for diversity. Nevertheless, given that the main goal of the third stage of cultivation is to extend one's sense of justice to those one does not have an existing relationship with, one will still benefit from experiences with those of ethnic and cultural backgrounds that are different from those represented in one's own family and community. This type of cultivation is especially important because it is often most difficult to feel for others in ways that move one to action when they are far removed from one's own context. This is why Rawls emphasizes that we can see most clearly that someone has a strong and fully developed sense of justice when she is willing to make sacrifices for members of society who are among the least advantaged, and the assumption here is that the one making the sacrifices is not among the least advantaged. One of the fundamental features of Rawls's sense of justice is that it leads us to feel for those who are marginalized as a result of various contingencies. These individuals are often (though not always) members of other ethnic and cultural traditions. As a result, we can see how experiences with diversity and the way in which those experiences shape us could assist in the development of a sense of justice. One who has experience with a particular culture or even a different position in society, such as that of migrant workers, will be more likely to care about the injustices that members of that culture or group encounter. However, and more important, the general sensibilities that encounters with diversity can instill in us contribute to the development of a stronger sense of justice—as well as to a range of other virtues. The basic ability to relate to those of different backgrounds seems to be one that we can reasonably expect to cultivate through encounters with different kinds of diversity.

It is important to remember that extending one's sense of justice to those outside of one's family and community, and especially to those who are severely marginalized, is something that is emphasized not only in Rawls's account but also in the *Analects*. This is significant especially because my aim in this section is to discuss the value of seeing diversity as a good in contemporary Chinese society, which is, as we have seen, informed in a number of important ways by Confucian understandings of self-cultivation. An important part of moral self-cultivation in the *Analects* is the ability to take a wider view and work to help those who are on the fringes of society. This is made clear, as we saw earlier in this work, in descriptions of cultivated persons, especially the *junzi*, who "provides for the needy but does not help the rich to become richer" (6.4) and takes everyone within the Four Seas as his brothers (12.5). These claims are significant, for they underscore the fact that the *Analects* is not narrowly concerned with family relationships; rather, for cultivated individuals, the moral capacities that are initially and continually cultivated within the context of family relationships enable them to reach out to others in significant ways. Kongzi tells us in 2.14 that the *junzi* associates openly with others and is not partial; he interacts not just with his family and friends but also with different kinds of people, not dismissing them simply on the basis of a bias or grudge or on the basis of their social status or notoriety. According to this vision, cultivated persons are fair-minded and exhibit a well-developed sense of justice and care that extends to all members of society. Although, in contrast, diversity is explicitly seen as a good in Rawls and is more generally a part of liberal values, the *Analects* does share the view that the ability to relate to and care widely for other members of society is a mark of a cultivated person.

Van Norden points out that among other things, Confucians emphasize "intellectual activities aimed at making oneself a better person," as well as caring for and helping other people.[72] In the *Analects*, the intellectual activities that contribute to making one a better person include artistic appreciation, which "has a morally edifying effect. Fine works of art 'teach' our emotions."[73] This point can be extended to ethnic and cultural diversity, which also can have a morally edifying effect by providing us with opportunities to become acquainted with those who are different from us and to come to appreciate their experiences. Encounters with members of other ethnic and cultural traditions can educate our emotions by helping us to cultivate the ability to feel for those of very different backgrounds as we cultivate a sense of justice. Because this type of emotional education is central to the task of self-cultivation in the *Analects* and in Confucianism more generally, one of the tasks of making this account of self-cultivation relevant in a contemporary setting is making use of the kinds of encounters one is likely to have. In contemporary China, as in other parts of the world, diversity is one part of this picture, seen not only in the increasing numbers of foreigners visiting and living in China but also in China's own ethnic minorities, as well as migrant workers.

Now that we have examined the way in which ethnic and cultural diversity can provide unique and valuable opportunities to cultivate a sense of justice, I want to turn to a second reason why ethnic and cultural diversity is a good: It provides distinctive opportunities for helping us to cultivate some of the things that Kongzi and other Confucians emphasized as being central to self-cultivation. I want to focus first on the importance of realizing how much one does not know and the need to learn more, and, second, on the resolve to work hard. In the course of my account I will also show how these things are considered a necessity for self-cultivationists in the Confucian tradition.

One thing that spending time in another culture or around members of other cultures helps to instill is a keen sense of how much one does *not* know. One who has never spent time in another culture or any significant length of time surrounded by those of different ethnic and cultural backgrounds might still know a great deal *about* other ethnic or cultural traditions and may even have a deep appreciation for some of the values and practices that are a part of those traditions. But being in or around members of another culture for significant periods of time typically leads to a deeper awareness of the limitations of one's knowledge than one would experience in one's own cultural setting.[74] In some cases, one will become aware of how little one really knows about the history of a particular people or culture because the vastness and complexity of the history of a people or culture become much more of a reality when one is surrounded by members of an ethnic or cultural tradition. One may become aware of how far one is from having real fluency in a language because the reality of how quickly languages are spoken, as well as the vast number of words and idiomatic expressions that are a part of a language, truly sets in when one is surrounded by native speakers. In other cases, spending time around those of other ethnic or cultural traditions will lead one to appreciate not just the specific body of knowledge found within such a history or a language but also the fact that one does not know the reasons why things are done in certain ways in a given culture. This sort of awareness often comes from noticing the nuances and subtleties that are a part of certain ways of doing things, such as the way in which laughter serves different social functions—and means very different things—in different situations in some cultures. In these latter kinds of cases, being in a different ethnic or cultural setting provides one with the opportunity to observe and come to understand details that would otherwise be difficult to appreciate or even have an awareness of. In all of these different kinds of cases, firsthand experiences in other ethnic or cultural traditions often lead one to a deeper awareness of how much one does not know than one would otherwise have.

In addition to instilling in us a deeper appreciation of how much we do not know, experiences with other ethnic and cultural traditions can also expand our estimation of how much we *should* know. For example, a non-Jewish person attending a Shabbat dinner at the home of her Jewish friends might become more aware that she does not know very much about the history of the Jewish people and the reasons why certain rituals are a meaningful part of Jewish culture, and she might also come to believe that one *should* learn about these things. These are distinct recognitions, and spending time around those of different ethnic and cultural backgrounds has a way of leading us to appreciate not just one but both of them, partly because there is a certain urgency that often accompanies firsthand experiences. In all of the examples described above, one is likely not just to become aware of how much one does not know about a history, language, or culture but also to develop the desire to learn more, in part because one has the immediate opportunity to do so and has established some relationship and rapport with those who live within and value the foreign history, language, or culture. Both the recognition of how much one still has to learn as well as the recognition that one should make an effort to learn those things represent important goods that can be attained as a result of encounters with those of diverse ethnic and cultural traditions. In addition, both of these things are an important part of Confucian self-cultivation. Confucians have tended to emphasize that one who does not recognize his limitations will find it very difficult to genuinely learn and improve. As Kongzi says in 2.17, "This is wisdom: to recognize what you know as what you know, and recognize what you do not know as what you do not know." Knowing what one does not know is an expression of intellectual humility, which is important for learning and self-cultivation. Students who know they still have much to learn are more likely to grow and improve than students who think they already know everything they need to know. But it is not enough simply for someone to know how much she does not know; one must have reasons to think that she *should* work to learn more. Experiences in different ethnic and cultural settings can lead to a deeper appreciation for both of these things.

Experiences with ethnic and cultural diversity can also play a unique role in developing the resolve to apply oneself to the task of learning in an intensive way, "as if you will never catch up, and as if you feared losing what you have already attained" (8.17). This is another hallmark of Confucian self-cultivation. *Analects* 8.7 emphasizes that for those who have devoted their lives to the path of self-cultivation, "the burden is heavy and the Way is long. They take up *Ren* as their burden—is it not heavy? Their way ends only with death—is it not long?"[75] Throughout the *Analects*, we are told that self-cultivationists exhaust their strength working to cultivate themselves (1.6, 1.7), and if their strength is insufficient to go the whole way, they "go at least halfway before giving up" (6.12). The ability to apply oneself in this way is something that everyone possesses, but the resolve to do it is what most people lack. Kongzi asks, "Is there someone who for a whole day is willing to use all his strength to achieve humaneness? I've never seen anyone who lacked the strength to do so—there may be such a person, but I've never seen one" (4.6).[76] One must have the willingness or resolve to apply oneself in a disciplined way and work hard. We have seen above how experiences in different ethnic or cultural settings can help us to recognize how much we do not know and the reasons why we should work to learn more, but in addition, these experiences provide unique opportunities to develop the resolve to do so. One reason why this is the case is that encounters with ethnic and cultural diversity highlight for us some of the practical reasons why learning is important. For example, when students are learning a foreign language, visiting a place where that language is spoken by all or most people can help them not only to learn the language by giving them practice speaking and listening; it can also help them to develop the resolve to apply themselves more seriously to studying on a daily basis. One's resolve to apply oneself intensively to developing certain skills, abilities, and virtues is likely to be strengthened when one is able to see firsthand the contexts in which those skills, abilities, and virtues will be helpful and meaningful. Because such a remarkably wide range of skills, abilities, virtues, and different kinds of knowledge is an important part of understanding and interacting in meaningful ways with those of different ethnic and cultural backgrounds, experiences with ethnic and cultural diversity provide a unique opportunity to strengthen one's resolve in learning and self-cultivation. Such experiences also give us the opportunity to enjoy firsthand the rewards of learning, such as being able to understand and respond in more effective and meaningful ways to those of different ethnic and cultural backgrounds. Experiencing these rewards also helps to strengthen one's resolve and dedication to learning.

The third and final reason I want to discuss concerning why ethnic and cultural diversity is a good is that it can help us to appreciate the diversity of good lives that are available to humans. One might understand this ability as "recognizing and admiring worthiness" (1.7) in a contemporary setting, and it is important to recognize that if we take moral self-cultivation in the *Analects* seriously, then we must take seriously the task of evaluating—and not merely tolerating—different forms of life. Philip J. Ivanhoe has argued that tolerance tends to fail to acknowledge and appreciate the good in other forms of life and, in addition to failing to respect adequately the people who live those lives, limits the range of goods that we might be able to appreciate both in our own lives and in the lives of those we care about.[77] In addition—and this is most important from the standpoint of a self-cultivationist—toleration can deform our character in certain ways, especially because it sometimes results in the view that the life we lead is the only good life possible for creatures like us.[78] For as Ivanhoe points out,

> Most advocates of tolerance do not require us to understand, in any substantial way, the views that we are asked to tolerate; rather, we only have to know enough about them to know that they do not violate some minimal level of moral acceptability. None insist that we work to appreciate the mad variety of values in the world and be open to the quest for new ones.[79]

Tolerance also sometimes offers "a convenient and appealing excuse for not engaging, learning about, and coming to appreciate the nature of these alternative forms of life."[80] As a substitute, Ivanhoe argues for "ethical promiscuity," which "celebrates ethical diversity as an important feature of good human lives."[81] Ivanhoe's work can help us to understand why ethnic and cultural diversity, which of course often includes ethical diversity, ought to be recognized as a good by contemporary self-cultivationists who are informed by Confucian views of self-cultivation.

Ivanhoe argues that ethical promiscuity rests on two supporting claims. First is the fact of ethical pluralism, or "the view that there are a variety of distinct ethical values in the world that cannot be reduced to one another or derived from any higher common source."[82] Second is "the recognition that no single human life or culture can realize all of the values that are possible for creatures like us," something that stems in part from the fact that humans are finite and can live only one life at a time, and "to access certain goods is a result of factors such as one's gender, race, tradition, or personal history, which are largely or wholly contingent matters. Chance offers us direct access to only a small sample of the full range of human values."[83] One key feature of ethical promiscuity that is of particular interest here is that those who embrace this view appreciate diversity in a particular way, for despite the fact that they have not lived the lives that those of other ethnic and cultural backgrounds have lived, they can, "with enough imagination, patience, and understanding, come to see and to some extent appreciate what is valuable" about at least some of these lives.[84] Further, not only can the contemporary self-cultivationist do this, but she is dedicated to this task as a part of the practice of moral self-cultivation. Now it is important to note that this sort of practice has political implications in a society. As Ivanhoe argues, "[I]t does not seem implausible to believe that at least a number of people who work to achieve a sympathetic understanding of other kinds of lives will ultimately come to see their own and the others' lives as in important ways mutually interdependent."[85] Recognizing the way in which one's life is interdependent with others' lives in a society is one of the ways in which an appreciation for diversity can deepen one's sense of justice and one's willingness to make sacrifices for other members of society. This helps to promote a range of other goods, including the fact that one who embraces ethical promiscuity will at least be much less likely to oppress, exploit, or attack those who are different.

In what ways does ethical promiscuity contribute to the task of self-cultivation? One way in which it clearly does this is by helping one to cultivate a healthy way of viewing one's own life and the various stages that are a part of it. When we work to appreciate the variety of good lives, we also develop a new appreciation for the variety of important experiences during different times in our own lives without longing to re-live or re-create them—that is, without longing to be somewhere (or someone) else. This is morally significant, for surely a part of living a full and rich life is appreciating and making the most of the goods that are uniquely a part of one's life at each particular time. Parents whose children are grown often remark to young parents that they wish they had savored their children's early years to a greater extent, and some even express a desire to return to that time now because, looking back, they see it as the best time in their lives. This is unfortunate because, at least in some cases, it suggests that they were not present in ways that would have been meaningful and enriching for them and their children in the past and also because they seem to regret being in the present, which fosters the very problem at hand: a lack of appreciation for each moment or stage and its unique value and richness. To be sure, this is something that one must attend to on a daily basis; a self-cultivationist will monitor herself and try to catch herself when she is dwelling too much on the past or future and not savoring and working to make the most of her present relationships and opportunities. There are, of course, extraordinarily practical implications of this sort of attentiveness: It leads us to have better relationships with our family and friends, and it leads us to do a better job in our professional and personal activities. Ivanhoe notes a connection between this sort of perspective on one's own life and an appreciation for diversity in one's society:

> [O]ne can look back with pride and satisfaction on a period in one's life when one worked in one's family business or served one's country without regretting or yearning for the distinctive goods one enjoyed during those times simply because they are absent from one's present life. The more sensible response to such reflection is the feeling that one has been remarkably lucky, even blessed, to have had these experiences as parts of one's life. In the same way, we can appreciate the lives of many people who live very differently from the way we do if we take the time and make the effort to come to appreciate—as well as simply understand—the lives they lead. This process not only honors them, which is fitting, but it can also improve and benefit us and those around us.[86]

As Ivanhoe argues, ethical promiscuity insists that celebrating the diversity and values of good lives both helps one to avoid deforming one's character and leads one to share and enjoy a more edifying life. Indeed, the very character of ethical promiscuity entails a commitment to a certain kind of self-cultivation: "Ethical promiscuity encourages us to keep our hearts and minds open, to look for and discover new value in human life, and to share these insights with others while incorporating them into our own lives."[87] This helps to make clear how a contemporary form of Confucian moral self-cultivation can be promoted and furthered through an appreciation for the goods associated with ethnic and cultural diversity.

There are certainly other resources in early Confucianism to explore in this regard. Van Norden argues that one way in which Mengzi's views should be modified is that "we should come to think of human ethical cultivation in pluralistic terms," and one aspect of that pluralism is that although good lives will be similar in certain respects, such as in the (Confucian) virtues they manifest, "these manifestations can take quite different forms in different kinds of good lives."[88] For our purposes, this could mean several different things. On the one hand, with this sort of modification, a view informed by early Confucian values could welcome ethnic and cultural diversity, at least as long as the diverse views had certain overlapping goods like shared virtues, even though those virtues would be cultivated in different ways and would have different manifestations. On the other hand, one of the values that would become a part of the modified Confucian view I am describing is diversity itself, and ethnic and cultural diversity would be a good worth having in part because it contributes to cultivating certain virtues in the members of a society. In addition, we might learn the importance of acquiring new virtues—ones we hadn't known about or considered—and acquire new and possibly richer or more accurate vocabularies for reflecting on virtues or aspects of virtues that we already recognize. One might even say that the value of diversity is one manner in which the Way could be "filled out," extended, or broadened (15.29).

Some of the things achieved through Confucian moral self-cultivation as it is described in the *Analects* can be deepened and enriched when one works to achieve them in the presence of ethnic and cultural diversity.[89] As we have seen, these things include the opportunity to cultivate a sense of justice, particularly in relation to those of different backgrounds, as well as one's awareness of how much one does not know, one's understanding of why one should work to learn more, and one's resolve and dedication to learning more. We have also seen how one's appreciation for the diversity of good lives that are available to humans can enrich one's own life in some important ways that contribute to the process of self-cultivation. All of these things help to show how encounters with other cultures, at least under the right circumstances and when one is ready, push one to become more than one is, prompting the kinds of growth that are a part of Confucian self-cultivation, and as a result they are enriching in a fundamental way. We can see, then, how the liberal value of diversity envisioned in the work of political philosophers like Rawls might have relevance in contemporary Chinese society.

It is important to recognize that in arguing that the value of diversity is a part of liberal democratic societies, I am not arguing that the goods associated with this value are fully realized in liberal democratic societies. Clearly, societies such as that of the United States still have a long way to go in helping citizens to appreciate the distinctive kinds of goods that are associated with diversity and in helping members of diverse racial, ethnic, and cultural backgrounds to live together in ways that reflect that sort of appreciation. Nevertheless, diversity is widely recognized as a good in liberal societies, and it is recognized as a good in Rawls's account. Indeed, Ivanhoe argues that ethical promiscuity not only is compatible with Rawls's view but even supplements and strengthens Rawls's account of reasonable pluralism in a number of ways. It gives greater content to the idea of what is "reasonable" by emphasizing the importance of working to understand one another's reasons for embracing different goods, which in turn allows us to see one another as reasonable. It also serves a practical political end by "reinforcing allegiance to our shared social life by making explicit the many different routes reason took to lead different members of society to the cause of liberal democracy." In addition, Ivanhoe argues, ethical promiscuity would raise the level of mutual respect among members of liberal democratic societies today, as a shared commitment to understanding and appreciating other views helps to bind together those of diverse backgrounds and perspectives.[90] Many of these points have relevance in a contemporary Chinese setting, as well, where ethical promiscuity can serve as a more constructive resource than tolerance concerning relationships with ethnic minorities as well as in international relations.

One specific way in which a greater appreciation for diversity could bring about positive change is through certain kinds of approaches to education. Daniel Bell argues that

> political thinkers need to consider the question of how to best educate the people so that they express desirable political virtues and help to sustain free and fair political institutions. It is widely recognized today that the educational system is crucial for the purpose of cultivating democratic virtues. One of the teaching methods designed to improve democratic virtues is the public recognition of the intellectual contributions of different groups, including those historically marginalized.[91]

In an East Asian context, Bell argues, this means including works by Asian thinkers that resonate with the backgrounds of students, with the aim being

> not so much to transmit specific moral content from particular traditions as to identify significant contributions by authors of scholarly traditions that students take pride in and that seem to address their concerns, thus increasing the students' desire to learn and participate in classroom discussion, and, it is hoped, improving their ability to participate intelligently as adults in the political processes that shape their society.[92]

Bell offers a helpful illustration of this sort of practice from his own teaching experience at the National University of Singapore, where he taught students of Chinese, Malay, and Indian descent and worked to include the contributions of Chinese, Muslim, and Indian thinkers in his curriculum. Bell writes that we should be cautious about "exporting this 'lesson' to other teaching contexts" because the right pedagogical approach depends on a number of different factors, including the particular course one is teaching, whether students' ethnic groups are clearly defined, and the number of ethnicities represented in a classroom. He also notes that in both Hong Kong and Beijing, one faces much more ethnically homogeneous settings.[93] He writes,

> One way of meeting the challenge of promoting in-depth learning of other cultures in homogeneous settings is to establish regular exchanges with students from other societies so that classrooms are composed of students from different backgrounds. In Hong Kong and mainland Chinese universities, there are increasing numbers of foreign exchange programs, but there is still a long way to go.[94]

How might we build on Bell's remarks here in light of the foregoing analysis of the goods associated with diversity in Chinese culture, especially given that Chinese universities are not very ethnically and culturally diverse? Bell maintains that the ideal classroom is composed of students from diverse ethnic and cultural backgrounds, because exposure to other cultures

> often leads people to question "the way things are done at home" and helps them to learn from other ways (i.e., it allows for moral and political progress). There are also economic advantages: individuals able to navigate between different cultures have competitive advantages relative to those intimately familiar with only one culture.[95]

I have argued above for a range of goods that come from interacting with those of different ethnic and cultural backgrounds, specifically focusing on those goods associated with Confucian views of self-cultivation, which heavily inform Chinese culture. It is thus clear that there are good reasons—and reasons with deep roots in Chinese culture, and not just in Western liberal democratic culture—for those in a contemporary Chinese setting to value diversity. But the crucial question is how Chinese students can benefit from diversity when they do not have regular opportunities to interact with those of different ethnic and cultural backgrounds. As Bell points out, one way of addressing this is to work to increase the opportunities for students to interact with those of different backgrounds by increasing foreign exchange programs. Another approach would be to work to increase the opportunities students have to interact with ethnic minorities within Chinese society, including opportunities to visit regions where ethnic minorities live, exchange programs that promote opportunities for ethnic minorities within and through Chinese universities, and curricular opportunities to study minority cultures and languages, which would of course help to prepare students for more meaningful encounters with ethnic minorities.

One might also approach this set of issues in a contemporary Chinese setting by focusing more on helping students to reflect on their own cultural background and the ways in which it is distinctive when compared with other cultures, with the aim of helping them to think more constructively about diversity. Specifically, it would be important for Chinese students to reflect on why diversity should not be seen as a threat to their own cultural values and practices and, to the contrary, how diversity can expand the opportunities to embrace and extend cultural values like self-cultivation. This in turn can help to prepare them for encounters with ethnic and cultural diversity in their own society and internationally as well. One way of doing this is to help make Chinese students more aware of the Confucian origins of their own views of learning and the reasons why seeing diversity as a good—and working to understand and appreciate other ethnic and cultural traditions—can help to strengthen some of the things that are most important to them.[96] This can help them to take pride in their own culture and to think more about the distinctive contributions their own cultural views and practices might make in the world. For example, there is much that those in Western countries might learn from Chinese views of learning, and it is worth thinking more about the ways in which Chinese views might fruitfully inform Western cultural attitudes and practices.[97] Recognizing that ethnic and cultural diversity is not a threat to one's own cultural values—and that it can even help one to embrace and cultivate cultural practices like self-cultivation more fully while helping those of other backgrounds to appreciate those practices, too—gives one good reasons to avoid embracing certain forms of cultural dominance. It should also lead one to work to preserve and promote ethnic and cultural diversity in one's own society. Greater reflection on these issues, could, in the future, lead to a deeper appreciation for the distinctive values and practices that are important to ethnic minorities in regions such as Tibet and Xinjiang. It could also be a potential resource for helping to improve the social standing of migrant workers. Because self-cultivation is already an important part of philosophical outlooks and everyday social practices in China, it is reasonable to think that social reformers can and should be more attentive to the positive function of self-cultivation as they work to address issues such as diversity.

I want to emphasize that I am not arguing that the *only* way to reach these conclusions is through a study of the liberal values associated with a Rawlsian sense of justice. One might argue that diversity is a good that is

consistent with the values associated with self-cultivation in Chinese society today without having studied the sense of justice in Rawls or the
Analects, and this would be a significant objection if my argument were that
the *only* way to appreciate these things is through the study of a sense of
justice. However, just as in the previous section of this chapter, my argument is more modest. I aim to show that Rawls's sense of justice *can* help
us to see how we might develop an account of Confucian self-cultivation
that is helpful in a contemporary Chinese setting because doing so can
promote an appreciation for ethnic and cultural diversity. However, it is
important to note that insisting that ethnic and cultural diversity are values
worth cultivating and protecting is a clear expression of a sense of justice,
as is the insistence that ethnic and cultural minorities ought to be treated
in certain ways.

International Justice and Moral Influence in Rawls and the Analects

In this chapter, we have examined some of the ways in which Rawlsian
and Confucian accounts of a sense of justice might have contemporary
relevance for China and for modern liberal democracies such as the United
States, but the foregoing analysis has focused primarily on ways to address
various challenges *within* these societies. Those who are interested in questions of contemporary relevance would be correct to note, however, that
issues concerning international relations are increasingly pressing today,
particularly for China. What relevance might a Confucian sense of justice
have for Chinese foreign policy, particularly concerning questions of international justice?[98] How does Rawls's sense of justice relate to his remarks
on international relations, and what contemporary relevance might it have
for the way both China and liberal democracies interact with the rest of
the world? These are timely questions as China becomes increasingly influential and begins to play a more cooperative role in international affairs.
In this concluding section of the chapter, I will explore these questions by
examining what sort of dialogue we might construct between Rawls and
Kongzi on the subject of international justice, and what further lessons
each side might learn from the other.[99] While it is clear that Kongzi did
not offer an account of *international* relations in the *Analects,* he did make
a number of remarks about interstate relations and moral influence in relation to foreign peoples, and in what follows I will use these as the basis
for my remarks.[100] I will focus on a particular aspect of Kongzi's view of
interstate relations, namely the role of *de* ("Virtue") and its relationship to

the capacity for a sense of justice. I go on to examine whether Rawls thinks a person's virtue can give her a unique way of influencing others in cases of international justice and, if so, what we might be able to learn from a comparison of these two accounts of moral and political influence in international relations. My goal is to show that although such practices as economic sanctions and military force will continue to be the norm in many areas of international relations, the influence of moral and political virtues is worth considering in greater depth, at least in relation to some questions of international justice. To be sure, this type of influence represents a desirable alternative to various kinds of force, and with a little more analysis and further argument we may be able to see how it does not represent a wholly unrealistic alternative in certain kinds of cases.

In multiple places in the *Analects*, Kongzi expresses his view concerning the Yi and Di tribes, groups of non-Chinese people who lived to the east and north of what is now China. In *Analects* 9.14, Kongzi expresses a desire to go and live among the Nine Yi Barbarian tribes. Elsewhere in the *Analects*, he remarks that "The Yi and Di tribes, even with their rulers, are no match for the Xia [Chinese] people without their rulers" (3.5). This makes it unsurprising that in 9.14 he is asked, "How could you bear their crudeness?" Kongzi replies, "If a *junzi* dwells among them, what crudeness could there be?"[101] Traditional commentators have linked this passage to the idea that a cultivated person has a powerful moral influence on others, for Kongzi clearly maintains that the Nine Yi Barbarian tribes can and will be transformed by the influence of a *junzi*. This idea very well may underlie his non-aggressive stance toward them. Nevertheless, Kongzi sees the moral, religious, and political views and practices of his own culture as superior to those of the Yi people, and this is why he maintains that they ought to adopt the views and practices of his culture. *Analects* 13.19 can be seen as lending additional support to this view, with Kongzi stating that even if one goes among the Yi or Di tribes, one can never put aside such virtues as reverence, respectfulness, and dutifulness. One implication of this passage is that there are no circumstances under which one ought to abandon the virtues and practices that are a part of the Way. One might draw the additional conclusion that these virtues and practices become especially important when one is in a place where others do not follow the Way, because it is the influence of virtue that leads people to follow the Way. Despite his non-aggressive stance toward them, Kongzi's view is not that he and his followers ought to work to appreciate the culture of the Yi and Di tribes; rather, he thinks they need to be transformed by his own culture.[102] This is part of a larger vision of the ideal society that we begin to see in the *Analects* and that is further developed in the work of thinkers like Mengzi and Xunzi. Joseph Chan has argued that this ideal is characterized by the Confucian conception of *tian xia* 天下, "an ideal moral and political order admitting of no territorial boundary—the whole world to be governed by a sage" and that "transcends the narrowness of states."[103] This ideal helps to explain the importance of *de* ("Virtue," "moral power") in relation to foreign cultures as well as interstate relations, for if the goal is to lead all to follow the Way, then one needs an account of how this transformation is both possible and likely in the midst of cultural and political differences.

As we saw earlier in this work, the idea that we gravitate toward and are influenced by those who are virtuous is related to the traditional Chinese understanding of *de* that takes a particular form in the *Analects*: A virtuous person's *de* is her inherent and spontaneous power to affect others.[104] *De* is a special kind of authoritative charisma that good rulers in particular were believed to possess and that was thought to arise from one's morally exemplary character. On this view, people naturally defer to those with *de* and freely support them. Accordingly, virtuous political leaders effortlessly "rule through the power of *de*," ordering society through their virtuous example instead of through regulations and punishments (2.3). When Kongzi is asked whether those who lack the Way should be executed in order to advance the Way, Kongzi replies, "[W]hat need is there for executions? If you desire goodness, then the common people will be good. The *de* ('Virtue') of a *junzi* is like the wind, and the *de* ('Virtue') of a petty person is like the grass—when the wind moves over the grass, the grass is sure to bend" (12.19). On this view, the *junzi*'s *de* can influence even members of another state to change and follow the Way.

De functions in an important way even in passages in which Kongzi is simply learning about the manner in which different states operate politically. In 1.10, Ziqin asks Zigong, "When the Master goes to a particular state, he is certain to learn about its government. Does he seek such information? Or do others just give it to him?" Zigong replies, "The Master goes about it by being cordial, forthright, respectful, modest, and deferential. The Master's way of seeking it is different from that of others."[105] Different traditional commentators point out the role of *de* in this passage. Zhu Xi maintains that rulers are attracted to Kongzi because of his *de*, and so the point of the passage is that they seek him out to discuss problems in governing, not vice versa. Huang Kan argues that Kongzi's virtue gives him a heightened sensitivity to people and situations, and as a result he does not need to make inquiries. By being attentive, he is able to perceive the sentiments of the people, which are the true measure of a state. This, too, is a way in which *de* might function: One does not have to seek after information, people, or things; whatever one needs simply comes, effortlessly. On such a view, one can understand the passage as describing the attractive power of *de* as well as the extraordinary degree of perceptiveness that—at least in part—enables cultivated persons to know without asking. According to the interpretations of both Zhu Xi and Huang Kan, Kongzi does not take an aggressive stance, even when he is learning about the affairs of another state. Rather, he allows things to come to light without forcing them, and part of the reason why this is effective is that he has *de*. Kongzi's moral charisma and the attractive power associated with it enable him to learn about other states effortlessly. In turn, just as the *junzi*'s influence can inspire members of another state to change their behavior and follow the Way, perhaps leaders are drawn to Kongzi and led to seek his advice in governing.

In the *Law of Peoples*, Rawls's primary question is "Should liberal societies tolerate and cooperate with nonliberal societies that are not just according to (political) liberalism, and if so, how far should toleration and cooperation extend? Or should liberal societies seek to shape in their own image all societies not yet liberal or democratic, intervening in their internal affairs and applying sanctions whenever effective?"[106] According to Rawls, the answer to this question depends heavily on the type of society one is dealing with. While Rawls does *not* think liberal societies should tolerate dictatorial, tyrannical, or other "outlaw" regimes, he argues that it is unreasonable to expect "unjust but nonetheless decent societies to conform to all the egalitarian norms of a constitutional democracy as a condition of peaceful coexistence and cooperation."[107] He maintains that requiring all societies to be liberal would fail to express due toleration for other acceptable ways of ordering society, and that this would be inconsistent with political liberalism, which is partly defined by a respect for citizens' comprehensive doctrines—religious, philosophical, and moral (*LP*, 59). Rawls also maintains that liberal peoples' not respecting decent peoples is actually likely to prevent change in decent societies. He writes that withholding respect from decent peoples might stifle change partly because doing so "may lead to great bitterness and resentment. Denying respect to other peoples and their members requires strong reasons to be justified," and Rawls maintains that those reasons simply do not exist in the case of decent peoples (*LP*, 61). "All societies undergo gradual changes, and this is no less true of decent societies than of others. Liberal peoples should not suppose that decent societies are unable to reform themselves in their own way" (*LP*, 61). Further, it is primarily through recognizing and showing respect for decent peoples that liberal peoples *encourage* this change. "Liberal peoples must try to encourage decent peoples and not frustrate their vitality by coercively insisting that all societies be liberal" (*LP*, 62).

Here we can begin to recognize the similarity between Rawls's view of decent peoples and Kongzi's view of foreign tribes such as the Yi and Di, for they both take a non-aggressive stance toward these peoples, and this stance is based primarily on the fundamental tenets of their respective views—political liberalism, in Rawls's case, and the Way, in Kongzi's case. In addition, clearly each of them wishes to see moral and political change in these peoples, and they each maintain that this change is possible and even likely under the right circumstances. Here is where we see an even more interesting point of resemblance: For both Kongzi and Rawls, the moral or political change they wish to see is likely to occur at least in part as a result of the influence of certain virtues. We have already seen Kongzi's view, but we need to further examine what Rawls says in order to appreciate his view on this matter.

To be sure, Rawls thinks decent societies should be respected, and he argues *against* the view that the guiding principle of liberal foreign policy should be to "gradually shape all not yet liberal societies in a liberal direction, until eventually (in the ideal case) all societies are liberal" (*LP*, 60). However, despite the fact that Rawls does not think this view should be the guiding principle of liberal foreign policy, he nevertheless maintains that liberal democracies are the best form of society. He makes this especially clear in relation to decent societies when he emphasizes that his view "does not imply that political liberalism endorses decent hierarchical societies as just and beyond criticism."[108] He encourages public criticism and critical assessment by liberal citizens, in contrast with hostile criticisms, sanctions, or other forms of coercive intervention. As Samuel Freeman has pointed out, according to Rawls's *Law of Peoples* liberal peoples "have a duty to cooperate with . . . decent nonliberal societies. This means that liberal peoples have certain moral duties to decent nonliberal peoples. . . ."[109] As we have seen, according to Rawls, "Liberal people must try to encourage decent peoples":

> Moreover, if a liberal constitutional democracy is, in fact, superior to other forms of society, as I believe it to be, a liberal people should have confidence in their convictions and suppose that a decent society, when

offered due respect by liberal peoples, may be more likely, over time,
to recognize the advantages of liberal institutions and take steps toward
becoming more liberal on its own. (*LP*, 62)

Rawls takes an important step here, arguing that if liberal democracy is
indeed superior to other forms of society, then, upon experiencing the
respect of liberal peoples, members of decent societies are likely to come
to see the advantages of liberalism and become more liberal themselves. A
couple of important presuppositions are present here, including the idea
that if liberal democracy is indeed superior, its appeal will be apparent to
others, and the idea that the respect shown by liberal peoples can lead to
political influence.[110]

An interesting comparison can be drawn with the *Analects* here: Both
Rawls and Kongzi offer an account of how members of one state or nation
can and should seek to influence and shape members of another state with
respect to a range of ethical and political issues, including questions of justice. In Rawls's case, the question is how to act so as to promote liberalism
in nonliberal but decent societies, while for Kongzi the question is how to
act so as to promote the Way among people without it.[111] Interestingly,
Rawls thinks the respect shown for members of a decent society by liberal
peoples, together with open discussion and critical reflection, is likely to
motivate decent peoples to embrace liberal democratic values. It is important to try to clarify what Rawls has in mind here when he talks about
respect, open discussion, and reflection, because he does not elaborate further. One way of fleshing this out is to turn to the resources in Rawls's
other work. His discussion of different kinds of political virtues seems especially relevant because for Rawls, the political virtues—many of which
grow from or are closely connected with a sense of justice—often enable
one to show this sort of respect for others and engage in open discussion
of political matters. As we saw in Chapter 2, in *Justice as Fairness: A Restatement* Rawls discusses "the cooperative virtues of political life: the virtues of
reasonableness and a sense of fairness, and of a spirit of compromise and a
readiness to meet others halfway" (*JF*, 116). He also discusses the judicial
virtues, which are "excellences of the moral power of a sense of justice"
and "involve intellect and imagination, the capacity to be impartial and to
take a wider and more inclusive view, as well as a certain sensitivity to the
concerns and circumstances of others" (*JF*, 170). Because these virtues are
in line with Rawls's description in *The Law of Peoples* of the respect shown
by liberal peoples toward decent peoples, they might be what ultimately
enable liberal peoples to influence decent peoples politically, on Rawls's

view. There seems to be a very important relationship, then, for Rawls, between a sense of justice and the capacity for liberal peoples to influence decent peoples with respect to questions of international justice, for the virtues that stem from or are closely connected with a sense of justice may actually facilitate this moral and political influence.

Here we can see how an understanding of *de* in the *Analects* can help us to notice that Rawls sees individuals who possess certain kinds of political virtues as having a particularly strong capacity to influence others. In both Rawls and the *Analects*, one's virtues seem to enable one to inspire significant political change internationally. Yet there are important differences between the *moral* influence of the *junzi* who possesses *the full range of virtues* and the *political* influence of *liberal peoples* who exhibit certain kinds of *political virtues*. The influence described in the *Analects* clearly involves not just political change but also thoroughgoing moral change, involving all of the Confucian virtues and the patterns of life associated with following the Way. Furthermore, individuals who can bring about this type of change are those who exhibit a profound mastery of the virtues and rituals associated with the Way and as a result possess *de* ("Virtue," "moral power," "moral charisma"), which gives them a deep and remarkable ability to influence others. The type of influence Rawls describes is mainly political in character, and those who can bring about this type of influence are exemplars of certain political virtues, seen in their various expressions of respect for decent peoples, as well as in such things as an openness to discussion and critical reflection on political questions.[112] On Rawls's view, then, a much wider range of individuals would be capable of having this kind of influence, and they would represent a cross-section of different comprehensive views, even though they would have overlapping values and commitments, namely those things that are central to liberalism. It also seems to be the case that it is not only exemplary individuals but also a certain way of life that is attractive, on Rawls's view. However, in order to accept the view that a certain political system (and the way of life that partially defines it) is better, one must find the people within it appealing.

Another important contrast between the accounts of moral and political influence found in Rawls and the *Analects* concerns the relationship between a sense of justice and moral influence. For Rawls, liberal peoples are able to influence decent peoples through the political virtues that grow from or are closely connected with a sense of justice, but in the *Analects*, the *junzi*'s *de* does not have its origins in a sense of justice, nor does it seem to be closely related to a sense of justice, even though it is clear that those with *de* also have a sense of justice. This is an important difference from the standpoint of moral psychology, because different virtues and moral capacities are seen as being foundational in relation to the capacity for moral and political influence. Now Rawls acknowledges that many different aspects of a person's moral education can play a role in the development of a sense of justice and the political virtues, but it appears that the virtues which develop from or in connection with a strong sense of justice can, on Rawls's view, enable liberal peoples to influence decent peoples politically.

In contrast, in the *Analects* filial piety is seen as having a foundational role in a person's moral development, seen for example in Kongzi's claim that filial piety and respect for elders constitute the root of *Ren* ("humaneness"), and that "once the roots are firmly established, the Way will grow" (1.2). As we saw earlier in this work, filial piety has a clear and direct relationship with political participation; Kongzi even goes so far as to say that in being filial, one contributes in important ways to a political society (2.21). At the same time, it is important to clarify some matters here. First, *de* ("Virtue," "moral power," "moral charisma") does not grow solely from filial piety; rather, *de* is described as a quality of the truly exemplary person, meaning that *de* involves the possession of the full range of virtues. Filial piety, though, plays a foundational role in the cultivation of those virtues. Second, even though a sense of justice is not seen as "the root" of one's moral or political influence, it is still an important part of the character of a person with *de*. Because having *de* has to do with having a particular sort of character, and a sense of justice is a part of that, then the *junzi*'s sense of justice surely is an important part of what makes the *junzi* attractive and influential.

Comparing these two accounts of moral and political influence can also help us to notice the different challenges they face. The Confucians must defend the view that *de* ("Virtue," "moral power," "moral charisma") actually works in the way the *Analects* says it does, namely that virtuous people have an attractive power and a profound influence on those around them, enough to accomplish the sort of ethical and political conversion that the Yi Barbarians are supposed to undergo in the presence of a *junzi*. The Confucian account of how other states could be brought to follow the Way (and thus have societies that are humane and just, among other things) depends in part on this account of the *junzi*'s *de* being true. In sorting out the reasons why this account might be difficult for some to accept, it is helpful to distinguish between different aspects of the conception of *de* in the *Analects*. On the one hand, there is a *practical* aspect of the account of *de* that most of us can accept fairly readily based on our experience. Many of the descriptions of *de* in the *Analects* simply seem to highlight genuine features of our experience, such as the fact that we are often inspired to behave in certain ways as a result of being treated in those ways by others, and that we have a tendency to want to reciprocate when someone shows us a particular kindness. In addition, most of us recognize that being around and interacting with good people often leads us to be better people. This is both because those who possess certain virtues provide an inspiring example of why it is good to possess those virtues, which prompts us to work harder at cultivating those virtues, and because we tend to mirror the behavior of those we admire. In these ways, the basic claim that virtuous people are likely to attract others, inspire them to respond in kind, and are able to lead others effortlessly seems to be true.[113] On the other hand, there is another side to the account of *de* in the *Analects*, one that we might call the *mystical* aspect. This aspect of the account of *de* is often seen most clearly in the *strength* of the claims made about the virtuous person's influence, for some passages make it sound as though virtuous individuals possess an almost supernatural or magical power. For example, the claim that "If you desire goodness, then the common people will be good," which precedes the claim that the *de* ("Virtue") of the *junzi* is like the wind blowing across the grass (12.19), simply does not seem realistic in the absence of some sort of mysterious, extraordinary power. The claim that simply desiring goodness—even if one takes that to mean pursuing goodness— will make the common people good is much stronger than the claim that virtuous people tend to have an inspirational effect on others. These kinds of claims suggest that an aspect of the virtuous person's influence is mystical in character.

This aspect of the conception of *de* in the *Analects* surely reflects the early origins of this idea, including the belief that *de* was a kind of power that accrued to those who acted favorably not only toward people but also toward ancestral spirits, and that this power consisted largely of receiving the favor of the spirits. Additionally, in Kongzi's time the idea that Heaven bestows its mandate on good rulers continued to be important, and this is another part of the religious sensibility that is a part of the view of *de*, for part of what it means to have Heaven's mandate is to be able to rule through the power of *de*. These views require faith in the existence of powerful unseen entities. Both the practical and mystical aspects of the conception of *de* in the *Analects* help to explain how, on Kongzi's view, it is possible for virtuous people to have a profound influence on those around them, and as a result they both play a key role in showing how Kongzi's moral and political vision can be realized. It would be wrong to reduce the conception of *de* in the *Analects* to either one of these aspects; my aim here is simply to point out that claims about *de* in the *Analects* on the one hand describe something most of us have experienced in our everyday lives but on the other hand describe something more extraordinary and which requires us to believe that some individuals possess a mysterious power. The latter requires a type of religious faith on our part.[114] As a result, if the conception of *de* in the *Analects* is to have relevance in a contemporary setting, we will need to emphasize and develop the practical aspect of *de* and show that it is not dependent on the mystical aspect of *de*. This would help to show how those committed to different religious views could still accept and learn from key aspects of the account of moral influence presented in the *Analects*.

Rawls's account also faces challenges in showing how political virtues such as respect can translate into political influence. Rawls's view seems to depend upon whether the political virtues exhibited by liberal peoples help to make clear the inherent attractiveness of liberal democratic regimes, enough to lead members of decent societies to embrace liberal values and institutions. As we have seen, Rawls is reasonably optimistic on this point, maintaining that "a decent society, *when offered due respect by liberal peoples*, may be more likely, over time, to recognize the advantages of liberal institutions and take steps toward becoming more liberal on its own," and also that, in a similar manner, withholding respect from decent peoples may prevent such change.[115] As this passage shows, Rawls thinks the appeal of liberal democratic institutions is often made clear through the respect that liberal peoples demonstrate for others. The crucial question, though, is whether the respect shown by members of liberal societies will indeed lead members of decent societies to see the appeal of liberal constitutional democracy—enough to convince them that political change is needed. It seems that in order for this to occur, members of decent societies would have to see this sort of respect as something that is unique to liberal democracy or at least something that liberal democracies encourage more effectively than other societies. Rawls appears to assume that some form of this claim is true, especially given his view that the respect shown by liberal peoples toward decent peoples will help to convince decent peoples of the value of liberal institutions.[116] Unfortunately, this is not an unproblematic assumption. There simply do not seem to be obvious reasons to think that liberalism offers a superior way of cultivating respect for others, compared with other kinds of societies. Even if we understand Rawls as referring to *particular expressions* of respect—such as a spirit of compromise, sensitivity to the concerns and circumstances of others, openness to criticism, and other qualities associated with the political virtues Rawls discusses—it remains difficult to substantiate the claim that these virtues and attitudes are in some way uniquely characteristic of, or more effectively cultivated within, liberal societies.

One way of strengthening the Rawlsian account here would be to argue that expressions of respect and the exercise of certain kinds of political virtues are effective ways for *any* society to highlight the goods associated with its institutions. This would require Rawls to grant that respect and the other political virtues he discusses are not uniquely associated with liberal institutions, while maintaining that they are a mark of a good society. Of course, this modification has important implications for Rawls's account of political influence, for it means that decent peoples will not likely be led to embrace liberal institutions solely or primarily as a result of respect and other political virtues expressed by liberal peoples. But such expressions of respect by liberal peoples could be seen as an important first step in leading decent peoples to explore further the goods associated with liberal institutions. If members of other kinds of societies expressed similar virtues, then decent peoples might also be led to explore their political culture and institutions. The point, though, is that on this view, when members of one society exemplify certain political virtues in their interactions with members of another kind of society, those political virtues can and should have the effect of leading members of the other society to consider more carefully the political institutions that may have helped to encourage those virtues in its people. On this modified Rawlsian view, liberal peoples should interact with decent peoples in ways that are respectful and sensitive to the concerns and circumstances of others and that show a willingness to meet others halfway and engage in open discussion. While we should not expect this to lead them to appreciate the unique appeal of liberal institutions (for such virtues and attitudes are not unique to or more effectively cultivated within liberal societies), we should anticipate that it may lead them to want to learn more about liberal institutions. Indeed, one should want to learn more about *any* society whose members consistently embody these kinds of political virtues in clear and compelling ways.

In considering whether this modification of Rawls's view would be consistent with his overarching view in *The Law of Peoples*, it is important to remember the reasons why Rawls claims we should work to influence decent societies through the cooperative virtues of political life instead of subjecting them to some form of sanction, despite the fact that they are not fully just by liberal principles. In addition to maintaining that such extreme measures are simply not warranted because we have a number of good reasons to respect decent societies, Rawls argues that this sort of response to decent peoples is self-defeating. It makes members of decent societies decidedly *less* likely to appreciate the goods associated with liberalism in part because they are not being shown the sort of respect that is supposed to be characteristic of liberalism. Even if this sort of respect is not seen as uniquely tied to liberal institutions in any way, the attempt to bring about political change in decent societies through force remains entirely inconsistent with political liberalism, according to which it is "a good for individuals and associations to be attached to their particular culture and to take part in its common public and civic life. In this way political society is expressed and fulfilled. This is no small thing. It argues for preserving significant room for the idea of a people's self-determination" (*LP*, 61). It is worth recognizing, then, that however liberal peoples seek to influence decent peoples, it must be in accord with allowing them to determine their own future. By insisting that liberal peoples focus on maintaining a spirit of respect and cooperation, Rawls contends that the best testament to liberal values is to apply them consistently so that the reasons why they are appealing *in practice*, and not just in theory, can be appreciated. In order to appreciate what is distinctive about liberalism, though, we must look beyond respect to the *results* of such respect. For example, a liberal society supports diversity through its political institutions, and this is an important part of the general, inherent attractiveness of the liberal form of life. Rawls notes that a basic feature of liberal democracy is the fact of reasonable pluralism—"the fact that a plurality of conflicting reasonable comprehensive doctrines, both religious and nonreligious (or secular), is the normal result of the culture of its free institutions," and the fact of democratic unity in diversity—"the fact that in a constitutional democratic society, political and social unity does not require that its citizens be unified by one comprehensive doctrine, religious or nonreligious" (*LP*, 124). As we have seen, individuals' dispositions—including the possession of a strong sense of justice—are an important part of what makes justice possible in a diverse society. What is distinctive is not the tendency of liberal peoples to exemplify certain political virtues; rather, it is the outcomes promoted by liberal institutions working together with citizens who possess these virtues.

Recognizing that the political virtues possessed by liberal peoples are not unique to liberal societies can also lead us to notice a related feature of the account of *de* found in the *Analects*. The virtues possessed by the *junzi* are not unique to a society that follows the Way of Kongzi. On both views, then, there is no guarantee that one who is influenced by a virtuous person's *de*, or by the political virtues of liberal peoples, will be led to pursue the same kind of life or the same kind of society. Both Kongzi and Rawls seem to have assumed that the sort of moral and political influence they envisioned would lead one to follow the Way (in Kongzi's case) and to endorse liberal political institutions (in Rawls's case). But neither of them seems to have been aware that the virtues they discussed were not unique to the Way (in Kongzi's case) and liberalism (in Rawls's case).

Examining the different challenges the Confucian and Rawlsian accounts of moral and political influence face allows us to notice a further feature of these two views. While the Confucian view of *de* enables even bad societies to be reformed through moral influence, according to Rawls's view, apparently only other *decent* societies are to be reformed through the influence of liberal peoples' political virtues. Societies with dictatorial or tyrannical regimes, for Rawls, often require intervention by force because of the depth of the injustice that is perpetuated in these societies. One of the strengths of Rawls's account here is that it does not seem overly idealistic in its reach. It is relatively easy to appreciate how a spirit of respect and open discussion might, over time, contribute to changes in cultural attitudes and practices in societies that are already decent. In contrast, Kongzi's belief that virtuous persons will have a transformative effect even on bad societies might strike one as implausible, especially if one does not accept the mystical aspect of the description of *de* in the *Analects*. On the other hand, one strength of the Confucian account of *de* is that it provides an account of *why* some individuals have a special sort of influence on others, whereas Rawls's account fails to offer a satisfying explanation for why decent peoples would be led to embrace liberal institutions as a result of political virtues that members of nonliberal societies often possess. This is where we can see that Rawls relies on the assumption that certain political virtues are in some way a unique part of liberal institutions. As we have seen, comparing the two views can lead us to see ways in which both accounts can be amended or further developed in order to become more appealing and workable in a contemporary setting. In the end, although we may not grant in either case that moral or political influence is always likely, surely we can grant that at least in some cases, it is a possibility and perhaps even a strong one.

The concept of *de* can help to remind us of the importance of having the right kinds of people in place—whether they are citizens or political leaders or both—if one hopes to influence others. Kongzi says much about this issue, while Rawls's account of how the political virtues enable liberal peoples to influence decent peoples is more subtle. But a comparison with Kongzi's account can help us to tease out, further develop, and appreciate these aspects of Rawls's view, while prompting us to think more about moral and political influence internationally. Similarly, comparing Kongzi's view of moral influence with Rawls's account of political and moral influence can help us to appreciate the contemporary relevance that Kongzi's view might have. For if the idea that we can influence and inspire others in an international setting through the virtues we possess has been defended by the most influential liberal political philosopher of the last century, then we have good reasons to believe that we should not too quickly reject this idea as archaic and inappropriate in a contemporary setting. To the contrary, we should be led to examine more carefully the accounts of this type of influence found in different traditions, in the hope that these conceptions might, with a little more analysis and further development, lead us to consider new approaches to the questions and challenges associated with international justice.

Conclusion

One of the original overarching aims of this study was to demonstrate some of the ways in which comparative work can be worthwhile. I have argued that a comparative study of the capacity for a sense of justice in Kongzi and Rawls helps us not only to understand each of their views and the nature of a sense of justice but also helps us to see new ways of applying and further developing Confucian and Rawlsian insights. This approach offers an alternative to those approaches that see comparative philosophy simply as an opportunity to compare and contrast two views without having clear goals or constructive aims. This model is also an alternative to those approaches that see comparative philosophy as an opportunity to show how one philosophical position can serve as a corrective supplement to another, or as an enterprise concerned primarily with arguing for the superiority of one philosophical tradition over another. Additionally, unlike some studies, my aim is not to demonstrate the compatibility or incompatibility of the two views under study. My comparative study of Rawls and the *Analects* is not purely descriptive; it recognizes merit in and seeks to help us to understand important aspects of both of these accounts, as opposed to simply using one to highlight the weaknesses or strengths of the other. It also has further constructive aims, especially with respect to the contemporary relevance of the two accounts of a sense of justice. Accordingly, the fruits of this comparison lie in a number of different areas, including political philosophy, ethics, and Chinese and comparative philosophy.

My discussion of the challenges and aims of comparative work and my discussion of a sense of justice in Rawls and Kongzi depend upon each other in important ways and are mutually enhancing. While I have not utilized a single, specific method in my comparison of the *Analects* and Rawls, I have worked to give attention to interpretive, thematic, and procedural issues. This "anti-method" approach has allowed me the flexibility to address the various challenges of comparative work in ways that are appropriate for my particular study. I discuss my thematic choices explicitly and in considerable detail in the Introduction, and one of the things I make clear both in discussing these choices and in reviewing other discussions of this topic is that this comparative study offers a response to other discussions of liberalism and early Confucianism. In light of the fact that my study highlights neglected features of both views under study, I devote separate chapters to Rawls and the *Analects* before proceeding with my comparative discussion. This procedural choice is important for multiple reasons. It provides a separate and distinct space for the discussion of differences and similarities, which is especially important in light of the attention that has been given to the dramatic contrast between liberalism and Confucianism and the tendency some readers will have to worry about the imposition of one view on the other. In addition, it provides the space for a more extended look at each of the views under study, which is necessary in order to provide textual evidence in support of my claims, including the claim that the family has an important role in cultivating a sense of justice in Rawls's thought and the claim that despite the absence of a term for "justice" in the *Analects*, the capacity for a sense of justice is considered important. I have also worked to address interpretive challenges by examining the various ways in which a variety of concepts and themes function together to show the importance of a sense of justice, which, as we have seen, contributes to a larger account of a well-ordered and stable society in Rawls and a harmonious and humane society in the *Analects*. Once again, this is especially important because so many contemporary interpreters of the *Analects* have focused on the absence of a single term for "justice," and my argument is that the importance of a sense of justice is seen in a wide range of different concepts and themes in the text. A comparison of the ways multiple concepts and themes function together in the two texts has also been a helpful way of approaching the subject of a sense of justice because it is one way to avoid creating the impression that a sense of justice is the only important thing in these two texts. Although I have argued that this idea has been neglected in both Rawls and the *Analects*, my goal is to show not that it is the only or most important idea in these works but rather to show how this idea plays an important role in the larger context of Rawlsian and early Confucian philosophies.

The central aim of this study is to show that certain aspects of the moral and political thought of Rawls and the *Analects* can be seen as expressions of the importance of the capacity for a sense of justice. Although the differences between the general views of society found in Rawls and the *Analects* are often more striking than the similarities between certain aspects of their views of moral development and moral psychology, it is important not to lose sight of what their accounts have in common. The fact that an account of a sense of justice is offered in these two very different philosophical contexts shows that thinkers of different times and places have found such a sense to play a critical role in human moral development and also in creating and maintaining a good society. These features of a sense of justice should lead us to be even more interested in exploring it.

My discussion of the nature and significance of a sense of justice should make clear not only how important this capacity is but also the variety of ethical and political theories in which it plays a critical role. Understanding a sense of justice and how it develops is important in part because, if Kongzi and Rawls are correct, a well-developed sense of justice makes a substantive contribution to the value and success of a wide range of societies, from pluralistic liberal democracies to societies defined by a comprehensive vision of the good life such as the Way. The different kinds of societies Kongzi and Rawls envision each address the need to provide assistance to members of a society who are marginalized by circumstances beyond their control. In addition, they each maintain that it is critical for other members of society, as well as political leaders, to understand why it is both necessary and appropriate to address these needs. This is why a well-developed sense of justice is so important, for it includes the disposition to feel for other members of society under certain circumstances, as well as the willingness if not the desire to make sacrifices for others in these kinds of circumstances. For Rawls, this capacity is one of the things that make a just society possible. For Kongzi, a sense of justice contributes to the achievement of larger goals such as humaneness and harmony.

While Rawls devotes the greatest share of his attention to the nature of just institutions that are designed to help address the inequalities that stem from natural and social contingencies, the *Analects* devotes the greatest share of its attention to the process of moral self-cultivation that members of society must engage in if they wish to achieve a harmonious, humane society—a society that embodies the Way. I have argued that cultivating a sense of justice is one part of what it means to follow the Way and that this capacity is seen in descriptions of the *junzi* and in a wide range of other ideas as well. Rawls's discussion, as we have seen, contains self-cultivationist dimensions that are underdeveloped and understudied. The *Analects*, as we have seen, does not address in detail the kinds of institutions that individuals who have a well-developed sense of justice might work to establish and maintain. The fact that Rawls does not develop further the self-cultivationist dimensions of his account is partly a function of his desire to provide a political account of justice that is broad enough to appeal to a plurality of reasonable comprehensive doctrines. It also reflects his participation and training in Western moral philosophy, which historically has neglected this aspect of ethical inquiry. Similarly, the fact that the *Analects* fails to discuss how political institutions might address natural and social contingencies more systematically is tied to the urgency of other concerns in early Chinese philosophy and culture, and to the way in which Kongzi viewed his own task. It seems clear that he sees himself as a moral teacher, as opposed to an official whose job is to design, establish, and maintain certain kinds of institutions, laws, or policies. As we have seen, he expresses concern over the tendency people have to focus exclusively or primarily on the latter.

Indeed, a critical difference in the overall aims of these two sources is that while Kongzi's goal is strongly therapeutic in that he aims to improve his students' character by teaching them about the Way, Rawls's primary aim is theoretical—that is, to explain what justice is and how the basic structure of society should be arranged. However, as we have seen, a comparative study helps us to more fully understand the features of both accounts. Kongzi's emphasis on self-cultivation, which is at the heart of his therapeutic program, might even help us to recognize and appreciate some of the more therapeutic aspects of Rawls's account, while Rawls's theoretical account of a sense of justice can help us to better understand certain features of Kongzi's view by making explicit a number of things that are only implicit in the *Analects*. Once we appreciate Rawls's emphasis on how a sense of justice is cultivated at various stages within a family, community, and society, and the extent to which a view of human nature is a part of this account, we can also come to appreciate the therapeutic side of Rawls's work. For although theoretical concerns are clearly at the forefront of Rawls's project, he also seems to hope that his analysis will move people to act in certain ways. At the very least, Rawls works to demonstrate why we should all take an interest in cultivating a sense of justice among members of our own families and communities. Just as the *Analects* can lead us to appreciate this side of Rawls, so too can his theoretical concerns lead us to recognize and understand important features of the *Analects*. We have seen how Rawls's distinction between a sense of justice, the concept of justice, and a conception or theory of justice can help us not to neglect the appreciation for justice that is seen in the *Analects*, despite the fact that the *Analects* does not offer anything like a theory of justice. I have argued that if we follow this basic distinction between a sense, concept, and theory of justice, then we can begin to appreciate how a number of institutions assume the basic role of justice in the society envisioned in the *Analects*, including the family and the rites.

In the midst of the many contrasts between these views, perhaps the most striking point of resonance between Rawls and the *Analects* is their insistence that a sense of justice must be cultivated first and foremost within the context of parent–child relationships. Although the family has a distinctive place in Kongzi's account that is obviously very different from its place in Rawls's account, it is still the case that both Rawls and the *Analects* emphasize the importance of role-specific duties and the abilities one cultivates with respect to thinking about and considering the needs of others in the context of the family. Both Kongzi and Rawls acknowledge in their own ways that it is in relationship with our parents that we begin to learn what it means to be a participant in a community and to value our obligations to others. As I argued in Chapter 5, we have good reasons to consider their insights on this matter. Their views on the role of the family in cultivating such capacities as a sense of justice ought to influence discussions in a variety of areas, including political philosophy, where concerns about the role of parent–child relationships and the family have largely been relegated to the private realm. Scholars such as Susan Moller Okin have worked to bring discussions of the family and justice into mainstream political philosophy, but even these discussions remain bound up with the accordance of rights to family members, and with little emphasis on the relationships between parents and children, the role these relationships play in moral development, and the subsequent impact they have on our political culture.[1] Here, different criticisms of the centrality of liberal rights discourse offered by communitarians and by scholars of Confucianism might serve as guiding voices in the conversation. As the discussions of a sense of justice in both Rawls and the *Analects* suggest, the family plays a critical role in moral development generally and in the development of the political virtues in particular, and this set of issues is worthy of more attention in both ethics and political philosophy. If members of our society do not tend to have a fully developed sense of justice, then on both Rawls's view and on the view presented in the *Analects* the family is the place to which we must return in an effort to address the problem.

Despite these areas of agreement, I have worked to emphasize throughout this study that deep and important differences exist between these two views. Indeed, I have argued that the differences between these two understandings of a sense of justice represent the reason why a comparison of them is so fruitful. One of the most significant differences is that Rawls is concerned primarily with establishing just political institutions and with the role that just institutions have in shaping citizens' sense of justice. The *Analects*, on the other hand, is more concerned with the development of a sense of justice as one of several moral capacities individuals must cultivate in order to follow the Way. Although both Rawls and the *Analects* each acknowledge that basic institutions and moral character are both important, their discussions move in very different directions on these matters. Kongzi explicitly rejects the view that political policies are a proper starting place for achieving the goal of a humane and harmoniously functioning society. Rawls, on the other hand, sees political principles of justice as one of the areas where a variety of reasonable comprehensive doctrines might achieve overlapping consensus, and as a result he sees it as a good starting place for achieving a just society. Here we are reminded of the very different tasks of achieving stability for the right reasons in a pluralistic liberal democracy and working to achieve the comprehensive vision of the good that is seen in the Way of Kongzi.

An important difference that emerges from Rawls's emphasis on political institutions as opposed to moral self-cultivation is that when it comes to the development of a sense of justice, Rawls continually talks in terms of class position. Throughout Rawls's discussion, he traces the development of one's capacities, including one's moral capacities, to one's social class of origin, as opposed to the sort of family in which one has been raised. Because Rawls discusses the critical role that parent–child relationships play in the development of good citizens, the kind of family one happens to be born into should be—but curiously is not—among the moral contingencies Rawls addresses. Like the other kinds of contingencies he discusses, different kinds of families are the source of especially deep inequalities that cannot be justified by appealing to notions of merit or desert and that affect people's initial chances in life. Yet as we have seen, Rawls outlines three kinds of contingencies that affect the inequalities in citizens' life-prospects: one's social class of origin, native endowments, and good or ill fortune over the course of one's life. But although one's life-prospects are certainly affected by the class position of one's family, the evidence suggests that they are even more deeply affected by the *kind* of family one is born into and raised in. There is not a neat correspondence between being born into an advantageous class position and having caring, attentive parents, or between being raised in a socially and financially advantaged home and developing good character.

In most of the cases Rawls describes, one's class position and the kind of parent–child relationships that exist in one's home are separate, though not unrelated, issues. For example, children who begin their lives in favorable class positions are not *necessarily* raised in families that value the development of their native endowments of intelligence or other abilities. Individuals are surely *more or less likely* to have material opportunities to develop their abilities and overcome weaknesses or disabilities as a result of class position, but much of a child's development ultimately rests in the hands of the family. Indeed, in many cases the most serious difficulties in an individual's development arise not from class position but from circumstances within the family. Children born into socially and economically privileged families sometimes receive *less* of the right kinds of attention and support from their parents than some children born into socially and economically disadvantaged families, while children born into less advantageous class positions sometimes have families that exemplify the best kinds of familial support. As we have seen in this work, evidence suggests that good families, broadly construed, play a greater role in an individual's overall flourishing than issues of social advantage or class, because they more reliably lead to good lives. This is one of the reasons why the Nurse-Family Partnership is able to more effectively intervene in the lives of individuals than programs that offer forms of assistance which do not directly address the quality of family relationships. The NFP's research shows that addressing family relationships, in turn, can lead to things that contribute to positive changes in class position, such as greater economic self-sufficiency; this helps to show how critically the quality of the family affects the other contingencies Rawls seeks to address. All of this suggests that the family ought to be recognized in Rawls's account as a fourth kind of contingency. Taking fuller account of the different kinds of families one might be born into and raised in is important for Rawls's account not only because the family is a source of inequalities that affect people's chances in life just as deeply as—and in most cases even more deeply than—class position, native endowments, and good or ill fortune but also because parents and their surrounding communities provide the earliest and most critical steps in developing a sense of justice, as well as a range of other important moral sensibilities, in citizens.

The *Analects* provides us with a particular model for discussing the critical role of the family in these matters. Kongzi frames the question of moral development in terms of the virtues one must cultivate in familial relationships in order to flourish as a human being, as opposed to framing the question primarily in terms of political matters like class position. However, that is not to say that class position is unimportant. The view found in the *Analects* could be deepened by a discussion of the way that natural and social contingencies such as class position affect the role of the family. Likewise, the kinds of moral contingencies Rawls discusses could be more fully addressed within the context of a more developed view of the role of familial relationships. Although Rawls and the *Analects* both acknowledge the important role that parent–child relationships play in the development of a sense of justice, their diagnosis of the general problem in human societies differs in that the *Analects* remains focused on self-cultivation and the important place of virtues like filial piety, while Rawls focuses primarily on the way in which political institutions can shape citizens' sense of justice while addressing moral contingencies like class position. This is one area where the *Analects* can make a significant contribution to ongoing discussions in political philosophy, in ethics, and even, perhaps, as we saw in Chapter 5, in the area of public policy. Indeed, the potential for these kinds of contributions is one of many things that a comparative study of a sense of justice in Rawls and the *Analects* can help us to see. It is not that it would be impossible to appreciate these things without comparing the two accounts; my point is that we come to appreciate a variety of important features of a sense of justice and of the two views under study, including their relevance for us today, as a result of studying them comparatively. It should be clear that one would not see precisely the same things if one compared other accounts.

The most important shared insight of Rawls and the *Analects* is that we stand on the shoulders of our parents as they cultivate, shape, and refine our initial sense of justice, alongside our other capacities as human beings. They give us our first images of what we can and should be as members of families, communities, and societies, and it is within the context of our relationship with them that we begin to learn about justice and injustice. The importance of this insight points the way to a more robust understanding of a sense of justice, and one about which both ancient Chinese and modern Western voices have much to say.

INTRODUCTION

1. Here I have in mind both the number of different cultures that it has influenced as well as the extent or depth of its influence in those cultures. If influence is measured in the number of people who have lived their lives according to a particular person's teachings (or the teachings attributed to that person), then a good argument can be made that Kongzi (the purported founder of Confucianism) has been the most influential thinker in human history, as Roger T. Ames and Henry Rosemont Jr. suggest (see Ames and Rosemont, trans., *The Analects of Confucius: A Philosophical Translation* [New York: Ballantine Books, 1998], p. 1). Here and in what follows, I associate the ideas found in the *Analects* with Kongzi, even though he is not the author of this work or the source of all of the ideas found in it. I discuss the textual history of the *Analects* and my approach to the text in greater detail below, but for now I want to note that my remarks should not be interpreted as an attempt to attribute all of the ideas found in the *Analects* to the historical Kongzi. In early China, philosophical texts typically were not the work of one author sitting down to write a systematic treatise but instead reflected a family and lineage of thinkers associated with a particular founding figure and philosophical vision. When I refer to Kongzi, I am referring to the family and lineage of thinkers and the philosophical vision that are associated with him in the *Analects*.

2. See Freeman's preface in the *Collected Papers* (ix–xii). Freeman provides a concise overview of the essays that have spanned Rawls's career.

3. Kongzi 孔子 is known to many Westerners as "Confucius," which is the latinization of a man whose surname was Kong 孔. It was common practice in early China to refer to philosophers by appending the honorific suffix *zi* 子 ("master") to their surnames, and so he became known as "Kongzi" ("Master Kong"). As a result of his exceptional influence, in time Kongzi was given the more elaborate honorific *fuzi* 夫子, and from "Kongfuzi" 孔夫子 we get the latinized name "Confucius." Although the title of this work refers to "Confucius" because that is his most recognizable name in English, I refer to

him as "Kongzi" throughout the body of the work because that is how he was known in ancient China and how he remains known in China and throughout East Asia today (the Japanese is "Kosi" and the Korean is "Kongja").

4. The earlier part of the Eastern Zhou (722–481 B.C.E.), during which Kongzi lived, is also known as the Spring and Autumn Period. The *Zuozhuan* 左傳, one of three traditional commentaries on the *Spring and Autumn Annals* (*Chunqiu* 春秋), paints a vivid picture of what life was like before and during Kongzi's time. See the translation by James Legge (*The Chinese Classics*, Vol. 5) and selected translations by Burton Watson (*The Tso Chuan* [New York: Columbia University Press, 1989]). For a survey covering Chinese history from the earliest times through the Qin unification, see Michael Loewe and Edward Shaughnessy, eds., *The Cambridge History of Ancient China: From the Origins of Civilization to 221 B.C.* (New York: Cambridge University Press, 1999). For general introductions to the philosophy of this period, see Benjamin I. Schwartz, *The World of Thought in Ancient China* (Cambridge, Mass.: The Belknap Press, 1985) and Angus C. Graham, *Disputers of the Tao* (LaSalle, Ill.: Open Court Press, 1989). For a study that focuses on the issues of violence and warfare in the Eastern Zhou, see Mark Edward Lewis, *Sanctioned Violence in Early China* (Albany: SUNY Press, 1990).

5. That is, he was the head of the department or ministry of crime in the state of Lu. This position (*si kou* 司寇) is sometimes translated as "police commissioner." There are references to Kongzi's having held this position in the *Zuozhuan*, the *Mozi*, and the *Mengzi*. Although Creel regards these accounts as apocryphal, I think Bryan Van Norden is correct in noting that it is hard to ignore the testimony of three independent sources. See Bryan W. Van Norden, "Introduction," in Van Norden, ed., *Confucius and the Analects: New Essays* (New York: Oxford University Press, 2002), 33 n. 51.

6. Ibid., 3.

7. A handful of essays have dealt with early Confucian views of justice. I discuss this work in the next section of this Introduction.

8. An example of the former view is seen in the work of Henry Rosemont Jr., discussed in the following section. Examples of the latter view are seen in works by Rosemont, Hall and Ames, and Peerenboom, all discussed in the following section.

9. Some examples include R. Randle Edwards, Louis Henkin, and Andrew J. Nathan, eds., *Human Rights in Contemporary China* (New York: Columbia University Press, 1986); Leroy S. Rouner, ed., *Human Rights and the World's Religions* (Notre Dame, Ind.: University of Notre Dame Press, 1988); Michael C. Davis, ed., *Human Rights and Chinese Values: Legal, Philosophical, and Political Perspectives* (New York: Oxford University Press, 1995); Peter R. Baehr, ed., *Human Rights: Chinese and Dutch Perspectives* (The Hague:

Martinus Nijhoff, 1996); Wm. Theodore de Bary and Tu Weiming, eds., *Confucianism and Human Rights* (New York: Columbia University Press, 1998); Wm. Theodore de Bary, *Asian Values and Human Rights: A Confucian Communitarian Perspective* (Cambridge, Mass.: Harvard University Press, 1998); Joanne R. Bauer and Daniel A. Bell, eds., *The East Asian Challenge for Human Rights* (New York: Cambridge University Press, 1999); Daniel A. Bell, *East Meets West: Human Rights and Democracy in East Asia* (Princeton, N.J.: Princeton University Press, 2000); Stephen C. Angle and Maria Svensson, eds., *The Chinese Human Rights Reader* (Armonk, N.Y.: East Gate, 2001); Stephen C. Angle, *Human Rights in Chinese Thought: A Cross-Cultural Inquiry* (Cambridge: Cambridge University Press, 2002); and Kwong-loi Shun and David B. Wong, eds., *Confucian Ethics: A Comparative Study of Self, Autonomy, and Community* (New York: Cambridge University Press, 2004).

10. For examples, see W. Theodore de Bary, "Neo-Confucianism and Human Rights," in Rouner, ed. (1988); Du Ganjian and Song Gang, "Relating Human Rights to Chinese Culture: The Four Paths of the Confucian Analects and the Four Principles of a New Theory of Benevolence" in Davis, ed. (1995); Julia Ching, "Human Rights: A Valid Chinese Concept?" in de Bary and Tu, eds. (1998); and Joseph Chan, "A Confucian Perspective on Human Rights for Contemporary China" in Bauer and Bell, eds. (1999).

11. For examples, see Jack Donnelly, "Human Rights and Asian Values: A Defense of 'Western' Universalism," in Bauer and Bell, eds. (1999); and Margaret Ng, "Are Rights Culture-Bound?" in Davis, ed. (1995).

12. For examples, see the essays by Henry Rosemont Jr., R. P. Peerenboom, and Ruiping Fan discussed in this section, as well as Roger T. Ames, "Rites as Rights: The Confucian Alternative," in Rouner, ed. (1988), and David L. Hall and Roger T. Ames, *The Democracy of the Dead* (Chicago: Open Court Press, 1999).

13. See the essays by R. P. Peerenboom, Alan Fox, Xunwu Chen, Yang Xiao, and Ruiping Fan discussed later in this Introduction.

14. Van Norden refers to this view as the *lexical fallacy*. See his *Virtue Ethics and Consequentialism in Early Chinese Philosophy* (New York: Cambridge University Press, 2007), 21–23. I discuss Van Norden's view below.

15. For a detailed study of the history of the idea of human rights in China, see Angle and Svensson, *The Chinese Human Rights Reader*. Angle and Svensson note that that until the mid–nineteenth century, there was no single term in Chinese that corresponded to the English term "rights" or its cognates in other European languages. They argue that "discussions of rights built upon Confucian ideas and concepts while at the same time trying to develop them by drawing on and incorporating foreign ideas" (xx). They note that the term *quanli* 權力 ("rights") has a history of being used in Confu-

cian literature to mean the "power and profit" that can tempt one away from morality. Such a meaning is obviously quite different from what we mean by "rights," an observation that has led some scholars to suggest that *quanli* is simply a bad translation for "rights." But, Angle and Svensson point out, "[t]he problem with calling *quanli* a bad translation, though, is its implication that the only process at work in the origins of Chinese rights discourse is a (failed) attempt to mirror and adopt Western concepts and standards. We believe that Chinese rights discourse shows a complex interaction between people discovering and interpreting foreign ideas that they take to be of universal significance, on the one hand, and people building from a foundation of native terms and concerns, on the other" (xvi). Angle develops and argues for this view in greater detail in his *Human Rights and Chinese Thought: A Cross-Cultural Inquiry* (Cambridge: Cambridge University Press, 2002).

16. The interest in certain kinds of rights and the relationship they have to Chinese philosophical views clearly has to do with the pressing nature of certain topics in contemporary international politics. In contrast with discussions of human rights, there has been virtually no philosophical work on the idea of property rights in ancient China, even though the Chinese had clear and publicly shared views about the ownership of land. However, discussions of intellectual property rights in China have generated a great deal of interest because Western companies want to avoid pirating. William P. Alford's monograph *To Steal a Book Is an Elegant Offense: Intellectual Property Law in Chinese Civilization* (Stanford, Calif.: Stanford University Press, 1995) suggests that traditional sources played such a strong role in the ethical, political, and social aspects of Chinese society that the Chinese could not have developed a notion of intellectual property rights. For a study and critique of Alford's view that offers a more historically and philosophically grounded account of why certain aspects of traditional Chinese thought and society made the development of a conception of intellectual property rights less likely, see Philip J. Ivanhoe, "Intellectual Property and Traditional Chinese Culture," in Joseph Keim Campbell, Michael O'Rourke, and David Shier, eds., *Topics in Contemporary Philosophy, Vol. 3, Law and Social Justice* (Cambridge, Mass.: MIT Press, 2005), 125–42.

17. For a careful study of concept of rights in relation to the thought of the early Confucian thinker Mengzi, see Justin Tiwald, "A Right of Rebellion in the *Mengzi*?" *Dao* 7.3 (2008), 269–82. Tiwald argues that Mengzi's account of how tyrannical rulers can be justifiably deposed falls short of a proper *right* of rebellion.

18. Angle and Svensson, *The Chinese Human Rights Reader*, xv.

19. R. P. Peerenboom, "Confucian Justice: Achieving a Humane Society," *International Philosophical Quarterly* 30:1 (March 1990), 17. Peerenboom

cites Roger T. Ames and David L. Hall, *Thinking Through Confucius* (Albany: SUNY Press, 1987). Much of Peerenboom's argument in this essay also appears in R. P. Peerenboom, *Law and Morality in Ancient China* (Albany: SUNY Press, 1993), 126–37.

20. Alan Fox, "The Aesthetics of Justice," *Legal Studies Forum* 19:1 (1995), 44.

21. Ruiping Fan, "Social Justice: Rawlsian or Confucian?" in Bo Mou, ed., *Comparative Approaches to Chinese Philosophy* (Hampshire, U.K.: Ashgate Publishing, 2003), 145. Like Peerenboom and Fox, Fan notes that *yi* is not an appropriate translation of "justice" (163 n. 2).

22. Yang Xiao, "Trying to Do Justice to the Concept of Justice in Confucian Ethics," *Journal of Chinese Philosophy* 24 (1997), 531.

23. Henry Rosemont Jr., "Which Rights? Whose Democracy?" *The Raven* 39 (1999), 219–20.

24. Henry Rosemont Jr., "Against Relativism," in Gerald James Larson and Eliot Deutsch, eds., *Interpreting Across Boundaries* (Princeton, N.J.: Princeton University Press, 1988), 41 n. 11. For a rebuttal of this type of position in relation to Western history, see Gad Prudhovsky, "Can We Ascribe to Past Thinkers Concepts They Had No Linguistic Means to Express?" *History and Theory* 36.1 (1997), 15–31.

25. Alasdair MacIntyre, *After Virtue, Second Edition* (Notre Dame, Ind.: University of Notre Dame Press, 1984), 69.

26. Peerenboom, "Confucian Justice: Achieving a Humane Society," 17; Rosemont, "Which Rights? Whose Democracy?" 219–20.

27. Italics mine.

28. "Term" in *Compact Oxford English Dictionary of Current English, Third Revised Edition* (Oxford: Oxford University Press, 2008), online edition: http://www.askoxford.com/concise_oed/term?view=uk (visited June 12, 2010).

29. Philip J. Ivanhoe, *Ethics in the Confucian Tradition: The Thought of Mencius and Wang Yang-ming, Second Edition* (Indianapolis: Hackett, 2002), 210–11 n. 2. Edward Slingerland appropriates this term in his essay "Conceptual Metaphor Theory as Methodology for Comparative Religion," *Journal of the American Academy of Religion* 72:1 (2004), 1–31. Slingerland discusses "word fetishism" and points to Rosemont's work as an example of this problem (36 n. 9).

30. Philip J. Ivanhoe, "Heaven as a Source for Ethical Warrant in Early Confucianism," *Dao* 6.2 (2007), 216 n.10.

31. *Mengzi* 3B9 discusses the competing teachings and ways of Mo Di 墨翟 (Mozi 墨子) and Yang Zhu 楊朱. This makes it clear that not only did Kongzi's followers understand themselves as Confucians but they also

understood that there were other distinct schools of thought. In 7B36, we find another good example of the Mohists and Yangists as competing schools with the Confucians, and in this passage the word *ru* 儒 clearly designates the followers of Kongzi as distinct from other groups. Also significant is *Mengzi* 3A4, which describes members of the Tillers and serves as an example of someone's studying a thinker and becoming committed to the life he advocates.

32. Some of the above-mentioned authors would, I think, agree that a number of Chinese characters have a broad semantic range. For example, Rosemont points out with Roger Ames that *li* has the following meanings: "ritual," "rites," "customs," "etiquette," "propriety," "morals," "rules of proper behavior," and "worship," and that "in classical Chinese the character carries *all* of these meanings on every occasion of its use" (Ames and Rosemont, *The Analects of Confucius*, 51).

33. This is the kind of argument Yang Xiao makes in "Doing Justice to the Concept of Justice in Confucian Ethics."

34. Bryan W. Van Norden, *Virtue Ethics and Consequentialism in Early Chinese Philosophy*, 22. Van Norden notes that Rosemont formulates this principle explicitly. He also discusses the lexical fallacy, together with some related issues, in his essay "Virtue Ethics and Confucianism," in Mou, *Comparative Approaches to Chinese Philosophy*, 101–2.

35. Ibid., 23.

36. Although *xiu shen* 修身 means "self-cultivation," it is not used in the *Analects*. Clearly, however, self-cultivation is one of the central concepts in the text. So although "self-cultivation" evidently has a lexical representative in classical Chinese, the early Chinese texts that describe self-cultivation do not rely on this lexical representative to express and describe the concept of self-cultivation. I will discuss this matter in detail in Chapter 3. For now I simply wish to point out that the account of self-cultivation is established by a number of passages about *fan xing* 反省 ("self-reflection"), *xue* 學 ("study"), and so on.

37. Some might object to the use of the English term "self-cultivation" in favor of an alternative term, but a purely terminological objection is different from the denial that there is an understanding of the concept that the term "self-cultivation" designates.

38. In 5.13 Zigong says "one does not get to hear the Master expounding on" the subject of human nature (*xing* 性), but there is agreement in the commentarial tradition that Kongzi *did* have views on human nature. This, though, seems to be the only thing the commentarial tradition reaches a consensus about on this passage. For a broad study of *Analects* 5.13, see Philip J. Ivanhoe, "Whose Confucius? Which Analects?", 119–33. Regarding

the other passages in the *Analects* that provide clarification on this matter, in 17.2 Kongzi says, "By nature (*xing* 性) people are similar; they diverge as the result of practice (*xi* 習)." At the very least, this suggests that Kongzi thought human nature did not determine people fully; their nature was malleable in some sense. Many other passages affirm the view that humans are malleable and can cultivate themselves (even though this process is long and difficult), without using a term for "human nature" (see, for example, 1.15). This, of course, ties Kongzi's view of human nature to his view of self-cultivation, which as we have seen does not have a single consistent lexical representative either.

39. The idea of human nature found in the *Shijing* 詩經 is also a good example. Although many poems in the *Shijing* give a sense of what the authors thought about human nature, the term for "human nature" (*xing*) appears in only one ode in the *Shijing* (Part III, Book II, Ode VIII, verses 2, 3, 4). The character is used three times in this ode, but even there, some commentators take the term in the sense of *ming* (life) and translate it as "span of life" or "years." (See James Legge, trans., *The Chinese Classics, Vol. IV. The She King or The Book of Poetry* [Hong Kong: Hong Kong University Press, 1960], p. 492. For a study that shows there is a complex and distinctive view of human nature in the *Shijing* despite the fact that the term *xing* is not prominent in the text, see Xu Fuguan 徐復觀, *Zhongguo renxing lun shi* 中國人性論史 ["A History of Human Nature in China"], xian qin pian 先秦篇 [Shanghai: Shanghai san lian shudian, 2001].)

40. Xunwu Chen seems to make an argument that multiple terms together specify an appreciation for justice in "Justice as a Constellation of Fairness, Harmony and Righteousness" (*Journal of Chinese Philosophy* 24 [1997], 497–519).

41. The more general point I am making is that ideas and theories can be expressed without terms that specifically represent them. The behavior of pre-linguistic children provides evidence in favor of the related view that one can have a concept or theory without a term. For example, if one places a ball on the floor and then covers it with a blanket, a young child will look under the blanket for the ball. The child does not assume that the ball has disappeared. The child must have had a theory that the ball was under the blanket, even without yet having terms for things. Rosemont argues against this position in his essay "Against Relativism," in Gerald J. Larson and Eliot Deutsch, eds., *Interpreting Across Boundaries* (Princeton, N.J.: Princeton University Press, 1988), 40 n. 11. He writes that "we may attribute prelinguistic awareness to babies . . . awareness of pain, heat, hunger, and so on, without talking of their having concepts; to be in pain is clearly distinguishable from having the concept expressed by the open English sentence '. . . is in pain.' And on

the basis of this distinction it can be maintained that people have both sensations and concepts and that we attribute specific sensations to people on the
basis of either their behavior or their speech, but that we attribute concepts
to them only on the basis of the latter." However, it seems to me that we
do indeed attribute concepts to people on the basis of their behavior, and it
should be noted that in the example I give above, it is not simply a question
of the child's *being* in pain or being hungry. Rather, the child draws certain
conclusions and acts based on what she sees, and that is certainly sufficient
for saying she has a theory about what she will find when she looks under the
blanket—that is, she *expects* to find the ball. For two excellent essays that take
account of the recent work in both philosophy of science and developmental
psychology on this subject, see Eric Schwitzgebel, "Children's Theories and
the Drive to Explain," *Science & Education* 8 (1999), 457–88, and "Theories
in Children and the Rest of Us," *Philosophy of Science, Supplemental Issue*, 63
(1996), s202–s210.

42. Most of the essays discussed here explore "Confucian justice" broadly,
without distinguishing between the views of, for example, Kongzi, Mengzi,
and Xunzi and later figures like Zhu Xi. I discuss these essays because the
Analects is one of the texts they discuss, but I do not discuss work that focuses
exclusively on texts other than the *Analects* (such as the *Mengzi*) because I
think there are important differences between the views presented in them.
To my knowledge, no studies have focused strictly on the understanding of
justice in the *Analects*.

43. There are a few other essays I would like to note but which I will not
discuss for particular reasons: Chung-ying Cheng, "Critical Reflections on
Rawlsian Justice Versus Confucian Justice," *Journal of Chinese Philosophy* 24
(1997): 417–26, provides editorial reflections on the other essays published
on justice in an issue of *JCP*, which are discussed in this section. Betty Yung,
"An Interplay Between Western and Confucian Concepts of Justice: Development of Hong Kong Housing Policy," *Housing, Theory and Society* 24.2
(2007): 111–32, focuses on justice in relation to a particular applied issue.
Finally, Jang Dong-jin, "A Confucian Deliberation on Rawls's Liberal Conception of International Justice" [*Sungkyun Journal of East Asian Studies* 4.1
(2004): 133–55], focuses on international justice in particular, which is one of
the topics addressed in Chapter 5 of this book; I briefly discuss Jang's essay in
that chapter.

44. My aim here is not to provide a summary of each of these essays, nor
is it to offer a critique, but rather to discuss some particular features of them
in order to highlight how my study differs in some significant ways from the
important work that has already been done by these scholars. I would like
to note, though, that I disagree with the claims some of them make about

Rawls and Western liberalism. For example, Peerenboom and Fan both seem to misunderstand the nature of the original position and Rawls's understanding of autonomy (see, for example, Peerenboom, "Confucian Justice," 18–19, 24, 30, and Fan, "Social Justice," 149–50). These aspects of Rawls's thought, as well as common misunderstandings of them, will be discussed in Chapter 2.

45. Peerenboom writes that Western understandings of justice are concerned with "securing a minimum level of basic rights for alienated individuals unable or unwilling to participate cooperatively in collective living" and that for Kongzi, this view amounts to failure because it assumes "that there is no way to overcome the self-interested passions and desires of the animal world and to move beyond the bestial level of the Hobbesian order" (23). This is an example of one place where I think there is considerable room for improvement and refinement in working to understand the differences between, and the diversity among, Western and Confucian views. As a first step, we need to consider the important differences and disagreements between, for example, Hobbes and Rawls on the fundamental character of human nature and the potential for moral cultivation. (It is likewise important to take account of the disagreement between Mengzi and Xunzi on these issues.) As we will see in Chapter 2, compared with other liberal theories of justice, Rawls takes one of the more optimistic and socially oriented views of human beings when he claims that humans have a fundamental capacity for cooperation and a "sense of justice" that leads them to make sacrifices for the least advantaged members of society.

46. Peerenboom, "Confucian Justice, 31.

47. Fan, "Social Justice," 145, 149.

48. Ibid., 145.

49. Ibid., 148.

50. Chen, "Justice as a Constellation of Fairness, Harmony and Righteousness," 498.

51. Fox, "The Aesthetics of Justice: Harmony and Order in Chinese Thought," 51.

52. In *Human Rights and Chinese Thought: A Cross-Cultural Inquiry*, Stephen C. Angle points out that a similar problem emerges with claims that a concern for rights can be found in classical Confucianism. He says, "Rights have a distinctive conceptual structure that sets them apart from other moral commitments, like duties or ideals. The humanistic ideals found in the populist chapters of the *Analects* certainly resonate with some of the ideals expressed in the more general assertions of the UDHR [Universal Declaration of Human Rights], but this is very different from finding 'rights' in the *Analects*" (21). I take the same general position with respect to justice, namely

that it has a distinct conceptual structure that sets it apart from other moral commitments and social ideals.

53. Xiao, "Justice in Confucian Ethics," 528–29.

54. Ibid., 540.

55. Ibid., 531.

56. John Rawls, *Justice as Fairness: A Restatement*, ed. Erin Kelly (Cambridge, Mass.: Harvard University Press, 2001), xvi. Hereafter cited as *JF* with page number.

57. For a strong criticism of the ambiguity of *Theory* on this fundamental matter, see Charles Larmore, *Patterns of Moral Complexity* (Cambridge: Cambridge University Press, 1987), 118–30. I will devote the following discussion to this aspect of the changes in Rawls's view because it is the source of most discussions of the degree of continuity in Rawls's early and later work. For a further discussion of the other shifts Rawls mentions, see *JF*, xvi–xvii.

58. John Rawls, *Political Liberalism* (New York: Columbia University Press, 1993, 1996), 177n. Hereafter cited as *PL* with page number.

59. The one exception I am aware of is Brian Barry, who argues that *Theory* does not ground justice as fairness on a comprehensive doctrine. See Barry, "John Rawls and the Search for Stability," *Ethics* 105:4 (1995), 874–915.

60. For a concise and helpful discussion of some of these issues, see Stephen Mulhall and Adam Swift, "Rawls and Communitarianism," in Samuel Freeman, ed., *The Cambridge Companion to Rawls* (Cambridge: Cambridge University Press, 2003), 460–87.

61. Michael Loewe, ed., *Early Chinese Texts: A Bibliographical Guide* (Berkeley, Calif.: Institute of East Asian Studies, 1993), 315.

62. I will return to the subject of the dates of composition of the *Analects* later in this section. However, readers may refer to Loewe, ed., *Early Chinese Texts*, 313–23 for an overview of discussions of authorship, date of composition, textual history, and edition.

63. D. C. Lau, trans., *Confucius: The Analects* (Harmondsworth, U.K.: Penguin Books, 1979).

64. Arthur Waley, trans., *The Analects of Confucius* (New York: Vintage Books, 1989).

65. Bryan W. Van Norden, "Introduction," in *Confucius and the Analects: New Essays*, 14–15.

66. Steven Van Zoeren, *Poetry and Personality* (Stanford, Calif.: Stanford University Press, 1991).

67. E. Bruce Brooks and A. Taeko Brooks, *The Original Analects* (New York: Columbia University Press, 1998).

68. There are a number of difficulties with the work of Brooks and Brooks. For example, in his review of *The Original Analects*, Edward Slingerland points out the highly speculative nature of the claim that there is a "rate of accretion" that applies to the strata of the *Analects*, and that on this theory, the text was composed at a fairly constant rate, in distinct bands that are each one chapter thick. He also discusses the philosophical weaknesses of the view of Brooks and Brooks, arguing that their

> lack of philosophical orientation reveals itself . . . in their resolutely political rendering of the text. Practicing a rather extreme hermeneutics of suspicion, they systematically discount the possibility that philosophical developments of early themes by later compilers might actually be genuine attempts to elucidate the Master's teachings and make them relevant to a new age. Rather, doctrinal innovations are generally seen in terms of political stratagems designed to enhance the prestige of one line of disciples over another. (140)

See Slingerland's review, the response from Brooks and Brooks, and Slingerland's reply, in *Philosophy East and West* 40:1 (2000), 137–47.

69. Van Zoeren, *Poetry and Personality*, 28.

70. Ames and Rosemont, trans., *The Analects of Confucius*, 9–10.

71. In his discussion of how a composite text can present a consistent vision, Ivanhoe uses the helpful analogy of a cobbler: "Just as a cobbler can make use of various scraps of leather to fashion a very fine pair of shoes, an editor can draw upon and augment material from a variety of different sources and shape these into a coherent and elegant composition. Indeed, this process can pass through numerous iterations and through the hands of a series of different editors, generating a number of related yet equally coherent texts." See Philip J. Ivanhoe, trans., *The Daodejing of Laozi* (Indianapolis: Hackett, 2002), xv.

1. METHODS IN COMPARATIVE WORK

1. Although most of my specific examples and illustrations in this chapter are drawn from comparative work related to the Chinese tradition (because that is my area of expertise), my remarks about the reasons for doing comparative work and the challenges comparativists often face are applicable to those studying and working on comparisons with other traditions as well.

2. Unlike work in comparative philosophy, comparative work in religious studies and theology is not best characterized as comparative studies of "non-Western" and "Western" religions but by comparisons across different religious traditions. Sometimes these comparisons are between "Western"

and "non-Western" religious traditions, but many studies in comparative
religion or comparative religious ethics focus on two Western religions, such
as Christianity and Judaism. It is important to note, though, that scholars
of religion tend not to use the categories of "Western" and "non-Western."
These categories are more appropriate in comparative philosophy partly
because comparative studies normally cross these boundaries and, as we will
see below, because non-Western philosophies are united by their systematic
exclusion from the mainstream discipline of philosophy. "Western philosophy" is an appropriate category because there are deep and important
historical connections between American, European, Greek, and Roman
philosophy, and as a result when philosophers are trained in the history of
Western philosophy (typically referred to as "the history of philosophy"),
they do not normally study these traditions separately, nor do they study
only one of them. Although philosophers specialize in particular fields,
all philosophers are expected to have training in the "canon" of Western
philosophy—that is, in a set of texts and thinkers widely recognized as important. In contrast, scholars of religion normally are not trained in a single
received "canon" that constitutes the history of religion. Although there is
an area of overlap in the training of most scholars of religion (in figures such
as Durkheim who have had significant influence in theory and method in
the study of religion), this area is *much* smaller than it is in the discipline of
philosophy.

3. The fact that most philosophy departments have failed to make the
study of non-Western traditions a part of how students are educated and
evaluated (at both the undergraduate and graduate levels) shows that many
philosophers continue to be guided by the view that non-Western philosophies are not worth serious study. This view is also reflected in the absence of
specialists in non-Western traditions in most philosophy departments. That
is not, of course, to deny that there are philosophers who would like to see
non-Western philosophy included in their offerings. Indeed, those who have
worked to convince colleagues that they ought to devote even one faculty line
to hiring a specialist in a non-Western philosophical tradition are aware of
the resistance one typically meets.

4. The academy's debt to Aristotle is especially apparent here. There are
some illuminating similarities and differences between the view found in
Aristotle and early Confucian thinkers such as Mengzi, who also saw reflection as having a critical (though different) role in the good life. For a helpful
discussion of some important differences between these accounts of human
flourishing, see Bryan W. Van Norden, *Virtue Ethics and Consequentialism in
Early Chinese Philosophy* (New York: Cambridge University Press, 2007), esp.
355–58.

5. Karen L. Carr and Philip J. Ivanhoe, *The Sense of Antirationalism: The Religious Thought of Zhuangzi and Kierkegaard, Revised Second Edition* (Charleston, S.C.: CreateSpace, 2010), xiii.

6. Ibid., xiii. Carr and Ivanhoe note the work of Melford Spiro, who argues that the true aim of anthropological study is to make the familiar strange and the strange familiar. See his *Anthropological Other or Burmese Brother?* (New Brunswick, N.J.: Transaction Publishers, 1992).

7. Ibid., xiii–xiv.

8. Ibid., xiv.

9. Ibid. Carr and Ivanhoe emphasize that in order to realize the advantages they discuss, comparative studies must bring together the right sorts of subjects. I discuss their view on this matter in the second section of this chapter.

10. It is, though, worth noting the fact that most of these things have *not* been previously appreciated.

11. Few studies of *any* sort could demonstrate this. Indeed, one could object to almost any study of a single thinker or tradition on the same grounds (namely that one *could* come to appreciate the things this study demonstrates by using another method or approach), and the objection would not be seen as evidence that a study is not valuable.

12. Lee H. Yearley, *Mencius and Aquinas: Theories of Virtue and Conceptions of Courage* (Albany: SUNY Press, 1990), 2.

13. Martha Nussbaum, "Comparing Virtues," *Journal of Religious Ethics* 21.2 (1993), 347.

14. Ibid.

15. Ibid., 349, 347. Nussbaum offers a detailed study of these and other vices that commonly plague comparative and cross-cultural study in her *Cultivating Humanity: A Classical Defense of Reform in Liberal Education* (Cambridge, Mass.: Harvard University Press, 1997), 118–39.

16. Ibid., 347; Yearley, *Mencius and Aquinas*, 195. I discuss Yearley's method of working with "similarities in differences and differences in similarities" in the next section of this chapter.

17. Yearley, *Mencius and Aquinas*, 203.

18. Nussbaum, "Comparing Virtues," 349.

19. Ibid., 348. Nussbaum mentions "topics ranging from global ecology to food provision and agriculture to gender and ethnic and racial equality" as examples. While most of us will not participate as representatives in global dialogues, most of us will participate in various kinds of conversations about issues facing our own communities and societies.

20. Ibid., 349. At least some forms of this view seem to deny the *humanity* of the "other" in an important sense. In treating the other as fully alien, one

often denies the capacity of other people to exercise reason, to reflect on and modify their views, to engage in meaningful dialogue, and so on. For further discussion of this kind of view, see Nussbaum's discussion of normative skepticism in *Cultivating Humanity*, 136–38.

21. Ibid, 350. Nussbaum mentions, for example, that these are features of good development practice. See Martha Nussbaum and Amartya Sen, eds., *The Quality of Life* (Oxford: Oxford University Press, 1993).

22. The apparent unwillingness of some who hold these views to seriously consider and offer clear responses to comparativists' arguments against their claims helps to confirm Nussbaum's view that these tendencies represent intellectual vices.

23. Some philosophers make an exception to this rule when it comes to studying the history of Western philosophy. On this view, the history of non-Western philosophy is apparently not seen as important because it is unrelated to the history of the philosophers who shaped the discipline of philosophy in the Western academy. However, a significant number of philosophers now reject the view that studying the history of philosophy is important in itself. This view is increasingly common not only in very analytical philosophy departments where a narrow set of philosophical issues is seen as worth studying but also in very continental departments where the traditional canon of works in the history of philosophy is rejected in favor of historically marginalized figures and movements. In both kinds of departments, study of the history of Western philosophy (at least as it is understood by most philosophers) is not treated as important.

24. Priest attributes the former claim to Marx. Priest, "Where Is Philosophy at the Start of the 21st Century?" *The Proceedings of the Aristotelian Society* CIII (2002), 98.

25. Priest writes that the United States is currently both the world's dominant economy and the center of gravity of the Western philosophical world. He bases this on the claim that although the dominant philosophical views of the past century came from elsewhere (he cites the examples of logical positivism and deconstructionism), "the US has appropriated them. One reason for this is that it can afford to buy good philosophers from elsewhere, either temporarily or permanently. And of course, good philosophers will want to go where other good philosophers are" (98–99).

26. See, for example, Henry Rosemont Jr., "Which Rights? Whose Democracy?" *The Raven* 39 (1999), 230.

27. Priest, "Where Is Philosophy at the Start of the 21st Century?" 99.

28. Indeed, Greece never achieved the kind of lasting and widespread economic and political dominance enjoyed by civilizations such as those of

Egypt, Babylon, Persia, and Rome. Greek philosophy, then, seems to represent a counter-example to the sort of view we are examining here.

29. A case could be made that if something does not play a decisive role in motivating one to study a philosophical tradition, then it is not a "reason" for studying it at all. However, in this discussion I include supporting reasons in order to accommodate those cases where one has more than one important reason for doing something, meaning that one has multiple sources of motivation. In most cases, though, I still think it is usually possible to identify a primary reason.

30. Although a number of scholars have linked Confucianism with capitalism in East Asia, their arguments do not always draw strictly on those dimensions of the Confucian tradition that deal with economic or political prosperity. For example, in support of their argument against the claim that Confucianism is concerned with upholding a particular kind of feudal society, Robert Bellah and Tu Weiming both argue that Confucianism is concerned with the good life for human beings generally. This viewpoint responds to Max Weber's claim that religion was a possible factor in the emergence of capitalism in the Protestant West and its failure to develop in Confucian China. On Weber's view, which was further developed by Joseph Levenson, Confucianism was incompatible with modernization defined in terms of industrial capitalism. Against this claim, Bellah and Tu have argued that Confucianism offers the kind of ideals that Weber argues are a necessary constituent of capitalism. They also argue that a deeper understanding of Confucianism sees hierarchical relationships as defining the set of obligations citizens owe to one another in a democratic society. These views, then, take Confucianism as a kind of ideology or worldview and argue that it has a direct impact on the economic success or failure of those countries in which it is a primary cultural influence. See Max Weber, *The Religion of China: Confucianism and Taoism*, trans., ed. Hans H. Gerth (Glencoe, Ill.: Free Press, 1951 [originally published in German, 1922]); Robert Bellah, *Tokugawa Religion: The Values of Pre-industrial Japan* (Glencoe, Ill.: Free Press, 1985 [originally published in 1957]); Joseph R. Levenson, *Confucian China and Its Modern Fate: A Trilogy* (Berkeley: University of California Press, 1968); Tu Weiming, "The 'Third Epoch' of Confucian Humanism," in Tu Weiming, ed., *Way, Learning, and Politics: Essays on the Confucian Intellectual* (New York: HarperCollins, 1993), 141–60; Tu Weiming, ed., *Confucian Traditions in East Asian Modernity: Moral Education and Economic Culture in Japan and the Four Mini-Dragons* (Cambridge, Mass.: Harvard University Press, 1996).

31. There will be considerable variety on this matter, and that is part of my point. For example, studying Sartre and Beauvoir—partly because of

their more recent dates and their engagement with social issues—might be more helpful in working to understand French culture than Hegel and Kant would be in relation to German culture.

32. One could make a case that it is more specifically a form of eurocentrism, because American pragmatism has been neglected as well. There are, though, some important differences between the place of pragmatism and non-Western philosophies. First, the relatively small amount of attention given to American pragmatism partly stems from the fact that there are fewer major figures in the pragmatic tradition compared with those in Western analytical and continental philosophy. Pragmatism also represents a single school of thought (even though there is considerable diversity within it), in contrast with the numerous and extremely diverse traditions and schools of thought in non-Western philosophies. Additionally, figures like Peirce, James, and Dewey are, at least in many departments, taught as a part of the history of (Western) philosophy, even if they are not given as much attention as other figures and movements.

33. As I indicated earlier, in the academy philosophy is now the exception rather than the rule in this case. For example, history departments typically have specialists in Japanese and Chinese history, and religious studies departments usually have specialists in such areas as Chinese religions, Buddhism, and Islam. It seems, then, that although the academy acknowledges that non-Western traditions have histories and religions, it does not yet fully acknowledge that non-Western traditions have philosophies.

34. It is important to note that this view accommodates a wide range of interpretations of and positions on Western and non-Western philosophies alike. For example, some comparative philosophers have argued that the Western tradition is essentially bankrupt by virtue of its failure to provide adequate answers to the most important questions of philosophy, and that this is why philosophers should study non-Western traditions. (See, for example, the work of Roger T. Ames, David L. Hall, and Henry Rosemont Jr.) Other comparative philosophers have argued that although there are compelling views in the Western tradition, significantly different and insightful alternatives in non-Western traditions can help us to resolve certain difficulties or to deepen and extend our views on certain matters. (See, for example, the work of Philip J. Ivanhoe, Joel Kupperman, and Bryan W. Van Norden.) Despite the differences between these views, in both cases the reason why non-Western philosophy is seen as worth studying is that there are true and valuable ideas in non-Western traditions.

35. J. S. Mill, "On Liberty," in *The Basic Writings of John Stuart Mill* (New York: The Modern Library of Random House, Inc., 2002), 22.

36. Ibid., 54.

37. Of course, as Mill argues, views need not be true in order to be valuable. I would not want to rule out the possibility of having good reasons to study views that are false. For example, encountering false views can sometimes help us to develop more plausible and compelling alternatives. However, I think philosophers will tend to have stronger reasons for studying views that are true or partially true.

38. For a discussion of these aspects of the early Confucian tradition and their contemporary relevance, see Chapter 5.

39. Here I am thinking of such areas as ethics, political philosophy, and the philosophy of religion.

40. I do not mean to imply that citizens are not affected by economic or political matters, only that economic and political concerns generally are not at the top of the list of people's priorities. For instance, although the high cost of gasoline affects most citizens financially, this matter is a minor annoyance compared with concerns about the well-being of one's children. I think that in most cases this is true even for those citizens who are most dramatically and seriously affected by such things.

41. I will confine my discussion of particular comparative studies in this section to book-length comparative studies of Western and Chinese philosophy, because that is the field I know best and my aim is simply to offer clear examples of these different types of issues in comparative work. Not only do I lack the training that would be necessary to carefully evaluate comparative works in other areas, but it would be impossible to discuss such a vast body of work in a single chapter. As it is, I have selected a small number examples from the large body of work comparing Western and Chinese philosophy because I think these particular works offer especially clear examples of different approaches to interpretive, thematic, and procedural issues (and, in some cases, questions about those particular issues have been raised by critics). I fully expect and encourage readers to find illuminating examples of these different kinds of issues in other works, as well. My goal is not to offer a review of the many interesting and stimulating approaches to these issues in comparative studies (for such a task would require a book-length study of its own) but rather to offer concrete illustrations that help to make clear how interpretive, thematic, and procedural issues represent distinctive kinds of issues, even though they are clearly related.

42. That is not to deny the possibility of productive misreadings. Sometimes, misreadings of texts provoke interesting and novel views, and so long as one does not attribute these views to thinkers who did not hold them, then misreadings can be philosophically productive. But one would then be engaged in a different type of project and would no longer be offering an interpretation of a particular figure or text.

43. The problem of adequate space is especially pronounced with journal articles. This is a reason to consider the view that book-length studies might be the best venue for comparative work. However, even in the case of book-length comparative studies, comparativists face the challenge of dividing the space they have between these various tasks.

44. A number of senior scholars in the field of Chinese and comparative philosophy have employed and defended a virtue ethical interpretation of Chinese ethics, including Philip J. Ivanhoe, Joel Kupperman, David Wong, and Lee Yearley. See Lee H. Yearley, *Mencius and Aquinas: Theories of Virtue and Conceptions of Courage* (Albany: SUNY Press, 1990); David B. Wong, "On Flourishing and Finding One's Identity in Community" in Peter A. French, Theodore E. Uehling Jr., and Howard K. Wettstein, eds., *Midwest Studies in Philosophy Volume XIII Ethical Theory: Character and Virtue* (South Bend, Ind.: University of Notre Dame Press, 1998), 324–41; Joel J. Kupperman, *Learning from Asian Philosophy* (New York: Oxford University Press, 1999); Philip J. Ivanhoe, *Confucian Moral Self Cultivation, Second Edition* (Indianapolis: Hackett, 2000) and *Ethics in the Confucian Tradition: The Thought of Mengzi and Wang Yangming, Revised Second Edition* (Indianapolis: Hackett, 2002). For critiques of virtue ethical interpretations of Confucian ethics, see Yuli Liu, *The Unity of Rule and Virtue: A Critique of a Supposed Parallel Between Confucian Ethics and Virtue Ethics* (Singapore: Eastern Universities Press, 2004), and Heiner Roetz, *Confucian Ethics of the Axial Age: A Reconstruction Under the Aspect of the Breakthrough Toward Postconventional Thinking* (Albany: SUNY Press, 1993). For an overview of critiques of virtue ethics generally, as well as responses to them, see Rebecca L. Walker and Philip J. Ivanhoe, eds., *Working Virtue: Virtue Ethics and Contemporary Moral Problems* (New York: Oxford University Press, 2007), 5–8.

45. Bryan W. Van Norden, *Virtue Ethics and Consequentialism in Early Chinese Philosophy*. See also Van Norden's earlier essay on this topic, "Virtue Ethics and Confucianism" in Bo Mou, ed., *Comparative Approaches to Chinese Philosophy* (London: Ashgate Publishing, 2003), 99–121. For other recent comparative studies that make use of or respond constructively to a virtue ethical interpretation of Confucianism, see May Sim, *Remastering Morals with Aristotle and Confucius* (New York: Cambridge University Press, 2007); Jiyuan Yu, *The Ethics of Confucius and Aristotle: Mirrors of Virtue* (Routledge, 2009); and Stephen C. Angle, *Sagehood: The Contemporary Significance of Neo-Confucian Philosophy* (New York: Oxford University Press, 2009).

46. Van Norden, *Virtue Ethics and Consequentialism*, 21. Drawing on Martha Nussbaum's account of how the distinction between thick and thin accounts can be a tool in cross-cultural ethical discussions, Van Norden ar-

gues for a thin characterization of virtue ethics here. See Martha Nussbaum, "Non-Relative Virtues: An Aristotelian Approach," in Peter French, Theodore E. Uehling Jr., and Howard K. Wettstein, eds., *Ethical Theory: Character and Virtue*, Vol. 13 of *Midwest Studies in Philosophy* (Notre Dame, Ind.: University of Notre Dame Press, 1988), 32–53.

47. Van Norden, "Virtue Ethics and Confucianism," 99. See Van Norden's discussion of this issue in *Virtue Ethics and Consequentialism in Early Chinese Philosophy*, where he offers several examples of what he means (see especially Ch. 5). For discussion of the challenges involved in reading early Confucianism as a form of virtue ethics, see Michael Slote, "Comments on Bryan van Norden's *Virtue Ethics and Consequentialism in Early Chinese Philosophy*," in *Dao: A Journal of Comparative Philosophy* 8.3 (2009), 289–95, and Stephen C. Angle, "Defining 'Virtue Ethics' and Exploring Virtues in a Comparative Context," 298–304. See also Van Norden's "Response to Angle and Slote," 305–9.

48. I will discuss this view as it is seen in the work of David Hall and Roger Ames because they are the most well-known proponents of it today and because their work continues to have considerable influence. For other works that follow this basic line of interpretation, see, for example, Sor-hoon Tan, *Confucian Democracy: A Deweyan Reconstruction* (Albany: SUNY Press, 2004) and Haiming Wen, *Confucian Pragmatism as the Art of Contextualizing Personal Experience and World* (Lanham, Md.: Lexington Books, 2009). For a study of different views that that adopt this kind of interpretation, including some earlier views, see Robert W. Smid, *Methodologies of Comparative Philosophy: The Pragmatist and Process Traditions* (Albany: SUNY Press, 2010).

49. For a helpful discussion of the views of Hall and Ames in relation to other views of the relationship between Chinese and Western thought, as well as a critique of the view of "correlative thinking" that in part defines their approach, see Michael J. Puett, *To Become a God: Cosmology, Sacrifice, and Self-Divinization in Early China* (Cambridge, Mass.: Harvard University Press, 2002), esp. 5–26. For a discussion of Hall and Ames's view in relation to other views in the field of Chinese and comparative philosophy, see also Bryan W. Van Norden, "What Should Western Philosophy Learn from Chinese Philosophy?" in Philip J. Ivanhoe, ed., *Chinese Language, Thought, and Culture*, (Chicago: Open Court Press, 1996), 233–35.

50. David L. Hall and Roger T. Ames, *The Democracy of the Dead: Dewey, Confucius, and the Hope for Democracy in China* (Chicago: Open Court Press, 1999), 95.

51. Roger T. Ames and David L. Hall, *Focusing the Familiar: A Translation and Philosophical Interpretation of the Zhongyong* (Honolulu: University of Hawai'i Press, 2001), 7, 14. See also 16–17, 6 n. 2. Ames and Hall also argue

that process philosophy (particularly Whitehead) is helpful for understanding early Daoism. See their *Daodejing "Making This Life Significant": A Philosophical Translation* (New York: Ballantine Books, 2003), 29–31.

52. I will refer to the "pragmatic-process" interpretation not because Hall and Ames fail to distinguish between them but because my sense is that Hall and Ames see them as compatible and mutually enhancing views, because each resonates with important features of Confucian thought.

53. Van Norden, *Virtue Ethics and Consequentialism*, 16; Van Norden cites Hall and Ames, *Anticipating China*, 153–54, 171–75.

54. Angle, *Sagehood*, 59.

55. One reason why it is important to distinguish between and account for the relationships between these different areas is that doing so enables one to more effectively recognize and respond to different kinds of objections. I examine some examples of this below.

56. For a study of this concept in early Confucianism, see Philip J. Ivanhoe, "Heaven as a Source for Ethical Warrant in Early Confucianism," *Dao* 6 (2007), 211–20.

57. The distinction between thick and thin accounts has its origins in the work of Gilbert Ryle (and then was picked up by Clifford Geertz and, later, by Bernard Williams). As I noted earlier, Martha Nussbaum applied this distinction to cross-cultural ethical discussions, using it to show that we can describe something in at least two ways: "Thin" descriptions have little theoretical content and thus are often widely shared, even between members of different traditions, whereas "thick" descriptions are detailed accounts that are framed in terms of more distinctive concepts and commitments, which are often unique to particular traditions. Van Norden offers the very helpful example of the "thin" description of the sun ("the large bright thing in the sky during the day that illuminates the Earth when it is not too cloudy") and various "thick" descriptions of the sun (such as that of Hesiod, which is that the sun is a god, and that of modern science, which is that the sun is a mass of fusing hydrogen and helium). See Van Norden, *Virtue Ethics and Consequentialism*, 17; and Nussbaum "Non-Relative Virtues," 32–53. For the earlier versions of this distinction, see Gilbert Ryle, "Thinking and Reflection" and "The Thinking of Thoughts," in his *Collected Papers, Vol. 2* (London: Hutchinson and Company, 1971), 465–79 and 480–96; Clifford Geertz, *The Interpretation of Cultures* (New York: Basic Books, 1973), 3–30; and Bernard Williams, *Ethics and the Limits of Philosophy* (Cambridge, Mass.: Harvard University Press, 1985).

58. For an illuminating discussion of the virtue of courage in Aristotle and Mengzi, see Philip J. Ivanhoe, "Mengzi's Conception of Courage," *Dao* 5.2 (2006), 221–34.

59. Carr and Ivanhoe, *The Sense of Antirationalism*, xiv.

60. Ibid.

61. Ibid., xv.

62. Yearley's *Mencius and Aquinas* is another example of this type of approach.

63. Carr and Ivanhoe, *The Sense of Antirationalism*, xv.

64. Robin W. Lovin, "Cue the Chorus," *Journal of the American Academy of Religion* 78.1 (2010), 263. See Aaron Stalnaker, *Overcoming Our Evil: Human Nature and Spiritual Exercises in Xunzi and Augustine* (Washington: Georgetown University Press, 2006).

65. David Decosimo, "The Ubiquity of Resemblance," *Journal of the American Academy of Religion* 78.1 (2010), 242–44, 249 n. 37.

66. Decosimo questions why Stalnaker did not choose to focus on Plato, Aristotle, the Stoics, or Ignatius of Loyola instead of Augustine. Obviously, if one were to take Decosimo's suggestion seriously, there would be many more thinkers to consider, from a wide range of traditions.

67. Carr and Ivanhoe discuss their expertise in different traditions because it is one of the reasons why they engage in collaborative work. Their approach serves as a potential model for other comparative studies. See *The Sense of Antirationalism*, xvi.

68. That is, their accounts of human nature and self-cultivation resemble one another in certain ways. Later in this chapter, I discuss the reasons for thinking that Augustine and Xunzi share a thin concept of human nature but offer different theories of human nature.

69. Stalnaker mentions these discussions (in the work of H. H. Dubs, A. C. Graham, and Philip J. Ivanhoe) and writes that he aims to deal with the full complexities of this comparison by giving sustained attention to both Xunzi and Augustine (*Overcoming Our Evil*, 56). However, he does not mention these studies in relation to his reasons for choosing Xunzi and Augustine in Ch. 1 (19–21).

70. Decosimo, "The Ubiquity of Resemblance," 242. Decosimo again mentions the "focus on spiritual exercises" in this work on p. 243.

71. Decosimo writes:

. . . even if we interpret "spiritual exercises" in the maximally broad way that Stalnaker occasionally does—to mean something like "practices aimed at self-transformation"—given Augustine's patience with mediocrity, suspicion of habit, disinclination to associate grace with moral integrity, anti-elitism, emphasis on and surrender to the self-disintegrating power of confessed sin, and focus on divine agency alone as transformative and capable of re-forming the self, we can wonder whether Augustine

actually offers much of a program for *self*-improvement—or, for that matter, much of a *self* to be improved. Supposing he does, we can still wonder
whether such a program is central to his thought—certainly, it is not what
he is famous for. (244–45)

72. Decosimo, "The Ubiquity of Resemblance," 244–47. He also raises
the objection that Hadot's view is flawed, historically. I do not think this
criticism has much bite, for even if Hadot is incorrect to trace the origins
of spiritual exercises to ancient philosophy, and even if Augustine did not
reconceptualize ancient spiritual exercises, as the evidence cited suggests, this
does not undermine the claim that spiritual exercises (or the practices that
Stalnaker calls spiritual exercises) were important for Augustine. This criticism may, however, undermine some of Stalnaker's historical claims.

73. Ibid., 247.

74. Ibid.

75. Stalnaker, *Overcoming Our Evil*, 159–60. Hereafter page numbers are
cited parenthetically.

76. Stalnaker refers readers in a footnote to discussions of other models
of self-cultivation in Ivanhoe, *Confucian Moral Self Cultivation* (53 n. 23).
Ivanhoe offers the most complete and detailed study of the many diverse
models of self-cultivation in the Confucian tradition. For a collection of essays on self-cultivation in different thinkers and traditions, see Brad K. Wilburn, ed., *Moral Cultivation: Essays on the Development of Character and Virtue*
(Lanham, Md.: Lexington Books, 2007). As these works show, self-cultivation
is perhaps one of the most promising areas to be explored in contemporary
ethics, and Chinese thought has a number of distinctive contributions to
make in this area.

77. Yearley, *Mencius and Aquinas*, 1–6. Carr and Ivanhoe as well as Stalnaker embrace aspects of this approach.

78. Monastic communities conceive of themselves as another kind of
family as evidenced by their adoption of familial terms such as "father,"
"mother," "brother," and "sister" to describe members of the institution.

79. Yearley, *Mencius and Aquinas*, 195.

80. Angle, *Sagehood*, 6.

81. Ibid.

82. Ibid., 7.

83. Ibid.

84. At times, it sounds as though Stalnaker is claiming that human nature
is a multifaceted concept, but at other times he clearly claims that human
nature is not one concept but a cluster of several different concepts. I discuss
this further below.

85. Readers will recognize the resemblance with thick and thin descriptions here. I adopt the language of concepts and theories from John Rawls, who invokes this distinction to describe the difference between the basic *concept* of justice and a *theory* (or *conception*) of justice. Rawls argues that it is possible to express an understanding of the basic concept of justice without having or expressing a fully developed theory of justice. According to Rawls, the idea that a society should, through its institutions, have standards for assigning privileges, advantages, and obligations to different members of society expresses a basic understanding of the concept of justice. Theories or conceptions of justice contain principles that explicitly address these issues (*TJ*, 5).

86. For a careful defense of this view that includes a discussion of other interpretations, see Philip J. Ivanhoe, *Confucian Moral Self Cultivation*, 29–42. See also Bryan W. Van Norden, "Mengzi and Xunzi: Two Views of Human Agency," in T. C. Kline III and Philip J. Ivanhoe, eds., *Virtue, Nature, and Moral Agency in the Xunzi* (Indianapolis: Hackett, 2000), 103–34.

87. Stalnaker, "Review of Bryan W. Van Norden, *Virtue Ethics and Consequentialism in Early Chinese Philosophy*," *Journal of Religion* 89 (2009), 281.

88. A second worry Stalnaker has about these kinds of cases is that concepts and theories "inextricably interpenetrate," which makes it difficult to distinguish between them in any given thinker's view (personal correspondence with the author, January 19, 2011). By this I think Stalnaker means that a specific concept and a specific theory always stand in relation to each other, which strikes me as true, for theories are always *about* something. However, even if one maintains that theories and concepts always inextricably interpenetrate, that does not mean it is impossible to distinguish between them or that it is unhelpful to do so, nor does it mean that a thin concept can be interwoven with only one theory. To the contrary, my argument is that thin concepts are often interwoven with multiple theories. On my view, this is the case with Mengzi's and Xunzi's accounts of human nature, as it is the case with Van Norden's example of different accounts of the sun.

89. When Stalnaker says that "bridge concepts multiply under comparative scrutiny to cover a cluster of ideas," I take him to mean that (for example) the more one studies Augustine's and Xunzi's concepts of *natura* and *xing* and compares them, the more one realizes how complex human nature is, and how many different concepts are actually a part of it. If this is correct, then bridge concepts *seem* to multiply as the comparativist realizes that they are not single concepts.

90. Stalnaker notes that when he refers to bridge concepts covering "a cluster of related ideas," he is focusing on "an apparently single idea like

'human nature' that when tracked into multiple accounts in different languages can be analyzed into various constituent ideas of no necessary mutual
relationship" (53 n.13).

91. Some of Wittgenstein's clearest remarks on family resemblance are
found in his *Philosophical Investigations*, trans. G.E.M. Ancombe (Upper
Saddle River, N.J.: Prentice Hall, 1973), paragraphs 65–67, where he sets up
his account of language games through a discussion of the defining features of
language, games, and numbers. He critiques the view that these phenomena
have just "one thing in common," instead emphasizing that we find several
different similarities between them—"sometimes overall similarities, sometimes similarities of detail" (par. 66). He illustrates this idea with the analogy
of woven thread, noting that "the strength of the thread does not reside in
the fact that some one fibre runs through its whole length, but in the overlapping of many fibres" (par. 67).

92. An example is seen in Stalnaker's use of the category "spiritual
exercises" and Decosimo's objections to this category, including not only
the question of whether the category is appropriate for Augustine but also
the relationship between Stalnaker's understanding of spiritual exercises and
Hadot's understanding of spiritual exercises, as well as the reason why Augustine is selected over Ignatius of Loyola, who also employed this category. My
point here is not to judge whether the gains outweigh the losses in Stalnaker's
study but rather only to point out a clear example of the additional set of
objections that are typically raised in these cases.

93. A variety of issues make some comparative studies more difficult to
conduct than others, such as the additional training required to work on
certain texts or figures, whether the central topic under study is picked out by
multiple terms or a single term, whether the study of a thinker's view requires
the study of multiple texts or one text, whether the relevant texts have been
translated before, and so on.

94. Van Norden, *Virtue Ethics and Consequentialism*, 2–3.

95. Ibid., 3–6.

2. THE SENSE OF JUSTICE IN RAWLS

1. "Commonweal Interview with John Rawls," *CP*, 622.

2. See Samuel Richard Freeman, *Rawls* (New York: Routledge, 2007);
Thomas Pogge, *John Rawls: His Life and Theory of Justice*, trans. Michelle
Kosch (New York: Oxford University Press, 2007); David Lewis Schaef-
fer, *Illiberal Justice: John Rawls vs. the American Political Tradition* (Colum-
bia: University of Missouri Press, 2007); Percy B. Lehning, *John Rawls: An
Introduction* (Cambridge: Cambridge University Press, 2009); Jon Mandle,

Rawls's 'A Theory of Justice': An Introduction (Cambridge: Cambridge University Press, 2009); Todd Hedrick, *Rawls and Habermas: Reason, Pluralism, and the Claims of Political Philosophy* (Stanford, Calif.: Stanford University Press, 2010).

3. John Rawls, *Lectures on the History of Political Philosophy*, ed. Samuel Freeman (Cambridge, Mass.: Belknap Press of Harvard University Press, 2008). Recent edited volumes of essays on Rawls's work include Rex Martin and David Reidi, eds., *Rawls's Law of Peoples: A Realistic Utopia?* (Oxford: Blackwell Publishing, 2006), and Thom Brooks and Fabian Freyenhagan, eds., *The Legacy of John Rawls* (London: Continuum, 2007).

4. John Rawls, *A Brief Inquiry into the Meaning of Sin and Faith*, ed. Thomas Nagel (Cambridge, Mass.: Harvard University Press, 2010).

5. Ibid., 4.

6. "Justice as Fairness: Political not Metaphysical," *CP*, 395.

7. Rawls, *TJ*, p. 5. Hereafter cited parenthetically.

8. I have italicized "concept" and "conceptions" in order to highlight Rawls's distinction. Conceptions of justice are examples of thick descriptions or thick accounts of justice.

9. In his articulation of justice as fairness, Rawls calls these features "fair terms of cooperation" (*JF*, 7).

10. Aristotle, *Nichomachean Ethics*, trans. Terence Irwin (Indianapolis: Hackett, 1985), 1129b–1130b5.

11. "Justice as Fairness," *CP*, 48.

12. "The Sense of Justice," *CP*, 97.

13. See MacIntyre, *After Virtue, Second Edition*, 68–69.

14. Rawls notes, for example, that churches can excommunicate heretics, but they cannot burn them (*JF*, 10–11). Later in this chapter I discuss this matter specifically in relation to the family.

15. "Justice as Fairness," *CP*, 47.

16. Ibid.

17. Ibid., 48.

18. Ibid., 59.

19. Rawls formulates the two principles of justice in the following way:

(a) Each person has the same indefeasible claim to a fully adequate scheme of equal basic liberties, which scheme is compatible with the same scheme of liberties for all; and (b) Social and economic inequalities are to satisfy two conditions: first, they are to be attached to offices and positions open to all under conditions of fair equality of opportunity; and second, they are to be to the greatest benefit of the least-advantaged members of society (the difference principle). (*JF* §13, pp. 42–43)

20. There are, of course, exceptional cases in which individuals are not *actually* free to leave these relationships or require extraordinary assistance to do so safely, such as in many cases of domestic violence.

21. Rawls also notes that our personal identity as this concept is understood by some in the philosophy of mind does not change when our moral identity changes.

22. "Justice as Fairness," *CP*, 61.

23. "The Sense of Justice," *CP*, 96. For Rousseau's view, see Book IV of *Emile*, trans. Allan Bloom (New York: Basic Books, 1979), 211–53, esp. 235, 253.

24. "The Sense of Justice," *CP*, 96.

25. Ibid. As we shall see in Chapter 4, there is an interesting resemblance between this aspect of Rawls's view and certain features of the early Confucian thinker Mengzi's account of human nature.

26. Ibid., 97.

27. Ibid., 100.

28. Ibid.

29. In the final formulation of his work on justice, Rawls says he would not make any substantial changes to the moral psychology behind the three-stage development of the morality of principles originally articulated in "The Sense of Justice" and also discussed in *Theory* (*JF*, 196). The only change Rawls makes to this account in *Theory* is terminological: Instead of referring to authority, associational, and principle forms of guilt, he refers to these stages as three different forms of morality. However, his basic argument concerning what defines these three areas does not change. In what follows, I occasionally refer to *Theory* simply because Rawls sometimes states things more clearly there.

30. Ibid. See Jean Piaget, *The Moral Judgment of the Child* (London: Routledge and Kegan Paul, 1932). One might have reservations about whether Rawls's psychological construction is consistent with his claim that "The conception of the person itself is meant as both normative and political, not metaphysical or psychological" (*JF*, 19). Rawls clearly bases his account of a sense of justice on Piaget's work, though Rawls's account is not a particularly controversial psychological account in the sense that it seems reasonably straightforward to say that children initially learn to follow rules and to feel guilty for violating them in the context of their relationship with their parents. In noting that he does not present a psychological conception of the person here, I think Rawls means that he is not offering the sort of comprehensive, systematic account that psychologists offer; rather, he focuses on a narrower range of issues given his particular interest in a sense of justice. Rawls is trying to avoid an account that is tied to a comprehensive

doctrine, which is why he avoids metaphysical commitments, but it is worth noting that not all psychological accounts are as controversial as metaphysical accounts tend to be. It is also the case that not all doctrines (psychological, philosophical, or otherwise) are plausibly comprehensive, in the sense of being life-directing.

31. "The Sense of Justice," *CP*, 101.

32. Ibid., 101–2.

33. It seems clear, Rawls says, that "the sense of justice is acquired gradually by younger members of society as they grow up. The succession of generations and the necessity to teach moral attitudes (however simple) to children is one of the conditions of human life" (*TJ* §70, p. 405). Additionally, he says, "given the nature of the authority situation and the principles of moral psychology connecting the ethical and the natural attitudes, love and trust will give rise to feelings of guilt once the parental injunctions are disobeyed" (*TJ* §70, p. 407). First, parents must love their children and be worthy objects of their children's admiration, thus arousing in them a sense of their own value and the desire to become the sort of person their parents are. That is, parents need to be moral exemplars. Second, they must enunciate clear and intelligible (and of course justifiable) rules that the child can comprehend, giving reasons for these injunctions so far as these reasons can be understood. Additionally, "The parents should exemplify the morality which they enjoin and make explicit its underlying principles as time goes on" (*TJ* §70, p. 407).

34. "The Sense of Justice," 102.

35. Ibid., 101.

36. Ibid., 103.

37. Ibid.

38. I discuss Rawls's understanding of stability at the end of this chapter.

39. "The Sense of Justice," 105.

40. Ibid.

41. Ibid.

42. Ibid.

43. Ibid., 105–6.

44. Ibid., 106. It seems clear that feelings of guilt do not restore joint activity, but rather the actions that can (and should) result from these feelings help lead to such restoration. I think Rawls means that the feelings of guilt are where the possibility of restoration begins, but he does not point out other feelings and dispositions that need to be present in order for this kind of restoration to occur. Shame seems to be more apropos here. A sense of falling short of some ideal is much more conducive to self-improvement than a recognition of disobeying or transgressing. Accordingly, the sort of guilt

Rawls discusses seems to be a necessary but not sufficient condition for a fully developed sense of justice.

45. Ibid.

46. Although Rawls thinks that association guilt "quite naturally leads up to" principle guilt, he also says that for some time at least, one's motive for complying with principles of justice "springs largely from his ties of friendship and fellow feeling for others, and his concern for the approbation of the wider society" (*TJ* §72, p. 414). But according to Rawls, these feelings provide a basis for fully developing a sense of justice, and the conception of acting justly is a natural outgrowth of those previous experiences with one's parents and associations with others.

47. "The Sense of Justice," 106. In *Theory*, Rawls stresses that "our natural attachments to particular persons and groups still have an appropriate place. . . . The violation of these ties to particular individuals and groups arouses more intense moral feelings, and this entails that these offenses are worse. To be sure, deceit and infidelity are always wrong. . . . But they are not always equally wrong. They are worse whenever bonds of affection and good faith have been informed . . . ." (*TJ* §72, p. 416). Rawls's remarks concerning the fact that these bonds serve as a basis for developing concern for others outside of one's immediate circle simply reflect the fact that not everyone in a modern liberal democracy (the subject of his analysis) knows everyone else personally, *and yet they still care when their actions have wronged others.* This is why principle guilt and a morality of principles constitute the third stage in one's development of a sense of justice. A mature sense of justice also functions in at least some relationships with individuals we know well, particularly with people we might know well but strongly dislike—perhaps for good reasons. A well-developed sense of justice in these cases helps one to view these other individuals as persons and helps one to treat them with justice.

48. This sort of view is reminiscent of how the Mohists understood the Confucians. Mozi criticizes the Confucians for caring only about their families and friends, and thus for "excessive partiality," which leads to the neglect and harm of those who are outside of one's inner circle. Furthermore, the Mohists thought we should have *only* principle guilt. Their conception of the good is exhausted by their conception of justice. It seems clear that the Mohists misinterpret the Confucian position as it is expressed in the *Analects*. My argument in Chapter 3 will show that the Confucian view is more moderate and certainly does not allow one to disrespect or disregard the well-being of those outside of one's immediate circle. As we will see, the most cultivated rulers and the most cultivated individuals are those who have a highly developed sense of respect and care for the well-being of all members of society.

49. "The Sense of Justice," 97.

50. Insofar as it is easiest to see that someone has developed a sense of justice when that person feels principle guilt, which concerns those with whom they do not have a special relationship, Rawls's view resembles Kant's view that it is easiest to tell that a person has moral motivations in those cases where we can be sure that they do not *feel* like doing the right thing, specifically when "all sympathy with the fate of others" has been extinguished. Of course, Kant does not mean to say that feelings are unimportant or that it is a good thing to feel indifferently toward others, only that one's feelings or inclinations are not a factor in determining the morality of one's actions. For Kant, a moral person must be "beneficent not from inclination but from duty." This is similar to how Rawls places emphasis on having a fully developed sense of justice that causes one to act justly toward those for whom one does not feel preferential love. The deep and important difference between Rawls and Kant here is that Rawls endorses the view that one's emotions are an indicator of moral development and that they play a crucial role in developing the ability to act morally toward others with whom one does not have a preexisting relationship that involves feelings of love, sympathy, and care. This understanding of moral development is the more Humean dimension to Rawls. For Kant's view, see Immanuel Kant, *Groundwork of the Metaphysics of Morals*, trans., ed. Mary Gregor (Cambridge: Cambridge University Press, 1997), esp. 11–12 (4:398–4:399 in the Academy Edition).

51. An ongoing body of feminist work criticizes liberal theory for its denigration of emotion. See, for example, Alison Jaggar, *Feminist Politics and Human Nature* (Totowa, N.J.: Rowman and Littlefield, 1983), 28–47; Virginia Held, *Feminist Morality: Transforming Culture, Society, and Politics* (Chicago: University of Chicago Press, 1993); Marilyn Friedman, *What Are Friends For? Feminist Perspectives on Personal Relationships and Moral Theory* (Ithaca, N.Y.: Cornell University Press, 1993).

52. "The Idea of Public Reason Revisited," *CP*, 595–96.

53. Still, some critics have maintained that the bonds of continuity in a society depend primarily on emotions or tradition as opposed to rationally justifiable principles. They argue that these two options are mutually exclusive and attribute the latter view to Rawls. See Bernard Williams, "Morality and Social Justice," Tanner Lectures given at Harvard University (1983); John Haldane, "The Individual, the State, and the Common Good," *Social Philosophy and Policy* 13 (1996), 59–79. I think these critics underestimate the role Rawls gives to the emotions.

54. For a critique that sees Rawls's account as relying *too* heavily on the emotional and relational ties the feminists criticize Rawls for neglecting, and which represents theoretical differences in psychology, see John Deigh, "Love, Guilt, and the Sense of Justice," in John Deigh, ed., *The Sources of*

Moral Agency: Essays in Moral Psychology and Freudian Theory (New York: Cambridge University Press, 1996), 39–64. Deigh argues that the "optimistic view" taken by Rawls is insufficient compared with the "pessimistic view" accepted by Hobbes, Hume, and, perhaps most significantly, Freud. He writes that on Rawls's optimistic view, "the sense of justice is itself a form of good will toward humanity, a sentiment of the heart, which grows out of the natural sentiments of love and friendship, as these mature in the context of a social order" (40–41). The pessmisitic view, Deigh says, maintains that "our sense of duty and justice results from society's turning to its advantage asocial and antisocial drives that are part of our natural endowment and that if left untutored and unharnessed would ruin whatever peace and harmony our capacities for goodwill and fellow feeling could establish" (40). Deigh bases his critique on the argument that Rawls conflates guilt and remorse, which, if correct, is an important objection because as we have seen, Rawls conceives of guilt as the characteristic emotion of the sense of justice. For a defense of Rawls against Deigh's criticisms, see Richard Kyte, "Guilt, Remorse, and the Sense of Justice," *Contemporary Philosophy* 14:5 (1992), 17–20. Kyte argues that even if Deigh's criticisms are correct, his critique does not have as great an effect on Rawls's overall account of moral development as Deigh implies, because remorse is as significant an indication of the moral sense as guilt.

55. Rawls qualifies this sentence in the 1999 revised edition of *Theory*, quoted here (p. 87, *TJ* 1999). In the original 1971 edition, this line reads, "[T]he difference principle represents, in effect, an agreement to regard the distribution of natural talents as a common asset . . . ." (*A Theory of Justice* [Cambridge, Mass.: Belknap Press of Harvard University Press, 1971], 101). Notice that in the revised edition, Rawls says citizens agree to regard "the distribution of natural talents *as in some respects* a common asset," which softens the claim slightly.

56. Thomas Nagel, "Rawls and Liberalism," in *The Cambridge Companion to Rawls*, 79.

57. Ibid., 79–80.

58. The objection that Rawls neglects the extent to which persons are indebted to their community for the way they think about themselves has been pursued at length by a number of scholars, including Michael Sandel. In their analysis of the communitarian critique of Rawls, Stephen Mulhall and Adam Swift point out that Rawls "explicitly concedes the validity of Sandel's claim about the phenomenology of our moral experience (*PL*, 31), and he is happy to see such constitutive values and communal attachments flourish in the context of family life, churches, and scientific societies; what he denies is their appropriateness for the realm of politics" (*PL*, 466). For a concise but detailed overview of communitarian critiques of Rawls, as well as a discussion

of Rawls's replies, see Mulhall and Swift, "Rawls and Communitarianism," in *The Cambridge Companion to Rawls*. For the communitarian critique of Rawls, see Michael Sandel, *Liberalism and the Limits of Justice, Second Edition* (Cambridge: Cambridge University Press, 1988). See also Charles Taylor, *Philosophical Papers, Vol. 1: Human Agency and Language* (Cambridge: Cambridge University Press, 1985); *Philosophical Papers, Vol. 2: Philosophy and the Human Sciences* (Cambridge: Cambridge University Press, 1985); *Sources of the Self: The Making of Modern Identity* (Cambridge: Cambridge University Press, 1989); and Alasdair MacIntyre, *After Virtue* (South Bend, Ind.: Notre Dame University Press, 1981).

59. Rawls's claim, then, is a *generic* and not strictly a *universal* claim. In this respect his claim resembles Mengzi's claim about the possession of moral sprouts: all healthy, normally raised members of the species possess them. For a discussion of the difference between generic and universal claims, and the significance of this difference for Mengzi's thought, see Philip J. Ivanhoe, "Confucian Self Cultivation and Mengzi's Notion of Extension," in Xiusheng Liu and Philip J. Ivanhoe, eds., *Essays on the Moral Philosophy of Mengzi* (Indianapolis: Hackett, 2002), 222–23.

60. "The Sense of Justice," *CP*, 114.

61. Scholars of early Confucianism may recognize the similarity here with Mengzi's distinction between acting according to benevolence versus acting out of benevolence (*ren*) and righteousness (*jyi*), seen in *Mengzi* 4B19.

62. This poses a dilemma for Rawls that resembles what I will call "Xunzi's Dilemma." Xunzi, who rejects Mengzi's claim that humans have innate moral tendencies and maintains that they need teachers and the traditions associated with the Way in order to become virtuous, faces the challenge of explaining why and how people came to commit themselves to following the Confucian Way and how the sages who created the Way turned themselves into beings who not only possessed knowledge of morality but loved and delighted in it. A similar dilemma arises for Rawls in explaining the origins of just institutions: If citizens must grow up under just basic institutions in order to fully develop a sense of justice, then where do just institutions come from in the first place? I discuss these issues in detail in Chapter 4.

63. Rawls, "Justice as Fairness: Political Not Metaphysical" in *CP*, 401.

64. Ibid., italics mine.

65. Rawls, *TJ*, 181.

66. Martha C. Nussbaum, "Rawls and Feminism," in *The Cambridge Companion to Rawls*, 492–93.

67. Ibid.

68. "The Sense of Justice," *CP*, 115.

69. Ibid.

70. At the end of the day, our tendency might simply be evolutionary good luck. Of course, one could also see this as a part of a divine plan.

71. There is an interesting similarity between the issues I am discussing here and the debate between Mengzi, who maintains that humans have innate moral "sprouts," and Xunzi, who thinks that humans are morally blind at birth. This similarity will be discussed further in Chapter 4.

72. "The Sense of Justice," *CP*, 97, 100.

73. Much more robust evidence supports this case than my very modest examples suggest. For a study of children's responses to distresses they caused and witnessed in others during the second year of life, including prosocial behaviors such as helping, sharing, and comforting, see Carolyn Zahn-Waxler, et al., "Development of Concern for Others," *Developmental Psychology* 28.1 (1992), 126–36. For a review of studies that cast doubt on conceptions of young children as primarily egocentric and uncaring toward others, see Carolyn Zahn-Waxler and Marian Radke-Yarrow, "The Origins of Empathic Concern," *Motivation and Emotion* 14.2 (1990), 107–30. For an argument that natural selection is unlikely to have given us purely egoistic motives, and a study of evidence for psychological altruism throughout the animal kingdom, see Elliott Sober and David Sloan Wilson, *Unto Others: The Evolution and Psychology of Unselfish Behavior* (Cambridge, Mass.: Harvard University Press, 1998).

74. Aristotle, *Nichomachean Ethics*, Book VII, Chapters 11–14, and Book X, Chs. 1–5.

75. For an essay that touches on some other dimensions of the Aristotelian side of Rawls, see Steven M. DeLue, "Aristotle, Kant and Rawls on Moral Motivation in a Just Society," *The American Political Science Review* 24:2 (1980), 385–93.

76. John M. Cooper, "Political Animals and Civic Friendship," in Neera Kapur Badhwar, ed., *Friendship: A Philosophical Reader* (Ithaca, N.Y.: Cornell University Press, 1993), 303–26. Cooper is also an appropriate source here because Rawls acknowledges his debt to Cooper for his formulation and interpretation of the Aristotelian Principle (*TJ* §65, p. 374 n. 20).

77. Cooper, "Political Animals and Civic Friendship," 303.

78. Ibid. See Aristotle, *Nichomachean Ethics* Book I:7 (1097b); *Politics* Book I:2 (1253a 2–3).

79. Ibid., 304.

80. Ibid., 314.

81. Ibid.

82. Ibid., 315.

83. Ibid. One needs only to think of the way most of us react to corporate corruption or political malfeasance in order to see that this is true.

84. Ibid., 316.

85. Ibid. The willingness to give to charitable organizations to aid fellow citizens who are the victims of natural disasters like hurricanes and earthquakes serves as an example here. We want to do our part to help because we feel bound to other members of our society in an important way, and we feel that it is part of our responsibility as citizens to help one another in such times of need.

86. Ibid., 316–18. For Aristotle's discussion of civic friendship, see *Eudemian Ethics*, Book VII: 9–10. See also Aristotle's distinction between different kinds of friendship in the *Nichomachean Ethics*, Book VIII.

87. Ibid., 319.

88. Ibid., 320.

89. Ibid. Cooper notes that citizens are obviously quite unlike a family in other respects. This poses a contrast to the view found in the *Analects*, according to which the family serves as the model for what a state should be like.

90. Rawls adopts Charles Taylor's definition of civic humanism from Taylor's *Philosophy and the Human Sciences* (Cambridge: Cambridge University Press, 1985), 334f. He notes that Taylor attributes this view to Rousseau, while noting that Kant does not accept it.

91. Rawls also notes that justice as fairness *is* compatible with classical republicanism, which differs from civic humanism. Classical republicanism is the view that the safety of democratic liberties requires the active participation of citizens who have the political virtues needed to sustain a constitutional regime. "The idea is that unless there is widespread participation in democratic politics by a vigorous and informed citizen body moved in good part by a concern for political justice and public good, even the best-designed political institutions will eventually fall into the hands of those who hunger for power and military glory" (*JF*, 144).

92. W. D. Ross, *The Right and the Good* (Oxford: The Clarendon Press, 1930).

93. Here, Rawls agrees with almost every thinker in the Chinese tradition. Simply having or satisfying a desire is not any reason to think that this is *good*, but most utilitarians seem to think that it is good, preference utilitarians being the clearest example.

94. "In justice as fairness, then, the general meaning of the priority of right is that admissible ideas of the good must fit within its framework as a political conception. Given the fact of pluralism, we must be able to assume: (1) that the ideas used are, or could be, shared by citizens generally regarded as free and equal; and (2) that they do not presuppose any particular fully (or partially) comprehensive doctrine" (*JF*, 141).

95. "The Sense of Justice," *CP*, 105.

96. For a discussion of this issue, see Samuel Freeman, "Congruence and the Good of Justice," in Samuel Freeman, ed., *The Cambridge Companion to Rawls* (New York: Cambridge University Press, 2003), 308–9 n. 4.

3. THE SENSE OF JUSTICE IN THE *ANALECTS*

1. *Analects* 16.1, my translation. Subsequent translations follow Slingerland unless otherwise specified.

2. I follow the He Yan commentary in taking this passage as Kongzi's lament for his personal hope of seeing the world attain the Way. [He Yan, *Lun yu ji jie* 論語集解, *Zhong yong shuo can ben [Zhang Jiucheng]. Lun yu ji jie [He Yan ji jie]*, et al. (compilation), (Taibei: Taiwan shang wu yin shu guan, 1981), 9.]

3. For an insightful study of the lively debates on this subject in early China, see Michael J. Puett, *The Ambivalence of Creation: Debates Concerning Innovation and Artifice in Early China* (Stanford, Calif.: Stanford University Press, 2001).

4. Cf. 7.2. Translation adapted from Slingerland.

5. My translation.

6. My translation.

7. Translation adapted from Slingerland.

8. My translation. Kongzi refers to a special kind of joy here, one that is available only to those who follow and live in harmony with the Way. For an illuminating discussion of this aspect of Kongzi's thought, see Philip J. Ivanhoe, "Happiness in Early Chinese Thought," in Susan David, Ilona Boniwell, and Amanda Conley Ayers, eds., *Oxford Handbook of Happiness* (Oxford: Oxford University Press, 2012). I examine the parallel between the early Confucian conception of joy seen in the *Mengzi* and what Rawls calls the Aristotelian principle later in this book.

9. Translation adapted from Slingerland.

10. I have left "junzi" untranslated in all passages using this term.

11. Translation adapted from Slingerland. I leave *Ren* untranslated in all passages using this term.

12. My translation.

13. My translation. I follow Waley's translation of *tu* as "soil" in the first line. *Huai tu* 懷土 ("cherishes the earth") connotes caring about one's land and material goods, as opposed to Virtue. [Arthur Waley, trans., *Lunyu The Analects* (Changsha, P.R. China: Hunan People's Publishing House, 1999), 35.] Legge translates the last line as "the small man thinks of favours which he may receive." [James Legge, trans., "Confucian Analects," in *The Chinese*

Classics, Vol. I (New York: Dover Publications, 1971. Originally published in Oxford, U.K.: Clarendon Press, 1893), 168.]

14. Roger T. Ames and Henry Rosemont Jr., trans., *The Analects of Confucius: A Philosophical Translation* (New York: Ballantine Books, 1998), 91.

15. Translation adapted from Slingerland.

16. I follow most traditional commentaries on the *Analects* here in maintaining that an emotional attitude and not just one's physical behavior is important when it comes to being filial. For a helpful sampling of a few commentaries on this issue, see Slingerland, *Confucius Analects*, 11.

17. Ibid., 67.

18. Translation adapted from Slingerland.

19. Translation adapted from Slingerland.

20. My translation.

21. I will discuss Kongzi's other remarks in 8.13 later in this chapter.

22. I follow David Nivison in capitalizing the translation of *de* as "Virtue," which helps to distinguish the distinctive Chinese idea from the more general sense of "virtue."

23. David S. Nivison, *The Ways of Confucianism: Investigations in Chinese Philosophy*, ed. Bryan W. Van Norden (LaSalle, Ill.: Open Court Press, 1996), 17–57.

24. Philip J. Ivanhoe, *Confucian Moral Self Cultivation, Second Edition* (Indianapolis: Hackett, 2000), ix–xvii. See also Ivanhoe, "The Concept of de ('Virtue') in the Laozi," in Mark Csikszentmihalyi and Philip J. Ivanhoe, eds., *Religious and Philosophical Aspects of the Laozi* (Albany: SUNY Press, 1999).

25. Ivanhoe, "The Concept of de ('Virtue') in the Laozi," x.

26. Cf. 13.11, 13.12, 13.13.

27. My translation.

28. The character is made up of two parts: *tu* 土 ("soil," "earth," "land") and *yun* 勻 ("even," "uniform"). See Tor Ulving, ed., *Dictionary of Old and Middle Chinese: Bernard Karlgren's Grammata Serica Recensa Alphabetically Arranged* (Goteborg, Sweden: Acta Universitatis Gothoburgensis, 1997), 242 (*jun*), 362 (*tu*), 199 (*yun*). See also Legge, "Confucian Analects," 309, 460.

29. My translation.

30. My translation.

31. Julia Tao, "Beyond Proceduralism: A Chinese Perspective on Cheng (Sincerity) as a Political Virtue," *Philosophy East and West* 55.1 (2005), 69.

32. Regarding this idea, Tu Wei-ming cites Michael Polanyi, *Personal Knowledge: Towards a Post-Critical Philosophy* (New York: Harper Torchbooks, 1964), 203–45. [Tu Wei-ming, *Centrality and Commonality: An Essay on Confucian Religiousness* (Albany: SUNY Press, 1989), 3, 124 n. 8.]

33. Tu, *Centrality and Commonality: An Essay on Confucian Religiousness*, 67.

34. I owe this point to Philip J. Ivanhoe.

35. My translation.

36. Zhu Xi (1130–1200 C.E.) is the most influential Chinese thinker since the classical period, and the most influential Confucian commentator on the *Analects*. For an introduction to Zhu Xi's philosophy and historical influence, see Ivanhoe, *Confucian Moral Self Cultivation*, 43–58, and Daniel K. Gardner, trans., *Chu Hsi: Learning to Be a Sage* (Berkeley: University of California Press, 1990), 3–81. In the passage discussed above, Legge translates *ai* 愛 as "love," but I have translated it as "care" because this seems more accurate in terms of what Kongzi expects individuals to show to those with whom they are not acquainted. That is, he expects sympathetic feelings and actions, as opposed to the emotion of love. See Legge, "Confucian Analects," 140.

37. My translation.

38. My translation.

39. That is, everyone in the world is his brother.

40. Here we should be reminded of Rawls's contention that having a fully developed sense of justice is seen in one's ability to feel for those with whom one is not immediately associated, in addition to one's family and friends.

41. My translation.

42. In the following discussion, I leave *yi* untranslated to more easily facilitate an exploration of what it means in the *Analects*.

43. This aspect of Confucian thought represents an important point of resonance with Aristotle.

44. My translation. I follow Legge's rendering of *yu yu yi* 喻於義 as "is conversant with *yi*" (Legge, "Confucian Analects," 170).

45. Legge translates this as "When he sees gain to be got, he thinks of righteousness" (Legge, "Confucian Analects," 314).

46. My translation.

47. My translation.

48. Translation adapted from Slingerland.

49. He Yan, *Lun yu ji jie* 論語集解, 4.

50. Slingerland, *Confucius Analects*, 12.

51. Zhu Xi, *Si shu ji zhu*, 四書集注 (*Changsha shi: yue lu shu she: Hunan sheng xin hua shu dian fa xing*, 1985), p. 170. For a detailed discussion of the ideal of impartiality in Confucianism, see the essays in Part I of Hahm Chaihark and Daniel A. Bell, eds., *The Politics of Affective Relations* (Lanham, Md.: Lexington Books, 2004).

52. Slinglerland, *Confucius Analects*, 180.

53. Another question to consider is whether Kongzi's decision is fair to his daughter. I thank Bonnie Mann for raising this issue. On the one hand,

his actions in selecting his daughter's spouse rest on what most of us would regard as a cultural practice that is unfair to women. On the other hand, it seems clear that Kongzi's decision about his daughter's spouse is not based on the desire for increased social status or wealth. If Kongzi's decision is based on Gongye Chang's moral character, then this would be to the advantage of Kongzi's daughter and may reflect a concern for her well-being. At the same time, it is important to acknowledge that the social stigma attached to her husband may make her life much more difficult than it might have otherwise been. It is worth noting, though, that if Kongzi did sacrifice his family's interests for a larger purpose here, this sort of practice is by no means unique to ancient China. Indeed, Daniel Bell has pointed out to me that Western thinkers have generally been far more willing to justify such sacrifices because the good of the family was not considered to be as important. He cites the examples of Socrates' neglect of his family in order to pursue truth and J. S. Mill's chiding of uneducated women because their "petty" family concerns held down public-spirited husbands.

54. My translation.

55. Cf. 11.6, which seems to take Nan Rong's carefulness in speech as the reason Kongzi gave his niece to him in marriage. For a study of the theme of carefulness in speech in the *Analects*, see my "Nameless Virtues and Restrained Speech in the *Analects*," *International Philosophical Quarterly* 49.1, no. 193 (2009), 53–69.

56. It should be noted that Kongzi is *providing instruction* in 8.13, while in 18.7 (discussed earlier in this chapter) he *describes* how the *junzi* "takes office and does what is *yi*, even though he already knows that the Way will not be followed." Throughout the *Analects*, the *junzi* is described, not instructed. Accordingly, although 8.13 and 18.7 may seem to be in tension with each other, the latter offers a description of what the *junzi* does when taking office, while the former offers instruction to others concerning entering or residing in states that are endangered or disordered. These instructions are not obviously or necessarily in tension.

57. My translation.

58. Waley follows this reading and groups these passages together into one paragraph in his translation (Waley, *Lunyu the Analects*, 155).

59. In 14.9 and 14.16 Kongzi is noncommittal in his remarks about Guan's character, even when Zilu explicitly asks if Guan was *Ren* ("humane") in 14.16. In 14.17, Zigong criticizes Guan and declares that he was not *Ren*, but Kongzi responds by explaining some of Guan's actions in a charitable light. However, in both 14.16 and 14.17, although Kongzi acknowledges that Guan Zhong did some good things, he never really praises Guan. And in 3.22, Kongzi pretty clearly criticizes Guan's moral failings. Perhaps this

rather mixed assessment is simply Kongzi being *fair* to Guan Zhong. That is, these passages may manifest a sense of fairness.

60. Trans. Slingerland, *Confucius Analects*, 158. See He Yan, *Lun yu ji jie* 論語集解, 38.

61. Legge, "Confucian Analects," 279 n. 11.

62. Aristotle thought it was unlikely that those who were not a part of the noble class would become virtuous. In contrast, Kongzi maintains that even though it may be more difficult for poor people to cultivate themselves, they are certainly capable of it. Yan Hui is an example of one who, despite his humble circumstances, dedicated himself to the path of self-cultivation and excelled.

63. He Yan, *Lun yu ji jie* 論語集解, 22.

64. Xunzi explicitly discusses the need for the government to take care of the handicapped, orphaned, ill, and destitute. For a discussion of this dimension of Xunzi's thought, see Henry Rosemont Jr., "State and Society in the Xunzi: A Philosophical Commentary," in T. C. Kline III and Philip J. Ivanhoe, eds., *Virtue, Nature, and Moral Agency in the Xunzi* (Indianapolis: Hackett, 2000), 1–38.

65. The CUHK *Concordance to the Lunyu* has the form of the character (*xiu* 脩) that was used in early editions of the *Analects* for both passages. I use the preferred (and more widely known) modern form of the character here.

66. The term *xiu shen* 修身 is not used in the *Analects*, although it is used in other Confucian texts. Additionally, *shen* 身 is not a term of art in this sense; it often simply means oneself or a body (one's own or another's).

67. As we saw in Chapter 2, Rawls points out that fairness is one aspect of justice but notes that fairness and justice are not equivalent (*TJ* §3, p. 11; "Justice as Fairness," *CP*, 47). On Rawls's view, fairness is the *fundamental* aspect of justice, but even if one does not accept this view, it seems to me that it is not particularly controversial to claim that fairness is one aspect of justice.

68. The translation is my own. Arthur Waley notes that the term for "upright one" (*zhi gong* 直躬) refers to "a legendary paragon of honesty" (Waley 1999, 267 n. 17). Indeed, *gong* 躬 is both a term meaning "person" and a name, and so it might also be translated as "Upright Gong." Legge maintains that it is not clear that the case of "Upright Gong" is an actual case: "We cannot say whether the duke is referring to one or more actual cases, or giving his opinion of what his people would do. [Kongzi's] reply would incline us to the latter view" (Legge, "Confucian Analects," 270 n. 18).

69. These issues are also raised in the *Mengzi*, which praises sage-king Shun's filial piety, noting that if his father had murdered someone, Shun "would have secretly carried him on his back and fled, to live in the coast-

land, happy to the end of his days, joyfully forgetting the world" (*Mengzi* 7A35, trans. Bryan W. Van Norden, *Mengzi: With Selections from Traditional Commentaries* [Indianapolis: Hackett, 2008], 181). Like *Analects* 13.18, there is more to this passage than first meets the eye, and it should not be seen as simply advocating a disregard for justice in favor of filial piety. First, Shun is described as abdicating the throne, which suggests his recognition that his actions, in taking his father into his care and fleeing the state, make him ineligible to serve as king. It certainly shows that he is unwilling to abuse his power: He does not simply pardon his father and continue to rule. Additionally, in taking his father to a remote area and remaining with him there, Shun protects the people from being harmed by his father. His actions can hardly be seen as excusing his father's wrongdoing: He does not simply turn his father loose. In these respects, he balances his filial and state duties while also exhibiting a sense of justice.

70. That is not to deny that there might be potential conflicts between filial piety and other values such as justice, or even between different filial obligations, based on other passages in the *Analects*. For example, one might ask whether Kongzi's instructions to remonstrate with one's parents but "follow their lead diligently without resentment" (2.5) ought to be followed if one's parents ask one to do something inhumane or unjust. Kongzi does not explicitly entertain this question. However, Mengzi and Xunzi both argue that there are times when it is appropriate to act contrary to traditional filial duties. Mengzi describes how sage-king Shun violated the traditional dictates of filial piety by not informing his parents of his marriage (*Mengzi* 5A2). Mengzi justifies Shun's actions by arguing that Shun *had* to violate this obligation because it was the only way he could avoid the *most* unfilial act: having no posterity (4A26). This passage shows that on Mengzi's view there are times when we must prioritize conflicting filial obligations, violating some in order to fulfill others. Xunzi's view is similar in some ways but also distinctive. He argues that there are times when not following orders—be they of the ruler or of one's father—is an instance of filial piety (*Xunzi*, Ch. 26, "The Way to Be a Good Son").

71. The latter term is used in passages like 12.18, where Ji Kangzi asks about the prevalence of thieves in the state of Lu. See also *Analects* 17.12, 17.23.

72. Zhu Xi, *Si shu ji zhu*, 四書集注, p. 178.

73. Karlgren confirms this and notes that the semantic range of *rang* includes "to pull away," "to expel," "to thrust aside," "to thrust forward." All of these connote a greater sense of urgency than the semantic range of *dao* ("thief," "robber," "scoundrel"), which implies an established habit or pattern of behavior. See Tor Ulving, ed., *Dictionary of Old and Middle Chinese: Bernard*

Karlgren's Grammata Serica Recensa Alphabetically Arranged (Goteborg, Sweden: Acta Universitatis Gothoburgensis, 1997), 299 (*rang*), 176 (*dao*).

74. In fact, we accord the U.S. military the power to do this. It is called "requisitioning," and it is considered good initiative for a military officer to order his or her troops to take the necessary goods to distribute to people when they are not able to get supplies after natural disasters. Of course, in such cases, the rule is to leave a notice describing what was taken and by whom so that the owner can be compensated by the government.

75. In his discussion of this passage, Van Norden argues that the Confucian view that we have special obligations to our parents "seems to capture the commonsense intuitions that many of us have, both in China and in the West." He offers the example of how we would react to the claim "People are going hungry tonight in New York, and Bryan isn't doing anything about it!" compared with "Bryan's *father* is going hungry tonight in New York, and he isn't doing anything about it!" Whereas the former claim would not, for most people, be taken to indicate a serious character flaw in Bryan (even though one might believe that we should all do more to feed the hungry), the latter would be seen as indicating a major character flaw, at least in the absence of an extraordinary explanation (Van Norden, *Virtue Ethics and Consequentialism in Early Chinese Philosophy*, 115–16).

76. The Duke of She's position reflects aspects of Legalism, and his disagreement with Kongzi illustrates some of the sharp disagreements between Confucians and Legalist thinkers like Han Feizi. Indeed, a version of the story of stolen sheep is recounted in Ch. 49 of the *Han Feizi* ("The Five Vermin"). For a translation, see Joel Sahleen, trans., "Han Feizi," in Philip J. Ivanhoe and Bryan W. Van Norden, eds., *Readings in Classical Chinese Philosophy, Second Edition* (Indianapolis: Hackett, 2005), 344. According to this version of the story, the upright son was put to death by the apparently Confucian officials in his state for being "upright in regard to his lord but crooked in regard to his father." The purpose of the story, for Han Feizi, is to highlight the tragic consequences of valuing filial piety over strict adherence to the law. On the view presented in the *Han Feizi*, the son is put to death by his backward culture when in fact he did the right thing by acting in accordance with the law. On the view presented in the *Analects*, the son is praised by his backward culture when in fact he did the wrong thing by failing to be filial. For an examination of Legalist critiques of Confucianism that also takes into account its significance for virtue ethics, see Eric L. Hutton, "Han Feizi's Criticism of Confucianism and Its Implications for Virtue Ethics," *Journal of Moral Philosophy* 5 (2008), 423–53.

77. See, for example, 11.22.

78. *Analects* 7.18, Burton Watson, trans., *The Analects of Confucius* (New York: Columbia University Press, 2007), 50.

79. Legge, "Confucian Analects," 270 n. 18. Similar views can be found in the Western tradition. The first-century B.C.E. Stoic thinker Hecaton argued that filial piety is decisive for many minor offenses (though not in cases like treason or blasphemy) because the consequences of citizens' standing by their parents outweigh the consequences of children's turning their parents in. For a discussion of this point in relation to the virtue of filial piety, see Philip J. Ivanhoe, "Filial Piety as a Virtue," in Rebecca Walker and Philip J. Ivanhoe, eds., *Working Virtue: Virtue Ethics and Contemporary Moral Problems* (New York: Oxford University Press, 2007), 309 n. 29.

80. My translation.

81. "Commonweal Interview with John Rawls," *CP*, 622.

82. For a helpful summary of the commentaries on this passage, see Slingerland, *Confucius Analects*, 82–83.

83. For a helpful discussion of the role the *Analects* played in inspiring the civil service examinations, see Thomas H.C. Lee, *Government and Examinations in Sung China* (Hong Kong: The Chinese University Press, 1985), 5–17. For a detailed historical study of the civil service examinations in China, see the monumental work by Benjamin A. Elman, *A Cultural History of Civil Examinations in Late Imperial China* (Berkeley: University of California Press, 2000). See also John W. Chaffee, *The Thorny Gates of Learning in Sung China* (Albany: SUNY Press, 1995).

84. Lee, *Government Education and Examinations in Sung China*, 11.

85. Elman, *A Cultural History of Civil Examinations in Late Imperial China*, 5.

86. Even though the examination system arose after the period of the *Analects*, it was well before any contact with the West. In fact, the West adopted this idea from China through Enlightenment thinkers like Voltaire.

87. "The Sense of Justice," *CP*, 115.

88. Lee, *Government Education and Examinations in Sung China*, 203. Lee includes documentation of the progress that some members of non-elite social classes made (see pp. 201–30). The overall picture is, of course, more complicated, and many members of the lower classes were effectively excluded by the educational curriculum and linguistic requirements of the examinations. Benjamin A. Elman points out that because they were "premised on a system of inclusion and exclusion based on tests of classical literacy that restricted the access of those in the lower classes (whose literacy was too vernacular to master the classical frames of language and writing tested in the local licensing examinations), the civil examinations concealed the resulting

process of social selection. By requiring linguistic mastery of nonvernacular classical texts, imperial examinations created a written linguistic barrier between those who were allowed into the empire's examinations compounds and those—the classically illiterate—who were kept out" (*A Cultural History of Civil Examinations in Late Imperial China*, xxx–xxxi. See Elman's discussion of the quota system in Ch. 5, pp. 239–94).

4. TWO SENSES OF JUSTICE

1. *Daodejing*, Ch. 77, trans. Philip J. Ivanhoe, *The Daodejing of Laozi* (Indianapolis: Hackett, 2002), 80.

2. Rawls, "The Sense of Justice," *CP*, 96.

3. I am indebted to Norman Daniels's discussion of these difficulties in his "Rawls's Complex Egalitarianism," in *The Cambridge Companion to Rawls*, 249. Daniels uses public education in the United States to illustrate how the principle of "careers open to talents" leaves in place the strong effects of unfair practices and morally arbitrary social contingencies. He points out that in many places, "[D]e facto residential segregation and unequal political power lead to basic inequalities between the best suburban schools, serving rich white children, and the worst rural and urban schools, serving poor minority and white children. . . ." As a result, "schools end up replicating, not reducing, class and race inequalities" (250).

4. This difference marks the fact that Rawls aims to focus strictly on *political concerns*, whereas the *Analects* does not.

5. I will discuss this issue further with respect to the *Analects*, *Mengzi*, *Xunzi*, and Rawls later in this chapter.

6. See 6.4 for another example of Ran Qiu's apparent *lack* of a sense of justice.

7. Kongzi says in 4.9: "A scholar-official who has set his heart upon the Way, but who is still ashamed of having shabby clothing or meager rations, is not worth engaging in discussion."

8. Daniel Bell even notes that "Confucius (if he were around today) may well have endorsed something like Rawls's difference principle." He goes on to note, however, that "Confucians might dispute Rawls's assumption that basic liberties should have priority over the fair distribution of material goods in cases of conflict—and here lies one basic contrast with liberalism." See his *Beyond Liberal Democracy* (Princeton, N.J.: Princeton University Press, 2006), 237 n. 23.

9. The extent to which Rawls shares this view is unclear. Clearly Rawls distinguishes between individuals suffering as a result of natural and social contingencies and those suffering as a result of circumstances they had control over. However, Rawls thinks natural and social contingencies *can*

determine a person's circumstances, at least to some degree, and prevent them from being able to cultivate themselves. He seems to think that individuals are not to blame in these situations, whereas the *Analects* maintains that individuals *are* to blame if they fail to cultivate themselves, which seems to mark an important difference between the two views.

10. One difference that emerges from this fact is that the *Analects* is primarily therapeutic, while Rawls's work is primarily theoretical and technical. That is, one of Kongzi's goals is to improve his students' character by teaching them about the Way, whereas Rawls's primary aims are theoretical and technical in that he focuses on what justice is and how the basic structure of society should be arranged. However, Rawls also seems to hope that his analysis will move people to act in certain ways, and Kongzi does discuss what things like *Ren* are, as well as the basic structure of society.

11. One might argue that Kongzi and Rawls present very different views of the self, and that this difference represents a much more important contrast than those I highlight here. I agree with scholars such as Henry Rosemont Jr. who emphasize the distinctive importance of roles and relationships in Confucian thought, but I take a more moderate view concerning what this means for Confucian views of the self. Rosemont argues that Confucians such as Kongzi understand humans as consisting entirely and only of their roles, to the extent that there is no "self" to speak of. As my discussion in Chapter 3 helps to make clear, I interpret the *Analects* as presenting the view that one's roles and relationships are a fundamental part of who one is, but not the only part, for a range of virtues and capacities is important here as well. For Rosemont's view, see his "Rights-Bearing Individuals and Role-Bearing Persons" in Mary I. Bockover, ed., *Rules, Rituals, and Responsibility: Essays Dedicated to Herbert Fingarette* (LaSalle, Ill.: Open Court Press, 1991), 71–101. For an argument in favor of a more moderate interpretation, see Philip J. Ivanhoe, "In the Shade of Confucius: Social Roles, Ethical Theory, and the Self," in Ronnie Littlejohn and Marthe Chandler, eds., *Polishing the Chinese Mirror: Essays in Honor of Henry Rosemont, Jr.* (New York: Global Scholarly Publications, 2008), 34–49. I discuss Rawls's view of the self and autonomy in relation to Rosemont's view of the Confucian self in my "Rawls, Rosemont, and the Debate over Rights and Roles" in *Polishing the Chinese Mirror*, 77–89.

12. See *Analects* 1.2, 1.6, and 2.21.

13. Later in this chapter I will specifically address the extent to which the rites may be considered basic institutions, on Rawls's definition.

14. In the next section of this chapter, I will return to this tension in Rawls and discuss some possible ways of resolving it.

15. Rawls is likely influenced by Kant on this point. For Kant, "ought implies can" does not minimize the *difficulty* of achieving a certain end.

16. "The Sense of Justice," *CP*, 96.

17. For a helpful discussion of these critics, especially the followers of Mozi and Yang Zhu, and Mengzi's response, see Ivanhoe, *Confucian Moral Self Cultivation*, 15–28.

18. "The Sense of Justice," *CP*, 114.

19. For studies of Mengzi's theory of human nature, see A. C. Graham, "The Background of the Mencian Theory of Human Nature," reprinted in *Studies in Chinese Philosophy and Philosophical Literature* (Albany: SUNY Press, 1990), 7–66, and D. C. Lau, "Theories of Human Nature in Mengzi and Xunzi," reprinted in Kline and Ivanhoe, *Virtue, Nature, and Moral Agency in the Xunzi*. For more general studies of Mengzi's moral philosophy, see David S. Nivison, *The Ways of Confucianism* (Chicago: Open Court Press, 1996); Kwong-loi Shun, *Mencius and Early Chinese Thought* (Stanford, Calif.: Stanford University Press, 1997); Philip J. Ivanhoe, *Ethics in the Confucian Tradition: The Thought of Mengzi and Wang Yangming, Second Edition* (Indianapolis: Hackett, 2002); and Bryan W. Van Norden, *Virtue Ethics and Consequentialism in Early Chinese Philosophy*, 199–314 (Ch. 4).

20. *Mengzi* 2A6 and 6A6. One could also interpret Mengzi as saying that there is one moral sense which manifests itself in four different ways. For this interpretation, see Liu Xiusheng, *Mencius, Hume, and the Foundations of Ethics* (Burlington, Vt.: Ashgate Publishing, 2003).

21. Mengzi 2A6, trans. Bryan W. Van Norden, "Mengzi (Mencius)" in *Readings in Classical Chinese Philosophy, Second Edition*, 130.

22. Ivanhoe, *Confucian Moral Self Cultivation*, 18; 25 n. 16.

23. Ibid., 25 n. 17.

24. Ibid., 19.

25. Mengzi 6A15, trans. Ivanhoe, in *Confucian Moral Self Cultivation*, 20.

26. Mengzi 6A7, trans. Van Norden, in *Readings in Classical Chinese Philosophy, Second Edition*, 148.

27. Mengzi 6A8, ibid., 149.

28. On the idea of "moral blindness" in Xunzi's thought, see Ivanhoe, *Confucian Moral Self Cultivation*, 32. The passages in which Xunzi outlines his view are quoted and discussed below.

29. Ibid., 29–32. See especially the beginning of Ch. 1 of the *Xunzi*.

30. *Xunzi*, trans. Eric L. Hutton, in *Readings in Classical Chinese Philosophy, Second Edition*, 256 (Ch. 1).

31. Ibid., 300 (Ch. 23).

32. Ivanhoe, *Confucian Moral Self Cultivation*, 33.

33. Xunzi (Ch. 1), my translation.

34. *Analects* 2.15 says, "Learning without reflection is a waste. Reflection without learning is a danger," while in 15.30 Kongzi says he once engaged in

reflection for an entire day without eating and an entire night without sleeping, ". . . but it did no good. It would have been better for me to have spent that time in learning."

35. What I am calling "Xunzi's Dilemma" was first pointed out by David S. Nivison in "Xunzi on 'Human Nature,'" in Nivison's *The Ways of Confucianism*, ed. Bryan W. Van Norden (Chicago: Open Court Press, 1996), 203–13. This set of issues is further analyzed by Bryan W. Van Norden in "Mengzi and Xunzi: Two Views of Human Agency," David Wong in "Xunzi on Moral Motivation," and T. C. Kline III in "Moral Agency and Motivation in the *Xunzi*," all in T. C. Kline III and Philip J. Ivanhoe, eds., *Virtue, Nature, and Moral Agency in the Xunzi* (Indianapolis: Hackett, 2000).

36. Trans. Hutton, *Readings in Classical Chinese Philosophy, Second Edition*, 298 (Ch. 23). For a comparison of Xunzi's view with that of Hobbes, see Eric Schwitzgebel, "Human Nature and Moral Development in Mencius, Xunzi, Hobbes, and Rousseau," *History of Philosophy Quarterly* 24 (2007), 147–68.

37. Ibid., 299 (Ch. 23).

38. Ibid. Although Xunzi maintains that the sage-kings are different from the common people (something I discuss below), he also claims in Ch. 23 that the people in the streets can all become like the sage-king Yu.

39. Ibid., 274 (Ch. 18).

40. Ibid., 300 (Ch. 23).

41. Ibid., 298 (Ch. 23), italics mine. As a number of leading interpreters of Xunzi have shown, there are resources in Xunzi's thought for developing an understanding of how the sages might have created the rituals and standards of righteousness. David S. Nivison has argued that we might take Xunzi's comments about the accumulated efforts of the sage as implying that "the 'manufacture' of 'rites and norms' *takes time*." As a result, perhaps Xunzi "does not need to have an 'individual genius' concept of 'sagehood'; the development of institutions under the fashioning hand of the sages may well take ages." Nivison adds, though, that although he thinks Xunzi's language "reveals this way of looking at the origin of 'rites and norms,' . . . Xunzi never develops this idea of historical process as a part of his philosophy." (David S. Nivison, "Critique of David B. Wong 'Xunzi on Moral Motivation,'" in Philip J. Ivanhoe, ed., *Chinese Language, Thought, and Culture: Nivison and His Critics* [Chicago: Open Court Press, 1996], 328–29.) T. C. Kline III has argued that on Xunzi's view, one means by which the sages came to have knowledge of the Way was by looking to the patterns and processes of the cosmos, as well as the behavior of humans and animals. By using their natural cognitive ability to perceive these patterns and fashion rituals and standards, over time they brought the human and natural orders into harmony with

each other. (T. C. Kline III, "Moral Agency and Motivation in the *Xunzi*," in *Virtue, Nature, and Moral Agency in the Xunzi*, 164–67.)

42. For example, Bryan W. Van Norden argues that on Xunzi's view, people were motivated because, as Xunzi argues, the Way is profitable and we would be worse off without it. Van Norden argues that people must have recognized this fact, and he goes on to argue that they were able to commit themselves to the path of self-cultivation by overriding their desires through "approval," which is the first step in self-cultivation, for Xunzi (Van Norden, "Mengzi and Xunzi," 121, 127–28). David Wong argues that there are significant difficulties with Van Norden's solution, and that from the standpoint of moral psychology Xunzi has serious problems explaining how we achieve virtue from a "self-seeking" nature. These problems lead him to suggest a reconstruction of Xunzi's theory that moves it closer to Mengzi's view (Wong, "Xunzi on Moral Motivation," 135–54). In addition, T. C. Kline III and Wong both suggest that the influence of rulers' *de* ("moral charisma," "Virtue") plays a key role in motivating people to take up the task of self-cultivation (Kline, "Moral Agency and Motivation in the Xunzi," 168–70, and Wong, "Xunzi on Moral Motivation," 136–37).

43. Indeed, the dilemma is not that there is no possible solution but that the various potential solutions appear to require Xunzi to change certain fundamental aspects of his view of human nature and moral psychology. Ivanhoe suggests calling this type of challenge a "dilemma" instead of a "paradox" partly because "paradox" implies that there is no solution to the challenge. See his discussion of Xunzi's dilemma and other similar dilemmas in early Chinese philosophy in his "The Paradox of Wuwei?" *Journal of Chinese Philosophy* 34.2 (2007), 277–87. For a detailed discussion of the possibility that Xunzi does not present a wholly consistent account of human nature, see Eric L. Hutton, "Does Xunzi Have a Consistent Theory of Human Nature?" in Kline and Ivanhoe, eds., *Virtue, Nature, and Moral Agency in the Xunzi*, pp. 220–36.

44. Such a view sees Xunzi's account as resembling, at least in certain respects, something like a Hobbesian view of moral psychology. For discussions of important differences between Xunzi and Hobbes on moral psychology and the difficulties they pose for resolving Xunzi's dilemma in this way, see Van Norden, "Mengzi and Xunzi," 121–22, and Wong, "Xunzi on Moral Motivation," 136–38. For a discussion of these aspects of Xunzi's thought, see also Ivanhoe, *Confucian Moral Self Cultivation*, 29–42.

45. For an account of this sort of view, see Wong, "Xunzi on Moral Motivation."

46. These questions include how, exactly, one might account for the abnormality of the sages in light of Xunzi's view that moral capacities are not in

any way genetic or inborn. Such a claim would seem to require a substantial modification of his view, if he were to maintain that the sages were human. As noted earlier, Nivison argues that one could account for the sages' extraordinary accomplishments by arguing that many different sages completed this work over a long period of time. Although I think Nivison is correct in noting that one need not see the sages as moral geniuses on such a view, I think it is difficult to defend the view that the sages possessed the same bad nature as other humans in light of the remarkable difference between what they did and what others failed to do, according to Xunzi's account. The fact that the sages hated the chaos and worked toward a moral solution clearly distinguishes them from other people, regardless of how long it took and how many sages participated in the process.

47. I thank Daniel Bell and Steve Angle for pressing me on the question of how and in what ways this set of issues represents a dilemma for Xunzi.

48. Mengzi 4A27, trans. Van Norden, in *Readings in Classical Chinese Philosophy, Second Edition*, 139. Xunzi, too, thinks our enjoyment in practicing the virtues increases the more the capacity is realized.

49. Mengzi 2A2, ibid., 127.

50. Wong, "Xunzi on Moral Motivation," 147.

51. For an examination of the importance of self-cultivation in a range of different philosophers, see Brad K. Wilburn, ed., *Moral Cultivation: Essays on the Development of Character and Virtue* (Lanham, Md.: Lexington Books, 2007).

52. For recent discussions of this aspect of Confucian thought, see Bryan W. Van Norden, *Virtue Ethics and Consequentialism in Early Chinese Philosophy*, 358, and Daniel A. Bell, *Beyond Liberal Democracy*, 145, 150, 253.

53. For a discussion of virtue ethical interpretations of Confucianism as well as dissenting views, see Chapter 1.

54. For a full account of this view, see my "The Way, the Right, and the Good," *Journal of Religious Ethics* 37.1 (2009), 107–29.

55. An example of this sort of view is seen in Book One of the *Mengzi*. Mengzi argues to King Hui that if one achieves good ends but achieves them at the expense of others, then one will never enjoy them as much as one could.

56. Samuel Scheffler calls this a holistic view of distributive justice. See his "Rawls and Utilitarianism" in *The Cambridge Companion to Rawls*, 445.

5. THE CONTEMPORARY RELEVANCE OF A SENSE OF JUSTICE

1. See Lee H. Yearley, "Confucianism and Genre: Presentation and Persuasion in Early Confucian Thought," *Journal of Ecumenical Studies* 40:1–2 (Winter–Spring 2003), 140. While the first two criteria are explicitly dis-

cussed by Yearley, Van Norden maintains that the third criterion is implicit in Yearley's account. Van Norden, *Virtue Ethics and Consequentialism in Early Chinese Philosophy* (New York: Cambridge University Press, 2007), 323.

2. Van Norden, *Virtue Ethics and Consequentialism*, 323.

3. Ibid. There is an important connection between Yearley's appropriateness criterion and my discussion of interpretive issues in comparative work in Chapter 1. In both cases, if one is to argue that a particular text or thinker either has relevance in a contemporary setting or can be fruitfully compared with another text, one's argument needs to be based on a defensible interpretation of the text or thinker under study. If one interprets the text or thinker in ways that are unrecognizable to others without a compelling defense of that interpretation, then one will not succeed in convincing others of the contemporary relevance or comparative potential of that text or thinker, for it will appear that one is presenting an argument for the contemporary relevance or comparative potential of something other than the text or thinker in question.

4. Ibid.

5. Daniel A. Bell, *Beyond Liberal Democracy: Political Thinking for an East Asian Context* (Princeton, N.J.: Princeton University Press, 2006), 18–19.

6. Ibid., 19.

7. Philip J. Ivanhoe, "'Heaven's Mandate' and the Concept of War in Early Confucianism," in Sohail H. Hashimi and Steven P. Lee, eds., *Ethics and Weapons of Mass Destruction: Religious and Secular Perspectives* (Cambridge: Cambridge University Press, 2004), 275.

8. Ibid., 276.

9. Interestingly, there are significant challenges in both the United States and China today regarding the treatment of migrant workers. Despite obvious and important differences between the circumstances of foreign migrant workers (primarily from Mexico) in the United States and migrant workers from rural parts of China who migrate to urban centers for work, successful resolution of the difficulties (both legal and social) in both countries will likely depend in part upon the ability of U.S. and Chinese citizens to work at understanding what it might be like to be in the shoes of a migrant worker. As I discuss below and as we will see again later in this chapter, exercising one's capacity for sympathetic understanding is an important part of what it means to have a sense of justice. For an essay that addresses some of these issues, see Qianfang Zhang, "Humanity or Benevolence? The Interpretation of Confucian Ren and Its Modern Implications," in Kam-Por Yu, Julia Tao, and Philip J. Ivanhoe, eds., *Taking Confucian Ethics Seriously* (Albany: SUNY Press, 2010), 53–72.

10. Some feminist discussions and critiques of Rawls have raised this point, particularly in relation to care ethics and feminist concerns. Carol Gilligan's work has, of course, played a pivotal role in shaping these discussions, as has the work of Susan Moller Okin. See Gilligan, *In a Different Voice: Psychological Theory and Women's Development* (Cambridge, Mass.: Harvard University Press, 1987); Okin, *Justice, Gender, and the Family* (New York: Basic Books, 1989); Marilyn Friedman, *What Are Friends For? Feminist Perspectives on Personal Relationships and Moral Theory* (Ithaca, N.Y.: Cornell University Press, 1993); and Virginia Held, *Feminist Morality: Transforming Culture, Society, and Politics* (Chicago: University of Chicago Press, 1993).

11. Martin L. Hoffman, *Empathy and Moral Development: Implications for Caring and Justice* (Cambridge: Cambridge University Press, 2000), 143. For an account that relates Hoffman's research to Neo-Confucian thought, see Stephen C. Angle, *Sagehood: The Contemporary Significance of Neo-Confucian Philosophy* (New York: Oxford University Press, 2009), 138–39.

12. See for example *Analects* 1.2.

13. Philip J. Ivanhoe, *Ethics in the Confucian Tradition: The Thought of Mengzi and Wang Yangming, Second Edition* (Indianapolis: Hackett, 2002), 3.

14. Mengzi 4A11, trans. Bryan W. Van Norden, in Philip J. Ivanhoe and Bryan W. Van Norden, eds. *Readings in Classical Chinese Philosophy, Second Edition* (Indianapolis: Hackett, 2005), 138. Unless otherwise noted, all subsequent translations from the *Mengzi* follow Van Norden and are cited by passage and page number in *Readings*. For Van Norden's full translation of the *Mengzi*, including a helpful introduction to Mengzi's thought and selections from traditional commentaries, see his *Mengzi: With Selections from Traditional Commentaries* (Indianapolis: Hackett, 2008).

15. The popularity of Greg Mortenson and David Oliver Relin's *Three Cups of Tea: One Man's Mission to Promote Peace . . . One School at a Time* (New York: Penguin Books, 2007) is an example. Tracy Kidder's *Mountains Beyond Mountains: The Quest of Dr. Paul Farmer, a Man Who Would Cure the World* (New York: Random House, 2003) in particular includes examples of the way in which humanitarian work can be a source of deeply felt tension between seeking the greater good and caring for one's own family. My intention is not to minimize the importance of the truly admirable work of such individuals. My aim here is simply to point out the kinds of individuals who are widely seen as a source of moral inspiration and to suggest that it tells us something important about the views of morality found in Western liberal societies today. It is worth noting that it is not impossible to find these types of exemplars in ancient China, either. Sage-king Yu, who was highly regarded by both the early Confucians and Mohists, left his family for several years

in order to work to stop the floods that had killed large numbers of people. Although his actions certainly promoted the best outcome for the greatest number and were seen as warranted, Confucians texts still emphasize the toll it took on his family. (See, for example, the biography of Tu Shan, Yu's wife, in the *Lienuzhuan*.) Although Confucians certainly admired individuals who made sacrifices for the greater good—which they tended to understand as expressions of humaneness—they also reserved deep admiration for good parents and children, and this is why many stories of good mothers, fathers, sons, and daughters are widely considered a source of inspiration throughout East Asia, even today. The story of Mengzi's mother is one example. There are relatively few well-known stories of this sort in American culture, by comparison.

16. Mengzi 4A5, pp. 152–53.

17. For an insightful discussion of how Confucian views of the relationship between the family and society differ from the classic liberal Western distinction between the private and public realms, see Pauline C. Lee, "Li Zhi and John Stuart Mill: A Confucian Feminist Critique of Liberal Feminism," in Chenyang Li, ed., *The Sage and the Second Sex: Confucianism, Ethics, and Gender* (Chicago: Open Court Press, 2000), 113–32.

18. See Rima Shore, *Rethinking the Brain: New Insights into Early Development, Executive Summary* (New York: Families and Work Institute, 1997); David Olds, Peggy Hill, JoAnn Robinson et al., "Update on Home Visiting for Pregnant Women and Parents of Young Children," *Current Problems in Pediatrics* 30 (2000), 109; David Olds, "Prenatal and Infancy Home Visiting by Nurses: Randomized Trials to Community Replication," *Prevention Science* 3.3 (2002), 153.

19. Olds et al., "Update on Home Visiting," 110. For studies of early-childhood interventions, see Lynn A. Karoly et al., *Investing in Our Children: What We Know and Don't Know About the Costs and Benefits of Early Childhood Interventions* (Santa Monica, Calif.: The RAND Corporation, 1998), and Lynn A. Karoly, M. Rebecca Kilburn, and Jill S. Cannon, *Early Childhood Interventions: Proven Results, Future Promise* (Santa Monica, Calif.: The RAND Corporation, 2005).

20. Olds et al., "Update on Home Visiting," 109, 115. The program was previously known as the Nurse Home Visitor Program.

21. David L. Olds, "The Nurse-Family Partnership: An Evidence-based Preventive Intervention," *Infant Mental Health Journal* 27.1 (2006), 11–13.

22. Ibid., 21.

23. Ibid., 5. For a sampling of the published results of the NFP, see David L. Olds, Charles R. Henderson Jr., and Harriet Kitzman, "Does Prenatal and Infancy Nurse Home Visitation Have Enduring Effects on Qualities of

Parental Caregiving and Child Health at 25 to 50 Months of Life?" *Pediatrics* 93.1 (1994), 89–98; David Olds, Harriet Kitzman, Robert Cole et al., "Theoretical Foundations of a Program of Home Visitation for Pregnant Women and Parents of Young Children," *Journal of Community Psychology* 25.1 (1997): 9–25; David Olds, Charles R. Henderson Jr., Robert Cole et al., "Long-term Effects of Nurse Home Visitation on Children's Criminal and Antisocial Behavior: 15-Year Follow-up of a Randomized Controlled Trial," *Journal of the American Medical Association* 280.14 (1998), 1238–44; Harriet Kitzman, David L. Olds, Kimberly Sidora et al., "Enduring Effects of Nurse Home Visitation on Maternal Life Course: A 3-Year Follow-up of a Randomized Trial," *Journal of the American Medical Association* 283.15 (2000), 1983–89.

24. Olds, Henderson, and Kitzman, "Does Prenatal and Infancy Nurse Home Visitation Have Enduring Effects on Qualities of Parental Caregiving and Child Health at 25 to 50 Months of Life?" 91–97; Olds, Henderson, Cole et al., "Long-term Effects of Nurse Home Visitation on Children's Criminal and Antisocial Behavior: 15-Year Follow-up of a Randomized Controlled Trial," 1241–43; Kitzman, Olds, Sidora et al., "Enduring Effects of Nurse Home Visitation on Maternal Life Course: A 3-Year Follow-up of a Randomized Trial," 1986–89.

25. Kitzman, Olds, Sidora et al., "Enduring Effects of Nurse Home Visitation on Maternal Life Course: A 3-Year Follow-up of a Randomized Trial," 1984; Olds, Henderson, Cole et al., "Long-term Effects of Nurse Home Visitation on Children's Criminal and Antisocial Behavior: 15-Year Follow-up of a Randomized Controlled Trial," 1240–43; Olds, Henderson, and Kitzman, "Does Prenatal and Infancy Nurse Home Visitation Have Enduring Effects on Qualities of Parental Caregiving and Child Health at 25 to 50 Months of Life?" 94.

26. Olds, "Prenatal and Infancy Home Visiting by Nurses," 164. See also Olds et al., "Effects of Prenatal and Infancy Nurse Home Visitation on Government Spending," *Medical Care* 31 (1993), 155–74.

27. Although Kongzi, Mengzi, and Xunzi did not devote a large share of their attention to early-childhood development, they still made a number of important points indicating their views on this issue, as we have seen. Additionally, a range of other sources associated with the early Confucian tradition support the view that the earliest years of a child's life represent a unique opportunity for moral development, including the *Record of Ritual* (*Liji*, especially Book 10, "*Neize*"), the *Discourse on the States* (*Guoyu*), *Collected Biographies of Women* (*Lienuzhuan*), and the *History of the Han* (*Hanshu*, especially Ch. 48, "*Baofu*"). These texts and the ideas they advocate played a causal role in how parents and children treated one another, and this remains true today. For a discussion of these sources in relation to my argument

concerning Confucian ethics and the NFP, see my "Confucian Ethics, Public Policy, and the Nurse-Family Partnership," *Dao* 11.3 (2012). For a helpful study of early Chinese views of childhood, see Anne Behnke Kinney, *Representations of Childhood and Youth in Early China* (Stanford, Calif.: Stanford University Press, 2004).

28. Lynn A. Karoly et al., *Investing in Our Children: What we Know and Don't Know About the Costs and Benefits of Early Childhood Interventions*, 106.

29. Olds, Kitzman, Cole et al., "Theoretical Foundations of a Program of Home Visitation for Pregnant Women and Parents of Young Children," 13; Olds, "Prenatal and Infancy Home Visiting by Nurses," 156.

30. Olds, "Prenatal and Infancy Home Visiting by Nurses," 156. Cf. Olds, "The Nurse-Family Partnership," 12. See Sara S. McLanahan and Marcia J. Carlson, "Welfare Reform, Fertility, and Father Involvement," *The Future of Children*, 12, 147–66. For a helpful discussion of the impact of marriage on children, see Derek Bok, *The Politics of Happiness: What Government Can Learn from the New Research on Well-Being* (Princeton, N.J.: Princeton University Press, 2010), 139–48. The NFP specifies that the quality of the possible relationship and risk for domestic violence be carefully considered in relation to whether the father or other prospective partner can be a good spouse and positive caregiver. See Olds, "The Nurse-Family Partnership," 12–13.

31. Olds et al., "Theoretical Foundations of a Program of Home Visitation for Pregnant Women and Parents of Young Children," 13.

32. For many traditional Western virtue ethicists, the family and state are important *in order to enable* the flourishing of individuals, whereas good families and states partly *constitute* Confucian conceptions of human flourishing. One way of understanding this difference is to see it as an expression of different conceptions of what constitutes the self.

33. Olds et al., "Theoretical Foundations of a Program of Home Visitation," 20.

34. Ibid., 19–20.

35. Studies of care ethics offer a range of important insights here. Nel Noddings has argued for a conception of caring that sees a relational sense of caring as underlying and giving meaning to caring as a virtue. See for example her "Caring as Relation and Virtue in Teaching" in Rebecca L. Walker and Philip J. Ivanhoe, eds., *Working Virtue: Virtue Ethics and Contemporary Moral Problems* (New York: Oxford University Press, 2006). Recently Michael Slote has argued in his *Ethics of Care and Empathy* (New York: Routledge, 2007) that the use of empathy allows care ethics to develop a compelling, comprehensive account of morality.

36. The contrast between this sort of view and Confucian views has been discussed extensively by Henry Rosemont Jr. See "Whose Democracy?

Which Rights? A Confucian Critique of Modern Western Liberalism," in Kwong-loi Shun and David B. Wong, eds., *Confucian Ethics: A Comparative Study of Self, Autonomy, and Community* (New York: Cambridge University Press, 2004), 49–71.

37. This is a point made by Philip J. Ivanhoe. For an insightful discussion of this issue that gives attention to both Western and Confucian perspectives, see his "A Confucian Perspective on Abortion," *Dao* IX.1 (Spring, 2010), 37–51.

38. Olds, "The Nurse-Family Partnership: An Evidence-Based Preventive Intervention," 12.

39. For a discussion of this aspect of the NFP, see the discussion of behavioral change in Olds, Kitzman, Cole et al., "Theoretical Foundations of a Program of Home Visitation for Pregnant Women and Parents of Young Children," especially 11–17.

40. Olds, "Update on Home Visiting," 110, 139.

41. See Owen Flanagan's "minimal psychological realism" condition, discussed in his *Varieties of Moral Personality: Ethics and Psychological Realism* (Cambridge, Mass.: Harvard University Press, 1991).

42. Derek Bok has pointed out that deep and sustained relationships between parents, and between parents and children, are one of the greatest factors influencing happiness. This evidence clearly supports the view that a government which wishes to help facilitate happiness in its citizens should support the formation and maintenance of families. See Derek Bok, *The Politics of Happiness: What Government Can Learn from the New Research on Well-Being*, 139–55.

43. An appeal to necessity in this sort of case may be motivated in part by a desire to avoid the force of the evidence, which may not square easily with certain liberal moral values, beliefs, and attitudes. But philosophical fallibilists and naturalists ought to be willing to revise their values, beliefs, and attitudes in order to bring them in line with our best science—even if this means moving in a more "communitarian" direction.

44. This is a neglected area of study, particularly compared with the extensive literature on good physicians. For two works focused on the qualities associated with good nurses, see Helga Kuhse, *Caring: Nurses, Women and Ethics* (Oxford: Blackwell Publishers, 1997), and Derek Sellman, *What Makes a Good Nurse: Why the Virtues Are Important for Nurses* (London: Jessica Kingsley Publishing, 2011).

45. Olds et al., "Home Visiting by Paraprofessionals and by Nurses: A Randomized, Controlled Trial," *Pediatrics* 110 (2002), 486–96.

46. Olds et al., "Home Visiting by Paraprofessionals and by Nurses," 486, 494; Olds et al., "Update on Home Visiting," 136.

47. Olds, "The Nurse-Family Partnership," 15; Olds et al., "Home Visiting by Paraprofessionals and by Nurses," 494. The NFP cites the Gallup organization, "Nurses Remain at Top of Honesty and Ethics Poll," November 27, 2000.

48. In *The Politics of Happiness*, Bok offers good support for this kind of argument, including a discussion of studies that provide compelling evidence for this type of claim.

49. See for example Nel Noddings, *Starting at Home: Caring and Social Policy* (Berkeley: University of California Press, 2002).

50. It is beyond the scope of this work to show precisely how these aspects of early Confucian views differ from the views that particular Western thinkers have advanced about the family and parent–child relationships, because the argument that specific views are different—or the argument that they are exactly the same—requires a detailed comparative study of the thinkers in question. However, anyone who engages in careful, sustained study of the Western and Chinese philosophical traditions will, I think, be struck by the distinctiveness of these features of Confucianism. Even in the midst of shared concerns and ideas there remain genuine differences between Confucian views and the views of Western philosophers (just as there remains genuine diversity *within* the Confucian and Western philosophical traditions). My aim here is to highlight some of the specific ways in which early Confucian views can, at least in some cases, make novel contributions to our consideration of contemporary moral problems.

51. Karoly et al., *Investing in Our Children*, 108.

52. Most other Western societies do much better on this count, and one thing the Confucian view might do is prompt us to look more closely at such policies and their benefits. The United States is unusual worldwide because it does not mandate paid parental leave, and it is unusual among Western countries (especially European countries) because of the short duration of parental leave. For example, the U.K. provides thirty-nine weeks of paid leave for mothers; Sweden provides sixteen months of paid leave, which is available to both mothers and fathers. These examples are important because they show how liberal democracies can do much better on these policies. I would like to stress here that I am *not* arguing that we should model all of our public policies after those of East Asian countries; rather, I am arguing that we have good reasons to think that the early Confucians were right about the formative nature of the early interactions between parents and children, and that as a result we have good reasons to invest more of our resources at this level. We should look for examples of how to do this in a range of different societies, and with respect to parental leave policies (including both the length of leave and the availability of paternal leave in addition to maternal leave),

European countries tend to do better than East Asian countries. Cultural factors in some East Asian countries help to account for this difference (such as the expectation that grandparents will provide in-home care for infants and children in China).

53. Van Norden, *Virtue Ethics and Consequentialism*, 337. It may, of course, require more than minimal virtue. This point has been stressed by communitarians.

54. Ibid., 336.

55. Ibid.

56. For discussions of some of the relevant issues relating to ethnic minorities in China, see Jule Teufel Dreyer, *China's Forty Millions: Minority Nationalities and National Integration in the People's Republic of China* (Cambridge, Mass.: Harvard University Press, 1976); Colin Mackerras, *China's Minorities: Integration and Modernization in the Twentieth-Century* (Hong Kong: Oxford University Press, 1994); Dru C. Gladney, "Ethnic Identity in China: The Rising Politics of Cultural Difference," in Susan J. Henders, ed., *Democratization and Identity: Regimes and Ethnicity in East and Southeast Asia* (Lanham, Md.: Lexington Books, 2004); He Baogang, "Minority Rights with Chinese Characteristics," in Will Kymlicka and He Baogang, eds., *Multiculturalism in Asia* (Oxford: Oxford University Press, 2005).

57. There is a basis for this type of reflection in the teaching 溫故而知新 ("Be thoroughly versed in the old, yet understand the new . . . ."), from *Analects* 2.11.

58. See for example C. S. Dweck, *Self-theories* (Philadelphia: Psychology Press, 1999); H. W. Stevenson and J. W. Stigler, *The Learning Gap* (New York: Simon and Schuster, 1992); R. G. Tweed and D. R. Lehman, "Learning Considered Within a Cultural Context: Confucian and Socratic Approaches," *American Psychologist* 57 (2002), 89–99.

59. Jin Li, "U.S. and Chinese Cultural Beliefs About Learning," *Journal of Educational Psychology* 95.2 (2003), 265. For an insightful book-length study of these and a variety of other fascinating issues, see Jin Li, *Cultural Foundations of Learning: East and West* (New York: Cambridge University Press, 2012).

60. Ibid., 261–62.

61. Jin Li, "Learning as a Task or a Virtue: U.S. and Chinese Preschoolers Explain Learning," *Developmental Psychology* 40.4 (2004), 600–2.

62. Ibid., 596. See also Jin Li, "A Cultural Model of Learning: Chinese 'Heart and Mind for Wanting to Learn,'" *Journal of Cross-Cultural Psychology* 33 (2002), 246–67.

63. In saying that this is a shared feature of self-cultivation I mean that even among Confucian thinkers who maintain that our nature is fundamentally good, we must work hard in order to extend, discover, or uncover our

original goodness. So even in these thinkers, being a cultivated person is an achievement because one's true nature requires further development or has been obscured in some way. For an insightful study of some of the most influential accounts of human nature and self-cultivation in the Confucian tradition, see Ivanhoe, *Confucian Moral Self Cultivation, Second Edition* (Indianapolis: Hackett, 2000).

64. Li, "U.S. and Chinese Cultural Beliefs About Learning," 263–64.

65. Li, "Learning as a Task or a Virtue: U.S. and Chinese Preschoolers Explain Learning," 600.

66. Li, "U.S. and Chinese Cultural Beliefs About Learning," 265. For further studies that show the importance of self-cultivation in Chinese views of learning, see A.-B. Yu, "Ultimate Life Concerns, Self, and Chinese Achievement Motivation," in M. Bond, ed., *The Handbook of Chinese Psychology* (Hong Kong: Oxford University Press, 1996), 227–46; Jin Li, "Chinese Conceptualization of Learning," *Ethos* 29 (2001), 111–37; Jin Li, "A Cultural Model of Learning: Chinese 'Heart and Mind for Wanting to Learn,'" *Journal of Cross-Cultural Psychology* 33 (2002), 246–67.

67. Trans. Edward Slingerland, *Confucius Analects* (Indianapolis: Hackett, 2003), 3. Subsequent translations from the *Analects* follow Slingerland unless otherwise specified.

68. For a helpful overview of the complexities surrounding the situation of migrant workers in China, see Bell, *Beyond Liberal Democracy*, 313–21. As Bell points out, the best way to improve the well-being of migrant workers is likely not complete abolishment of the *hukou* but significant reforms that increase wages and provide guarantees for such things as health insurance and work accident insurance. See also his discussion of how common rituals involving managers or bosses can help to improve the social standing of migrant workers in his *China's New Confucianism*, 50. Bell's remarks help to underscore the fact that social as well as legal changes are needed in order to address the plight of migrant workers and that social change can (and should) occur at a variety of different levels and in ways that draw upon existing cultural resources for addressing social injustice.

69. There is an interesting parallel here with the way in which some U.S. citizens view migrant workers from Mexico. For a discussion of the plight of migrant workers in China, see Dorothy J. Solinger, "Human Rights Issues in China's Internal Migration: Insights from Comparisons with Germany and Japan," in Joanne R. Bauer and Daniel A. Bell, eds., *The East Asian Challenge for Human Rights* (New York: Cambridge University Press, 1999), and Tan Shen, "Rural Workforce Migration: A Summary of Some Studies," *Social Sciences in China* (Winter 2003).

70. Solinger critiques the *hukou* system for precisely some of these reasons.

71. This is one example of how a sense of justice can have an important role in efforts to resolve a problem where a liberal policy solution based on liberal principles of justice might have a negative impact. Bell argues that securing access to permanent residency rights for migrant workers would be counterproductive for a variety of reasons, including the fact that it would likely result in further migration from the countryside, more competition for jobs among migrant workers, and a resultant decrease in their salaries. In this case, then, "the good intentions of liberals would harm the very constituency they are supposed to be helping" (Bell, *Beyond Liberal Democracy*, 320).

72. Van Norden, *Virtue Ethics and Consequentialism*, 317.

73. Ibid., 357.

74. Martha Nussbaum has written extensively on the value of studying other cultures. See for example her *Cultivating Humanity: A Classical Defense of Reform in Liberal Education* (Cambridge, Mass.: Harvard University Press, 1997). See also her discussion of the value of cosmopolitanism (as well as critical responses and Nussbaum's replies) in her *For Love of Country?* ed. Joshua Cohen (Boston: Beacon Press, 2002).

75. My translation.

76. I follow Burton Watson's translation here. See his *Analects of Confucius* (New York: Columbia University Press, 2007), 32–33.

77. Philip J. Ivanhoe, "Pluralism, Toleration, and Ethical Promiscuity," *Journal of Religious Ethics* 37.2, 311–29.

78. For contemporary perspectives on tolerance, see David Heyd, ed., *Toleration: An Elusive Virtue* (Princeton, N.J.: Princeton University Press, 1996).

79. Ivanhoe, "Pluralism, Toleration, and Ethical Promiscuity," 320.

80. Ibid., 321.

81. Ibid., 314.

82. Ibid., 311.

83. Ibid., 315.

84. Ibid., 316.

85. Ibid., 317.

86. Ibid., 319.

87. Ibid., 322.

88. Van Norden, *Virtue Ethics and Consequentialism*, 341.

89. My argument is not that Kongzi or classical Confucians would accept the view I am presenting here. Rather, my focus is on developing and extending in a contemporary setting aspects of the view presented in the *Analects*.

90. Van Norden, *Virtue Ethics and Consequentialism*, 324.
91. Bell, *Beyond Liberal Democracy*, 206.
92. Ibid., 206–7.
93. Ibid., 218 n. 26.
94. Ibid.
95. Ibid.
96. Such an approach would build upon the existing interest in Confucianism among Chinese college students. Bell writes that courses on Confucianism are now among the most popular on university campuses in China and that many students come with a solid background in the Chinese classics, as well. See Daniel A. Bell, *China's New Confucianism: Politics and Everyday Life in a Changing Society* (Princeton, N.J.: Princeton University Press, 2008), 11, 136.
97. Jin Li, one of the leading researchers studying Chinese and American attitudes and beliefs about learning, has noted several reasons why we ought to take an interest in this type of cross-cultural research, including the fact that Asian children achieve higher than their Western peers, especially in math and science (Li, "Learning as a Task or a Virtue," 595). Li's research suggests that cultural attitudes and beliefs about learning are important factors in helping us to understand this difference. For studies of the achievement gap between Asian and Western children, see R. D. Hess, C.-M. Chang, and T. M. McDevitt, "Cultural Variations in Family Belief About Children's Performance in Mathematics: Comparisons Among People's Republic of China, Chinese American, and Caucasion American Families," *Journal of Educational Psychology* 79 (1987), 179–88; C. C. McKnight et al., *The Underachieving Curriculum: Assessing U.S. School Mathematics from an International Perspective* (Champaign, Ill.: Stipes, 1987); H. W. Stevenson and S. Y. Lee, "Context of Achievement," *Monographs of the Society of Research in Child Development* 55, 1–2, serial no. 221 (1990); H. W. Stevenson and J. W. Stigler, *The Learning Gap* (New York: Simon and Schuster, 1992); D. C. Kwok and H. Lytton, "Perceptions of Mathematics Ability Versus Actual Mathematics Performance: Canadian and Hong Kong Chinese Children," *British Journal of Educational Psychology* 66 (1996), 209–22; M. Harmon et al., *Performance Assessment in IEA's Third International Mathematics and Science Study* (Chestnut Hill, Mass.: Boston College, TIMSS International Study Center, 1997).
98. Although my remarks here focus specifically on the relationship between a sense of justice and international justice, a number of other studies examine related issues. For an insightful study of just war theory in the thought of the early Confucian Mengzi, including issues of contemporary relevance in relation to international justice, see Daniel A. Bell, "Just War

and Confucianism: Implications for the Contemporary World," in *Beyond Liberal Democracy*, 23–51. For a more general discussion of some issues in relation to Confucianism and international relations, see Cho-yun Hsu, "Applying Confucian Ethics in International Relations," *Ethics and International Affairs* 5 (1991). Finally, Jang Dong-jin's "A Confucian Deliberation on Rawls's Liberal Conception of International Justice," [*Sungkyun Journal of East Asian Studies* 4.1 (2004), 133–55] claims that Confucianism is "a non-liberal but decent political theory" (135, cf. 147) and appears to explore how a Confucian society might fit into Rawls's Law of Peoples. Because Jang's article deals with a different set of questions from those I examine here and does not discuss the *Analects*, and also because it regards Confucianism as representing a single, unified view on moral and political questions—a view that is substantially different from the view I defend in this work—I will not discuss it in further detail here.

99. I am indebted to Eric L. Hutton for initially raising this question in relation to my work on a sense of justice in his paper "Rawls and Confucius Revisited," presented at a panel sponsored by the Association of Chinese Philosophers in America at the 2009 Pacific Division meeting of the American Philosophical Association. His remarks have helped me to develop the ideas I discuss here.

100. While there is obviously not an understanding of "international relations" in the contemporary sense in the *Analects*, it is nevertheless important to remember that Kongzi's teachings come from a time prior to the unification of China, when there were clear borders between different states in the region now known as China. Kongzi moved from state to state trying to convince rulers to follow the Way, at a time when these various states were not infrequently at war with one another. (He lived during the time just prior to the beginning of the "Warring States Period.") These states shared a number of important features with modern nation-states, such as the fact that they each had their own government, taxation policies, and military. There was also considerable discussion of inter-state relations in classical China and an awareness of important cultural and ethnic differences between peoples, evidenced in references to tribes such as the Yi and Di, discussed below. Indeed, Benjamin Schwarz has argued that the multi-state system in ancient China resembles the emerging multi-state system of fifteenth- and sixteenth-century Europe, including "a rudimentary science of international politics and efforts to achieve collective security." See Benjamin Schwarz, "The Chinese Perception of World Order, Past and Present," in John Fairbank, ed., *The Chinese World Order: Traditional China's Foreign Relations* (Cambridge, Mass.: Harvard University Press, 1968), 278–79.

101. My translations.

102. My aim here is to describe Kongzi's view, which is an obvious contrast to the way of thinking about other ethnic, cultural, and value traditions that I examined in the previous section of this chapter (Ivanhoe's "ethical promiscuity"). That is not to say that there are not resources in the *Analects* for constructing a different position. For example, one might argue for a different understanding of what it means to embody virtues such as reverence and respectfulness in one's encounters with other cultures, based on the view that one ought to work to learn from and appreciate other cultures. But it is important to distinguish between the task of working out new understandings of Confucian texts and values, and describing the views that thinkers like Kongzi actually held.

103. Joseph Chan, "Territorial Boundaries and Confucianism," in David Miller and Sohail H. Hashmi, eds., *Boundaries and Justice* (Princeton, N.J.: Princeton University Press, 2001), 96. See *Analects* 8.18. 12.11, 14.5. For different views on how to interpret the phrase *you tianxia*, see essays by Joseph Chan and Michael Nylan in Daniel A. Bell, ed., *Confucian Political Ethics* (Princeton, N.J.: Princeton University Press, 2007).

104. Philip J. Ivanhoe, *Confucian Moral Self Cultivation, Second Edition* (Indianapolis: Hackett, 2000), ix–xvii, and "The Concept of de ('Virtue') in the Laozi," in Mark Csikszentmihalyi and Philip J. Ivanhoe, eds., *Religious and Philosophical Aspects of the Laozi* (Albany: SUNY Press, 1999). See also David S. Nivison, *The Ways of Confucianism: Investigations in Chinese Philosophy*, ed. Bryan W. Van Norden (LaSalle, Ill.: Open Court Press, 1996), 17–57.

105. Trans. Watson, *The Analects of Confucius*, 17.

106. Samuel Freeman, "Introduction," in *The Cambridge Companion to Rawls*, ed. Freeman (Cambridge: Cambridge University Press, 2002), 45. See John Rawls, *The Law of Peoples* (Cambridge, Mass.: Harvard University Press, 1999).

107. Rawls, *The Law of Peoples*, 46. Rawls understands a decent society as a nonliberal society whose basic institutions "meet certain specified conditions of political right and justice and lead its people to honor a reasonable and just law for the Society of Peoples" (Rawls, *The Law of Peoples*, 59–60). Decent peoples recognize and protect human rights, offer their members the right to be consulted or a substantial political role in making decisions and a right of dissent, and require a respectful reply to dissenters according to the rule of law as interpreted by the judiciary (61). For a detailed discussion, see *The Law of Peoples*, 62–78. For a study that appeals to understandings of decency in order to argue for the view that societies need more than justice, see Avishai Margalit, *The Decent Society*, trans. Naomi Goldblum (Cambridge, Mass.: Harvard University Press, 1996).

108. Freeman, "Introduction," 46.

109. Ibid., 47.

110. One could object here by saying that part of respect is the acknowledgment that we might find the other culture or society better than ours, all things considered. This possibility is cut off, though, by the trumping value of justice.

111. On this basis, it seems reasonable to speculate that Kongzi and Rawls would each seek to change the other's society.

112. In saying that the type of influence Rawls describes is mainly political, I mean that the primary goal seems to be getting people to commit themselves to a particular form of government and not primarily to a moral way of life. However, it is nevertheless important to recognize that a commitment to modern liberal democracy entails certain kinds of moral commitments, and this is something that many liberals tend to minimize.

113. My point here is based on Philip J. Ivanhoe's study of these three features of *de* in the *Analects* in comparison with the related but distinct conception of *de* in the *Daodejing*. See his "The Concept of *de* ("Virtue") in the *Laozi*," in Csikszentmihalyi and Ivanhoe, eds., *Religious and Philosophical Aspects of the Laozi*.

114. Ivanhoe notes that these kinds of beliefs entail "heroic metaphysical commitments."

115. *LP*, 62, italics mine.

116. In the absence of the view that respect is in some way uniquely tied to liberal institutions, it would be difficult to see *why* decent peoples would come to appreciate the appeal of liberal institutions as a result of liberal peoples' expressions of respect.

CONCLUSION

1. Susan Moller Okin, *Justice, Gender, and the Family* (New York: Basic Books, 1989). For a response to Okin's critique of Rawls, see Martha Nussbaum, "Rawls and Feminism," in *The Cambridge Companion to Rawls*, 499–507.

Alford, William P. *To Steal a Book Is an Elegant Offense: Intellectual Property Law in Chinese Civilization*. Stanford, Calif.: Stanford University Press, 1995.

Ames, Roger T. "Rites as Rights: The Confucian Alternative." In *Human Rights and the World's Religions*, ed. Leroy S. Rouner, 199–216. Notre Dame, Ind.: University of Notre Dame Press, 1988.

Ames, Roger T., and David L. Hall, trans. *Daodejing "Making This Life Significant": A Philosophical Translation*. New York: Ballantine Books, 2003.

——, trans. *Focusing the Familiar: A Translation and Philosophical Interpretation of the Zhongyong*. Honolulu: University of Hawai'i Press, 2001.

——. *Thinking Through Confucius*. Albany: SUNY Press, 1987.

Ames, Roger T., and Henry Rosemont Jr., trans. *The Analects of Confucius: A Philosophical Translation*. New York: Ballantine Books, 1998.

Angle, Stephen C. "Defining 'Virtue Ethics' and Exploring Virtues in a Comparative Context." *Dao: A Journal of Comparative Philosophy* 8:3 (2009), 298–304.

——. *Human Rights in Chinese Thought: A Cross-Cultural Inquiry*. Cambridge: Cambridge University Press, 2002.

——. *Sagehood: The Contemporary Significance of Neo-Confucian Philosophy*. New York: Oxford University Press, 2009.

Angle, Stephen C., and Maria Svensson, eds. *The Chinese Human Rights Reader*. Armonk, N.Y.: East Gate, 2001.

Aristotle. *Nichomachean Ethics*. Trans. Terence Irwin. Indianapolis: Hackett, 1985.

Baehr, Peter R., ed. *Human Rights: Chinese and Dutch Perspectives*. The Hague: Martinus Nijhoff, 1996.

Barry, Brian. "John Rawls and the Search for Stability." *Ethics* 105:4 (1995), 874–915.

Bauer, Joanne R., and Daniel A. Bell, eds. *The East Asian Challenge for Human Rights*. New York: Cambridge University Press, 1999.

Bell, Daniel A. *Beyond Liberal Democracy: Political Thinking for an East Asian Context*. Princeton, N.J.: Princeton University Press, 2006.

———. *China's New Confucianism: Politics and Everyday Life in a Changing Society*. Princeton, N.J.: Princeton University Press, 2008.

———. *East Meets West: Human Rights and Democracy in East Asia*. Princeton, N.J.: Princeton University Press, 2000.

Bell, Daniel A., ed. *Confucian Political Ethics*. Princeton, N.J.: Princeton University Press, 2007.

Bellah, Robert. *Tokugawa Religion: The Values of Pre-industrial Japan*. Glencoe, Ill.: Free Press, 1985 (originally published in 1957).

Bok, Derek. *The Politics of Happiness: What Government Can Learn from the New Research on Well-Being*. Princeton, N.J.: Princeton University Press, 2010.

Brooks, E. Bruce, and A. Taeko Brooks. *The Original Analects*. New York: Columbia University Press, 1998.

Brooks, Thom, and Fabian Freyenhagen, eds., *The Legacy of John Rawls*. London: Continuum, 2007.

Carr, Karen L., and Philip J. Ivanhoe. *The Sense of Antirationalism: The Religious Thought of Zhuangzi and Kierkegaard*. Charleston, S.C.: CreateSpace, 2010. Originally published in New York: Seven Bridges Press, 2000.

Chaffee, John W. *The Thorny Gates of Learning in Sung China*. Albany: SUNY Press, 1995.

Chan, Joseph. "A Confucian Perspective on Human Rights for Contemporary China." In *The East Asian Challenge for Human Rights*, ed. Joanne R. Bauer and Daniel A. Bell, 212–37. New York: Cambridge University Press, 1999.

———. "Territorial Boundaries and Confucianism." In *Boundaries and Justice*, ed. David Miller and Sohail H. Hashmi, 89–111. Princeton, N.J.: Princeton University Press, 2001.

Chen, Xunwu. "Justice as a Constellation of Fairness, Harmony and Righteousness." *Journal of Chinese Philosophy* 24 (1997), 497–519.

Cheng, Chung-ying. "Critical Reflections on Rawlsian Justice Versus Confucian Justice." *Journal of Chinese Philosophy* 24 (1997), 417–26.

Ching, Julia. "Human Rights: A Valid Chinese Concept?" In *Confucianism and Human Rights*, ed. Wm. Theodore de Bary and Tu Weiming, 67–82. New York: Columbia University Press, 1998.

Cline, Erin M. "Confucian Ethics, Public Policy, and the Nurse-Family Partnership." *Dao* 11.3 (2012).

———. "Nameless Virtues and Restrained Speech in the *Analects*," *International Philosophical Quarterly* 49:1, no. 193 (2009), 53–69.

———. "Rawls, Rosemont, and the Debate Over Rights and Roles." In *Polishing the Chinese Mirror: Essays in Honor of Henry Rosemont, Jr.*, ed. Ronnie L. Littlejohn and Marthe Chandler, 77–89. New York: Global Scholarly Publications, 2008.

———. "The Way, the Right, and the Good." *Journal of Religious Ethics* 37:1 (2009), 107–129.

Cooper, John M. "Political Animals and Civic Friendship." In *Friendship: A Philosophical Reader* ed. Neera Kapur Badhwar, 303–26. Ithaca, N.Y.: Cornell University Press, 1993.

Daniels, Norman. "Rawls's Complex Egalitarianism." In *The Cambridge Companion to Rawls*, ed. Samuel Freeman, 241–76. New York: Cambridge University Press, 2003.

Davis, Michael C. *Human Rights and Chinese Values: Legal, Philosophical, and Political Perspectives*. New York: Oxford University Press, 1995.

De Bary, Wm. Theodore. *Asian Values and Human Rights: A Confucian Communitarian Perspective*. Cambridge, Mass.: Harvard University Press, 1998.

———. "Neo-Confucianism and Human Rights." In *Human Rights and the World's Religions*, ed. Leroy S. Rouner, 183–98. Notre Dame, Ind.: University of Notre Dame Press, 1988.

De Bary, Wm. Theodore, and Tu Weiming. *Confucianism and Human Rights*. New York: Columbia University Press, 1998.

Decosimo, David. "The Ubiquity of Resemblance." *Journal of the American Academy of Religion* 78:1 (2010), 226–58.

Deigh, John. *The Sources of Moral Agency: Essays in Moral Psychology and Freudian Theory*. New York: Cambridge University Press, 1996.

DeLue, Steven M. "Aristotle, Kant and Rawls on Moral Motivation in a Just Society." *The American Political Science Review* 24:2 (1980), 385–93.

Donnelly, Jack. "Human Rights and Asian Values: A Defense of 'Western' Universalism." In *The East Asian Challenge for Human Rights*, ed. Joanne R. Bauer and Daniel A. Bell, 60–87. New York: Cambridge University Press, 1999.

Dreyer, Jule Teufel. *China's Forty Millions: Minority Nationalities and National Integration in the People's Republic of China*. Cambridge, Mass.: Harvard University Press, 1976.

Du, Ganjian, and Song Gang. "Relating Human Rights to Chinese Culture: The Four Paths of the Confucian Analects and the Four Principles of a New Theory of Benevolence." In *Human Rights and Chinese Values: Legal, Philosophical, and Political Perspectives*, ed. Michael C. Davis, 35–56. New York: Oxford University Press, 1995.

Dweck, C. S. *Self-theories*. Philadelphia: Psychology Press, 1999.

Edwards, R. Randle, Louis Henkin, and Andrew J. Nathan, eds. *Human Rights in Contemporary China*. New York: Columbia University Press, 1986.

Elman, Benjamin A. *A Cultural History of Civil Examinations in Late Imperial China*. Berkeley: University of California Press, 2000.

Fan, Ruiping. "Social Justice: Rawlsian or Confucian?" In *Comparative Approaches to Chinese Philosophy*, ed. Bo Mou, 144–68. Hampshire, U.K.: Ashgate Publishing, 2003.

Flanagan, Owen. *Varieties of Moral Personality: Ethics and Psychological Realism.*
  Cambridge, Mass.: Harvard University Press, 1991.

Fox, Alan. "The Aesthetics of Justice." *Legal Studies Forum* 19:1 (1995), 44.

Freeman, Samuel, ed. *The Cambridge Companion to Rawls.* New York: Cambridge University Press, 2003.

———. "Congruence and the Good of Justice." In *The Cambridge Companion
  to Rawls*, ed. Samuel Freeman, 277–315. New York: Cambridge University
  Press, 2003.

———. *Rawls.* New York: Routledge, 2007.

Friedman, Marilyn. *What Are Friends For? Feminist Perspectives on Personal Relationships and Moral Theory.* Ithaca, N.Y.: Cornell University
  Press, 1993.

Gardner, Daniel K., trans., *Chu Hsi: Learning to Be a Sage.* Berkeley: University of California Press, 1990.

Geertz, Clifford. *The Interpretation of Cultures.* New York: Basic Books, 1973.

Gilligan, Carol. *In a Different Voice: Psychological Theory and Women's Development.* Cambridge, Mass.: Harvard University Press, 1987.

Gladney, Dru C. "Ethnic Identity in China: The Rising Politics of Cultural
  Difference." In *Democratization and Identity: Regimes and Ethnicity in East
  and Southeast Asia*, ed. Susan J. Henders, 133–51. Lanham, Md.: Lexington Books, 2004.

Graham, A. C. "The Background of the Mencian Theory of Human Nature."
  Tsing Hua *Journal of Chinese Studies* 6.1–2 (1967), 215–74. Reprinted
  in Studies in Chinese Philosophy and Philosophical Literature. Albany:
  SUNY Press, 1990.

———. *Disputers of the Tao.* LaSalle, Ill.: Open Court Press, 1989.

Hahm, Chaihark, and Daniel A. Bell, eds., *The Politics of Affective Relations.*
  Lanham, Md.: Lexington Books, 2004.

Haldane, John. "The Individual, the State, and the Common Good." *Social
  Philosophy and Policy* 13 (1996), 59–79.

Hall, David L., and Roger T. Ames. *The Democracy of the Dead: Dewey,
  Confucius, and the Hope for Democracy in China.* Chicago: Open Court
  Press, 1999.

Harmon, M., et al., *Performance Assessment in IEA's Third International Mathematics and Science Study.* Chestnut Hill, Mass.: Boston College, TIMSS
  International Study Center, 1997.

He Baogang. "Minority Rights with Chinese Characteristics." In *Multiculturalism in Asia*, ed. Will Kymlicka and He Baogang, 56–79. Oxford: Oxford
  University Press, 2005.

He Yan 何晏. *Lun yu ji jie* 論語集解. *Zhong yong shuo can ben [Zhang Jiucheng].
  Lun yu ji jie [He Yan ji jie]*, et. al. (compilation). Taibei: Taiwan shang wu
  yin shu guan, 1981.

Hedrick, Todd. *Rawls and Habermas: Reason, Pluralism, and the Claims of Political Philosophy*. Stanford, Calif.: Stanford University Press, 2010.

Held, Virginia. *Feminist Morality: Transforming Culture, Society, and Politics*. Chicago: University of Chicago Press, 1993.

Hess, R. D., et al. "Cultural Variations in Family Belief About Children's Performance in Mathematics: Comparisons Among People's Republic of China, Chinese American, and Caucasion American Families." *Journal of Educational Psychology* 79 (1987), 179–88.

Heyd, David, ed. *Toleration: An Elusive Virtue*. Princeton, N.J.: Princeton University Press, 1996.

Hoffman, Martin L. *Empathy and Moral Development: Implications for Caring and Justice*. Cambridge: Cambridge University Press, 2000.

Hsu, Cho-yun. "Applying Confucian Ethics in International Relations." *Ethics and International Affairs* 5 (1991), 15–31.

Hutton, Eric L. "Does Xunzi Have a Consistent Theory of Human Nature?" In *Virtue, Nature, and Moral Agency in the Xunzi*, ed. T.C. Kline III and Philip J. Ivanhoe, 220–36. Indianapolis: Hackett, 2000.

———. "Han Feizi's Criticism of Confucianism and Its Implications for Virtue Ethics." *Journal of Moral Philosophy* 5 (2008), 423–53.

Hutton, Eric L., trans. "Xunzi." In *Readings in Classical Chinese Philosophy*, Second Edition, ed. Philip J. Ivanhoe and Bryan W. Van Norden, 255–309. Indianapolis, Ind.: Hackett, 2005.

Ivanhoe, Philip J. "The Concept of de ('Virtue') in the Laozi." In *Religious and Philosophical Aspects of the Laozi*, ed. Mark Csikszentmihalyi and Philip J. Ivanhoe, 239–57. Albany: SUNY Press, 1999.

———. *Confucian Moral Self Cultivation*, Second Edition. Indianapolis: Hackett, 2000.

———. "A Confucian Perspective on Abortion." *Dao* IX:1 (Spring, 2010), 37–51.

———. "Confucian Self Cultivation and Mengzi's Notion of Extension." In *Essays on the Moral Philosophy of Mengzi*, ed. Xiusheng Liu and Philip J. Ivanhoe, 221–41. Indianapolis: Hackett, 2002.

———. *Ethics in the Confucian Tradition: The Thought of Mengzi and Wang Yangming*, Revised Second Edition. Indianapolis: Hackett, 2002.

———. "Filial Piety as a Virtue." In *Working Virtue: Virtue Ethics and Contemporary Moral Problems*, ed. Rebecca Walker and Philip J. Ivanhoe, 297–312. New York: Oxford University Press, 2007.

———. "Happiness in Early Chinese Thought." In *Oxford Handbook of Happiness*, ed. Susan David, Ilona Boniwell, and Amanda Conley Ayers. Oxford: Oxford University Press, 2012.

———. "Heaven as a Source for Ethical Warrant in Early Confucianism." *Dao: A Journal of Comparative Philosophy* 6:2 (2006), 211–20.

————. "'Heaven's Mandate' and the Concept of War in Early Confucianism." In *Ethics and Weapons of Mass Destruction: Religious and Secular Perspectives*, ed. Sohail H. Hashimi and Steven P. Lee, 270–76. Cambridge: Cambridge University Press, 2004.

————. "In the Shade of Confucius: Social Roles, Ethical Theory, and the Self." In *Polishing the Chinese Mirror: Essays in Honor of Henry Rosemont, Jr.*, ed. Ronnie L. Littlejohn and Marthe Chandler, 34–49. New York: Global Scholarly Publications, 2008.

————. "Intellectual Property and Traditional Chinese Culture." In *Topics in Contemporary Philosophy, Vol. 3, Law and Social Justice*, ed. Joseph Keim Campbell, Michael O'Rourke, and David Shier, 125–42. Cambridge, Mass.: MIT Press, 2005.

————. "Mengzi's Conception of Courage." *Dao: A Journal of Comparative Philosophy* 5:2 (2006), 221–34.

————. "The Paradox of Wuwei?" *Journal of Chinese Philosophy* 34:2 (2007), 277–87.

————. "Pluralism, Toleration, and Ethical Promiscuity." *Journal of Religious Ethics* 37:2, 311–29.

————. "Whose Confucius? Which Analects?" In *Confucius and the Analects: New Essays*, ed. Bryan W. Van Norden, 119–33. New York: Oxford University Press, 2002.

Ivanhoe, Philip J., trans. *The Daodejing of Laozi*. Indianapolis: Hackett, 2002.

Jaggar, Alison. *Feminist Politics and Human Nature*. Totowa, N.J.: Rowman and Littlefield, 1983.

Jang, Dong-jin. "A Confucian Deliberation on Rawls's Liberal Conception of International Justice." *Sungkyun Journal of East Asian Studies* 4:1 (2004), 133–55.

Kant, Immanuel. *Groundwork of the Metaphysics of Morals*, trans. Mary Gregor. Cambridge: Cambridge University Press, 1997.

Karoly, Lynn A., M. Rebecca Kilburn, and Jill S. Cannon, *Early Childhood Interventions: Proven Results, Future Promise*. Santa Monica, Calif.: The RAND Corporation, 2005.

Karoly, Lynn A. et al. *Investing in Our Children: What We Know and Don't Know About the Costs and Benfits of Early Childhood Interventions*. Santa Monica, Calif.: The RAND Corporation, 1998.

Kidder, Tracy. *Mountains Beyond Mountains: The Quest of Dr. Paul Farmer, a Man Who Would Cure the World*. New York: Random House, 2003.

Kinney, Anne Behnke. *Representations of Childhood and Youth in Early China*. Stanford, Calif.: Stanford University Press, 2004.

Kitzman, Harriet, et al., "Enduring Effects of Nurse Home Visitation on Maternal Life Course: A 3-Year Follow-up of a Randomized Trial," *Journal of the American Medical Association* 283:15 (2000), 1983–89.

Kline, T. C., III. "Moral Agency and Motivation in the *Xunzi*." In *Virtue, Nature, and Moral Agency in the Xunzi*, ed. T. C. Kline III and Philip J. Ivanhoe, 155–75. Indianapolis: Hackett, 2000.

Kuhse, Helga. *Caring: Nurses, Women and Ethics*. Oxford: Blackwell Publishers, 1997.

Kupperman, Joel J. *Learning from Asian Philosophy*. New York: Oxford University Press, 1999.

Kwok, D. C. and H. Lytton. "Perceptions of Mathematics Ability Versus Actual Mathematics Performance: Canadian and Hong Kong Chinese Children." *British Journal of Educational Psychology* 66 (1996), 209–22.

Kyte, Richard. "Guilt, Remorse, and the Sense of Justice." *Contemporary Philosophy* 14:5 (1992), 17–20.

Larmore, Charles. *Patterns of Moral Complexity*. Cambridge: Cambridge University Press, 1987.

Lau, D. C., trans. *Confucius: The Analects*. Harmondsworth, England: Penguin Books, 1979.

Lau, D. C., and Fong Ching Chen, eds. *A Concordance to the Lunyu* 論語逐字索引. Hong Kong: The Commercial Press, 2006.

———. "Theories of Human Nature in Mengzi and Xunzi." Reprinted in *Virtue, Nature, and Moral Agency in the Xunzi*, ed. T. C. Kline, III and Philip J. Ivanhoe, 188–219. Indianapolis: Hackett, 2000.

Lee, Thomas H.C. *Government and Examinations in Sung China*. Hong Kong: The Chinese University Press, 1985.

Lee, Pauline C. "Li Zhi and John Stuart Mill: A Confucian Feminist Critique of Liberal Feminism." In *The Sage and the Second Sex: Confucianism, Ethics, and Gender*, ed. Chenyang Li, 113–32. Chicago: Open Court Press, 2000.

Legge, James, trans. "Confucian Analects." In *The Chinese Classics, Vol. I*. New York: Dover Publications, 1971. Originally published in Oxford, U.K.: Clarendon Press, 1893.

———. *The Chinese Classics, Vol. IV. The She King or The Book of Poetry*. Hong Kong: Hong Kong University Press, 1960.

Lehning, Percy B. *John Rawls: An Introduction*. Cambridge: Cambridge University Press, 2009.

Levenson, Joseph R. *Confucian China and Its Modern Fate; A Trilogy*. Berkeley: University of California Press, 1968.

Lewis, Mark Edward. *Sanctioned Violence in Early China*. Albany: SUNY Press, 1990.

Li, Jin. "Chinese Conceptualization of Learning." *Ethos* 29 (2001), 111–37.

———. *Cultural Foundations of Learning: East and West*. New York: Cambridge University Press, 2012.

———. "A Cultural Model of Learning: Chinese 'Heart and Mind for Wanting to Learn.'" *Journal of Cross-Cultural Psychology* 33 (2002), 246–67.

———. "Learning as a Task or a Virtue: U.S. and Chinese Preschoolers Explain Learning." *Developmental Psychology* 40:4 (2004), 595–605.

———. "U.S. and Chinese Cultural Beliefs About Learning." *Journal of Educational Psychology* 95:2 (2003), 258–67.

Liu, Xiusheng. *Mencius, Hume, and the Foundations of Ethics.* Burlington, Vt.: Ashgate Publishing, 2003.

Liu, Yuli. *The Unity of Rule and Virtue: A Critique of a Supposed Parallel Between Confucian Ethics and Virtue Ethics.* Singapore: Eastern Universities Press, 2004.

Loewe, Michael, ed. *Early Chinese Texts: A Bibliographical Guide.* Berkeley, Calif.: Institute of East Asian Studies, 1993.

Loewe, Michael, and Edward Shaughnessy, eds. *The Cambridge History of Ancient China: From the Origins of Civilization to 221 B.C.* New York: Cambridge University Press, 1999.

Lovin, Robin W. "Cue the Chorus." *Journal of the American Academy of Religion* 78:1 (2010), 259–64.

MacIntyre, Alasdair. *After Virtue,* Second Edition. Notre Dame, Ind.: University of Notre Dame Press, 1984.

Mackerras, Colin. *China's Minorities: Integration and Modernization in the Twentieth-Century.* Hong Kong: Oxford University Press, 1994.

Mandle, Jon. *Rawls's 'A Theory of Justice': An Introduction.* Cambridge: Cambridge University Press, 2009.

Margalit, Avishai. *The Decent Society,* trans. Naomi Goldblum. Cambridge, Mass.: Harvard University Press, 1996.

Martin, Rex, and David Reidi, eds. *Rawls's Law of Peoples: A Realistic Utopia?* Oxford: Blackwell Publishing, 2006.

McKnight, C. C., et al. *The Underachieving Curriculum: Assessing U.S. School Mathematics From an International Perspective.* Champaign, Ill.: Stipes, 1987.

McLanahan, Sara S., and Marcia J. Carlson. "Welfare Reform, Fertility, and Father Involvement." *The Future of Children* 12, 147–66.

Mill, J. S. "On Liberty." In *The Basic Writings of John Stuart Mill.* New York: The Modern Library of Random House, Inc., 2002.

Mortenson, Greg, and David Oliver Relin. *Three Cups of Tea: One Man's Mission to Promote Peace . . . One School at a Time.* New York: Penguin Books, 2007.

Mulhall, Stephen, and Adam Swift. "Rawls and Communitarianism." In *The Cambridge Companion to Rawls,* ed. Samuel Freeman, 460–87. Cambridge: Cambridge University Press, 2003.

Nagel, Thomas. "Rawls and Liberalism." In *The Cambridge Companion to Rawls,* ed. Samuel Freeman, 62–85. Cambridge: Cambridge University Press, 2003.

Ng, Margaret. "Are Rights Culture-Bound?" *Human Rights and Chinese Values: Legal, Philosophical, and Political Perspectives*, ed. Michael C. Davis, 59–71. New York: Oxford University Press, 1995.

Nivison, David S. "Critique of David B. Wong, 'Xunzi on Moral Motivation.'" In *Chinese Language, Thought, and Culture: Nivison and His Critics*, ed. Philip J. Ivanhoe, 323–31. Chicago: Open Court Press, 1996.

———. *The Ways of Confucianism: Investigations in Chinese Philosophy*, ed. Bryan W. Van Norden. LaSalle, Ill.: Open Court Press, 1996.

Noddings, Nel. "Caring as Relation and Virtue in Teaching." In *Working Virtue: Virtue Ethics and Contemporary Moral Problems*, ed. Rebecca L. Walker and Philip J. Ivanhoe, 41–60. New York: Oxford University Press, 2006.

———. *Starting at Home: Caring and Social Policy*. Berkeley: University of California Press, 2002.

Nussbaum, Martha C. "Comparing Virtues." *Journal of Religious Ethics* 21:2 (1993), 345–67.

———. *Cultivating Humanity: A Classical Defense of Reform in Liberal Education*. Cambridge, Mass.: Harvard University Press, 1997.

———. *For Love of Country?* Ed. Joshua Cohen. Boston: Beacon Press, 2002.

———. "Non-Relative Virtues: An Aristotelian Approach." In *Ethical Theory: Character and Virtue*, Vol. 13 of *Midwest Studies in Philosophy*, ed. Peter French, Theodore E. Uehling Jr., and Howard K. Wettstein, 32–53. Notre Dame, Ind.: University of Notre Dame Press, 1988.

———. "Rawls and Feminism." In *The Cambridge Companion to Rawls*, ed. Samuel Freeman, 488–520. Cambridge: Cambridge University Press, 2003.

Nussbaum, Martha, and Amartya Sen, eds. *The Quality of Life*. Oxford: Oxford University Press, 1993.

Okin, Susan Moller. *Justice, Gender, and the Family*. New York: Basic Books,1989.

Olds, David, et al. "Does Prenatal and Infancy Nurse Home Visitation Have Enduring Effects on Qualities of Parental Caregiving and Child Health at 25 to 50 Months of Life?" *Pediatrics* 93:1 (1994), 89–98.

———. "Effects of Prenatal and Infancy Nurse Home Visitation on Government Spending." *Medical Care* 31 (1993), 155–74.

———. "Home Visiting by Paraprofessionals and by Nurses: A Randomized, Controlled Trial." *Pediatrics* 110 (2002): 486–96.

———. "Long-term Effects of Nurse Home Visitation on Children's Criminal and Antisocial Behavior: 15-Year Follow-up of a Randomized Controlled Trial." *Journal of the American Medical Association* 280:14 (1998), 1238–44.

———. "The Nurse-Family Partnership: An Evidence-based Preventive Intervention." *Infant Mental Health Journal* 27:1 (2006), 5–25.

————. "Prenatal and Infancy Home Visiting by Nurses: Randomized Trials to Community Replication." *Prevention Science* 3:3 (2002), 153–72.

————. "Theoretical Foundations of a Program of Home Visitation for Pregnant Women and Parents of Young Children." *Journal of Community Psychology* 25:1 (1997), 9–25.

————. "Update on Home Visiting for Pregnant Women and Parents of Young Children." *Current Problems in Pediatrics* 30 (2000), 107–41.

Peerenboom, R. P. "Confucian Justice: Achieving a Humane Society." *International Philosophical Quarterly* 30:1 (1990), 17–32.

————. *Law and Morality in Ancient China*. Albany: SUNY Press, 1993.

Piaget, Jean. *The Moral Judgment of the Child*. London: Routledge and Kegan Paul, 1932.

Pogge, Thomas. *John Rawls: His Life and Theory of Justice*, trans. Michelle Kosch. New York: Oxford University Press, 2007.

Polanyi, Michael. *Personal Knowledge: Towards a Post-Critical Philosophy*. New York: Harper Torchbooks, 1964.

Priest, Graham. "Where Is Philosophy at the Start of the 21st Century?" *The Proceedings of the Aristotelian Society* CIII (2002), 85–99.

Prudhovsky, Gad. "Can We Ascribe to Past Thinkers Concepts They Had No Linguistic Means to Express?" *History and Theory* 36.1 (1997): 15–31.

Puett, Michael J. *The Ambivalence of Creation: Debates Concerning Innovation and Artifice in Early China*. Stanford, Calif.: Stanford University Press, 2001.

————. *To Become a God: Cosmology, Sacrifice, and Self-Divinization in Early China*. Cambridge, Mass.: Harvard University Asia Center, 2002.

Rawls, John. *A Brief Inquiry into the Meaning of Sin and Faith*, ed. Thomas Nagel. Cambridge, Mass.: Harvard University Press, 2010.

————. *Collected Papers*, ed. Samuel Freeman. Cambridge, Mass.: Harvard University Press, 1999.

————. *Justice as Fairness: A Restatement*, ed. Erin Kelly. Cambridge, Mass.: Harvard University Press, 2001.

————. *The Law of Peoples*. Cambridge, Mass.: Harvard University Press, 1999.

————. *Lectures on the History of Political Philosophy*, ed. Samuel Freeman. Cambridge, Mass.: Belknap Press of Harvard University Press, 2008.

————. *Political Liberalism*. New York: Columbia University Press, 1993, 1996.

————. *A Theory of Justice*. Cambridge, Mass.: Belknap Press of Harvard University Press, 1971.

————. *A Theory of Justice*, Revised Edition. Cambridge, Mass.: Belknap Press of Harvard University Press, 1999.

Roetz, Heiner. *Confucian Ethics of the Axial Age: A Reconstruction Under the Aspect of the Breakthrough Toward Postconventional Thinking.* Albany: SUNY Press, 1993.

Rosemont, Henry Jr. "Against Relativism." In *Interpreting Across Boundaries*, ed. Gerald J. Larson and Eliot Deutsch, 36–70. Princeton, N.J.: Princeton University Press, 1988.

———. "Rights-Bearing Individuals and Role-Bearing Persons." In *Rules, Rituals, and Responsibility: Essays Dedicated to Herbert Fingarette*, ed. Mary I. Bockover, 71–101. LaSalle, Ill.: Open Court Press, 1991.

———. "State and Society in the Xunzi: A Philosophical Commentary." In *Virtue, Nature, and Moral Agency in the Xunzi*, ed. T. C. Kline III and Philip J. Ivanhoe, 1–38. Indianapolis: Hackett, 2000.

———. "Which Rights? Whose Democracy?" *The Raven* 39 (1999), 217–34.

———. "Whose Democracy? Which Rights? A Confucian Critique of Modern Western Liberalism." In *Confucian Ethics: A Comparative Study of Self, Autonomy, and Community*, ed. Kwong-loi Shun and David B. Wong, 49–71. New York: Cambridge University Press, 2004.

Ross, W. D. *The Right and the Good.* Oxford: The Clarendon Press, 1930.

Rouner, Leroy S., ed. *Human Rights and the World's Religions.* Notre Dame, Ind.: University of Notre Dame Press, 1988.

Rousseau, Jean-Jacques. *Emile*, trans. Allan Bloom. New York: Basic Books, 1979.

Ryle, Gilbert. *Collected Papers, Vol. 2.* London: Hutchinson and Company, 1971.

Sahleen, Joel, trans. "Han Feizi." In *Readings in Classical Chinese Philosophy*, Second Edition, ed. Philip J. Ivanhoe and Bryan W. Van Norden, 311–61. Indianapolis: Hackett, 2005.

Sandel, Michael. *Liberalism and the Limits of Justice*, Second Edition. Cambridge: Cambridge University Press, 1988.

Schaeffer, David Lewis. *Illiberal Justice: John Rawls vs. the American Political Tradition.* Columbia: University of Missouri Press, 2007.

Scheffler, Samuel. "Rawls and Utilitarianism." In *The Cambridge Companion to Rawls*, ed. Samuel Freeman, 426–59. Cambridge: Cambridge University Press, 2003.

Schwartz, Benjamin I. "The Chinese Perception of World Order, Past and Present." In *The Chinese World Order: Traditional China's Foreign Relations*, ed. John K. Fairbank, 276–91. Cambridge, Mass.: Harvard University Press, 1968.

———. *The World of Thought in Ancient China.* Cambridge, Mass.: The Belknap Press, 1985.

Schwitzgebel, Eric. "Children's Theories and the Drive to Explain." *Science & Education* 8 (1999), 457–88.

———. "Human Nature and Moral Development in Mencius, Xunzi, Hobbes, and Rousseau." *History of Philosophy Quarterly* 24 (2007): 147–68.

———. "Theories in Children and the Rest of Us." *Philosophy of Science, Supplemental Issue,* 63 (1996), s202–s210.

Sellman, Derek. *What Makes a Good Nurse: Why the Virtues Are Important for Nurses.* London: Jessica Kingsley Publishing, 2011.

Shore, Rima. *Rethinking the Brain: New Insights into Early Development, Executive Summary.* New York: Families and Work Institute, 1997.

Shun, Kwong-loi. *Mencius and Early Chinese Thought.* Stanford, Calif.: Stanford University Press, 1997.

Shun, Kwong-loi and David B. Wong, eds. *Confucian Ethics: A Comparative Study of Self, Autonomy, and Community.* New York: Cambridge University Press, 2004.

Sim, May. *Remastering Morals with Aristotle and Confucius.* New York: Cambridge University Press, 2007.

Slingerland, Edward. "Conceptual Metaphor Theory as Methodology for Comparative Religion." *Journal of the American Academy of Religion* 72:1 (2004), 1–31.

———. "Why Philosophy Is Not 'Extra' in Understanding the *Analects*: A Review of *The Original Analects.*" *Philosophy East and West* 40:1 (2000), 137–47.

Slingerland, Edward, trans. *Confucius Analects.* Indianapolis: Hackett, 2003.

Slote, Michael. "Comments on Bryan van Norden's *Virtue Ethics and Consequentialism in Early Chinese Philosophy.*" *Dao: A Journal of Comparative Philosophy* 8:3 (2009), 289–95.

———. *The Ethics of Care and Empathy.* New York: Routledge, 2007.

Smid, Robert W. *Methodologies of Comparative Philosophy: The Pragmatist and Process Traditions.* Albany: SUNY Press, 2010.

Soanes, Catherine, ed. *Compact Oxford English Dictionary of Current English, Third Revised Edition.* Oxford: Oxford University Press, 2008.

Sober, Elliott, and David Sloan Wilson. *Unto Others: The Evolution and Psychology of Unselfish Behavior.* Cambridge, Mass.: Harvard University Press, 1998.

Solinger, Dorothy J. "Human Rights Issues in China's Internal Migration: Insights from Comparisons with Germany and Japan." In *The East Asian Challenge for Human Rights,* ed. Joanne R. Bauer and Daniel A. Bell, 285–312. New York: Cambridge University Press, 1999.

Spiro, Melford. *Anthropological Other or Burmese Brother?* New Brunswick, N.J.: Transaction Publishers, 1992.

Stalnaker, Aaron. *Overcoming Our Evil: Human Nature and Spiritual Exercises in Xunzi and Augustine.* Washington: Georgetown University Press, 2006.

———. "Review of Bryan W. Van Norden, *Virtue Ethics and Consequentialism in Early Chinese Philosophy.*" *Journal of Religion* 89 (2009): 280–82.

Stevenson, H. W., and S. Y. Lee. "Context of Achievement." *Monographs of the Society of Research in Child Development* 55:1–2, serial no. 221 (1990).

Stevenson, H. W., and J. W. Stigler. *The Learning Gap*. New York: Simon and Schuster, 1992.

Tan, Sor-hoon. *Confucian Democracy: A Deweyan Reconstruction*. Albany: SUNY Press, 2004.

Tan Shen. "Rural Workforce Migration: A Summary of Some Studies." *Social Sciences in China* (Winter 2003), 83–101.

Tao, Julia. "Beyond Proceduralism: A Chinese Perspective on *Cheng* (Sincerity) as a Political Virtue." *Philosophy East and West* 55:1 (2005), 64–79.

Taylor, Charles. *Philosophical Papers, Vol. 1: Human Agency and Language*. Cambridge: Cambridge University Press, 1985.

———. *Philosophical Papers, Vol. 2: Philosophy and the Human Sciences*. Cambridge: Cambridge University Press, 1985.

———. *Philosophy and the Human Sciences*. Cambridge: Cambridge University Press, 1985.

———. *Sources of the Self: The Making of Modern Identity*. Cambridge: Cambridge University Press, 1989.

Tiwald, Justin. "A Right of Rebellion in the *Mengzi*?" *Dao* 7:3 (2008), 269–82.

Tu, Weiming. *Centrality and Commonality: An Essay on Confucian Religiousness*. Albany: SUNY Press, 1989.

———, ed. *Confucian Traditions in East Asian Modernity: Moral Education and Economic Culture in Japan and the Four Mini-Dragons*. Cambridge, Mass.: Harvard University Press, 1996.

———. "The 'Third Epoch' of Confucian Humanism." In *Way, Learning, and Politics: Essays on the Confucian Intellectual*, ed. Tu Wei-ming, 141–60. New York: HarperCollins, 1993.

Tweed, R. G., and D. R. Lehman. "Learning Considered Within a Cultural Context: Confucian and Socratic Approaches." *American Psychologist* 57 (2002), 89–99.

Ulving, Tor, ed. *Dictionary of Old and Middle Chinese: Bernard Karlgren's Grammata Serica Recensa Alphabetically Arranged*. Goteborg, Sweden: Acta Universitatis Gothoburgensis, 1997.

Van Norden, Bryan W., ed. *Confucius and the Analects: New Essays*. New York: Oxford University Press, 2002.

———. "Mengzi and Xunzi: Two Views of Human Agency." In *Virtue, Nature, and Moral Agency in the Xunzi*, ed. T.C. Kline, III and Philip J. Ivanhoe, 103–34. Indianapolis: Hackett, 2000.

———. "Response to Angle and Slote." *Dao: A Journal of Comparative Philosophy* 8:3 (2009), 305–9.

———. "Virtue Ethics and Confucianism." In *Comparative Approaches to Chinese Philosophy*, ed. Bo Mou, 99–121. Hampshire, U.K.: Ashgate Publishing, 2003.

———. *Virtue Ethics and Consequentialism in Early Chinese Philosophy*. New York: Cambridge University Press, 2007.

———. "What Should Western Philosophy Learn from Chinese Philosophy?" In *Chinese Language, Thought, and Culture*, ed. Philip J. Ivanhoe, 224–49. Chicago: Open Court Press, 1996.

Van Norden, Bryan W., trans. "Mengzi (Mencius)." In *Readings in Classical Chinese Philosophy*, Second Edition, ed. Philip J. Ivanhoe and Bryan W. Van Norden, 115–59. Indianapolis: Hackett, 2005.

———. *Mengzi: With Selections from Traditional Commentaries*. Indianapolis: Hackett, 2008.

Van Zoeren, Steven. *Poetry and Personality*. Stanford, Calif.: Stanford University Press, 1991.

Waley, Arthur, trans. *The Analects of Confucius*. New York: Vintage Books, 1989.

———. *Lunyu* 論語 *The Analects*. Changsha, P.R. China: Hunan People's Publishing House, 1999.

Walker, Rebecca L., and Philip J. Ivanhoe, eds. *Working Virtue: Virtue Ethics and Contemporary Moral Problems*. New York: Oxford University Press, 2007.

Watson, Burton, trans. *The Analects of Confucius*. New York: Columbia University Press, 2007.

———. *The Tso Chuan*. New York: Columbia University Press, 1989.

Weber, Max. *The Religion of China: Confucianism and Taoism*, trans. Hans H. Gerth. Glencoe, Ill.: Free Press, 1951 (originally published in German, 1922).

Wen, Haiming. *Confucian Pragmatism as the Art of Contextualizing Personal Experience and World*. Lanham, Md.: Lexington Books, 2009.

Wilburn, Brad K., ed. *Moral Cultivation: Essays on the Development of Character and Virtue*. Lanham, Md.: Lexington Books, 2007.

Williams, Bernard. *Ethics and the Limits of Philosophy*. Cambridge, Mass.: Harvard University Press, 1985.

———. "Morality and Social Justice." Tanner Lectures given at Harvard University, 1983, Boston, Mass.

Wittgenstein, Ludwig. *Philosophical Investigations, Third Edition*. Trans. G.E.M. Anscombe. Upper Saddle River, N.J.: Prentice Hall, 1973.

Wong, David B. "On Flourishing and Finding One's Identity in Community." In *Midwest Studies in Philosophy Volume XIII Ethical Theory: Character and Virtue*, ed. Peter A French, Theodore E. Uehling Jr., and Howard K. Wettstein, 324–41. South Bend, Ind.: University of Notre Dame Press, 1998.

———. "Xunzi on Moral Motivation." In *Virtue, Nature, and Moral Agency in the Xunzi* ed. T. C. Kline III and Philip J. Ivanhoe, 135–54. Indianapolis: Hackett, 2000.

Xiao, Yang. "Trying to Do Justice to the Concept of Justice in Confucian Ethics." *Journal of Chinese Philosophy* 24 (1997).

Xu, Fuguan 徐復觀. *Zhongguo renxing lun shi* 中國人性 論史 ("A History of Human Nature in China"), xian qin pian 先秦篇. Shanghai: Shanghai san lian shudian, 2001.

Yearley, Lee H. "Confucianism and Genre: Presentation and Persuasion in Early Confucian Thought." *Journal of Ecumenical Studies* 40:1–2 (2003), 137–52.

———. *Mencius and Aquinas: Theories of Virtue and Conceptions of Courage.* Albany: SUNY Press, 1990.

Yu, A.-B. "Ultimate Life Concerns, Self, and Chinese Achievement Motivation." In *The Handbook of Chinese Psychology*, ed. M. Bond, 227–46. Hong Kong: Oxford University Press, 1996.

Yu, Jiyuan. *The Ethics of Confucius and Aristotle: Mirrors of Virtue.* New York: Routledge, 2009.

Yung, Betty. "An Interplay Between Western and Confucian Concepts of Justice: Development of Hong Kong Housing Policy." *Housing, Theory and Society* 24:2 (2007), 111–32.

Zahn-Waxler, Carolyn, et al., "Development of Concern for Others," *Developmental Psychology* 28:1 (1992), 126–36.

Zahn-Waxler, Carolyn, and Marian Radke-Yarrow, "The Origins of Empathic Concern," *Motivation and Emotion* 14:2 (1990), 107–30.

Zhang, Qianfang. "Humanity or Benevolence? The Interpretation of Confucian Ren and Its Modern Implications." In *Taking Confucian Ethics Seriously*, ed. Kam-Por Yu, Julia Tao, and Philip J. Ivanhoe. Albany: SUNY Press, forthcoming, 2010.

Zhu Xi 朱熹. *Si shu ji zhu* 四書集注. Changsha: yue lu shu she: Hunan sheng xin hua shu dian fa xing, 1985.

Adams, Robert M., 74
Alford, William P., 276n16
Ames, Roger T., 21, 51, 273n1, 278n32, 288n34, 291n48, 291n49, 291n51, 292n52
Analects (Lunyu), 14–15; textual issues, 20–23, 150, 158, 166, 273n1, 283n68
Angle, Stephen C., 9, 52, 61, 63–64, 69, 275n15, 281n52, 290n45, 291n47, 321n11
antirationalism, 56, 61
Aristotle, 53–54, 78–80, 106–9, 111, 196–97, 284n4, 305n86, 308n43, 310n62
assensus, 135–36
Augustine, 56–60, 64–67

Barry, Brian, 282n59
Bell, Daniel A., 213, 248–49, 314n8, 328n68, 328n69, 329n71, 330n96, 330n98
Bellah, Robert, 287n30
Bok, Derek, 325n42
Book of Odes (Shijing), 123, 126, 148, 279n39
Brooks, A. Taeko, 20–21, 283n68
Brooks, E. Bruce, 20–21, 283n68
Buddhism, 54

Carr, Karen L., 31–33, 55–56, 61, 63, 70, 285n9, 293n67
Chan, Joseph, 253
Chen, Xunwu, 15–17, 279n40
children, 216–17, 219–30, 235–36, 245, 269, 271, 279–80n41, 304n73, 325n42, 326n52; Confucian views of, 46, 123, 127, 131, 136, 137–38, 217–19, 269, 322n15, 323–24n27, 326n50; Rawls's view of, 90–91, 95, 102–3, 105, 171, 196, 269, 298n30, 299n33
Christianity, 3, 32–33, 54, 135–36, 179
civil service examinations, 165–67, 313n83, 313n86, 313n88
Cohen, Joshua, 74
communitarianism, 18–20, 269, 302n58
comparative philosophy, 24–25; challenges in, 48–68, 266–67, 296n92, 296n93,

320n3; contrasted with comparative religion, 29–31, 36–37, 283–84n2; methods and approaches to, 48–73, 265–67, 289n41; reasons for doing, 2–8, 28–47, 265–66, 270, 272, 288n34
concepts: shared, 54, 64–68, 156–57, 295n88; terms and, 4, 7, 9–15, 48, 54, 60, 72, 119, 150–57, 266, 269, 277n24, 277n29, 278n36, 278n37, 279n41; theories and, 4, 66–68, 204–5, 269, 279n41, 295n88; thin and thick, 54, 65–67, 110, 206, 290n46, 292n57, 293n68, 295n85, 295n88, 297n8
Confucius. *See* Kongzi
Cooper, John, 107–8, 304n76
Cui, Shu, 20

Daniels, Norman, 314n3
dao. See Way (*dao*), the
Daoism, 32, 168
de. See Virtue
decent societies, 254–63, 332n107, 333n116
Decosimo, David, 56–60, 293n66, 293n71, 294n72, 296n92
Deigh, John, 301–2n54
Dewey, John, 51
difference principle, the, 96, 297n19, 302n55, 314n8
diversity, 75, 233–34, 238–51, 333n112
education, 248–50. *See also* learning
Elman, Benjamin A., 313n83, 313n88
ethical promiscuity, 244–48
exemplary person. See *junzi*

families, 107–8, 321–22n15, 325n42; Confucian views on, 123, 126, 130–31, 134, 136–38, 143–44, 146, 153, 157–63, 165, 176, 200, 203, 217–19, 222–23, 226, 229, 240, 269–70, 272, 300n48, 305n89, 308–9n53, 311n70, 322n15, 322n17, 326n50; Rawls's views on, 4, 5, 75, 80,

families (*continued*)
  81, 85–87, 89–92, 94–98, 103, 105–6,
  196, 200, 202–3, 238–40, 266, 268–72,
  301*n*50, 302*n*58
family resemblance. *See* Wittgenstein,
  Ludwig
Fan, Ruiping, 10, 15–17, 277*n*21, 281*n*44
fiducia, 135–36
filial piety, 126–28, 132, 136–37, 157–63,
  200, 203, 217–19, 221, 229, 258, 272,
  307*n*16, 310*n*69, 311*n*70, 312*n*76, 313*n*79
Flanagan, Owen, 325*n*41
Fox, Alan, 10, 15–17
Freeman, Samuel, 112, 273*n*2
friendship, 107–8, 121, 129–30

Geertz, Clifford, 292*n*57
gentleman. See *junzi*
governing, 126, 130–41, 145–46, 163–66,
  182–83, 207, 209, 253

Hall, David L., 51, 288*n*34, 291*n*48,
  291*n*49, 291*n*51, 292*n*52
Han Feizi. *See* Legalism
harmony (*he*), 121, 126, 128, 131–34,
  143–44, 164, 205, 207, 209, 267–68,
  270
He Yan, 20, 23, 141, 149, 306*n*2
Heaven (*tian*), 54, 120–21, 124, 259,
  292*n*56
Hegel, G.W.F., 41
Hobbes, Thomas, 112, 281*n*45, 317*n*36,
  318*n*44
Hoffman, Martin, 216–17, 321*n*11
human nature, 65–68, 304*n*73; Confucian views of, 173, 278–79*n*38, 279*n*39;
  Rawls's views of, 4, 6, 83, 89, 97–110 ,
  112, 187–89, 195–98
Hume, David, 187, 301*n*50, 316*n*20
Hutton, Eric L., 312*n*76, 318*n*43

inequalities, 1, 81, 88–89, 96, 133–34,
  171–72, 270–71, 314*n*3
Ivanhoe, Philip J., 12, 31–33, 55–56, 61,
  63, 70, 130–31, 190–91, 213–14, 217,
  244–48, 283*n*71, 285*n*9, 288*n*34, 293*n*67,
  294*n*76, 315*n*11, 316*n*28, 318*n*43,
  325*n*37, 333*n*113–14

junzi (exemplary person), 123–26, 128–29,
  131, 133, 137–43, 145, 151, 164, 185,
  209, 240, 252–54, 257, 259, 262, 268,
  309*n*56

justice
  as fairness: 82–84, 109–10, 115, 305*n*91,
    305*n*94, 310*n*67. *See also* justice:
    theory of
  background: 79, 82, 89, 99, 104–6, 117,
    183, 198, 303*n*62
  concept of: 76–82, 154, 295*n*85
  conceptions of: 76–81, 85, 111–12,
    114–17, 206, 295*n*85, 297*n*8. *See also*
    justice: theory of
  distributive: in the *Analects*, 119, 133–34,
    136, 139, 145, 155, 165–67, 207,
    307*n*28; in Rawls, 79. *See also* differ-
    ence principle, the
  legal: in the *Analects*, 141–44, 146–48,
    151, 157–64
  international: 251–64, 330–31*n*98
  principles of: 76–81, 84, 93–96, 98–99,
    101, 104, 109–17, 206, 230–32, 238,
    270, 297*n*19
  sense of. *See* sense of justice
  terms for. *See* concepts: terms and
  theory of: in the *Analects*, 151, 204–5,
    269; in Rawls, 4, 75–77, 80, 82, 95, 97,
    188, 295*n*85, 297*n*19

Kant, Immanuel, 41, 80, 101, 187, 301*n*50,
  315*n*15
Kierkegaard, Søren, 56, 61, 63
Kline, T. C. III, 317*n*41, 318*n*42
Kongzi, 2–3, 13, 120–25, 164–65, 273*n*1,
  273*n*3, 274*n*4, 274*n*5. See also *Analects*
  (*Lunyu*)
Kupperman, Joel, 288*n*34
Kyte, Richard, 302*n*54

Lau, D. C., 20
learning, 123, 234–44, 247
Lee, Thomas H.C., 167, 313*n*83, 313*n*88
Legalism, 312*n*76
Legge, James, 137, 148, 158, 310*n*68
Levenson, Joseph, 287*n*30
lexical fallacy, 13–14, 275*n*14, 278*n*34. *See
  also* concepts: terms and
li (ritual). *See* ritual (*li*)
Li, Jin, 234–36, 330*n*97
liberal societies. *See* liberalism
liberalism, 2, 76, 80, 96, 107–8, 115, 118,
  171, 179, 187–88, 233–34, 247–48,
  254–57, 260–63, 267, 301*n*51, 329*n*71,
  333*n*112, 333*n*116; and Confucianism,
  7–9, 15, 164, 266, 269, 314*n*8, 322*n*17,
  324–25*n*36

Liu, Xiusheng, 316*n*20
Lunyu. See *Analects*

MacIntyre, Alasdair, 11, 76, 79
Margalit, Avishai, 332*n*107
Mencius. *See* Mengzi
Mengzi, 3, 5, 13–14, 23, 53–54, 59, 66–67,
    151, 187, 189–92, 195–200, 218–22,
    229, 246, 253, 276*n*17, 284*n*4, 295*n*88,
    303*n*59, 303*n*61, 304*n*71, 310*n*69,
    311*n*70, 316*n*20, 330*n*98
migrant workers, 238–39, 241, 250, 320*n*9,
    328*n*68, 329*n*71
Mill, J. S., 44–45, 80
modus vivendi, 113–15
Mohism, 151, 277*n*31, 300*n*48
moral self-cultivation, 14, 59–60, 105, 200,
    294*n*76, 327–28*n*63, 328*n*66
    Confucian views of: 121–32, 134–38,
        145, 147–49, 151–52, 155, 157, 159,
        166, 173–76, 185–86, 217, 229–31,
        233–38, 240–47, 250–51, 268, 272,
        278*n*36, 310*n*62, 310*n*66; and the emo-
        tions, 127–28, 132, 136, 138, 142–43,
        151, 155, 240–41, 307*n*16
    Rawls's views of: 4, 76, 90–95, 97–112,
        117–18, 184, 186–89, 196–200,
        238–39, 258, 268–72, 314–15*n*9
Mulhall, Stephen, 20, 302*n*58

Nagel, Thomas, 74, 96
Neo-Confucianism, 61, 64
Nivison, David S., 130, 307*n*22, 317*n*35,
    317*n*41, 318–19*n*46
Noddings, Nel, 324*n*35
non-Western philosophy, marginalization
    of, 29–30, 37–39, 42–43, 283–84*n*2,
    284*n*3, 286*n*23, 288*n*33
Nurse-Family Partnership, 220–30, 271
Nussbaum, Martha C., 34–36, 100,
    285*n*15, 285*n*19, 285–86*n*20, 286*n*21,
    286*n*22, 290*n*46, 292*n*57, 329*n*74,
    333*n*1

Okin, Susan Moller, 269, 333*n*1
Olds, David, 224
original position, 99–101
overlapping consensus, 114–15, 270

parents. *See* children; families
Peerenboom, R. P., 10, 15–17, 276–77*n*19,
    281*n*44, 281*n*45
Piaget, Jean, 90, 298*n*30

pluralism. *See* diversity; reasonable plural-
    ism, fact of
poverty, 1, 138–39; in the *Analects,* 119,
    133–34, 136, 145–49, 164, 176, 207,
    310*n*62, 314*n*7
pragmatism, 51–53, 69, 288*n*32, 291*n*48,
    292*n*52
Priest, Graham, 37–38, 286*n*25
principle of reversibility, 92, 138, 215–17,
    245, 320*n*9. *See also* reciprocity
process philosophy, 51–53, 69, 291–92*n*51,
    292*n*52
public policy, 219–30, 271–72
Puett, Michael J., 291*n*49, 306*n*3

Rawls, John, 2, 74–75; autonomy, view
    of, 75–76; communitarian critics of,
    5, 18–20, 76, 86–87, 96–97, 301*n*53,
    302*n*58; early *vs.* later work, 18–19, 178,
    205, 207; feminist critics of, 5, 86–87,
    95, 301*n*51, 301*n*54, 321*n*10; on free
    and equal persons, 84–85, 87, 89, 100;
    Law of Peoples, 254–64, 332*n*107; moral
    powers, views on, 84–85, 87, 98, 104,
    106, 184; moral psychology, views on,
    2, 4, 23–24, 75, 87–112, 117, 187–88,
    199, 216–17, 231, 258, 298*n*29, 298*n*30,
    299*n*33, 299*n*44, 300*n*46, 300*n*47,
    301*n*50, 301*n*53, 301–2*n*54; religion,
    views on, 74, 80, 85–86, 97, 114, 116,
    178–79, 188, 262, 297*n*14, 302*n*58;
    self, view of, 100, 298*n*30, 302*n*58,
    315*n*11; on social cooperation, 83, 87,
    89, 98, 111–12, 115–17; on stability, 75,
    111–18, 205, 270; theory of justice (*see*
    justice); on the well-ordered society, 78,
    82, 84–85
reasonable pluralism, fact of, 75, 80,
    178–79, 247–48, 262, 305*n*94
reciprocity: in the *Analects,* 136, 138–39,
    149–50, 152–53, 155; in Rawls, 83–84,
    99, 104, 113
Ren (humaneness), 121–24, 126, 128–29,
    136–38, 145, 149–50, 153, 155, 173,
    185, 243, 258, 267–68, 270
right, relationship to the good, 205; in
    Confucianism, 207–8, 319*n*55; in Rawls,
    109–11, 205–8, 305*n*94
rights, 79–80; Chinese views of, 8–10, 269,
    275–76*n*15, 276*n*16, 276*n*17, 281*n*52;
    terms for, 11, 275–76*n*15
ritual (*li*), 120–21, 127–28, 132, 147–48,
    153, 203–4, 269, 278*n*32

Rosemont, Henry Jr., 10–11, 21, 273*n*1,
    277*n*24, 277*n*29, 278*n*32, 278*n*34,
    279–80*n*41, 288*n*34, 310*n*64, 315*n*11,
    324*n*36
Ross, W. D., 109
Rousseau, Jean-Jacques, 89
Ryle, Gilbert, 292*n*57

Sandel, Michael, 302*n*58
Scheffler, Samuel, 319*n*56
Schwartz, Benjamin, 331*n*100
Schwitzgebel, Eric, 280*n*41, 317*n*36
self-cultivation. *See* moral self-cultivation
sense of justice, 169–72; in the *Analects*
    (basic view), 23, 132–67, 173–76; and
    contemporary China, 231–51, 329*n*71;
    difficulties with each view, 182–201;
    and international justice, 251–64; and
    modern liberal democracies, 214–30;
    in Rawls (basic view), 84–85, 87–118;
    in Rawls and the *Analects*, compared,
    176–87, 199–200, 204–5, 230–32,
    239–40, 251–64, 267–72, 314–15*n*9,
    315*n*10, 315*n*11
shu. See principle of reversibility; reciprocity
Shun, sage-king, 310–11*n*69, 311*n*70
Sim, May, 290*n*45
Slingerland, Edward G., 23, 141, 277*n*29,
    283*n*68
Slote, Michael, 291*n*47, 324*n*35
Smid, Robert W., 291*n*48
Socrates, 3, 15, 47, 178
Solinger, Dorothy J., 328*n*69, 329*n*70
Spiro, Melford, 285*n*6
Stalnaker, Aaron, 56–60, 64–69, 293*n*69,
    294*n*76, 294*n*84, 295*n*88, 295*n*89,
    295*n*90, 296*n*92
Stoicism, 313*n*79
Svensson, Maria, 9, 275*n*15
Swift, Adam, 20, 302*n*58
sympathetic understanding. *See* principle of
    reversibility; reciprocity

Tan, Sor-hoon, 291*n*48
Tao, Julia, 135
Taylor, Charles, 305*n*90
tian. See Heaven (*tian*)
Tiwald, Justin, 276*n*17
tolerance, 244, 248, 329*n*78
trustworthiness (*xin*), 134–36, 141, 146, 153
Tu, Weiming, 135–36, 287*n*30

upright one (*zhi gong*), 157–63, 202,
    310*n*68, 312*n*75, 312*n*76

utilitarianism, 76, 80, 82, 101, 110, 113,
    205–8, 305*n*93, 319*n*56

Van Norden, Bryan W., 3, 13–14, 20, 50–
    52, 66, 71–72, 211–12, 232, 240, 246,
    274*n*5, 275*n*14, 278*n*34, 284*n*4, 288*n*34,
    290*n*44, 290*n*45, 291*n*47, 291*n*49, 292*n*57,
    295*n*88, 312*n*75, 318*n*42, 320*n*1
Van Zoeren, Steven, 20–21
veil of ignorance. *See* original position
Virtue (*de*), 122–23, 125, 129–33, 150, 165,
    180, 182–83, 209, 251–64; practical and
    mystical aspects of, 258–60, 263
virtue ethics, 50–53, 205, 207–8, 225–27,
    290*n*44, 290*n*45, 324*n*32
virtues: in the *Analects*, 120–22, 126, 148,
    155, 173–74, 205, 208–9, 223, 230–31,
    236, 247, 252, 257–59, 262, 272; in
    Rawls, 79, 103–5, 110, 116, 208, 231,
    239–40, 256–57, 260–63, 269–70

Waley, Arthur, 20, 306*n*13, 310*n*68
Way (*dao*), the, 13, 120–22, 126–27, 129–
    30, 133, 145–47, 149, 163–65, 173–74,
    185–86, 207, 218, 243, 247, 252–54, 256,
    258, 262–63, 267–68, 270, 314*n*7
Weber, Max, 287*n*30
Whitehead, Alfred North, 51
Wilburn, Brad K., 294*n*76
Wittgenstein, Ludwig, 68, 296*n*91
Wong, David, 198, 318*n*42, 318*n*45

Xiao, Yang, 10, 15, 17, 278*n*33
xin (heart-mind), 23, 124
Xunzi, 3, 5, 14, 23, 56–60, 64–67, 151,
    189, 191–96, 198, 253, 295*n*88, 304*n*71,
    310*n*64, 311*n*70, 316*n*28, 317*n*36,
    317*n*38, 319*n*48
Xunzi's dilemma, 183, 187, 192–95, 198,
    303*n*62, 317*n*35, 317*n*41, 318*n*42,
    318*n*43, 318*n*44, 318–19*n*46

Yan Hui, 124–25, 176, 185–86
Yang Zhu, 277*n*31
Yearley, Lee H., 34–36, 62–63, 69, 211–12,
    320*n*1, 320*n*3
yi (rightness), 10, 13, 17, 125, 139–41, 150,
    152, 155, 173–74
Yu, Jiyuan, 290*n*45

Zhu Xi, 23, 137, 142, 158, 160, 162,
    253–54, 308*n*36
Zhuangzi, 56, 61, 63